The Politics of War

The
POLITICS
of WAR

The Story of Two Wars Which
Altered Forever the Political
Life of the American Republic
(1890–1920)

Walter Karp

HARPER & ROW, PUBLISHERS

New York, Hagerstown,

San Francisco, London

FIRST EDITION

Designed by Stephanie Winkler

Library of Congress Cataloging in Publication Data

Karp, Walter.
  The politics of war.
  1. United States—Politics and government—1865–1933.
2. United States—Foreign relations—1865–1921.
I. Title.
E661.K22   1979   320.9′73′08   78–20170
ISBN 0–06–012265–X

---

79 80 81 82 83 10 9 8 7 6 5 4 3 2 1

For my parents, Morris and Libby Karp

Contents

Acknowledgments

I would like to express my gratitude to the John Simon Guggenheim Memorial Foundation for its generous help in financing the research for this book, and to Mary Harron, who helped me prepare the manuscript for publication.

Preface

In American history the years from 1890 to 1920 have often been called the age of reform. Those same years might with equal propriety be called the age of war. During those years America fought two foreign wars, one against Spain, the other against Germany; fought a quasi-war in Mexico; fought a war of colonial repression in the Philippines; stood on the brink of war with Chile and Great Britain; intervened with military force dozens of times in Latin America. During those years the reform movement waxed and waned, waxed and died while America itself became by turns, an imperial power, an Asian power, and lastly a world power. Yet no substantial connections have ever been made between the turbulent domestic politics of the age and the increasingly ambitious foreign politics of that age. It is as if they were two separate historical sequences, each flowing through its own watertight channel, one labeled "domestic" and the other "foreign."

Such is the way American history—ideological, Marxist history excepted—has come to be written. The diplomatic historian traces the history of foreign affairs as if domestic politics were offstage disturbances; the historian of domestic politics treats the explosions of war as if *they* were offstage disturbances. The historian who copes with both in the confines of a single book puts them into alternate chapters, as if it were virtually unthinkable that domestic and foreign politics could possibly be elements of a single unified history.

I say "as if" because no one, so far as I know, has ever argued explicitly that foreign affairs and domestic affairs could not possibly be related. Stated baldly, the proposition is absurd. Were it true, we would have to believe, for example, that Presidents who have faced a mounting sea of troubles at home have nonetheless conducted their foreign policy without the slightest regard for those troubles. We would have to believe, in other words, that individual American Presidents were themselves divided into watertight compartments, one labeled "domestic" and the other "foreign." We would have to believe, too, that public men faced with a dangerously divided country could not possibly want to see it united by a patriotic struggle against a foreign foe; that men of power forced to cope with bitter and burning domestic questions would not wish to change the question before the country by pushing foreign affairs forward. Such propositions are not only contrary to common sense, they are falsified by the overwhelming evidence of history, for the political history of mankind records innumerable examples of rulers using foreign affairs for domestic ends. As Alexander Hamilton pointed out in *Federalist* #6, there have been innumerable wars "which take their origin entirely in . . . the attachments, enmities, interests, hopes and fears of leading individuals in the communities of which they are members." Such being the case in general, we would have to believe that only in America, by some inexplicable self-denying ordinance, have men of power invariably refrained from using foreign affairs in general and war in particular as a useful political instrument.

America's historians do not, as I said, state such propositions plainly. They simply treat foreign and domestic affairs as if they were separate categories. Our history, in consequence, rests heavily on an absurdly begged question, and the question quite simply is this: What relations have in fact existed between domestic and foreign affairs, between a turbulent domestic politics and war?

What follows is the story of two American wars that altered forever the political life of the American Republic. It is not two distinct stories, but one. In narrating the events that led up to each war a single dramatic story emerges, I believe: the story of the last great popular struggle in America to maintain a genuinely free republic—a republic free of oligarchy, monopoly, and private power—and the defeat and final obliteration of that struggle in two foreign wars.

PART I

1

"The Eve of a Very Dark Night"

On April 20, 1898, President William McKinley signed a congressional resolution directing him to use the armed forces of the United States to drive the Spanish from Cuba and establish an independent government for the rebellious island. A few days later the United States was formally at war with Spain and within three months the badly beaten Spanish sued for peace. It had been, as McKinley's Secretary of State John Hay put it, "a splendid little war." Yet that little war against a fifth-rate power marked one of the major turning points in American history. At its end, the United States supplanted the broken Spanish Empire as the colonial overlord of Puerto Rico and the Philippine Islands, thus making a radical break with one of America's oldest republican traditions—its repudiation of empire and colonial hegemony. At the war's end America became for the first time a recognized world power, thus marking a break in yet another venerated republican tradition—America's deliberate self-isolation from the perilous international arena and its rejection of what John Quincy Adams had called "the murky radiance of dominion and power."

A war fought against Spanish colonial rule had ushered in a new and unprecedented era of American colonial rule. A war fought over an offshore Atlantic island had turned America into a force to be reckoned with as far east as China. Such disparities between causes and their apparent effects, between professed purposes and actual results suggest that powerful political motives had their expression in and through the Spanish-American War. If so, the conventional account of that war gives us no hint of them.

Our official memory of the Spanish War, the version told and retold in countless American history texts, is a remarkably simple one. The United States went to war with Spain because the American people, sympathetic to the Cuban struggle for independence and roused to hatred of Spain by a sensation-mongering press, clamored irresistibly for war when the US battleship *Maine* exploded in Havana harbor on February 15, 1898. Ever responsive to majority sentiment, Congress in turn joined the clamor and forced a peace-loving McKinley to fight a war he had done his best to avoid. Precipitated by the force of sheer accident—the still unexplained destruction of the *Maine*—the war then produced its far-reaching results through the force of sheer circumstance. A naval victory over the Spanish fleet in Manila Bay broke the Spanish power in the Philippine Islands and left President McKinley with no choice but to annex the archipelago, thus reluctantly inaugurating the new era of colonial expansion. We entered a war through accident and became a world power by accident, thus graphically demonstrating, as McKinley himself put it, that "the march of events rules and overrules human action." In no major episode of American history has so little been attributed to the intentions of political leaders and so much to forces beyond their control.[1]

Such is the official picture of the Spanish-American War, its causes and its consequences. The picture is grossly misleading. For one thing, the story of the Spanish-American War is not simple, but extraordinarily complicated. It is a story in which, as will be seen, every actor on the American political stage and every political current of the period played a part one way or another. Nor is it the story of "events" overruling men's actions and intentions. That was President McKinley's official version—which in itself ought to invite skepticism. The truth is, America's political leaders took the first steps toward war with Spain several years before the *Maine* exploded, several years before the public clamored for war, and paradoxical though it may seem, some years before there was even a rebellion in Cuba. The chief elements in the story are not the public sentiments of the American people, the warmongering of a sensational press, nor an explosion in Havana's harbor, but two national political parties, one ruthlessly determined to rule, the other equally determined to survive in the general political crisis of the 1890s.

Until 1890 the American electorate had been, for a generation, a predictable and readily managed body of voters. In the off-year election of 1890, however, they delivered a stunning rebuke to the long-dominant Republican Party, reducing its House majority to a mere rump of 88 representatives and sweeping the party out of power in states that had gone Republican since the first election of Abraham Lincoln. If the origin of the Spanish War can be given a fixed date, that date is Election Day 1890, for the election prompted the Republican Party, at once, to take the first major step that ultimately led to that war. It was also the first serious warning that a political crisis was brewing, for it revealed a sudden weakening in the electorate's once ardent loyalty to one or the other of the two major parties, the most distinctive feature of the post–Civil War party system.

This passionate attachment to party, little known before the Civil War, had been forged by the Civil War itself. If was as if, in the cauldron of civil strife, every American had been melted down into one or the other of two elementary political particles, one Republican, the other Democrat. To its massed and devoted partisans the party was a church, whose creeds and slogans supplied men with their political principles, whose celebrations supplied them with their holiday outings. To its massed and devoted partisans the party was also a standing army perpetually arrayed for battle, an army whose orders men gladly obeyed, whose rudest tricks its partisans cheered, as patriots will cheer the night raids and ambushes of the nation's fighting men. Identifying themselves with a party, Americans looked on their chosen party as a kind of end in itself; its victories were their victories, its prosperity their prosperity. For themselves they asked little, for the identification with party was strong and passionate. In the Middle West in the 1880s, "the Republican Party," recalled the urban reformer Brand Whitlock, "was not a faction, not a group, not a wing, it was an institution . . . a synonym for patriotism, another name for the nation. One became, in Urbana and in Ohio for many years, a Republican just as the Eskimo dons fur clothes." If the Democrats' supporters did not harbor such grandiose sentiments, their attachment to the Democracy was nonetheless deep, in part because the self-vaunting Republicans treated their party rivals with arrogant contempt.[2]

Because the party was a church, questioning one's party's creed was looked upon as heresy. Because the party was a standing army, rebellion within a party stood condemned as base treachery and was almost unknown until the decline of the old party loyalties. This, too, was part of the unfolding political crisis—the emergence of insurgency, or intraparty rebellion, during the 1890s. Before then independent voters aligned to neither party were looked upon either as boodlers—"floaters" who voted for the party that offered the larger election-day bribe—or self-important cranks. When a number of socially prominent Republicans campaigned for the Democrats' Grover Cleveland in the election of 1884, they were branded with the quirky label of "mugwumps," which conveyed in itself how quirky the commonality thought them to be.

For the post–Civil War party leaders the advantages of what Whitlock called "those days of silly partisanship" were many. The electorate's fidelity to party enabled the leaders to pursue on the state and local levels corrupt and self-serving policies in the certain knowledge that exceedingly few of their supporters could stomach the prospect of voting for the rival party. It enabled them to overawe independent-minded politicians with crushing assaults on their disloyalty to the party that had chosen to advance them. Most important, it allowed the two national parties, for almost a generation, to keep significant economic issues out of the political arena— issues that might split a party organization and weaken its hold on the voters' elected representatives. As long as men adhered to their party on the basis of Civil War passions, as long as they "voted as they shot," the two major parties could refight the Civil War in their election campaigns and leave the electorate reasonably appeased. Since both parties benefited by keeping Civil War passions alive, both parties cooperated in doing so. The sudden waning of party loyalty, the sudden unpredictability of the voters, was cause for alarm among the leading politicians, for it had been the chief prop of the postwar party system.[3]

In part the new phenomenon of the disloyal voter arose through the sheer passage of years. A quarter of a century is a long time to keep alive the passions of even the most passionate of wars. In greater part it was due to the failure of the two parties, despite their best efforts, to keep genuine economic issues out of the political arena. As the 1890s began, millions of Americans had begun pressing their economic grievances upon politicians and office-holders. They demanded to know why, for example, an expanding economy had a deflated currency advantageous chiefly to New York bankers; why manufacturers grew rich through special legislation while farm prices continued to fall; why the evils of monopoly went unchecked; why a few private banks in New York controlled so much of the nation's credit while land bore almost the whole burden of taxes. Men looked around them and saw the free enterprise system falling into the hands of a few powerful capitalists, saw special privilege dispensed to the rich and general privileges denied to the rest. America's farmers, a near-majority of the country, saw in the mighty owners of the railroads men with a death grip on their farms and their fates and an equally deadly grip on their elected representatives. Industrial expansion, which almost all Americans had wholeheartedly welcomed, had ceased by 1890 to be a glowing promise and had become, instead, the source of innumerable burning and bitter questions. The sum of those questions was, in essence, the reassertion of the republican standard in economic affairs. Content no longer with mere industrial growth, Americans now began asking. what *kind* of industrial growth and what kind of industrialized economy suited the needs of a free and self-governing people. What kind, they asked, would preserve free enterprise, secure equality of opportunity, prevent the formation of monopoly, and ensure the freedom and independence of the citizenry. To that question, millions of Americans, as if awakening from a generation of slumber, knew the answer at least in a general way. It was not the industrial expansion and the general economic conditions they had hitherto tolerated.

In brief, a quarter of a century after a searing Civil War, the American people were casting off the war-forged manacles of party loyalty and regaining, as it were, their voice and their franchise. The awakening struck with particular force against the Republican Party, for it was the Republicans, far more than the Democrats, who had promoted industrial expansion as the highest goal of American life and the panacea for all temporary ills and injustices.

What was more ominous yet for Republican leaders, the voters in 1890 had risen up in wrath against the Republicans' vaunted instrument for promoting industrial expansion, the protective tariff. The public anger was understandable. Throughout the 1880s it had become increasingly clear that the prevailing high duties on imports had completely lost their original purpose, protecting "infant" American industries from destructive overseas competition. By 1890 America's industries had not only ceased to be infants, they had become so efficient that American manufacturers were prepared to undercut their European rivals in the markets of the world. The Republicans' best vote-getting argument for protection, namely that it protected the American wage earner, was losing its factual basis. If American industrialists could pay so-called "American wages" and still compete abroad, then obviously they could do so at home without any need for high tariff walls. The only just and sensible tariff policy was a reduction in the prevailing rates, since every unnecessary penny of duty meant unearned windfall profits for the protected manufacturer.[4]

This the leaders of the Republican Party had not the slightest intention of doing. That the protective tariff had become a special privilege was precisely the reason Republican leaders were determined to maintain it. It was the basis of their power within the Republican Party itself. By dispensing corrupt tariff favors to the "manufacturing interests," they had turned them into clients of the party oligarchy, tied to that oligarchy by the strong ligaments of greed, dependent on the oligarchy for the protection of their unearned profits, and consequently committed, in turn, to protecting the power of the party leaders. With such wealthy clients committed to the Republican leadership's interests, the oligarchy could draw upon their wealth as needed—"frying the fat out of them," as a Republican fund raiser put it in 1888—for all the manifold political ends that money can serve. With such wealth—and the attendant social influence—allied to them, Republican leaders hoped not merely to win elections—there are other ways to win elections—but to do so while tightening their control over the Republican Party, its thousands of party workers and citizen adherents, its state and congressional legislators. By dispensing corrupt tariff favors, the party leaders expected to enjoy not only the fruits of office but irresponsible oligarchic power, the power to control the dominant party in the country.

With these self-serving considerations in mind, what the Republican-controlled Congress did in 1890 had the quality of sheer, brazen impudence. Knowing full well the political risks they were running—"Such movements as this for protection," Secretary of State James G. Blaine had warned his party colleagues, "will protect the Republican Party into speedy retirement"—the Republican leaders in Congress raised the tariff rates *higher* than ever, deliberately bestowing on the privileged manufacturers even greater windfall profits than they had previously enjoyed. That the Senate Republicans killed a House bill to protect Negro voting rights in the South in order to win votes for the 1890 tariff only underscored the waning virtue, to put it mildly, of the erstwhile party of Lincoln.[5]

If Republican Party leaders were cynically self-serving, it was because the Republican Party by 1890 was led by a small circle of cynically ambitious men. In its passage through the post–Civil War years, the party had become little more than a syndicate of power-grasping state party bosses, many of whom used their control over state legislatures to appoint themselves to the Senate, thereby transforming the upper chamber into the national headquarters of the Republican oligarchy. The party's typical managers were men such as Senator Matthew Quay, boss of the powerful Pennsylvania machine, and Thomas Platt, the "Easy Boss" of New York, the keystone of whose power lay in collusion with the Democrats of Tammany Hall. Its legislative leaders were men such as Senator Nelson Aldrich of Rhode Island, who frankly viewed any kind of politics save the politics of corrupt privilege as sentimental rot. Here and there, men of old-fashioned scruples survived in the higher councils of the Republican Party—Senator George Hoar of Massachusetts, Senator Eugene Hale of Maine, for example—but by 1890 such men had followed the twists and turns of Republican Party politics for too long, had been too thoroughly broken to party discipline, to seriously disrupt their more unscrupulous colleagues.[6]

The self-serving cynicism of the Republican leaders, however, had far stronger roots than mere cynicism. Ultimately it rested on a belief shared by all Republicans of note that the Republican Party was not merely superior to the Democrats but that it alone was entitled to rule the Union it had formerly saved. The capacity of the Republican Party for sustained, active, and insolent self-serving stemmed in great measure from that belief and precisely because it was not entirely hypocritical. In the long political history of mankind the moments of glory have been few. Fewer still are the moments of glory for which a political party can claim credit. The Republican Party, the party that had raised to the presidency one of the noblest figures in history, which had saved a sundered Republic, which had emancipated a nation's slaves and established them, if only briefly, on a footing of political equality with their former masters, had written one truly glorious chapter in the political history of mankind. Legitimated by the party's historic glory, the Republicans' belief in their title to rule America was readily understandable. Nonetheless, a political faction that regards itself as a nation's rightful ruling elite forms a dangerous element in a free republic, and the Republican Party of the 1890s comprised a dangerous body of men.

The disastrous election of 1890 left the Republican oligarchy on the horns of a serious dilemma. Despite the electorate's rebuke, the party leaders had no intention of modifying, let alone abandoning, their protectionist policy. It was the chief prop of their power over the Republican Party. They also had no intention of turning the party into a mere opposition, a party of perennial "outs." That, all Republicans agreed, was the proper role only for Democrats. For the moment, however, the two ambitions of the Republican oligarchy—serving their power through the politics of corrupt tariff privilege and ruling the country by winning elections—were each an obstacle to the other. For the Republicans the skies had darkened suddenly and they seemed likely to grow darker still with the electorate's reassertion of the republican standard in economic affairs. To question the virtues of mere industrial expansion was to question the Republican Party's very reason for being.

It was Secretary of State Blaine—a man always one step ahead of his party colleagues—who pointed the way out of the dilemma. The renewal of the Republican Party, the restoration of its former power and glory, the recovery of an acceptable national purpose could indeed be accomplished, Blaine believed. It would require the party leaders to undertake a course of action far bolder than protectionism and far more consequential for the future of the country. According to Blaine, the party's salvation—and for all his ability, Blaine never thought beyond the interests of party—lay in launching under the Republican aegis a new assertive foreign policy for the United States, one that would put an end to its isolation and place it once and for all in the international arena as a major world power. Such a status the United States was so far from enjoying in 1890 that the European powers kept only legations at Washington, D.C., reserving their embassies for nations of greater international consequence.

There were daunting difficulties in the way of such a policy. For one thing it meant a radical break with the traditions of the country, traditions backed by the immense authority of the founders themselves. Moreover, it would mean a complete reversal, too, in the Republicans' own party traditions. Before the Civil War Republicans had vehemently denounced an expansionist foreign policy as one of the more contemptible deceits of the hated "Slavocrats." Most important, such a policy had no support in the country, either among ordinary citizens or the business classes. There was no demand for such a policy, no practical need for such a policy, and given America's geographical position, precious few opportunities for launching such a policy.[7]

Most Republican leaders were willing to brave the difficulties. An aggressive foreign policy, although it served no national interest whatever, promised to solve all their major problems at a stroke. For one thing it would change—and change fundamentally—the question before the country. An electorate growing restive over economic conditions would find its attention riveted to the spectacle of America's overseas power and pursuits, its republican sentiments diluted and deformed by jingo nationalism, its political energies absorbed by overseas problems and perplexities. There were other party advantages as well. As the future apostle of national grandeur, as the future defender of the national honor abroad, the Republican party might regain its former role as the party of the Union, enable it to persuade the rising generations to believe what the party's older adherents had believed, that the Republican Party "was not a faction, not a group, not a wing, [but] a synonym for patriotism, another name for the nation."

There was yet a third party advantage. The Republicans, unlike the Democrats, had been from the start an active governing party with clear-cut national policies and national legislative programs. Without such an active national purpose the national Republican Party could scarcely hold together. Even its powerful state machines could not survive. The reason for this lay in a distinctive feature of the Republican Party's structure. Unlike the Democracy, which consisted chiefly of professional politicians, the Republican Party had always numbered among its active workers a large number of "substantial citizens," as Theodore Roosevelt called them, who served the party not for the sake of graft, patronage, or advancement, but because they believed in the party and respected its national purposes. They neither believed in nor respected the Republican state machines. For the sake of the national party, the party's citizen adherents tolerated the malfeasances of the party's machine politicians; for the sake of electing Republican senators, they supported for the state legislature the corrupt minions of the state Republican bosses. Without a compelling national purpose the "substantial citizens" would become dangerously restive, were already becoming rebellious, especially in the major machine parties of New York and Pennsylvania. A new active national party program was essential to the Republican oligarchy's power. If nothing else, an aggressive foreign policy would certainly be active enough, national enough, and comprehensive enough to overcome the dangers of factionalism, to divert the discontents of the electorate, to restore the fading glory of the party of the Union and bind it together under its rulers with sinews of steel.[8]

The Republicans' new disposition toward foreign adventures reflected itself at once in the second half of Benjamin Harrison's administration. After the 1890 elections, a new kind of propaganda began to emanate from Republican leaders. In 1891, for example, the public heard from the secretary of the navy, Benjamin Tracy, a line that was to become increasingly familiar in the next few years. "To [gain] a preeminent rank among nations," he advised a people that had not wanted preeminence among nations, "colonies are the greatest help." In the winter of 1891–1892 President Harrison escalated a street brawl in Valparaiso between Chileans and American sailors into a near war with Chile, to avenge, as the President put it in his annual message to Congress, an "insult . . . to the uniform of the United States." Only the conciliatory action of the Chilean government averted a military clash. At the 1892 national convention, the Republican Party committed itself formally to an expansionist foreign policy. The platform that year pledged the party to "the achievement of the manifest destiny of the Republic in its broadest sense." Republican leaders apparently hoped to discover what kind of response the old expansionist slogan of the antebellum Democracy would get from Republican voters with long memories. The platform prudently specified no particular policy, but during 1892 a number of Republican newspapers set to work to win popular support for a concrete step in achieving America's "manifest destiny . . . in its broadest sense"—the absorption of the Hawaiian Islands, an archipelago 2,000 miles from our shores but with close economic and cultural ties to America.

The annexation itself was not of primary importance. Republican leaders saw it chiefly as the first available step in launching a more general policy of overseas expansion. The annexation of Hawaii, said the New York *Tribune,* a Republican Party house organ, would help overcome "the traditional hostility of the United States toward an extension of authority, if not also of territory, among the islands near our coasts." It would, said the Philadelphia *Press,* "familiarize the public mind with the acquisition of other territory." Annexing Hawaii was not the most dramatic example of America's new self-assertion in the international arena, but it was the best that Republicans could muster on short notice. Encouraged and abetted by the Harrison administration, a band of proannexationist Americans overthrew the native Hawaiian government in January 1893. A month later, barely two weeks before his departure from office, President Harrison signed a treaty of annexation with the leaders of the coup. Submitted to the Senate the next day, it was hastily approved two days later by the Republican-controlled Committee on Foreign Relations. The new Republican foreign policy was now emphatically launched with overseas territorial expansion as its immediate objective. Although the newly elected President Cleveland withdrew the treaty, it was not lost on the European powers that the United States, after a century of continental isolation, was about to assert its long dormant power, if not under the Democrats then certainly when the Republicans once more regained the presidency. By the end of 1892 they all replaced their Washington legations with full-scale embassies.[9]

Superficially, the electoral troubles of one party redound to the benefit of the other. With the reelection of Grover Cleveland in 1892 (he had been elected President in 1884 as well), the Democratic Party, for the first time since the days of Buchanan, controlled both houses of Congress and the executive branch, a remarkable achievement for a party that had, by and large, taken the losing side in a fratricidal war. The Democrats were nothing if not survivors. If the Republican Party had the bold self-assurance of a governing elite, the Democrats had the survivors' sly cunning. The two parties differed markedly. If the overriding need of the Republican oligarchy was to find some active national policy, the overriding need of the Democrats was to avoid as far as possible doing anything at all.[10]

In its essential, stripped-down, irreducible historic core, the Democratic Party was a mere congeries of local parties, principally a number of urban strongholds in the North and several state-ruling "rings," as they were known, in the old Confederacy. Each local party satrapy survived by making appropriate local gestures to its voters, often with scant regard for the contrary gestures made by party colleagues elsewhere. Where low tariffs had local support, local Democrats preached the unconstitutionality of the Republican protective tariff. Where high tariffs had local support, as in Pennsylvania, Democrats favored high duties. Where inflationary policies had local appeal, the local party talked up currency inflation. Where it lacked such support, Democrats preached the virtues of "sound money" and the New York bankers' view of economics in general. In rural Protestant areas the party made itself hospitable to local religious prejudices. In the northern urban areas the Democracy was the noisy foe of Sunday blue laws, temperance, and Protestant "nativism" in general. Frightening Catholic immigrants with the bogie of "nativism" was a particularly favored device of northern machine Democrats.[11]

Since almost any national legislative program would swiftly sunder so motley a band of political allies, the central national tenet of the Democrats was the principle of doing nothing, which party leaders often described as "True Democracy." Democrats dressed up the principle in a number of wrappings. They preached it as the very essence of constitutional rule: "states' rights," "home rule" and "strict construction" of the Constitution ostensibly forbade the general government from doing almost anything. As Republican House leader Thomas Reed scornfully remarked of the Democracy, it was a party "struggling with its own inertia and mistaking it for the Constitution." It was not a mistake, however, since "inertia" was essential to the party's survival. Another Democratic version of the do-nothing principle was to ascribe it to the binding traditions of the founders. Had not Thomas Jefferson said that "that government is best which governs least"? The Democracy also cast the principle into more modern economic terms: The laissez-faire doctrines of English liberalism proved that any governmental disruption of the laws of economics could only prove harmful in the long run.[12]

By uniting on the principle of doing nothing whatever and attacking the Republicans for doing anything at all, the Democratic Party, through the do-nothing principle, was able to keep up, for electoral purposes, a reasonable semblance of national unity. It also gained them the support of the major New York bankers, who found the Republican Party too active, arrogant, and presumptuous to suit either their sentiments or their interests. The do-nothing principle, moreover, was equally essential to the party's local survival, for at every level of government Democratic Party bosses and rings could not carry out policies that served the interests of their constituents without grave risks to their power.

In the South, the Democracy's dependence on the do-nothing principle was little short of desperate. Ruling over a population of wretched, debt-ridden farmers—peons, in fact—the South's ruling state cliques could cling to power only as long as the farmers remained politically inert, and southern Democrats had but two ways to keep them that way. One was to preach the doctrine of "White Supremacy," sometimes referred to in the South as "the spirit of true patriotism." This enabled the South's state rulers to cry down any political rebel as a traitor to white "solidarity" who was paving the way for "Negro rule," a threat that by the 1890s was inevitably growing weaker as Negroes brave enough to vote grew fewer. The second was simply to persuade the rural populace by sheer iteration that it was unpatriotic, un-Jeffersonian, and grossly improper for them to expect from their state governments any relief from their multifarious economic woes. By thus stultifying political hope, the southern Democrats hoped to stifle any unruly political activity on the part of the most wretchedly misgoverned people in America.[13]

The northern city machines, too, depended for their security on the do-nothing principle and for much the same reason. Reform raises political hopes, encourages independent men to enter politics, and threatens the power of the local machine to control the actions of party members. For this reason, New York's Tammany Hall was unwilling to carry out even the simplest municipal functions, such as collecting the garbage or providing recreational facilities for the New York poor who supported it so faithfully. After a Republican reform mayor won authorization to build playgrounds in New York City, Tammany, returning to power, declined for years to build them. After all, if the municipal government could build parks and collect a poor man's garbage it would only encourage the needy to make further demands, and a demanding electorate, no longer meanly grateful for free beer at party picnics, was something with which Tammany had no wish to cope. In 1894 when a 2 percent federal tax on incomes over $4,000 was added to a Democratic tariff bill, Tammany's congressional minions led the opposition to it, although few of Tammany's adherents would have had to pay a cent in taxes. It was the principle that aroused Tammany's opposition. Mocking the Fifth Avenue "silk stockings" was one thing, but taxing them might give poor New York voters dangerous ideas. On the other hand, by doing nothing, the party machine could provide its supporters with politically safer outlets, such as denouncing Protestants, bluenoses, "nativists," and the British, a concentration on cultural and ethnic attitudes that was quite analogous to the White Supremacy creed of Tammany's southern allies. Tammany Hall, as the famous Emporia, Kansas, editor William Allen White was to observe in 1901, was a beneficial force for stability because, in White's words, "Tammany preaches contentment"—to people with nothing to be content about.[14]

What was true of the Tammany machine was true of most of the Democracy's lesser Tammanys. In Democratic Detroit, for example, a Republican reformer named Hazen Pingree won the mayoralty in 1889 and proceeded to put through several basic municipal reforms. The only response of the Democratic machine to this intrusion of genuine issues was to cry up the virtues of economy in government. Pingree won reelection three times against the combined efforts of the Detroit Democrats and the Republican state boss, Senator James McMillan, who worked in collusion with the Detroit Democracy just as the Republican boss of New York State, Tom Platt, worked in collusion with Tammany.[15]

In the rural Midwest, the Democratic do-nothing principle had all the preceding advantages and one other. It was a policy deliberately designed to repel rural voters, always a source of unruly agitation since they had no compunction about demanding remedial action from the government. By thus repelling rural majorities in the Midwest and West, the local Democratic machines in Omaha, St. Paul, and elsewhere enjoyed a far more prominent place in their state parties than they would otherwise have enjoyed had farmers and farm spokesmen been represented in the state party. The general result of repelling rural votes was that most Midwest states were Republican bastions and the losing Democratic parties of the region, dependent for money and patronage on the New York Democracy, were little more than rotten boroughs in the pocket of the New York party. The local heterogeneity of the Democratic Party was always belied by the tight inner unity of the local leaders themselves. If the national Democratic Party began to prosper in the 1880s, it was principally because, given a choice between active Republican corruption and passive Democratic corruption, more voters began choosing the latter. That was the essential choice the two national parties had been offering the voters since the Civil War, and for some time the electorate had been content with the choice. Those days, however, were now coming to an end, although few Democrats knew it when they renominated Cleveland in 1892.[16]

Grover Cleveland's devotion to the "principles of True Democracy"—one of his favorite phrases—was beyond all question. He was a laissez-fairist of the most rigid and doctrinaire kind. In his improbably swift rise to power—he was an obscure Buffalo lawyer in

1879 and President of the United States six years later—Cleveland
had chiefly distinguished himself by vetoing legislation regardless
of its utility or popularity. He had been known in turn as the "Veto
Mayor" of Buffalo and the "Veto Governor" of New York. During
his first term as President, he reached some sort of doctrinaire's ze-
nith by vetoing an emergency bill providing seed for drought-
stricken farmers. Only a remarkably dogmatic President would
deny succor to desperate men by so drastic an application of principle, but Cleveland's astonishing political success had only confirmed him in his righteous devotion to sound principles and in a
corresponding contempt for political expedience. "It is no credit to
me to do right," he once confided to friends. "I am never under any
temptation to do wrong!"[17]

Politically, however, Cleveland's self-righteous dogmatism was a
two-edged sword. It ensured that his devotion to True Democracy,
a creed, could never be matched by a similar devotion to the interests of the Democratic Party, a mere organization. The most truly
bourgeois President the United States ever had, Cleveland shared,
to a remarkable degree in a public man, the historic middle-class
contempt for professional politicians. An honest man himself, he
was painfully aware that the old-line Democratic Party leaders—
the city bosses and the southern rings—were not, like himself, prin-
cipled believers in True Democracy. At bottom, he wrote a friend
in late 1890, the old-line Democracy was the party of "shiftiness
and cheap expediency." He was privately determined to carry out
during his second term a complete reformation of the party, weak-
en its local machines and rings—"the base element" as he called
them—and "plant our party upon principle instead of shallow expediency." Cleveland's ideal seems to have been a party composed
of well-to-do citizens and public-spirited businessmen united by a
common devotion to laissez-faire economics, tariff reduction,
"sound money," the international gold standard and economy in
government.[18]

During his first term of office Cleveland had used his power and
patronage to plant a Clevelandite or business faction alongside the
old-line party leaders in almost every state party. In a few western
states where the Democrats rarely won—Nebraska, Iowa, and
Wisconsin, for example—the Cleveland faction was dominant.

Where the old-line Democracy had large local bastions—in Illinois, Michigan, and Ohio, for example—it was a mere auxiliary. In the South, the Clevelandites formed the junior partners of the old-line Bourbon rulers—the "young progressive element of the South," as they liked to call themselves. The old-line Democrats disliked the diversion of federal patronage to the newcomers, but the Clevelandite, or "reform," faction (as reform was understood in the 1880s) was quite useful to the old party of "shiftiness and cheap expediency." It was one of its cheap expedients. Devoted as heartily as the Democratic professionals were to the do-nothing principle, the business elements provided money for the party coffers, lucrative jobs and attorney's fees for the local leaders, and a cover of respectability for the Democracy as a whole. The cover was sufficiently convincing to persuade Republican mugwumps such as Carl Schurz that the Democracy had truly been transformed by Cleveland into an honorable party of principle. Although the old-line Democrats liked Cleveland no more than he liked them, he was undoubtedly useful to them. His renomination in 1892 was itself a party effort to use Cleveland, despite himself, to preserve the old-line Democracy, particularly in the South.[19]

The politics of that region had felt the brewing crisis in 1890 when a pressure group known as the Farmers' Alliance swept one million rural Southerners onto its membership rolls and began demanding that southern office seekers pledge their support to the Alliance program of agrarian reforms. Initially, the southern oligarchy decided to bend. Before the 1890 elections, numerous southern politicians gave the required pledge. As a further sop to the Alliance, every southern state party in 1890 endorsed the free and unlimited coinage of silver, an inflationary measure with considerable appeal to debt-burdened farmers. Once safely elected, the pledgees promptly betrayed their pledges, judging that the time had come to resist dangerous popular demands for reform. The nomination of Cleveland was to be the continuation on the national level of the same policy of resistance, for a more tenacious foe of silver coinage and of agrarian reform in general could not have been found anywhere on the American political scene. At the time of Cleveland's renomination, Democratic leaders hoped, not without trepidation, that Cleveland's rigid adherence to True Democra-

cy and the gold standard, combined with his astonishing resistance
to popular sentiment, would reduce southern farmers to their customary state of abject despair and enable the southern oligarchy to
weather the rural storm. Instead they brought themselves to the
brink of ruin. Never in American history were a band of political
engineers so swiftly hoist on their own petard.[20]

For the ruling southern rings, trouble began even before Cleveland's reelection. The prospect of a "gold" Democrat, so-called, in
the White House, far from discouraging the Farmers' Alliance, encouraged them to make a momentous decision, a decision more important in our history (and in the history of the Spanish-American
War) than many American Presidents ever made. Alliance leaders
decided to break with the party of White Supremacy and bring into
southern politics a new political entity, known as the People's Party. As a Virginia Allianceman put it, Cleveland's nomination had
snapped "the last cord which binds free men to the Democratic
Party." In the volatile western prairie states, local People's parties
had sprung up as early as 1890 and had quickly won the endorsement of the Northern Farmers' Alliance. The Southern Alliancemen had held back, however. To break with the Democracy, to
defy the doctrine of racial solidarity, was a prospect to daunt the
bravest heart. No one knew better than Southerners what the
Democratic oligarchs were capable of doing should anyone dare
challenge their monopoly of politics and power. In the summer of
1892, however, the Alliancemen made their historic plunge and
hastily began organizing the new party for the forthcoming fall
campaign. For the first time since 1850 the southern Democracy
was facing electoral opposition from a party of nearly equal
strength, for the Populists' rural appeal was instantaneous.[21]

So was the Democracy's response. In all America there were no
loftier rhetoricians than the ruling politicians of the southern Democracy. No men spoke more eloquently of the Constitution, the
founders, and the great Jeffersonian principles of liberty and self-
rule. It was all the hollowest sham, like the crocodile tears they
would soon be shedding for Cuban guerrillas. For daring to contest
an election in a free republic, the Populists were met with every vicious political weapon at the southern Democrats' command—with
thugs, mobs, threats, terror, intimidation at the polls, coercion of

voters; with ballot stuffing; with vile scurrilities; with scandals concocted by a servile party press. The elections, a Virginia newspaper conceded, were a "bacchanalia of corruption and terrorism" unleashed against the upstart People's Party. As one southern Democrat lamely put it, "We *had* to do it. Those damned Populists would have ruined the country." Temporarily in 1892, corruption and terror secured victory at the polls for most Democrats, but the party was shaken to its foundations. The Populists had openly appealed for Negro votes on the promise of equal political liberty for all; they had dared to defy "the true spirit of patriotism." White "solidarity" lay in ruins and the southern Populists, though barely a few months old, had done alarmingly well. They had no intention whatever of quitting the field. As a Mississippian wrote to President-elect Cleveland in December 1892, Northerners had no idea "how close many of the congressional districts in the South were" to going Populist.[22]

With the decision of the Southern Farmers' Alliance to endorse the new party, the People's Party became a national political entity—it nominated a presidential candidate, General James Weaver, in 1892—with a complex program of reform that stood out in sharpest contrast to the obfuscations, panacea-mongering, and bluster of the two established parties. The party program was based on a truly prescient, if doleful, economic insight: that private economic power—monopolies in transport and communications, industrial trusts and combinations, private banking control of American currency and credit—was no longer an incidental evil. It was one that would soon overwhelm the economy and the Republic if it were not extirpated at once. The Populists understood with perfect clarity that the already existing monopolies provided the basis for further monopolization. Their ultimate solution was therefore both drastic and logical. They called for direct government ownership of all "natural monopolies" in transport and communication, as well as government control of currency and credit. The government, as the Populists insisted, to the horror of laissez-fairists, was "not a foreign entity, governed by some outside power with which we have no connection ... [it] is simply the agent of the people." In effect, what the Populists were telling their fellow countrymen was this: If we Americans want what we all say we want, the maintenance of genuine free enterprise; if we agree, as we all say we do, that only an economy free of privilege and private power is consonant with republican liberty, then these draconian measures are required and anything less is self-deluding. If economic power were not wrested *now* from the hands of a few, the Populists warned, it would soon be too late—fatally late—for the citizenry to do so.[23]

The realism of the Populist program was remorseless, too much so for the widest acceptance. The economic prescience of the Populists was too far-seeing even for the more prosperous farmers; it was certainly so for the "respectable classes," who were not to awaken to the perils descried by the Populists until a dozen more years passed by. It was easier in 1892 to mock the Populists as "calamity howlers," ignorantly pessimistic about the future of the country. Undaunted either by guns or by ridicule, however, Populists by the many thousands swore by the party program, preached it to all comers, and spread it across the South and West with the zeal of religious evangelists. As one participant at an early Populist convention observed: "It was a religious revival, a crusade, a pentecost of politics in which a tongue of flame sat upon every man." A Dallas newspaper warned the established politicians in 1892 that "it would be supreme folly to despise and belittle a movement that is leavened with such moral stuff as this."[24]

To the established politicians it must have seemed by 1893 that Providence itself was conspiring to bring victory to the People's Party. A few months after Cleveland's inauguration, a financial panic struck the country, followed shortly after by the most severe and prolonged depression America had ever known. Farm prices, already so low it had inflamed the rural population, fell lower still, inflaming farmers still further. By late 1893 the entire national economy ground to a halt. Five hundred banks and some 16,000 business firms were forced into bankruptcy. Two and a half million men were pushed out of work. During the wretched winter of 1893–94 untold thousands of hungry people were kept alive by local charity and local soup kitchens, bitterly referred to as "Cleveland cafes." "Boston," recalled Henry Adams, "grew suddenly old, haggard and thin," and the same could be said for dozens of other American cities. "Uncertainty and fear," said the Washington *Post,* "spread like a pall over a hitherto prosperous land." Even before the depression the electorate had grown restive and exacting, a radical third party had already entered the lists, and now economic calamity of shocking proportions had stricken every section of the country. All the elements of a full-scale political crisis had come together and the presidency was in the hands of Grover Cleveland, perhaps the single greatest incitement to radical political action ever to inhabit the White House in a critical moment.[25]

To President Cleveland, an honorable man of the narrowest purview, the revolt of the farmers, the incursions of the People's Party, the tottering of the southern Democracy, the financial panic, the whole storm brewing beyond his doorstep, held only the narrowest significance. He saw it as a threat to America's adherence to the gold standard and to the sharply deflated currency which that adherence secured. This was an interpretation of events that in all of America only the major New York banks fully shared. At their urging, Cleveland even persuaded himself that the sole cause of the economic crisis lay in America's compromised adherence to the gold standard. The compromise had been effected by an innocuous piece of legislation known as the Sherman Silver Purchasing Act. Passed by Republicans in 1890 in order to win mining state votes for their fateful tariff bill, it called upon the government to purchase a certain amount of silver bullion each month in exchange for silver Treasury certificates. Here, according to Cleveland, lay the source of all the nation's soluble problems, a conclusion that came easily to the former veto mayor of Buffalo, who ascribed most of the world's public woes to acts of legislation. Cleveland's prescription for the financial panic was simple: Repeal the Silver Purchasing Act and all would be well. A more shallow analysis of the economic crisis could scarcely be imagined. A proposal more infuriating to debt-ridden farmers or better calculated to deepen their suspicion of Wall Street's power the President could not have put forward. Such popular reactions meant nothing to Cleveland. All through his public life he found it impossible to understand how anyone could hold views contrary to his own. There seemed to be no accounting for such human folly. In 1893, therefore, Cleveland called Congress into special session to effect the repeal of the cause of the depression. In that one stroke Cleveland transformed the old-line Democracy into his bitter antagonists. Like the Republican tariff of 1890, Cleveland's repeal efforts were to have far-reaching effects on American foreign policy and bring America yet another step closer to war.

By 1893, the southern Democrats' policy of resistance had been utterly overtaken by events. With the People's Party so surprisingly in the field, what they desperately needed now was some sop to southern farmers, some sign that the Democratic Party, a Democratic Congress, and a Democratic President held out some hope for, or at least had sympathy with, the aroused and aggrieved rural population. Either that or the Populists might well sweep the Democracy out of power in the South, a prospect the Democrats had already used shotguns to forestall. Instead, here was President Cleveland virtually demonstrating what an alarming number of southern farmers already believed, that the Democratic Party was the cat's-paw of the Wall Street "money power," and the Democratic President the "360-pound tool of plutocracy," as an Arkansas stump speaker put it. What made matters worse, Cleveland's argument for repeal was almost as infuriating as repeal itself. The object of repeal, according to Cleveland, was to obviate the Treasury's need to redeem bank-held silver certificates in gold, which was severely draining the Treasury's gold reserves. The certificates, by law, could also be redeemed with silver, but Cleveland refused to compromise the gold standard by doing so. Repeal, in other words, was Cleveland's Wall Street solution to a problem created by his Wall Street policies. Was any further proof needed that the New York money power controlled the President?[26]

In the House of Representatives, western and southern Democrats vehemently attacked Cleveland's "goldbug" policies. "Would you crush the people of your own land," asked Representative Richard Bland of Missouri, "and send them abroad as tramps . . . to satisfy the greed of Wall Street, the mere agents of Lombard Street?" In the Senate, Arthur Gorman of Maryland, one of the Democrats' most powerful state bosses, toiled desperately to effect a compromise repeal measure that would help southern Democrats save face. Even J. P. Morgan counseled compromise, but Cleveland was adamant. He wanted repeal, absolute and unconditional. For the whining of the old-line Democrats he had nothing but contempt. The President even seemed to relish their anger and chagrin. He had been a firm adherent of the gold standard when the party had nominated him. Did the "base element" expect him to follow "cheap expedience" now after a public career devoted to principle? The Georgia governor who warned Cleveland in 1893 that "every election held in this State for the past three months has gone against the Democrats and in favor of the Populists" might as well have addressed his warning to a wall.[27]

Understandably, the old-line Democrats did not share Cleveland's viewpoint or relish any longer his rigid adherence to the True Democracy. To them he was a base ingrate, a man they had lifted from obscurity to the highest office who was now turning his beefy back on the party in its hour of dire need. "I hate the ground that man walks, on" said the veteran Alabama ring politician Senator John Morgan, voicing a sentiment genuinely felt by hard-pressed southern Democratic leaders. Governor Ben Tillman of South Carolina publicly likened Cleveland to Judas. In Congress, Cleveland nonetheless prevailed. With the help of Republican votes and the sharp lash of patronage, Cleveland got the Silver Purchasing Act repealed in October, but the breach between him and his party was almost complete.[28]

By then Cleveland was well on his way to becoming one of the most detested Presidents in American history. To Democrats with nothing better to offer the voters, denouncing Cleveland was becoming a stock-in-trade, defying him in Congress proof of devotion to the plain people. Self-pity overwhelmed the President: "There was never a man in this high office," he confided to a friend in April 1894, "so surrounded with difficulties and so perplexed and so treacherously treated, and so abandoned by those whose aid he *deserves* as the present incumbent." When Cleveland's cherished tariff reduction measure came before the Senate in 1894 it became the turn of the northern machine Democrats, led by Gorman and David Hill of New York, publicly to defy the Democratic President. In committee and on the Senate floor they macerated the administration bill so thoroughly that Cleveland let it pass into law unsigned, while publicly accusing Senate Democrats of "party perfidy and party dishonor." Democrats answered him in kind. As an administration official sadly observed: "Former southern supporters in the Senate . . . cannot abuse him too much." One Democrat denounced the President as a monster of "belly and brass." The rancorous Governor Tillman won national prominence and the life-long nickname of "Pitchfork Ben" by promising to go to Washington "with a pitchfork and prod him in his old fat ribs."[29]

If Cleveland's fanatical devotion to the gold standard enraged the rural population, his defense of the industrial magnates enraged the nation's factory workers. During the Pullman strike of the summer of 1894, Cleveland, a professed adherent of states' rights, trampled on the legitimate rights of states by sending federal troops to quell the strikers without permission from Illinois's Democratic governor, John Peter Altgeld, who vainly protested the breach of party principle. Although a professed believer in the niceties of law, Cleveland allowed his attorney general, Richard Olney, to transform a minor legal device known as the judicial injunction into a major weapon of repression, one that allowed the government to arrest a union leader for acts not prohibited by law and to be tried by his accuser—the judge issuing the injunction—without benefit of a jury trial. Unnerved by the growing disorder, Cleveland was rapidly turning True Democracy into a purblind defense of the status quo and persuading millions of Americans, while doing so, that he was literally a traitor to the people.[30]

Month after month, the temper of the country grew more bitter and disaffected. In addition to rural agitation, industrial unrest in 1894 was registered in a record 1,394 strikes, in the formation of seventeen "hobo armies," which set forth in protest to Washington to the cheers of those they passed by. To many, revolution itself seemed imminent, a revolution of debtors against creditors, of employees against employers, of all the underprivileged against all the overprivileged. "If this keeps on long," a correspondent wrote to Secretary of State Walter Gresham shortly after the suppression of the Pullman strike, "fire and sword will sweep the country with flames." In Washington, Henry Adams summed up the inflammatory conditions with an apt classical allusion. "The public temper here," he reported to an English friend, "is, in my opinion, a very ugly one and likely on the smallest pretext to become exceedingly bitter, not to say dangerous. . . . We are the Rome of the Gracchi." In October 1894, a Wall Street supporter of the President gravely warned him that "we are on the eve of a very dark night unless a return of commerical prosperity relieves the popular discontent."[31]

The Republican oligarchy, however, displayed its customary self-possession. The growing radicalism of the country, the deepening of the depression, the inflammatory denunciations of the "money power," left the Republican leaders singularly unmoved. All the depression meant to the party was a chance to retrieve the fortunes of the protective tariff. Judging that industrial workers were at least as confused as they were angry, Republicans calmly laid the entire blame for the depression on Democratic tampering with the Republican high tariff. They continued to preach the virtues of an expansionist foreign policy, which was considerably safer, in any case, than meeting demands for reform with proposal for reform. Republicans felt no need to appeal to the electorate. They expected to ride the depression to victory anyway, since Cleveland and his party had performed the singular feat of alienating virtually every major category of voter. Even so, the results of the 1894 elections were electrifying. It remains to this day the most sweeping rebuke any President and his party ever suffered in an off-year election. Punished by a volatile electorate, the Democrats lost a total of 113 seats in Congress. In the Northeast, the Democrats' congressional contingent was reduced from 88 to 9; in twenty-four states the party no longer had congressional representation at all. In the South, despite the Democrats' increased use of terror and corruption, the People's Party now stood on the verge of victory throughout the Old Confederacy. Whatever else lay in store for the country, the post–Civil War party system had been destroyed forever.[32]

2

"The Malevolent Change in Our Public Life"

In mid-February 1895, a small group of Cuban-Americans landed secretly in Cuba and raised the banner of armed revolt against Spanish rule in the island, the last remaining possession of any value in the once mighty Spanish Empire. Calling themselves the "Republic of Cuba" and gathering round their flag small bands of guerrillas, whom they designated the "Army of Liberation," rebel leaders began at once a two-front assault on Spanish rule, one in Cuba, the other in New York City.

On the Cuban front, the rebels, led by Maximo Gomez, unleashed a campaign of destruction in the rural areas designed to reduce Cuba to a wilderness and its sugar economy to ashes. Sugar mills were to be destroyed, cane fields set ablaze, cane-field workers shot, railroads dynamited, food supplies to the cities cut off. The idealism of the Cuban rebels was avowedly ruthless. It would be a "crime," said General Gomez, to fail "because of puerile scruples." He was determined, he announced, "to unfurl triumphantly, even over ruin and ashes, the flag of the republic of Cuba."[1]

The guerrillas did not expect their scorched-earth tactics to drive the Spanish from Cuba or their revolt to win widespread popular support. Not independence but home rule under Spanish sovereignty was the cause supported by most discontented Cubans. In 1895 the chief Cuban advocates of independence lived in New York and Tampa, Florida. The main objective of the rebels' guerrilla warfare was to create conditions so atrocious in Cuba that the United States in due course would intervene. Securing that intervention was the second prong in the rebels' twofold assault on Spanish rule. For this purpose the civilian arm of the rebellion, the so-called Cuban Junta, set up its headquarters in New York to raise money, purchase arms, and carry out a campaign of agitation and political lobbying for American intervention, the rebels' only secure hope of success.[2]

On the face of it, that hope appeared bleak. The rebels, it seemed, could hardly expect Republican imperialists to lend support to a cause whose guiding spirit was anti-imperialist when they were trying to wean Americans from their traditional aversion to colonial rule. Neither, it seemed, could the rebels, whose guerrillas were chiefly black ex-slaves, expect support from the party of White Supremacy, which was, at that very moment, fulminating against the Populists for threatening the South with "Negro rule." Nor could they expect, on the face of it, powerful eastern Republicans to embrace a cause that aroused among "substantial citizens" little more than antipathy and disgust. Nine months before the Cuban revolt broke out, scarcely a single American politician had protested against Cleveland's lawless and unwarranted suppression of the Pullman strike. Even Cleveland's bitterest party enemies had praised his "prompt and vigorous measures" in the cause of property in general and the Pullman Company in particular. General Gomez and his incendiary guerrillas did not seem likely on the face of it to command the sympathy of political leaders such as these.[3]

There were other obstacles to the rebels' hopes. By every canon of international law, the conflict between Spain and the guerrillas was strictly an internal affair of Spain's. American intervention under any pretext would violate the single most important rule in the code of nation-states: the rule of noninterference in other nations' domestic affairs. If conditions grew truly atrocious international law allowed for intervention on the ground of "humanity," but only by a coalition of nations, which the isolated United States was extremely unlikely to forge. The proviso itself was based on the worldly political understanding that when one nation only is spurred to intervene by inhuman conditions in another country those conditions are more likely to be a pretext than anything else.

More important from the point of view of rebel hopes, the mere fact of rebellion and destruction in Cuba did not necessitate American involvement. Rebellion in Cuba was not a new story. Between 1868 and 1878 Cuban guerrillas and Spanish soldiers had fought one another, committed atrocities against one another, and brought untold suffering to the innocent while doing so. Yet for ten years the ruling Republican oligarchy, then in the high tide of its power and prestige, had remained aloof from the struggle. Since it did not serve their interests to support intervention, neither the protracted sufferings of Cubans nor popular American sympathy for the rebels had stirred Republican leaders to act. In consequence, President Grant had maintained strict fidelity to the principle of nonintervention in the internal affairs, however deplorable, of other nations.

That was a generation past, when the Republican oligarchy stood unchallenged and the American electorate had been easily managed. In fact the Cuban émigrés had timed their revolt well. Republicans who were openly betraying the cause of American Negroes would laud the guerrillas' struggle as a crusade for "republicanism"; politicians avid to forge corrupt ties with Wall Street would denounce New York's "money changers" for refusing to support the rebel cause. Democrats would take time out from threatening black Populists with mayhem in the South to sing the praises of black arsonists in Cuba. Republican expansionists, eager to annex the remnants of Spain's Caribbean empire, would cry up *"Cuba libre"* and the sacred cause of Cuban independence. The same politicians (and newspapers) who had lauded Cleveland's military assault on the law-abiding Pullman strikers would hurl abuse at Spain for daring to suppress guerrillas who were trying to turn Cuba into "ruin and ashes." Party politicians, professing themselves stricken with grief over the plight of Cubans, would insist that the "dictates of humanity" compelled the United States to end the suffering on an island a mere ninety miles from our shores, while overlooking as best they could the gross inequities, the widespread suffering, and the just demands for reform then pulsing through a great and prostrated republic ninety miles from the shores of Cuba.

The motives of the two parties differed greatly, but war and war agitation held out considerable advantages to both. The Republicans, as E. L. Godkin, famed editor of the New York *Evening Post* put it, were eager to "get up a foreign war if possible" because "they have tremendous and urgent domestic questions to confront and settle, but find the work dangerous politically." So much was obvious enough. In fact, however, Republican motives were deeper and much more far-reaching than even Godkin realized. Since the onset of the political crisis Republican leaders had been determined to transform America into an active world power and thereby make foreign affairs the preeminent factor in American politics. Politically speaking, it was to be the permanent functional equivalent of the no-issue politics of the precrisis years. The Republicans' "large policy," as Senator Henry Cabot Lodge of Massachusetts aptly called it, had as yet no support in the country. Aside from unconvincing talk about controlling the "Pacific trade"—an economic figment of politicians and party scribblers—the "large policy" offered no inducement whatever to the American people. Strictly speaking the large policy was not even a policy, in the sense of constituting a determinate means of serving the determinate interests of America. Even on its own terms it was not a means but an end in itself. Its essential purposelessness was well expressed by Godkin in a May 1895 issue of the *Nation*. What its advocates really wanted, he wrote, was to bring the United States "into contact with considerable foreign powers at as many points as possible." The object of the large policy was to have a large policy; the reason for making the United States a world power was that it might exercise power in the world. Such power, as Senator Lodge put it, is "essential to the greatness of every splendid people." Other Republican leaders resorted to the same jingo bluster. "A vigorous foreign policy is necessary to the strength and dignity of any nation," insisted Senator Joseph Gallinger, boss of the New Hampshire Republican machine. To gain popular support for so useless a policy Republicans were unrelenting in their efforts to arouse jingo sentiment in the country. After four years their efforts were making themselves felt. By the autumn of 1895 the New York *Journal of Commerce*, for example, would complain bitterly of the "artificial patriotism being carefully worked up at the present time" and note with particular disgust the new "remarkable fashion of hanging the flag over every schoolhouse and of giving the boys military drill."[4]

It takes considerably more than bluster and flag-waving, however, to persuade a nation of seventy million to discard overnight its historic renunciation of "the murky radiance of dominion and power." What Republican expansionists needed was some large and decisive action that would safely launch the large policy once and for all. Through a successful war, as one San Francisco newspaper put it, "almost without knowing it we shall have started forth on our colonizing ventures fully equipped with widely scattered possessions, a navy strong enough to protect them, and a newly roused martial spirit in our hearts made strong and enduring by victory." For many advocates of the large policy the rebellion in Cuba presented itself at once as the signal opportunity for transforming America into a world power "almost without knowing it," amid the confusions and fevers of war. As young Theodore Roosevelt confided to a correspondent in the course of explaining the benefits of a future war with Spain: "our people are not yet up to this line of policy in its entirety and the thing to be done is to get whatever portion of it is possible at the moment."[5]

Cuba was by no means a perfect opportunity. In many ways it was problematical. The rule of nonintervention in the internal affairs of other nations was not to be broken lightly; the rebellion affected no important American interests and the fearful Spanish were unlikely to provide any pretexts, let alone a *casus belli,* on which American interventionists might seize. Moreover, eastern commercial interests, always fearful of foreign adventures, were likely to oppose intervention on the side of the guerrillas with considerable fervor. Opportunities, however, come seldom to a nation which had no "points of contact" with "considerable foreign powers" and certainly faced no dangers from any of them.

If Democrats, too, wanted to "get up a foreign war, if possible," they did not share the Republicans' far-reaching objectives. Their motives were merely expedient. In the aftermath of the 1894 elections the Democratic Party was literally fighting for its life. If it failed to win southern farmers back to the party there was no doubt what the ultimate result would be—complete political disaster. As a Texas Democrat bluntly put it: "A number of Southern states will elect populist or fusion [Populist-Republican] state tickets and the Democratic Party will lose its power, prestige and machinery in the South." The entire national party faced imminent collapse. If the People's Party broke up the "Solid South" the northern Democrats could not survive either. Reduced to a hapless sectional rump holding out in a few urban bastions, they would be doomed to extinction as surely as the Whig Party of old. Shotguns and fraud had failed to halt the southern Populists' advance, but the Democratic Party, risen like a phoenix from the ashes of civil war, had no intention of being sent to extinction by an upstart party of rural stump-speakers, farm journalists, and untried politicians of no great political acumen.* After the 1894 elections the Democrats began concerting a plan, a desperate stratagem by which they intended to trap and ultimately destroy the People's Party in the South.[6]

The major elements in the Democratic plan were, first, to unleash across the rural South and West an intense and minutely organized propaganda campaign designed to persuade poor farmers that the free and unlimited coinage of silver bullion at the ratio of 16 to 1 to gold (twice the market value) would cure all their ills and remedy all their grievances; second, to make free silver coinage the major tenet of the Democratic Party's 1896 platform; third, to nominate for the presidency a well-recognized champion of free silver coinage. The ultimate purpose of the switch to free silver was to persuade a majority of the Populists at their 1896 convention to nominate the Democrats' own presidential candidate and, by that act of "fusion" in the cause of free silver to effect their own demise as an independent party. "Fusing" with a third party for the sole purpose of destroying it was an old party trick on the state level. This time, however, the Democrats were trying to accomplish it on a national scale and they had two considerable obstacles to overcome: the growing radicalism of rural voters and the wariness of the Populists themselves.[7]

As an inflationary measure, free silver had obvious appeal to farmers submerged in debt, but, as the Oregon *People's Post* observed in December 1894, it was a "very small reform" compared either to traditional agrarian demands or to the Populist program, which summed up and extended that tradition. The free coinage of silver bullion, in fact, was no more than the minimal departure

---

* The one major failing of the People's party was that its economic prescience was never matched by a corresponding political acuity. Politically, Populist leaders, particularly those from the western states, would prove themselves naive and shortsighted.

from the Democrats' do-nothing principle. Free silver coinage, for one thing, would not have established governmental control of the currency, one of the major objectives of agrarian reformers. Instead it would compel the federal government to coin all the bullion brought to the mint without the slightest regard for the needs of the economy. It was, in a word, inflationary laissez-faire, in contrast to the gold standard, which was deflationary laissez-faire. To overcome this handicap, Democrats intended to devote a major portion of their free silver propaganda to the elaborate pretense that free silver was a revolutionary measure whose enactment would mark the overthrow of the "money power" and the restoration of the "producing classes" to their rightful place in American society. The Democrats intended, that is, to wrap "a very small reform" in the radical sentiments of the People's Party and so transform a dubious panacea into a pseudo-Populist crusade.[8]

To overcome the Populists' suspicion of the established parties, the self-styled silver Democrats had to add yet another ingredient to their free silver propaganda. They would insist that their "movement" for free silver constituted a supreme rebellion against the Democratic Party's northern overlords, the New York Democracy in particular. Victory in that intraparty insurrection, the silver Democrats would then aver, would mean the complete and revolutionary transformation of the Democratic Party, a transformation that would make it worthy of "fusion" with the People's Party. To obscure the fact that the leaders of the "free silver movement" were in fact old-line southern ring politicians, often representatives of "the worst type of Bourbon Democracy," as one southern Populist put it, the Democrats intended to hold a number of free silver conferences and conventions designed to impress western Populists (southern Populists knew the Democrats too well to be fooled by anything they said or did) that they cared more for free silver than they did for the Democratic Party, when in fact the very opposite was true. The Democrats' fake insurrection would find its leaders returning to their former policies the moment their "revolution" had served its purpose.[9]

Since a genuine revolution obviously cannot be achieved with ease, Democrats bombarded western Populist leaders with a constant stream of lying reports about the insuperable difficulties they faced in their efforts to "capture" the Democratic Party and their almost certain prospect of defeat at the hands of the "gold" Democrats, who by now were a mere hapless rump. Since all efforts to promote fusion would be futile if the Populists held their nominating convention *before* the Democrats held theirs, Democrats frantically urged western Populists to wait until the Democratic convention was over. The bait they dangled was the prospect that they, the silver Democrats—who allegedly cared nothing for the Democratic Party as such—would bolt in a mass to the People's Party after the gold Democrats defeated them. Should the silverites, against all odds, triumph over the common foes—Wall Street, New York Democrats, the money power—would the Populists care or dare to reject fusion with a revolutionized Democratic Party that was linked to the old party merely by its name? Such, in brief, was the elaborate trap that old-line Democracy began laying for the People's Party as soon as the 1894 elections were over. If nothing else, it was a testament to the tight inner cohesion of the Democratic Party leadership. By June 1895, Chicago wardheelers from the Cook County machine would be chanting "16 to 1" at a party conference as if they were sharecroppers at the fork of a creek.[10]

It was the Democrats' free silver stratagem that set the party firmly on the road to war. Free silver was a dangerous stratagem to which the Democrats would never have resorted were it not for the still greater danger of Populism. It meant a drastic disruption of party routines; it would set a perilous precedent for genuine party rebellions in the future; it would attract to the Democratic Party agitators and reformers of every sort and description. Most important, it was forcing the southern Democrats, mainstay of the national party, to reverse the very policy on which their power for a generation had rested, that of keeping the rural populace in a state of apathy, despair, and inertia. Advocating free silver did not placate southern farmers, it made them hopeful and active. Crying up free silver as a revolutionary measure lured angry famers from the People's Party, but it left them no less angry. Moreover, to bring the free silver campaign to the voters, the Democrats were forced to create innumerable grass-roots "free silver clubs," thereby bringing thousands of southern farmers into organized political life. The entry of so many new men into the narrow ranks of the southern Democracy was itself a serious menace to the power of the southern state oligarchies. Little wonder, then, that the Richmond *Dispatch,* a voice of the Virginia oligarchy, looked forward to "swapping off the free coinage of silver for the Cuba question," that Cleveland's own consul general in Havana, Fitzhugh Lee, urged him to wage war against Spain because it "might do much toward directing the minds of the people away from imaginary ills," or that a Texas Democrat would beg the President to start a war with England at once in order to knock the "pus" out of this "anarchistic, socialistic and populistic boil." The prospect of war or even the mere rousing of war fever were simply promising popular distractions for a party forced to open its doors to angry farmers and not even sure that an eventual triumph over the People's Party might not prove a Pyrrhic victory in the end.[11]

That both parties were ready to "get up a foreign war, if possible," was not lost on President Cleveland. Personally, the President had never been a warmonger, a jingo, or an expansionist. Consistent with his belief in minimal government, he had long adhered to America's traditionally modest foreign policy. On the Cuba question, in fact, he was to maintain throughout his harrowing term of office a policy of strict neutrality and nonintervention. The President, however, was a desperate man. To Cleveland, the free coinage of silver was the ultimate economic menace, the final proof, as he had put it in September 1894, that his party was "returning to the wallowing in the mire." He had no direct means of stopping the Democrats. Cleveland's power in the party was now virtually nil. Even "gold" Democrats he had trusted to defend "sound money" with his own stubborn fidelity were prudently moving into the camp of the old-line party bosses. He was determined, nonetheless, to forestall the free silver stratagem. If the party of "cheap expediency" favored war as well as free silver, then perhaps they might accept war in place of free silver. In that way, at any rate, "sound money" would be saved. For the sake of sound money Cleveland had already sacrificed, quite unselfishly, his power and his popularity. In the aftermath of the 1894 elections, Cleveland was prepared to sacrifice the scruples of a lifetime and foment a war crisis with

England. The result was to be a temporary detour on the road to war with Spain, a detour which revealed that the political motives for the Spanish-American War predated every reason American politicians would give for starting it.[12]

Cleveland took the first public step toward crisis with England on December 3, 1894, in his annual message to Congress. In the message the President pledged himself to resolve by diplomacy an ongoing dispute between Venezuela and Britain, a dispute over the boundary of British Guiana that had sputtered on and off for half a century. At Venezuela's request he was going to try to "induce" Great Britain to refer the entire matter to arbitration, a proposal that Britain had rejected but "which is so earnestly sought by her weaker adversary." A puny nation, seeking justice, was being bullied by a great imperial power, and the United States, as a disinterested third party, was going to help rectify the wrong.[13]

Cleveland's decision to intervene in the Venezuela dispute was a sharp reversal of policy. A year before Cleveland had felt no obligation to help settle Venezuela's quarrel with Britain. To Venezuela's formal bid for American help in securing arbitration, Secretary of State Gresham had curtly replied, in January 1894, that Venezuela ought to resume its sundered diplomatic ties with Britain and reach "a good understanding." That cool reply and the standoff policy behind it had been understandable enough. The United States had no stake whatever in the dispute, no treaty obligations to fulfill, no national interest to serve, no threatened honor to uphold. Moreover the Venezuelan government, a corrupt dictatorship, had ulterior motives of its own for stirring up the dispute, which was as tawdry as it was tangled. It stemmed from conflicting territorial claims which each party had inherited from predecessors. Britain's claim, later upheld by an international tribunal, was based on the Dutch estimate of the boundaries of its Guiana colony, part of which the Dutch had ceded to Britain in 1810. Venezuela's claim, far more extreme than Britain's, was inherited from the Spanish Empire, whose pretensions in the region had been founded in large measure on the vague reports of Spanish adventurers. The overlapping claims left a vast area, much of it wilderness, in permanent if sporadic dispute. Between January and December 1894, all that had really changed in the affair was that a half-century-old quarrel had grown ten months older and the President of the United States was bent on stirring up trouble.[14]

Since Cleveland had never been a warmonger, the press at first took little notice of his pledge to "induce" a major power to do what it had adamantly refused to do. The lame-duck Democratic Congress, however, took the President's cue with alacrity. On January 10, 1895, a Georgia Democrat introduced into the House a joint resolution urging the President to secure arbitration of the Anglo-Venezuelan boundary dispute. By February 22 it had passed both houses of Congress unanimously, an encouraging response to the President's message. It is doubtful if anyone in Congress knew how far Cleveland intended to go, but the nation's legislators clearly approved the direction he was taking. Trouble with Britain was the one species of international wrangling that was certain at any time to win the electorate's approval.[15]

By the end of 1894 Britain had become a target particularly well suited to Cleveland's purpose, that of providing the Democrats with a vote-getting substitute for the "mire" of free silver. Among rural voters, hatred of the British had grown singularly intense. To the nation's angry farmers, it was British gold, British capital, and British influence which seemed to block every effort at reform. Time and again they were warned that some agrarian reform or other would frighten British investors, compelling them to withdraw their capital from America and bringing our economy to a halt. That anger the silver Democrats had been exploiting for some time. "Shall we bow the knee to England?" Democratic Senator Francis Cockrell of Missouri had declaimed during the silver-repeal fight. Other Democrats took up the cry. "It is time we act for ourselves and not be consulting England," asserted Representative William Jennings Bryan of Nebraska, a rising young politician who made it one of his leading themes on the stump. "War with England," declared the free silver publicist William "Coin" Harvey, would be the most "just war ever waged by man." War with England, said Nevada's Republican Senator William Stewart, a tenacious foe of reform as well as an ardent free silverite, would "rid the country of the English bank rule." Blaming British influence for the nation's economic ills, millions of rural voters were ready to regard war with England as an economic panacea in itself. This was the sentiment that Cleveland hoped to exploit. His diplomacy now proceeded steadily down the path toward war.[16]

On January 23, 1895, the State Department formally requested Thomas Bayard, America's Ambassador to England, to convey to the British government the President's wish to see the Venezuela boundary dispute settled by arbitration. On February 4, the British replied that they were willing to arbitrate all territory in dispute up to what was known as the Schomburgk line, behind which British subjects had been settled for fifty years. Given the dubious grounds of Venezuela's claims, Britain's response was by no means unreasonable. Had he wished to avoid trouble, Cleveland could easily have turned around and urged Venezuela to accept Britain's offer. He could even have hailed the British offer as proof of its respect for the wishes of the United States. Hoping to bring about a crisis Cleveland took the very opposite tack. After concluding, without warrant, that Venezuela's inflated claims were absolutely valid and Britain's entirely false, Cleveland rejected the British proposal. It is a measure of the corrupting effects of the political crisis that Cleveland, an essentially honorable man, had reached that self-serving conclusion by taking the word of a rascal named William Scruggs, the paid Washington lobbyist for the Venezuela government, whose sole distinction was his ill repute. A few years before, as ambassador to Venezuela, Scruggs had been discharged by President Harrison for financial misconduct in office. To such shabby makeshifts had the self-righteous Cleveland been driven. A President who regarded patronage-seeking politicians as despicable knaves was determined to risk the peace of his country on evidence supplied by the corrupt tool of a notorious dictator.

To increase his pressure on Britain, however, Cleveland needed a far stronger position in the Anglo-Venezuelan dispute than his original modest role as a disinterested third party. The only way he could bring to bear in due time the full weight of the American government, the full support of Congress, the press, and the people was to lay claim to a national stake in the dispute. Since none existed, Cleveland's next step was to fabricate one. The ingredients were at hand, as they usually are in diplomatic affairs. In 1823 President James Monroe had declared in a celebrated address that any effort by a European monarchy to "extend" its system of rule to the New World would be regarded as dangerous to the United States. The Monroe Doctrine, as it came to be known, had long held an honored place among the public sentiments of the American people, although it had been honored but intermittently by American administrations and had never been formally recognized by any act or resolution of Congress. Committed in the past to a restrained foreign policy, Cleveland himself had shown no interest in the Monroe Doctrine. As he later admitted to Ambassador Bayard, his "inclination" had been "to avoid a doctrine which I knew to be troublesome." Cleveland now viewed it more hospitably. From Monroe's speech he now saw implications that no previous President had hitherto detected. It had not occurred to anyone before Cleveland that a mere boundary dispute between an American republic and an established European colony could possibly violate the Monroe Doctrine. Such was the implication Cleveland now drew from Monroe's seventy-two-year-old utterance. Having entered the Anglo-Venezuelan dispute as a disinterested third party, Cleveland was ready to plunge into it further in the far more formidable role of defender of America's national interest—namely, our national interest in enforcing the Monroe Doctrine. It only remained to inform the British, as provocatively as possible, that they were no longer disputing with puny Venezuela but with the United States in all its might and majesty.[17]

In the meantime the leading politicians of both parties began smoothing the path for Cleveland's intervention in Venezuela. When it came to fomenting trouble abroad, the President, who otherwise had few supporters, had almost no opponents. Eager for a fresh foreign venture, the Republicans were not about to neglect the new issue of Venezuela's boundary which Cleveland had injected so abruptly into national politics. Republicans quickly made it their own. In March 1895, Republicans began in earnest to attack British policies in Latin America and to call for strong U.S. action in defense of Venezuela. The party press, which had ignored the issue before, now took up the Republicans' cry and treated its readers to the Venezuelan view of the dispute which Scruggs had been assiduously propounding on Capitol Hill. When the Cleveland administration on April 5 made public the British offer to arbitrate claims west of the Schomburgk line, the press, now coached in its duties, raged in fury over Britain's alleged rebuff to the United States. By April 12 the anti-British agitation had grown so intense that the British ambassador complained bitterly in private that "every sort of lie is propagated about British aggression."[18]

Like President Cleveland, the Republicans, too, saw ripe opportunities for intervention in a suitably expanded version of the Monroe Doctrine. The party's rising foreign affairs spokesman, Senator Lodge, well known for his scholarly bent and well hated by his fellow Boston Brahmins for his servility to the Republican oligarchy, published in June a learned essay entitled "England, Venezuela and the Monroe Doctrine." Replete with gross historical errors, the article accused Britain of violating the doctrine in Venezuela and therefore of committing nothing less than an act of hostility against the United States. Not for the last time would Senator Lodge make a mock show of learning to fabricate pretexts for war and aggression.[19]

The Democrats, too, were eager for a foreign adventure. On April 10, the party's chief spokesman on foreign affairs, Senator Morgan of Alabama, chairman of the Foreign Relations Committee, announced that he was certain of British aggression in Venezuela. Two weeks later the New York *Sun* reported that "the Old Guard of the Democracy" was disgusted with the President's flaccid conduct of foreign affairs; they were impatient to see him push further into the Venezuelan dispute. Avid for war with *someone* three years before the *Maine* exploded, the nation's political leaders had transformed a foreign quarrel of no consequence to the United States into a major political issue and had distorted it beyond recognition. Indeed, among the country's leading politicians bellicosity was reaching out in every direction during the early months of 1895. In March, when Spanish authorities in Cuba, suspicious of gun runners, shot at an American merchant ship for not stopping at their command, Democrats and Republicans raised a hue and cry out of all proportion to the incident. "The outrage would not have been more flagrant," said the Republican New York *Tribune,* "if [the Spanish] had entered the harbor of New York and bombarded the City Hall." Senator Morgan called indignantly for the "dispatch of a fleet of warships to Havana." Referring to Cuba, Republican Senator Shelby Cullom of Illinois announced that "it is time someone woke up and realized the necessity of annexing more property." The cause of Cuban *independence* had not yet become the official Republican line. Indeed, in the spring of 1895 war with England seemed a far likelier prospect than war with Spain. Any war agitation would do, however, for in the early months of 1895, explosive events were taking place on the domestic front that roused the public temper, already bitter and disaffected, to a pitch of fury rarely matched in our history.[20]

In January 1895, the Supreme Court decided an antitrust suit in favor of one of the country's most thoroughgoing monopolies, the American Sugar Refining Company. The decision not only virtually nullified the 1890 Sherman Antitrust Act, it was openly connived at by Cleveland's Attorney General Richard Olney, mastermind in the suppression of the Pullman strike, who prosecuted the suit with the collusive intention of losing it.[21]

In early February the public received an even greater shock. Faced for a third time with a dwindling Treasury gold reserve, Cleveland made a private gold-buying deal with J. P. Morgan and August Belmont. Forcing the President to accept harsh terms, the two bankers netted themselves a windfall profit of some $7 million within a matter of hours. The humiliating spectacle of the United States government at the mercy of two greedy bankers "stirred millions of Americans," a contemporary historian recalled, "to a pitch of acrimonious frenzy for which there are few parallels in our history." Had debt-ridden farmers doubted the existence of the money power, there it was at a White House conference table forcing a President to his knees.[22]

That furor had scarcely died down when on April 8 the Supreme Court declared a federal income tax on landed property an invalid "assault upon capital" and ultimately decided on May 20, in one of the worst decisions in Court history, that no federal income tax was valid. In the space of a mere fourteen years the Court had overturned a unanimous prior holding of the Court. The tortuous special pleading of the Court majority, its gross partiality to the propertied, sent a thrill of rage even through the opinions of the dissenting judges. "The decision," declared Justice Henry Brown in the hushed, packed courtroom, "involves nothing less than the surrender of the taxing power to the moneyed classes." Millions of Americans, thrown into yet another spasm of rage, now saw their worst suspicions confirmed—the government, the laws, the Constitution itself, were no longer the people's. The rich and the privileged had appropriated everything, and the Supreme Court had become their shameless tool.[23]

By then the Republican Party, deaf to the popular clamor, was beginning to eye with some interest the progress of the rebellion in Cuba and to lay plans for devoting the first session of the new Republican-controlled Congress as far as possible to foreign affairs. At the same time, President Cleveland, emboldened by the politicians' welcome response to his preliminary dealings with England, took the next step on the road to international crisis.

On May 1 a fatal illness removed the last minor impediment to Cleveland's Venezuela diplomacy, namely Secretary of State Gresham, who was as strongly anti-interventionist as Cleveland had been when he appointed him two years before. With Gresham on his deathbed—he died on May 28—Cleveland called upon Olney to take charge of the Venezuela business and prepare a diplomatic note to the British that would precipitate the crisis. With his shyster lawyer's mind, his unflinching audacity, and his forehead of brass, Olney, a former corporation lawyer, was perfectly suited to the task. When he completed the note on July 2 the President pronounced it "the best thing of its kind I ever read."[24]

It was a remarkable document, remarkable for its specious reasoning, its vulgar swagger, its insulting bellicosity, and most of all for its extraordinary escalation of America's alleged interest in the Anglo-Venezuelan boundary dispute. Simply put, Olney's note to the British was a dire threat harshly expressed: If Britain rejected the American demand that it submit the entire Venezuela claim to arbitration, the United States was prepared to go to war. "Today," Olney warned the British government, in an unprecedented assertion of American hegemony in Latin America, "the United States is practically sovereign on this continent, and its fiat is law upon the subjects to which it confines its interposition."[25]

According to Olney, who was now secretary of state, it was the Monroe Doctrine that gave the United States so large a stake in the Venezuela dispute and so authoritative a "fiat" in resolving it.

Just how the Monroe Doctrine applied in the case presented no problem to Olney. If the British refused arbitration, then the United States, said the note, would conclude that the British had committed an "invasion and conquest of Venezuela territory." Britain, in consequence, would stand guilty of attempting to "extend" a monarchical system of government to this hemisphere, thereby violating Monroe's "rule." Since the violation of that "rule"—the presumption that Monroe's 1823 speech was an ironclad rule of international law would particularly irk the British—would be "injurious to the interests of the people of the United States," Congress stood ready, warned Olney, to take "measures necessary or proper for the vindication" of the American people's interests. The threat of war was plain and the threat, warned Olney, was no bluff. The United States was "practically invulnerable against any and all other powers." With this and other truculent admonitions, Olney concluded his note, ostensibly dedicated to the peaceful adjudication of international disputes.

What Cleveland wanted, plainly, was not arbitration but provocation, the provocation implicit in Olney's proposition that Britain abase itself before America's meddlesome fiat or prepare itself for war. It fell to the unfortunate Ambassador Bayard, who could not understand how a boundary dispute could be deemed an "invasion," to deliver his government's note to the Tory ministry of Lord Salisbury, which received it on August 7.

While the Tory government disdainfully took its time in replying, tension over Venezuela began mounting in America. In October, Republicans got wind of the Olney note, which encouraged them to revive their spring agitation of the Venezuela question. Representative Charles Grosvenor of Ohio reminded the public of "our duty in the Venezuela crisis," while the Republican governor of Pennsylvania publicly denounced Cleveland's failure to enforce the Monroe Doctrine, a typical example of what might best be described as partisan bipartisanship, for it consisted in attacking the rival party's President for not doing what in fact he was doing. On December 3, one day after the new Congress convened, Republicans obliged the Democratic President still further by subscribing fully to Olney's expansion of Monroe's "rule." On December 10 Senators Lodge and Cullom introduced joint resolutions designed to make the Monroe Doctrine the official policy of the United States and to define it so broadly that it covered the Anglo-Venezuelan boundary dispute. A Republican President could hardly have gotten more support from the minions of his own party.[26]

Four days later the British reply to America's note reached the administration and the stage was set, predictably, for a crisis. The British government refused to comply with the U.S. demand that it submit to arbitration British-held land east of the Schomburgk line. It noted, correctly, that Monroe's Doctrine had undergone a "strange development" in Olney's hands and that the disputed frontier of Venezuela "has nothing to do with any questions dealt with by President Monroe." It also noted, again quite correctly, that Olney's presentation of the dispute was based entirely on "*ex parte* statements emanating from Venezuela." It also noted, among other particulars, that it was scarely fair for the British to submit to the perils of arbitration territory that had been occupied continuously for two centuries by the Dutch and their British heirs.[27]

Cleveland, needless to say, was not persuaded. On December 17, in a special message to Congress that bristled with jingo truculence, Cleveland publicly precipitated the crisis. The British reply, reported the President, was wholly unsatisfactory to the American government, whose stake in the dispute was great. "The doctrine on which we stand is strong and sound because its enforcement is important to our peace and safety . . . and can not become obsolete while our Republic endures." Since Britain had refused arbitration, said Cleveland, the United States would determine the true boundary between Venezuela and British Guiana. Once that was done, Cleveland warned, "It will in my opinion be the duty of the United States to resist by every means in its power, as a willful aggression upon its rights and interests, the appropriation by Great Britain of any lands or the exercise of governmental jurisdiction over any territory which after investigation we have determined of right belongs to Venezuela." The United States, formerly indifferent, then a third party, had now become the only party to the Anglo-Venezuelan boundary dispute. And our armed might was ready to back up our fiat. In his conclusion Cleveland endorsed a principle of intervention more extreme than anything even Republicans had thus far invoked. If the risks of war with Britain were great, said the President, they were well worth taking: "There is no calamity which a great nation can invite which equals that which follows from a supine submission to wrong and injustice." It was America's duty to redress the world's wrongs.[28]

After the message was read, a wild tumult of cheering swept across an overjoyed Congress. Almost everywhere the response of the politicians was overwhelming, exultant approval. "Republicans vied with Democrats," recalled a historian of the day, "in praising the boldness and patriotism of the President." Democrats who had been reviling Cleveland a few days before rushed to register their approval of his truculent diplomacy. From all over the country public men wired their congratulations to the White House, including Governor William McKinley of Ohio, the rising star of the Republican Party, who praised Cleveland for upholding "the honor of the nation." The President's admirers were deeply disturbed. Godkin wrote in disgust that the "jingoes" were "circling hand in hand around Cleveland and cheering him till their voices crack." Carl Schurz lamented the "grievous break in Mr. Cleveland's otherwise so dignified and statesmanlike foreign policy." Poor Ambassador Bayard, shaken to the core, wondered in private why Cleveland "should abandon suddenly his attitude of conservatism and go apparently into the camp of aggressiveness." The elegant John Hay had his own explanation: The President was in "a disturbed state of mind," driven mad, presumably, by popular hatred, party malfeasance, and what Cleveland himself called "the malevolent change in our public life."[29]

In the country at large, pent-up anger against Britain vented itself in popular, if short-lived, war fever, and Henry Adams shrewdly put his finger on its source. It was due, he wrote an English friend three days after the President's message, to "the bitterness excited by the silver struggle." Although Senator Marion Butler, Populist-Republican from North Carolina, accused Cleveland of deceitfully exploiting hatred of Britain to further his own Wall Street policies, silver Democrats did not mind the deceit. Senator John Daniel, a chieftain of the reactionary Virginia oligarchy and a leader of the free silver movement, rejoiced at the popular war clamor. He thought it "a sublime spectacle to behold how the call of patriotism made the people one," which is to say, how it relieved the political pressure from reformers, agitators, and angry farmers.[30]

The President and Olney, as Adams remarked in late December, had pulled off a major political coup: "They have the country on the run and will force foreign affairs forward as the issue in the general election." Cleveland, in fact, could have done so easily, but it required a measure of ruthlessness that, to his credit, was beyond him. Having brought the United States to the brink of war Cleveland did not seem to harbor any further discernible intentions. To carry warmongering further, to take direct personal responsibility for useless bloodshed was more than the President dared. What he did instead was let the British decide for him the issues of war and peace. Given the British government's own truculent temper at the time, the prospects for peace were by no means propitious. As the veteran diplomat Henry White remarked, the President's message to Congress was "calculated to render a modification of the English position more difficult." If there was to be peace, said White, "it will be rather in spite of than because of the Cleveland diplomacy." Given the temper of Congress and the country, any provocative move by the British—a diplomatic rebuke to the United States, a preparatory movement of battleships—and the dogs of war would surely have slipped from the President's control. Since Cleveland had created the explosive situation he certainly did not shrink from the prospect, but he did shrink from lighting the match himself. That no explosion occurred was chiefly due to the intercession of a wholly fortuitous event.[31]

On January 3, 1896, Germany's Kaiser Wilhelm sent his famous telegram to President Paul Kruger of the Transvaal Republic, congratulating him on repulsing a British-led raid. With that cable, which opened up a new chapter in European affairs, the Kaiser inadvertently secured peace between the United States and Britain. Faced with the new menace of Imperial Germany, Lord Salisbury was persuaded by his cabinet on January 11 to make himself agreeable to America and drop the dispute over Venezuela's boundary. A completely unpredictable occurrence had put an end to the crisis.

The effects of the crisis did not pass quite so swiftly. In after years a friend of Cleveland's would bluntly accuse the former President of being "the father of the spirit of imperialism," meaning that he had paved the way, quite unintentionally, for the Span-ish-American War. There was much truth in the charge. With his Venezuela adventure Cleveland had forced a major breach in America's traditional foreign policy; he had endorsed with the prestige of the presidency the proposition that it was America's duty to right wrongs abroad; he had laid sweeping claim to Ameri-can hegemony in Latin America. Most important, he had revealed to the nation's political leaders that the American people could in-deed be diverted from their domestic concerns if the right sort of foreign crusade was offered.[32]

3

"The Broad Ground of a Common Humanity"

One effect of the Venezuela crisis was short-lived. It delayed for a few months the efforts of interventionists in Congress to foment a crisis over Cuba, a somewhat more difficult task than crying up war with Britain. In the country at large, popular sympathy for the Cuban rebels was widespread, but in 1895—and for a long time thereafter—it was a passive, onlooker's sympathy. Witnessing a contest between republicans and imperialists, the great majority of Americans rooted for the republicans, but they had a rooting interest only. Despite their sympathy for the rebel cause, Americans neither expected nor demanded the government to intervene militarily on the rebels' behalf. They had no reason to do so. War with Spain, unlike war with England, promised no economic advantage to any portion of the American electorate. Nor were Americans, still engrossed in their own troubles, yet convinced that it was their government's obligation to alleviate the sufferings of foreigners. To alter those sentiments was the first and most important task of interventionist politicians. By inciting hatred of Spain, by crying up interventionist pretexts, by encouraging the rebels to prolong their struggle, by entangling America officially in Cuban affairs, the interventionists bent themselves to the task of turning passive, if promising, sympathy into active, fighting support.

As early as the summer of 1895, during a lull in the Venezuela agitation, the Republicans—though by no means unanimously in favor of intervention—made it clear that they intended to oppose, disrupt, and render untenable President Cleveland's declared policy of nonintervention in Spain's Cuban problems. With summer's end, organized agitation over the Cuban question burst on the public scene like a series of bomb explosions. In the North, Republicans (and Democrats to a lesser extent) began marshaling support for the Cuban rebels by staging mass rallies in their honor. From September to December 1895 hardly a week passed without news of a pro-rebel rally or a resounding declaration of support for the rebels from some prominent senator, governor, or local party organization. In organizing the rallies, Republicans not only pressed into service their long-standing auxiliary, the Grand Army of the Republic, they found a new ally in Samuel Gompers's fourteen-year-old American Federation of Labor, which now began what would prove to be an unbroken career of favoring foreign wars.

The autumn campaign had its obvious purposes: to strengthen public sympathy for the rebels, to render it visible at mass meetings, and to give it the imprimatur of reputable political endorsement. It also had a specific political objective. At the rallies people were urged to petition Congress with demands that President Cleveland grant belligerency rights to Cuban rebels. The demand sounded innocent enough. On the surface it seemed like a modest show of national accord with the rebels and one, moreover, without any overt interventionist implications. The organizers of the petition campaign knew better. Were Cleveland forced to grant such recognition, it would have quickly supplied the interventionists with a useful pretext for armed intervention. Granting belligerency rights to the rebels would give Spain the right, under international law, to search American ships—gun runners—on the high seas for contraband of war. This was the surest way to provoke an incident likely to inflame public passions. As a member of the Cuban Junta candidly put it: "If the Spanish cruisers should stop the American vessels the skippers are not very patient men, and it would not be long before a shot would be fired. Both countries would be plunged into war and then our business is done and you take care of it." For that very reason, President Grant in 1870 had denied belligerent status to Cuban rebels, who wanted, said Grant, to "embroil this government in complications and possible hostilities with Spain . . . carefully covered under the deceptive and apparently plausible demand for a mere recognition of belligerency." What had been a dangerous measure to leaders bent on nonintervention had, understandably, become desirable to those determined to create "complications and possible hostilities."[1]

Despite the political organization behind it, the petition campaign proved a popular failure, a testament to the passive nature of American sympathy for the Cuban rebels.* The petitions trickled fitfully into Congress for four months. Most of them were of the order of "sundry citizens" of Maple Hill, Illinois, or "76 citizens" of Canton, Pennsylvania, begging, in the stereotyped language of centrally organized agitation, for "the speedy recognition of the belligerency rights of Cuban patriots in their struggle for freedom." During the same period Congress received, far more spontaneously, about ten times as many petitions calling for immigration restrictions. Since the belligerency petitions were chiefly a pretext for agitating the Cuban question in Congress, congressional leaders described the trickle as an irresistible flood of public sentiment which compelled them to speak out against the neutral diplomacy of Cleveland and begin the task of persuading Americans that their government had a major stake in the internal conditions of Cuba.

The main headquarters of that effort was the floor of the United States Senate, where from February to April 1896—after a two-month delay over the Venezuela crisis—the first and most important battle on the Cuba question took place.

It began on February 20, when the Senate Foreign Relations Committee favorably reported out a concurrent (nonbinding) resolution calling on the President to recognize the belligerency rights of the Cuban rebels as well as an amendment to the resolution calling on him to use his good offices to secure Cuba's independence. Completely dominated by interventionists, the committee had gone about its work in a noteworthy manner. Rejecting efforts by the Spanish ambassador to submit a Spanish view of the Cuba question, the committee took all its information from the Cuban Junta,

---

*Evidence for that passivity, cited by Senator Hale of Maine, the leading Republican foe of intervention, was the fact that throughout the prewar period scarcely a single non-Cuban American volunteered to fight with the rebels.

which readily persuaded committee members that the "Republic of Cuba" was a functioning government, which it was not; that the Spanish were committing barbarous atrocities, which they were not; that the "Army of Liberation," by contrast, was a regularly organized military force which strictly adhered to the rules of war, which was even more grotesquely untrue. Thus armed with the Junta's propaganda and news clippings from the more sensational newspapers, the senators on the committee began their propaganda assault on Spain and on Cleveland's policy of nonintervention. Senator Lodge, who had previously favored the annexation of Cuba, now called for American efforts to secure Cuban independence by any means necessary. The bloodshed on the island, he insisted, was more than the human heart could bear. Other senators agreed. "How long," cried George Grey, a Democrat from Delaware, "are we to listen to the cries of outraged humanity that every southern breeze wafts across the straits that separate Cuba from Florida?" Spain was "the most wicked despotism there is today on this earth," thundered Senator William Frye of Maine, one of the most outspoken of Republican interventionists. "I have but one desire," said Frye, "and that is to see Cuba an independent Republic." The Democrats' Senator Morgan, who took charge of the debate for the committee, cried out in one of several inflammatory speeches that America's neutrality was "a stain upon our national honor." Democratic Senator George Vest of Missouri deemed it a crime to let Spain destroy the island of Cuba. By a curious inversion, the Senate orators managed to convey the impression that Spain had invaded the island and was bent on destroying the cane fields which the "Republic of Cuba" was trying to protect.[2]

Since international law posed a considerable obstacle to American intervention, Senate warmongers were quick to discern higher laws and more transcendent duties. Senator Lodge, who had already called a boundary dispute in Venezuela an act of hostility against America, insisted that intervention to achieve Cuban independence was justified "on the broad ground of a common humanity." Senator Roger Mills, Democrat of Texas, thought the newly expanded Monroe Doctrine gave the United States the duty to force Spain out of Cuba. Senator Vest invoked the deity. Securing Cuba's independence, he said, is "the task assigned us by Providence." To the objection that congressional demands for Cuban belligerency rights would anger Spain and might well lead to war, Senator Morgan replied, correctly enough, that "I contemplate war at the end of any resolution that we pass." The responsibility for it, however, would be Spain's, for "Spain has no real legitimate right to hold the province of Cuba" whereas the United States had "a very peculiar relation . . . to the government and people of Cuba."[3]

On February 28, the day set aside for the Senate vote, John Sherman of Ohio, an elder statesman of the Republican party and the Republicans' successor to Morgan as chairman of the Foreign Relations Committee, summed up the interventionists' line in one of the more mendacious speeches of the session. Assertions that the guerrillas had formed no government (which meant they had no legal title to belligerency rights) were "absolutely untrue," declared Senator Sherman. Assertions that the rebels were inflicting great misery on their fellow Cubans, an understandable sore point with the interventionists, were equally false. The rebel army, said Sherman, was "humane." It was Spain's newly appointed Captain General of Cuba, Valeriano Weyler, who was a fiend in human guise. As proof Sherman offered a translation of an alleged Spanish history book which had appeared in William Randolph Hearst's newly acquired New York *Journal*—"one of the great journals of the country," noted Sherman—and which chronicled the atrocities allegedly committed by General Weyler during the earlier Cuban revolt. To Sherman the conclusion was inescapable. "The intervention of the United States must sooner or later be given to put an end to crimes that are almost beyond description."[4]

Both the belligerency resolution and the amendment calling on the President to help secure Cuban independence passed the Senate by the lopsided margin of 64–6. On March 2, the House of Representatives passed its own resolution, one that also called for "intervention if necessary," by a vote of 262–17. When Senate members of the House-Senate conference committee reported in favor of the more bellicose House resolution, however, a few opponents of intervention felt constrained to speak out.

Senator Hoar of Massachusetts exposed the falsity of the Foreign Relations Committee's evidence and humiliated Senator Sherman by noting that his authoritative history of General Weyler's past crimes "turns out to be a statement of the agent or counsel of the Cuban belligerents." Democratic Senator Donelson Caffery of Louisiana exposed the hypocrisy of those senators who denied any desire for war. What was the purpose of their savage attacks on Spain, he asked, "if it is not to inflame the warlike passions of the American people and embroil us in a controversy with a friendly state?" Why else, asked Caffery, were so many senators trying to replace our obligations under international law with the "propaganda of republicanism"? Senator Hale of Maine, in a powerful speech delivered on March 9, also attacked the "inflammatory appeals that were made to this body by Senators . . . based upon alleged statements of atrocities and horrors on the Island of Cuba." Hale, the most politically influential of Republican opponents of war, reminded the Senate of President Grant's stand against belligerency rights. He even dared mention what the interventionists were at some pains to deny—that it was the guerrillas whose conduct was cruel and destructive. "It is incendiarism; it is the torch of destruction; it is pillage; it is murder; it is outrage." Summing up the political events of the preceding twelve months, a year in which the reform agitation of the electorate seemed to be running a match race with the war agitation of their elected representatives, Hale professed himself deeply disturbed "by the growth of what I may call the aggressive spirit as shown particularly within the last year . . . the desire to incite trouble, the desire to make difficulties with foreign powers, the dealing with the discussion, the imagery of war rather than of peace."[5]

Hale's Maine party colleague in the House, Representative Charles Boutelle, hit off well the glaring hypocrisy of the propagandists of "republicanism." We were, he said, a nation where millions of black people "are still denied some of the most sacred rights guaranteed to the people of this country in the Declaration of Independence. With this condition confronting us, it is strange, indeed, for us to dash across the Gulf of Mexico [sic] and establish and maintain the independence and freedom of the insurgents in the Island of Cuba. I can not so understand it. I do not believe it to be our duty."[6]

Stung by the criticism, interventionist leaders delivered a savage riposte to their congressional critics, numerically insignificant though they were. Senator Morgan denounced opponents of the belligerency resolution as nothing less than "hired traitors." Senator Mills discovered fresh grounds for armed intervention in the death of naturalized Cuban-Americans fighting in Cuba: "The blood of our citizens butchered by Spain is crying from the earth to us and I for one am for calling her to account." It was a flimsy pretext, but the interventionists were urgently in need of a patriotic as opposed to a humanitarian reason for war. A half-dozen senators thundered in wrath against the Spanish ambassador for pointing out in a public letter that some of the committee's sources were not altogether reliable.[7]

The opposition, although few in number, won a partial victory. With a presidential election in the offing, a majority of senators agreed with New York's Senator Hill that the House resolution threatening armed intervention was going too far "at this time." On April 6, the House adopted the Senate's milder resolution by a vote of 247–27.[8]

The damage, however, was done. By an overwhelming vote, Congress had endorsed the rebel cause, had virtually branded Spain the aggressor in Cuba, and had legitimated in principle America's right and duty to intervene in Cuban affairs. By their actions, congressional leaders had deliberately infuriated Spain, filled it with mistrust of America's intentions, and effectively destroyed Cleveland's efforts to end the rebellion by winning Spanish concessions for Cuba. Hoping to forestall the interventionists in Congress, Cleveland tried in April 1896 to persuade Spain to grant home rule to Cuba in return for American efforts to get the rebels to lay down their arms. The Spanish government rejected the offer. Given the attitudes of the American Congress, Spain could scarcely expect anything from America's diplomatic intervention in Cuba except the ultimate termination of its sovereignty. Indeed, the open hostility of the American Congress made it difficult for the Spanish government even to appear to be bowing to American demands.[9]

The actions of Congress, moreover, made it impossible for President Cleveland to fulfill the obligations of neutrality. It was not lost on federal judges who tried violations of the neutrality laws that laxity was the policy in congressional request. The latter was no small concern since American gunrunning to Cuba, a lucrative if illicit enterprise, helped the hard-pressed rebels continue their fight. Grasping what Congress required of them, federal judges gave the neutrality laws a sufficiently loose interpretation to keep from discouraging the arms traffic. The Spanish authorities in Cuba also found themselves debarred from imprisoning Cuban-American rebels arrested in Cuba. Apprehended, they demanded the rights and immunities of American citizens—which in fact they had forfeited—and the State Department had no recourse but to press Spain for their release. Had it failed to do so, the administration would have invited savage denunciation in Congress, for the Spanish imprisonment of American citizens—naturalized Cubans—was a favorite war cry of the interventionists. In their struggle to put down a rebellion, the Spanish government found itself fighting guerrillas who were armed, protected, and encouraged to struggle on indefinitely by leading American politicians determined to thwart as best they could any peaceful resolution of the guerrilla warfare in Cuba. It was the prospect of war, not the "cries of outraged humanity" that had stirred the interventionists in the first place.[10]

The events on Capitol Hill did not take place in a vacuum. From the outset of the Cuban rebellion the great majority of American newspapers expressed their sympathy for the rebel cause, their support for gunrunning, and their opposition to Cleveland's neutrality. In New York City, only Godkin's *Evening Post* remembered the sanctity of property, forgotten by the press since the Pullman strike, and castigated the guerrillas for violating it. When it became clear that interventionist sentiment ran strong in both parties, pro-Cuban editorial opinion quickly found its way into the news. Much of the Cuban news, in fact, the American press received directly from the Junta in New York, and the Junta, anxious to draw American attention away from the rebels' terrorist tactics, was ready to offer an endless stock of "eyewitness" reports of Spanish atrocities: the rape of defenseless women, the burning of hospitals, and the bayoneting of babies before the eyes of their horror-stricken parents—the standard "boiler plate" of every modern war's war propaganda. American newspaper readers would learn, day after day, that the Spanish were "feeding prisoners to the sharks," that "old men and little boys were cut down and their bodies fed to the

dogs," that General Weyler—"butcher Weyler" in the press—had
been overheard to threaten his resignation if he were "not allowed
to quench his thirst in American gore." As purveyors of sensational
Cuba stories, Joseph Pulitzer's New York *World* and Hearst's rival
Journal blazed all the journalistic trails. Newspapers in the hinter-
lands passed their stories along to the rest of the country, just as
during the Pullman strike the entire press had echoed the hysterical
antistriker lies of the Chicago *Tribune*, not merely because the
Tribune had been nearest the scene but because it had also taken
the correct line.[11]

America's newspapers did not invent the line on the Cuba question; still less did they force it upon politicians. Of all the myths
about the Spanish-American War, none is more frivolous than the
assertion that the inflammatory reporting of the American press
(or in the extreme view, the reporting of two rival New York newspapers) was an independent cause of the war. Nothing could be
further from the truth, for there was nothing independent about the
American press. It was, overwhelmingly, a party press, a press that
echoed to the point of slavishness the policies and propaganda of
one or the other major party. The majority of American newspapers were little more than quasi–house organs of the party organizations, "the strongest buttress of the machine and the Bosses," as
a contemporary foreign observer of American party politics put it.
Where a state machine was very powerful, virtually the entire news
coverage in the state was effectively in its hands. Senatory Quay's
formidable Pennsylvania machine, for example, "controlled much
of the news reporting machinery of the larger cities of the state. . . .
It was so managed that seldom did an Associated Press story get on
the wires of which the machine gang hadn't first approved." Less
powerful political machines exerted less strict control; a few headstrong editors such as Godkin followed their own bent; newspapers
read chiefly by the rich had to modify the party line to suit their
readers' tastes; but the American press in general was an instrument and a mouthpiece of party, including Pulitzer's *World*, which
was the Democracy's national house organ, and Hearst's *Journal,*
which Hearst was using to further his personal ambitions within
the Democratic Party.[12]

Since the press in its Cuba reporting followed the propaganda line of leading politicians, the politicians, in turn, gave official endorsement to the most effective organs of that propaganda, namely the two most sensational newspapers. Throughout the prewar period, senators would take the floor to read aloud a fresh clipping from the *World* or the *Journal*, demand an investigation or call for a resolution on the basis of the clipping, and even praise the newspaper for its general excellence. By giving senatorial endorsement to the *Journal* and the *World,* interventionist politicians did more than confirm the validity of their barely credible stories: they effectively nationalized their distribution. Staid newspapers that hesitated to repeat verbatim some particularly gruesome item from the *Journal* would relay it to its readers the next day as a statement made on the floor of the Senate or as testimony before the Senate Foreign Relations Committee, which treated the reporters from the most avidly prowar papers as their most reliable sources. As one disgruntled American correspondent put it, the typical American "star" reporter would arrive in Havana and duly interview a rebel publicist. Then "filling up his notebooks with stories of atrocities, battles, rapes, and other horrors attributed to the Spanish troops by interested parties ... he returns to the United States and in due course of time drifts into Washington, there to offer his collection of 'takes' as evidence before the committees."[13]

Of the mendacious warmongering journalism of the American press, suffice to say that everything that would inflame public sentiment against Spain was prominently reported, exaggerated, or fabricated. Whatever might weaken sympathy for the rebels or support for intervention was pretty well kept out of the news. For the interventionists it was imperative, for example, to sustain the electorate's belief in the military success of the guerrillas, although their rebellion was flagging badly throughout 1896. When one of the leading rebel generals, Antonio Maceo, was killed in a skirmish—a severe blow to the military prestige of the guerrillas—Junta publicists hit upon an old propaganda ruse to undo the damage. They reported that Maceo had actually been killed by treacherous Spaniards while approaching under a white flag of truce. Apprised of this discovery by the Junta, the American press clamored for days over the "murder" of Maceo and the "inherent cowardice and brutality of that human hyena" General Weyler. To confirm the story, the Senate, after its customary fashion, appointed a special committee to investigate what now officially became known as the "Maceo Assassination." So it went with the party-directed press, week after week, month after month, a ceaseless drumbeat of interventionist propaganda, a "cause" of war indeed, but only in the limited sense that a loaded pistol can be termed the cause of a shooting.[14]

Despite the agitation of the press and the oratory of the Senate, the Cuban question was completely overshadowed in 1896 by a matter of imcomparably greater concern to the American people— the forthcoming presidential election, the climactic event in the political crisis of the 1890s and the ultimate test of the two parties' ability to serve their own interests in the face of a disaffected electorate.

The silver Democrats' crusade to "capture" the Democratic Party from themselves proved, not surprisingly, a complete success. Between April and June one state party convention after another endorsed the free coinage of silver, while the sound money or gold Democrats, the ostensible party overlords, put forth only the most meager, fitful, and halfhearted resistance. The New York Democracy, the alleged archfoe of free silver, had obliged its silverite "enemies" by holding its convention in late June, conveniently too late to obstruct their plans. By the time New York Democrats met it was clear that the silver Democrats would control the national convention. "The most astounding feature of all this matter," Cleveland wrote to an ally on June 10, "is the lethargy of our friends, and the impossibility of stirring them to action."[15]

This, in truth, was the only serious hitch in the Democrats' scheme. Silver Democrats had been telling western Populist leaders for two years that they were almost certain to be overcome by the all-powerful Democratic "goldbugs." Western Populist leaders, bent on fusion with the Democrats, kept relaying the same story to their skeptical followers right up to the day the Democratic convention began. Unfortunately, the suspicious ease with which the party's alleged rebels had routed the enemy struck a false note in the proceedings. Where was the awesome money power? Where were the party's eastern masters? Where were the victims for the revolution's papier-mâché guillotine? The enemy's absence was so potentially embarrassing that the New York Democrats were compelled to call on the services of William C. Whitney, a New York financier and Cleveland's former campaign manager. Dramatically canceling a trip to Europe on June 17, three weeks before the Democratic convention, Whitney gathered the gold wing of the party into a luxurious private train for an alleged last-ditch stand against the party's self-styled agrarian revolutionaries. To ensure their recognition as the eastern plutocracy incarnate, Whitney and his colleagues ostentatiously sipped fine wines and feasted on luxurious meals as they proceeded to the Chicago convention site, picking up millionaires en route. At the convention, which began on July 7, Whitney's gold Democrats decided not to vote for a candidate, allegedly in sulky protest against the entire proceedings—in reality because their three hundred votes would actually have influenced the nomination, thereby fatally tainting the party's future standard-bearer and ruining the chances of fusion with the Populists, the very last thing either Whitney or his sound money colleagues wanted.[16]

As to whom the convention would nominate, it had to be, perforce, a complete suprise, its revelation the final triumphant scene in the complicated theatrics the Democracy had arranged for the Populists. Consequently, the man favored by a majority of the delegates and by the small clique of senators who tightly ran the convention was the very man whom the press and the public had been told to regard as the darkest of dark horses, thirty-six-year-old William Jennings Bryan, the "Boy Orator of the Platte." As Bryan himself later remarked, quite truthfully, his nomination was simply "the logic of the situation." He was the only aspirant for the Democratic nomination who met the peculiar requirements of 1896. The Democracy's needs were quite precise. Their candidate had to be, first, a recognized champion of free silver; second, he had to maintain sufficiently friendly relations with the Populists to enable Populist proponents of fusion to put him across at the People's Party convention. Third, and for the same reason, he had to appear a man uncontaminated by too many years of loyal truckling to the Democratic Party; fourth, he had to be a loyal servant of the Democratic Party. For three years, with a superb understanding of the "logic of the situation," Bryan had gone about qualifying himself on all counts. He had tirelessly campaigned for free silver, had addressed every Populist gathering he could locate, had sounded the call for "principles first" in order to suggest to suspicious Populists that he cared nothing for the Democratic Party as such.* In making himself acceptable to the Populists, Bryan's youth was one of his best assets. Since no Democratic rival came close to meeting the requirements, the senatorial clique in control of the convention pushed Bryan forward and allowed him to sweep the nomination with his famous "Cross of Gold" speech, which Bryan, in fact, had delivered many times before. No one was astonished except the public and the press, which, as always, relied on self-serving politicians to tell them the "news." "We have revolutionized the Democratic Party," a party spokesman told reporters at a press conference, and the message was duly relayed to the country. As Pulitzer's *World* obligingly reported: "The scepter of political power passed from the strong, certain hands of the East to the feverish, headstrong mobs of the West and South." [17]

Fifteen days later, the People's Party convention at St. Louis became the scene of bitter and fatal dissension as western Populist leaders used every trick of convention management to push the party's delegates into the Democracy's silver trap. For a variety of reasons—opportunism, naiveté, pessimism about the People's Party—most western Populist leaders and officeholders had long since decided that their future lay not with the struggling Populists, but with the newly silver-coated Democracy. Living as they did in Republican-controlled states and being themselves, for the most part, renegade Republicans, they were inclined, perhaps understandably, to regard the Republican Party as the one true enemy of reform, a view their southern colleagues in no way shared. For two years the Westerners had tried in vain to persuade Populist conferences to abandon the full party program and concentrate exclusively on free silver. For two years they had been telling their followers, none too scrupulously, that the Democracy would never endorse free silver, that the People's Party, swelled by bolting silver Democrats, would

---

*One of the real ironies of the situation was that Bryan, the ostensible party rebel, was incomparably more loyal to the Democratic Party and its leaders than Cleveland, the target of the supposed rebellion.

stand alone in the national arena as the party of free silver coinage. The presidency of the United States would be in its grasp. For a four-year-old national party that was a heady prospect indeed, but only to those who believed, or professed to believe, in the professions of old-line Democrats. Southern Populists knew better. Nevertheless, in January 1896, the Populists' national committee, dominated by fusionists, had managed to schedule the party's nominating convention after the Democrats' in order to "take advantage of the errors of the old parties," as Bryan had slyly put it.[18]

Since the western fusionists were willing to abandon the Populist program, secure the party's demise, and put its reforming zeal into the hands of the Democrats, they were Populists in name only and not even in that; they were often described as "Popocrats." By every political test they were now indistinguishable from Democrats—Populist Senator William V. Allen of Nebraska, for one, being little more than a mouthpiece for Bryan. Nominal Populists though they had become, it was they who ran the convention, and they forced the enemies of fusion, a majority of the delegates, into a cruel dilemma. If the party rejected Bryan's nomination, the western fusionists would desert to Bryan and destroy the People's Party outright. If they nominated Bryan, the Populist cause in the South would suffer terribly. How could southern Populists campaign against the party of White Supremacy with that party's standard-bearer at the top of their ticket? Out of that dilemma there was no escape this side of ruin. In the end, as the lesser of two evils, the convention nominated Bryan. Southern Populists returned from St. Louis angry, embittered, and profoundly demoralized. The whole affair, wrote an angry southern Populist editor, was a "deep-laid conspiracy to ruin our party and destroy the reform movement." So it was and so it did.[19]

"Free silver," wrote Henry Demarest Lloyd, a wealthy Chicago radical, "is the cowbird of the Reform movement. It waited until the nest had been built by the sacrifices and labor of others, and then laid its eggs in it, pushing out the others which lie smashed on the ground." More precisely, the old-line Democrats were the cowbirds of the reform movement and now the ardent hopes of rebellious farmers rested with them. The party that had deliberately spurned the votes of midwestern farmers for a generation, that had tried to manage southern farmers with racist threats and racial fears, still remained in the hands of men as opposed to reform in 1896 as they had been in 1886. Yet the party had become, out of sheer necessity, the champion of disaffected farmers, the hoped-for agency of radical reform, the magnet for agitators, dissenters, and reformers from New England to the Gulf of Mexico. The Democracy was still not out of the woods. The election campaign itself was a danger. To make sure that Bryan's campaign did minimal damage to the local party bosses—by attracting too many amateur zealots, for one thing—the Democratic convention chose Senator James K. Jones of Arkansas, a Bourbon Democrat of "the worst type," to manage his campaign. Jones's task was to see that the candidate's appetite for votes did not blind him to the party's local interests, which were at variance with and often antithetical to Bryan's personal interest in winning. Party leaders instructed Bryan, for example, not to make inflammatory speeches in the East, although, in truth, only inflammatory attacks on the rich and privileged could possibly have secured the votes of industrial workers; monetary inflation itself offering no economic inducement to men whose wages would inevitably lag behind rising prices. Democratic leaders, to put it bluntly, hoped to see Bryan lose.[20]

The Republican convention was an altogether different affair, for the party's nominee, Ohio's Governor William McKinley, was anything but a dark horse. Three years of economic depression under a Democratic President who had tried to reduce tariffs had given the Republicans a temporary reprieve for high tariffs. Industrial workers, desperate for some way out of the economic stagnation, were willing to give protection another try, and McKinley was nothing if not the champion of protection. Morever, "the Major," as he was called, was a genuinely popular figure, sweet-tempered, reassuring, and superbly tactful, a politician who had managed as governor of Ohio to handle bitter industrial strife without offending either industrial workers or their employers, a considerable feat of political management. McKinley, in truth, had a genius for alienating nobody as he made his way with apparent ease through the deadly factional struggles of Ohio's Republican Party. A Republican wheelhorse, a regular among regulars, a man never known to have uttered a heterodox remark—on all subjects save protection and patriotism, McKinley kept a discreet silence—the Major was, by 1895, not merely the Republican front-runner but, as John Hay, observed at the time, "almost certain of the nomination." [21]

In addition to his personal assets, McKinley had in his service the superb organizing skills and the deep open pocket of Marcus Alonzo Hanna, a wealthy Cleveland businessman who had entered politics when he discovered, to his chagrin, that a politician who took his bribe was too corrupt to stay bribed. It was a lesson in the predominance of power over money which sank deep. In his political dreams Hanna envisioned an America governed by a party— the Republicans—entirely in accordance with the sentiments, the interests, and the rational progressive spirit, as he saw it, of the nation's leading industrialists, with due regard for the more modest demands of their employees. But Hanna did not confuse his dreams with reality. His real contribution to American politics was his clear understanding that America's overprivileged business magnates had become, for the first time, a pack of frightened men. Grown fearful of an angry electorate, they would pay and pay dearly for the Republican oligarchy's political protection. That Hanna was widely regarded as the all-powerful representative of the all-powerful money power is one of the minor ironies of American history.

Since the Republican bosses had no reason to oppose McKinley's nomination, the two most important among them, Pennsylvania's Quay and New York's Platt, offered McKinley in early 1895 the usual political deal for their convention support—namely, whatever the two bosses needed to maintain uncontested control of their state machines, both of which were under severe attack from rank-and-file Republicans grown increasingly disgusted with boss rule. Given the low state to which the Democracy had fallen, the two major state bosses were apparently offering Mckinley nothing less than uncontested entry into the Presidency. A mere nod was all that was needed, but the two bosses never received it from the Major—the first sign that the sweet-tempered McKinley was a far deeper man than either his friends or his detractors supposed. McKinley not only turned down the offer, he boldly directed Hanna to turn publicly against the two men who had made it. He even had a slogan ready at hand, "The People Against the Bosses," with himself representing the people and Platt and Quay incarnating all the evils of boss rule. Since McKinley won the support of most state bosses except the notorious two, both the slogan and McKinley's antiboss campaign for the nomination, funded almost entirely by Hanna, were nothing more than flummery, analogous to, if not quite as dramatic as, the pseudorebellion of the silver Democrats. That fact does not diminish, however, the audacity of McKinley's stratagem. With so great a prize at stake, very few ambitious politicians would have borrowed trouble at all from powerful party managers. It took a superbly self-confident man to do what McKinley did and an exceedingly astute one to grasp its necessity. What McKinley understood far better than his party colleagues was that, however low in public esteem the Democracy had sunk, a mere creature of the Republican oligarchy, a candidate who represented in no way the spirit of reform coursing through the country, could well lose the election. The voters, oscillating wildly between the two parties, having rebuked both in two successive off-year elections, could not be taken for granted in 1896. By his daring campaign against the Republican bosses, a campaign that rallied every reform-minded Republican to his side, McKinley succeeded at a stroke in undercutting Bryan's claim that he and he alone carried the banner of a party transformed by the spirit of reform.[22]

There was one major surprise at the Republican convention. The platform pledged the party to maintaining for the present the existing financial policy of the country, meaning, significantly, the gold standard. The fruit of intense deliberation and complicated calculation, the Republicans' bold decision to meet free silver head on was to have enormous political repercussions for the country. In reaching it, Republican leaders were prepared to see free silver Republicans bolt the party outright at the national convention, which they did; they were prepared to abandon entirely the Populist-tinged prairie states. In return, however, they brought under the Republican aegis the frightened bankers of New York, hitherto supporters of the Democratic Party. In 1896 the Republican Party went before the voters with a personally popular candidate, a victorious foe of boss rule, an apparent representative in his own way of the reform spirit in the country, but it had succeeded for the first time in capturing for the uses of oligarchy the entire body of business magnates in the country. Pitted against McKinley was the "Boy Orator of the Platte," armed with a dubious panacea which appealed most strongly to the debt-ridden and shackled by a sham reform party determined as soon as the elections were safely over to return to its customary policies.

Sweeping every state in the industrial Northeast, where free silver meant little and where the Democratic machines gave Bryan only token support or less, McKinley won a resounding election victory. The Republican Party, seemingly bankrupt in 1890, had returned to national power with greater popularity than ever. The Democratic Party had survived the Populist menace, which was all its leaders really cared about. The People's Party, as its vice-presidential candidate, Tom Watson, observed when the election was over, "does not exist anymore. Fusion has well nigh killed it. The sentiment is still there, but confidence is gone." Judging by their votes, industrial workers looked to McKiney to restore prosperity; judging by the huge sums Hanna extracted from them, the major eastern businessmen looked forward to a business-minded administration with zeal neither for domestic reforms nor for any drastic departure from America's traditionally modest foreign policy, a topic on which McKinley never spoke.[23]

The Republican platform, it is true, had pledged the party for the first time to the outlines of the large policy: annexation of Hawaii, the "continued enlargement of the Navy," the reassertion of the Monroe Doctrine "in its fullest extent," and "the ultimate union of all the English-speaking parts of the continent by the free consent of its inhabitants," The platform also declared even more truculently that "everywhere American citizens and American property must be absolutely protected at all hazards and at any costs." It also pledged the party to securing the independence of Cuba, albeit by peaceful means. To the Republicans' business supporters, however, all this had the appearance of mere platform bluster. During the campaign itself both the Cuba question in particular and foreign affairs in general had plummeted completely out of sight, as if even Republican expansionists regarded them as matters of no genuine importance. Moreover, foreign adventures, jingoism, expansion, and the Cuban guerrillas were all equally abhorrent to Mark Hanna, the new national chairman of the Republican Party and, as Wall Street interests supposed, the real power behind the mild-mannered McKinley, or "McHanna," as Democrats scornfully referred to him. McKinley himself went out of his way to tell Carl Schurz that "you may be sure that there will be no jingo nonsense under my administration." Those who favored the traditional American foreign policy—mugwumps such as Schurz and eastern commercial interests—had good reason to expect under McKinley the peaceful, familiar political atmosphere of precrisis days.[24]

If so, they sadly misjudged the Republican Party oligarchy and grossly underestimated its determination to transform the politics of the American Republic. They had their first rude shock at once. As soon as the elections were safely out of the way, the Republicans at once began stirring up the Cuban question, this time with a fury and vehemence unhindered by election-year caution. The party was determined, it seemed, through one furious spasm of agitation, to force a war upon President Cleveland. That, indeed, would have been the Republican Party's ideal solution: on Wall Street the Democrats would be blamed for starting the war and Republicans would reap the glory of winning it. The Republican Party's auxiliaries were once again pressed into action. In the winter of 1896 the Grand Army of the Republic organized what were virtually war rallies from New York to South Dakota. The Republican press clamored daily for intervention; a few newspapers actually announced to their readers that Spain was planning to attack the United States. A slew of inflammatory resolutions (including one calling for an investigation of the "stripping of women" by Spanish officials, another journalistic mare's nest) were submitted to the lame-duck 54th Congress, where interventionists of both parties all but dropped the pretense that they sought no trouble with Spain. The most important resolution called for outright diplomatic recognition of the "Republic of Cuba." A virtual act of war against Spain, the resolution was reported out favorably by the Senate Foreign Relations Committee on December 21. With that, yet another war scare swept the country. The Republican New York *Tribune* reported that the United States stood on "the brink of war." The stock market duly collapsed (as it had done during the Venezuela crisis) and "the financial interests of the great eastern cities," as

Senator Lodge recalled after the war was over, "rose in wrathful opposition. They declared without any reservation that 'war would unsettle values'. . . ." Businessmen, a Boston stockbroker complained to Lodge, want "peace and quiet . . . if we attempt to regulate the affairs of the whole world we will be in hot water from now until the end of time"—exactly the object of the Republican large policy. Unfortunately for Republican plans, Cleveland, coming to the end of one of the more harrowing terms in presidential history, made it clear that nothing could force him to intervene in Cuba. With that, the Republicans called off their war campaign and America's second war scare within twelve months vanished like a puff of smoke, though not without leaving the half-beaten Cuban rebels determined to refuse any Spanish offers of reform in Cuba until, as seemed likely, the Republicans led America into the fray.[25]

The Cuba question was now in McKinley's hands, but just where McKinley stood on the Cuban question nobody had any idea. The Inauguration Day proceedings provided no clue, or rather they provided clues leading to contrary conclusions. On the one hand there was McKinley's brief Inaugural Address, which was obviously intended to reassure the Republicans' new banking allies. The President promised to carry out a "policy of noninterference with the affairs of foreign governments." He roundly declared that "we want no wars of conquest; we must avoid the temptation of territorial aggression." He looked forward to "the restoration of confidence and the revival of business." It was all pacific, routine, and reassuring. The Republican Party's large policy seemed to have sunk without a trace within the portly frame of President William McKinley. So, at any rate, it seemed. That impression was belied, however, by a curious and revealing alteration in the traditional inaugural review. Gone in March 1897 were the scraggly lines of civilian militia and the amiable republican disarray. This inaugural, McKinley's inaugural, was an altogether different affair. Column after column of crack regular army troops paraded in strict array down Pennsylvania Avenue; the smartest cavalry units rode by in impresssive review. It was a display of force, of discipline, of military might and the military virtues; but just what it portended only the equivocal McKinley knew.[26]

4

"An Uncommonly Dangerous Politician"

To most of his contemporaries, William McKinley was an insoluble puzzle. Men never knew quite what to make of him either as a man or as a leader. What were his political intentions? Nobody could say for certain. Did he even have any intentions of his own? A good many people doubted it. McKinley's public utterances—vague, windy, and oracular—never disclosed his real aims. His actions—ambiguous and self-contradictory—never quite revealed his policies. Those who visited him at the White House came away impressed with his sweetness of temper, his soothing disposition, his willingness to please, to placate, to agree, but they saw few signs of personal force or deeply held conviction. On the whole, men thought him amiably weak. It was the obvious conclusion to draw from cautious speeches, ambiguous actions, and the personal manner of the professional charmer who shrinks from giving offense. Since the President never sought to correct such impressions, men could well conclude that he was not only weak but supine. Few American Presidents were so widely regarded in their own time as the instrument of other men's visions, the tool of other men's ambitions, or the victim of sheer, inescapable circumstance.

A few men knew better. One of them was McKinley's future secretary of state, John Hay, who wrote to Henry Adams shortly after visiting McKinley during the 1896 election campaign: "I was more struck than ever by his mask. It is a genuine Italian ecclesiastical face of the fifteenth century. And there are idiots who think Mark Hanna will run him." Hay's physiognomical insight was particularly keen. The White House has rarely known a President more devious, crafty, or subtle than the amiable, mild-mannered McKinley and few so adept at getting what he wanted. He was, remarked Adams, "easily first in genius for manipulation." That was exactly the truth. McKinley *was* a political genius, and manipulation was the mode of his genius. Among American Presidents he is the supreme example of the political wirepuller, the leader who gets things done without ever seeming to lead.[1]

If contemporaries never knew McKinley's intentions it was because the President never candidly avowed them to anyone. If he seemed to be the victim of events, it was because he was master of the fait accompli, the patient contriver of circumstances which, as he would ruefully announce, gave him no choice but to do exactly what he privately wanted. Although he kept his goals secret, McKinley was superbly adept at letting those who had to divine them divine them correctly and at getting them to do what he wanted without ever openly declaring that he wanted it. Inevitably the men McKinley bent to his purposes often stole the limelight from the President, but McKinley cared nothing for the limelight. "He was a man of great power," his secretary of war Elihu Root recalled after his death, "because he was absolutely indifferent to credit . . . but McKinley always had his way." McKinley's lack of personal vanity—a lack bordering on shamelessness—was his greatest political asset. Few Presidents would have tolerated as McKinley did so complacently the insulting charge of being Mark Hanna's puppet. McKinley, however, had every reason to tolerate the insult for Hanna, in fact, was the President's front man, the one who did all his political dirty work and who suffered all the consequent abuse. During the 1896 election campaign Democrats brutally assailed Hanna while "the Major" went through the campaign virtually uncriticized. If McKinley appeared weak, vacillating, and passive, the tool of others and the slave of circumstance, it was because he wished to appear that way. The appearance was a political necessity. In order to get what he wanted, McKinley had to go to great lengths to deny that he wanted anything at all.

There was nothing safe or conservative about President McKinley's political objectives. By the standards of the nineteenth century he was not conservative but radical. Conservatism in the 1890s still retained a republican form: It meant adherence to the teachings of the founders; it meant disdain for the "murky radiance" of world power; it meant respect for constitutional forms; it meant protecting the free enterprise system from the new menace of trusts and monopolies; it meant—especially among rank-and-file Republicans—opposition to the growing power of the state party machines. On the road to the White House McKinley had been careful to heed the canons of conservatism, or least make no departures from them. On the Republican large policy he had kept silent, preferring to preach the safer theme of patriotism. On the issue of boss rule he had enthralled the party's citizen adherents with his unprecedented antiboss nominating campaign. In his Inaugural Address he had vowed to combat trusts and big business combinations just as he had vowed nonintervention in the internal affairs of other countries. On every count McKinley intended to betray both his followers and his pledges. "The Major," remarked Henry Adams, "is an uncommonly dangerous politician," more so than even Adams could foresee on Inauguration Day 1897.[2]

What guided the new President was a determination to forge a new "national unity and cohesion" for America. That unity and cohesion, however, the new President conceived in terms that differed sharply from traditional American conceptions. The unity of the American people rested—and rests still—on universal adherence to the Constitution, on respect for the law, on a shared faith in republican institutions. In 1897 that unity was completely unbroken. When McKinley took office it had just withstood the severest of tests. In a period of unparalleled discontent, the most exacting organ of disaffection, the People's Party, had shown unfailing devotion to the Constitution and a humble respect for law that was all the more poignant in view of the lawless conduct of its Democratic adversaries. At the end of a bitter election campaign the American electorate had accepted the result with its unfailing respect for the decision of the ballot box, and McKinley himself took office with a remarkable reservoir of good will to draw upon. The inevitable accompaniment of republican unity, however, is a large measure of popular unruliness; an exacting, vocal electorate; an ineffaceable dislike of special privilege, monopoly, and irresponsible power. It means dissent, conflict, insurgency. Liberty, as Jefferson remarked, is not for the nervous. The "national unity" McKinley hoped to forge was of an altogether different sort. He wanted a higher or transcendent unity, a unity that would quell discontent, eliminate dissension, and weaken the troublesome republican spirit which had revived so alarmingly during the preceding half-dozen years. He wanted to impose order and discipline on the Republic's unruly politics, order and discipline on its sprawling economy. Above all, he wanted to replace loyalty to the American Republic with loyalty to that very different thing, the Nation; love of liberty with love of the flag and the mystique of proud bunting. To these far-reaching aims, all the efforts of his administration were to be directed.[3]

To impose greater order on American politics, McKinley hoped to transform the Republican Party itself into a rigidly disciplined national political machine—aloof, dominating, and impregnable. Of all McKinley's betrayals none was more marked than his determination to quash Republican insurgents, the very people he had so captivated with his antiboss campaign. With few exceptions all the patronage, power, and prestige of the presidency McKinley was to put at the disposal of the state party bosses in their fight against rank-and-file party rebels. To McKinley the only defect of Republican boss rule was the independent power of the major state bosses. Under his leadership steps would be taken to centralize party management through the centralized control of party funds. By commanding the party purse strings, McKinley, for one thing, could keep the smaller Republican state parties under the control of the Republican National Committee, whereas in the past they had usually been the satrapies of the New York and Pennsylvania machines. By stripping the most powerful state bosses of their out-of-state power, the Republican oligarchy under McKinley was to become what it had long aspired to be, a tightly knit counsel of state, with the massed legions of a disciplined national party ready to support its policies.[4]

As part of his grand design for "national unity and cohesion," McKinley would even take steps to weaken the constitutional independence of the Senate. In the noontime of his power, he would begin the policy, quite shocking at the time, of giving senators lucrative seats on public commissions, a species of executive jobbery in the legislative branch which the framers of the Constitution had both feared and forbade. By the time of his death in 1901, President McKinley would establish a personal ascendancy over Congress which was, according to Republican Senators Hoar and Cullom, without parallel in our history.[5]

McKinley's economic policy, quite simply, was to encourage the concentration of economic power in the hands of a few. This was partly a reflection of his desire for order and partly an extension of his party aims. The rise of great interstate trusts and monopolies made the centralization of the Republican Party possible, for the monopolists were beholden not to particular state bosses, but to the national Republican Party and its policies. Consequently, McKinley, despite his inaugural pledge to combat the trusts, did nothing to enforce the Sherman Act, while making it abundantly clear to Wall Street financiers that he favored the making of combinations, a complicated endeavor that could not readily be carried out without tacit governmental approval.[6]

What McKinley envisioned for the American Republic was a genuine new order of things, a modern centralized order, elitist in every way, profoundly alien to the spirit of the Republic, and imposed from above on its indestructible constitutional forms. Doubtless McKinley's vision was all light to the President but it was not so to the American people. Had McKinley submitted his grand design for a new modeled republic to the judgment of the American electorate, only a small minority would have approved of it.* Republican sentiment remained too strong in the country. Of necessity, therefore, the key to McKinley's grand design for national unity and cohesion was the Republican large policy. It was the only way to supplant the republican spirit with the spirit of nationalism, to replace love of liberty with love of the flag, and to make the Nation a political presence strong enough to overwhelm the Republic and supplant it in popular affections. Only by transforming America into an active world power "in contact with considerable foreign

---

* The political history of the pre-World War I period, as will be seen in the second part of this book, is largely a register of that disapproval.

powers at as many points as possible" could the Nation (which exists only in relation to other nations) become the unifying force that McKinley and the Republican oligarchy intended to make of it.

The new President had urgent personal reasons of his own to launch the large policy quickly, for the Republican Party chieftains allowed the President extremely few resources for managing a still discontented electorate. Aside from the protective tariff, temporarily rescued by the depression, the Republicans had no domestic resources whatever. McKinley needed the large policy, for one thing, to maintain the uncertain coalition that had brought him victory in 1896: a coalition between capitalists and laborers who were unlikely to remain long united if domestic concerns remained paramount. More urgently, McKinley needed the large policy to overawe the growing opposition of rank-and-file Republicans—his own followers—to political oligarchy and economic monopoly. When the National League of Republican clubs met in the summer of 1897 to cheer Hazen Pingree's denunciation of trusts and the maldistribution of wealth, the audience little knew what their presidential champion had in store for them, or that Pingree, the antimachine governor of Michigan, was on the President's list of party enemies. Without a large foreign policy to cover his intended betrayal of every republican sentiment coursing through the country, McKinley's victory in 1896 could well turn to ashes just as Cleveland's victory in 1892 had done.[7]

If the large policy was essential to McKinley's ambitions there was only one certain way to launch it—through armed intervention in Cuba. It was the only opportunity at hand and McKinley intended to seize it. That intention he dared not avow; indeed it was imperative to disavow it, for in the aftermath of a resounding election victory, some of the most powerful people in Republican ranks opposed intervention. The party's new Wall Street allies strongly opposed war, chiefly out of shortsighted complacency. Fearful that war would prolong the depression, they were unaware after the 1896 elections how politically insecure they still remained. A number of New England party leaders also opposed intervention. They included old-fashioned Republicans such as Hale, Speaker Reed of Maine, and old Senator Justin Morrill of Vermont, who saw no reason for the victorious Republicans to pursue the expansionist policies of the old slave party; they included powerful members of the Senate oligarchy such as Aldrich and Senator Orville Platt of Connecticut, who thoroughly supported the large policy, but who deemed it folly to risk the alliance they had just forged with the major New York bankers. McKinley, however, shared neither the shortsighted views of New York bankers nor the provincial complacency of New England Republicans. As with his quest for the presidential nomination, McKinley saw far more clearly than did his eastern party colleagues the dangerous implications of the electorate's reawakening. It was the very alliance that Republicans had forged with Wall Street which required the protection of war and a forward foreign policy.

McKinley, however, could ill afford to defy the peace faction openly without risking a split in the Republican oligarchy itself. It was the President's plan to reassure the peace faction of his pacific intentions while he pursued a course of action that would slowly but surely reduce it to a nullity. McKinley's Cuban policy, a shrewd and subtle feat of political manipulation, was shaped from the start not by his fear of warmongers—the conventional historical view—but by his fear of Republican and Wall Street proponents of peace.

McKinley's immediate problem, in fact, was to rally the interventionists and keep alive their hopes. Even before his inauguration, McKinley began privately reassuring key Republican interventionists that his Cuban policy was not quite what the peace faction expected it to be. Meeting with the President-elect, Senator Lodge, for one, came away convinced that McKinley's foreign policy views were "broad," and that he intended to do something "far-reaching." Without quite saying so openly, McKinley also left Lodge with the impression that he intended to go to war over Cuba but wanted to wait for economic recovery when business opposition would be weaker. More explicit assurances McKinley was not prepared to give; he trusted nobody to keep his secrets.[8]

In his public appointments, too, McKinley weaved his way deftly between the interventionists and the peace faction, obliquely encouraging the former without arousing the suspicions of the latter. His appointment of Senator Sherman, a notorious warmonger, as secretary of state augured ill for peaceful relations with Spain but the appointment explained itself away. The peace faction could console itself with the fact that McKinley had appointed Sherman to create a Senate vacancy in Ohio for Mark Hanna—which was true—and that Sherman, growing senile, would have little influence on McKinley's diplomacy. Appointing the thirty-nine-year-old Roosevelt as assistant secretary of the navy was not so readily explained away. Not only was Roosevelt a well-known jingo and expansionist, his influence in the Navy Department was bound to be great since the secretary of the navy, John Long of Massachusetts, was a weak, stuffy hole in the air. To keep from alarming the peace faction, McKinley made an elaborate pretense of resisting Roosevelt's appointment. Then, after months of mock resistance, he pretended to succumb to the entreaties of Roosevelt's friends, a typical McKinley maneuver. Having thus relieved himself of personal responsibility for Roosevelt, McKinley now had at his disposal a man eager to undertake the boldest actions with a mere wink and nod from the President.[9]

McKinley's shrewdest appointment was his retention of a Democrat, Fitzhugh Lee, as consul general in Havana. On the face of it this looked like a guarantee that McKinley was continuing Cleveland's anti-interventionist policies. It was nothing of the kind, however. Privately McKinley had been warned that Lee was a warmonger of the most mendacious sort, a man who, as Cleveland himself put it, had "fallen into the style of rolling intervention like a sweet morsel under his tongue." Lee's retention by the ostensibly peace-loving McKinley understandably aroused the ex-President's suspicions. "There's something queer about all this business," Cleveland commented privately, and his suspicions were amply justified. Lee would prove an important cog in McKinley's interventionist apparatus.[10]

Despite his veiled assurances, it quickly became clear to McKinley that the interventionists needed firmer guarantees that he stood behind them. Their position during the first weeks of the new administration had grown weak. Given the President's pacific inaugural pledges, it was the peace faction, not they, who could claim to be the administration loyalists. In the House of Representatives Speaker Reed could rely on party loyalty to the administration to marshal votes for his own personal policy of stifling war agitation. In the Senate during the opening weeks of the first session, Republican interventionists seemed listless and demoralized. In the press, too, the President's pacific reputation made itself felt. Republican newspapers which had howled for war in December now loyally supported McKinley's apparently peaceful designs. In the country at large interventionist sentiment had never been strong, and now in the spring of 1897 even popular interest in Cuban affairs had begun to wane. "I wish to heaven we were more jingo about Cuba and Hawaii," the bellicose Roosevelt complained to a friend in April. "The trouble with our nation is that we incline to fall into mere animal sloth and ease." Senator Morgan, it was reported, even accused the American people of behaving "supinely" toward Cuba.[11]

There was some justification for Morgan's reproach. It is one of the ironies of the Spanish-American War that when public excitement over Cuba was ebbing, the humanitarian grounds for intervening were strongest. Under General Weyler's command the rebels were a half-beaten force, confined largely to the wilder eastern portion of the island, and reduced to mere roving bands more frightening to the neutral population—the *pacíficos*—than to the Spanish Army. Weyler's methods were draconian, however, and their side effects horrific. A ruthless technician of counterinsurgency, Weyler met rebel efforts to starve the cities with countermeasures to starve the rebels. To do so, he ordered the rural population "reconcentrated" within the precincts of Cuba's fortified towns, leaving the burnt-out countryside deserted. The American press, oddly enough, had made no outcry at first against Weyler's *reconcentrado* policy. For one thing the policy was a legitimate mode of conducting warfare. For another the spectacle of Cubans fleeing to the protection of the Spanish Army made a poor advertisement for the rebel cause. The horrors of *reconcentrado* lay not with the policy but with Spain's brutal neglect to care for the *reconcentrados*. Left to the meager resources of local civil officials, they lived in squalid, disease-ridden misery until the Spanish government later reversed its policy.[12]

It was with reconcentration in mind that McKinley in May delivered the well-timed stroke that decisively revived the interventionists, a stroke that bore marks of preconcert between the Presi-

dent and the Senate Foreign Relations Committee, chief
headquarters of the interventionist cause.

The stage was set on May 4 by Senator Morgan, the ranking
Democrat on the committee. Speaking in favor of his new resolution favoring belligerency rights for Cuban rebels, Morgan announced that he had definite proof that American citizens in Cuba
"are now literally starving to death in numbers for this want of provisions and supplies." American citizens, in a word, were now the
victims of Weyler's reconcentration policy. In a speech delivered
May 10, Senator Hale insisted that Morgan's assertion was utterly
unfounded, which in fact it was. The Maine senator professed himself puzzled, however, by the conduct of his fellow Republican senators. Here was Morgan, a Democrat, advocating a diplomatic action—recognition of belligerency rights—that ran counter to the
policy of a Republican President. Yet it had not been met, said
Hale, by a single Republican "caveat." Public opinion, he pointed
out, could scarcely account for Republican silence. As far as the
American people are concerned "the war is being fought mainly in
the Senate chamber." Some peculiar sort of collusion, Hale hinted,
existed between Morgan, the interventionist Democratic leader,
and a number of Senate Republicans. What it was he could not
specify. That the peace-loving McKinley had been giving secret assurances to Republican interventionists, Senator Hale, of course,
was totally unaware. Nor was he aware that the ground under the
peace faction was just about to crumble.[13]

On May 12, Republican Senator Gallinger, in support of Morgan, submitted a resolution calling for a $50,000 appropriation to
feed suffering Americans in Cuba. It was a typical propaganda tactic. A half-dozen times interventionists had taken an inflammatory
rumor, made a speech about it, submitted an appropriate resolution, and transformed it into a senatorial fact. If the members of
the peace faction were concerned they gave no sign of it. Five days
later the blow from the White House fell. On the morning of May
17, President McKinley sent Congress a special message announc-
ing that, according to Consul General Lee, who was already proving his usefulness, "a large number of American citizens in the island are in a state of destitution." The President asked for a
$50,000 appropriation to relieve them. That very morning, not co-

incidentally, the Senate Foreign Relations Committee favorably reported out the Gallinger resolution, now backed so surprisingly by
the authority of the President.[14]

McKinley's message created, as expected, an immediate nation-
wide sensation. At once the war spirit revived in the press, which
hailed the message as the first logical step toward armed intervention. "The relief-bearer," Hearst's *Journal* observed, "is but the
American camel intruding its head in the Spanish tent in Cuba."
Since the relief funds, by reluctant consent of the Spanish authorities, were to be distributed by the United States, intervention of
sorts had already begun. The New York *Mail and Express,* an administration paper, openly concluded that McKinley's policy is "to
secure Cuban independence," by arms if necessary.[15]

For Republican interventionists that was the real import of the
President's message. It had deftly confirmed McKinley's veiled assurances, precisely as McKinley had intended it to do. Why else,
interventionists reasoned, would the President have supported so
dramatically a charge against Spain of the most inflammatory
kind? In the Senate, the Republican war faction suddenly regained
its voice and the change was electrifying. Senator Joseph Foraker
of Ohio called the President's message a powerful argument for
Morgan's belligerency resolution. Citing the President's message
again and again, Senator William Mason of Illinois called for protecting American rights in Cuba with "bayonets." On May 20, a
number of Republican legislators actually outlined the policy Mc-
Kinley was in fact pursuing, that of preparing for war by slowly
grinding down the Republican and Wall Street peace faction. "I
am not asking or urging intervention at the present time," said
Senator John Thurston of Nebraska. "The grounds are not properly laid. We can not intervene in Cuba now. We can not carry out
the ultimate declaration of the Republican Party now. We must
first lay the foundation." Senator Charles Fairbanks of Indiana,
McKinley's Senate lieutenant, proposed that the government attempt to secure Cuba's independence by diplomacy, and failing
that, "I would have no hesitancy" about using armed force. The
theme of "laying the foundation" was sounded that day in the
House as well. Charles Grosvenor of Ohio, a confidant of McKinley's, promised that "when the right time comes, in the right order

of things . . . [Republicans] will be found voting not only for belligerent rights to Cuba, but they will be found demanding liberty and national independence for the men of Cuba who have suffered." The Republicans, as Representative Robert Adams of Pennsylvania put it some months later, would secure Cuban independence "in our own way and in our own time." With painful, if necessary, obliquity, Adams assured administration loyalists that the administration stood behind intervention. "You need have no fear that when the proper time comes there will be any lack of nerve and force in the Republican administration. . . . You need have no fear that when that time comes Cuba will rise up and will bless the Republican Party that has guided itself so that when the time came she could assert her independence."[16]

On May 20, Morgan's belligerency resolution passed the Senate by a vote of 41 to 14. The Republican peace faction, previously outspoken, was silent and subdued. Yet McKinley, with his artful message, had given them no solid grounds for reproach and had done nothing they could possibly oppose. All the kindly President had done, after all, was proffer a modest sum of charity to suffering fellow citizens in Cuba whose nonexistence they were no longer in a position to assert. Nor could they justly complain that not once since Inauguration Day—nor indeed throughout 1897—had the President publicly supported his avowed policy of nonintervention or used his great influence to counteract war propaganda in the press. The President presumably had the right and duty to keep silent while conducting delicate negotiations with Spain. Had the peace faction been privy to McKinley's diplomacy they would have known at once that the President was bent on intervention, but McKinley, for that very reason, conducted his diplomacy in secret.[17]

There was nothing subtle about McKinley's dealings with Spain. From the start he claimed the right to dictate Spain's conduct in Cuba and to intervene by force should that conduct fail to meet the American government's approval. In a harsh and hostile note to Spain's Ambassador de Lome, dated June 26, the President informed Spain for the first time of his intentions. Spain, the ambassador was told, would have to achieve peace in Cuba or the American government would intervene to secure it. That was not all. Peace alone, McKinley warned, would not suffice to stay America's hand. It would have to meet two fundamental conditions. First, the Spanish government would have to revoke the reconcentration order which, said McKinley, violated the "military code of civilization" and against which the United States government was forced to protest "in the name of the American people and in the name of common humanity." Secondly, Spain must enact reforms in Cuba that would presumably persuade the rebels to lay down their arms. Taken together, the two conditions complicated Spain's problems immensely. To end reconcentration, a successful strategy, could only strengthen the rebels militarily. Having been strengthened by the intercession of America's President, they would be less likely than ever to accept any reforms short of independence. Put simply, the only way Spain could forestall American intervention was to meet certain conditions that made intervention inevitable. That was McKinley's intention and "common humanity" had little to do with it.* A noninterventionist President moved by the plight of the *reconcentrados* could well have demanded on humanitarian grounds that Spain feed and tend them. Unfortunately, a purely humanitarian diplomacy would have removed the moral grounds for American intervention while leaving a successful military strategy intact. That was why McKinley was forced to insist, quite falsely, that reconcentration, even under humane conditions, violated the "military code of civilization," which America was constrained to enforce in Cuba. The false assertion was essential to McKinley's goal, that of preventing Spain from achieving peace on its own.[18]

The most important feature of the note was what it failed to say. President Cleveland, too, had asked Spain, though more politely, to enact reforms in order to secure peace, but he had promised American help in getting the rebels to accept them. That assurance, essential to any peaceful settlement, McKinley omitted, although a peaceful settlement ostensibly was his sole object in Cuba. To the Spanish government, McKinley's motives were obvious enough. Replying to the American government, the Spanish summed up in

---

* McKinley's "humanitarianism" disappeared the moment it went against his interests. In 1899 when news began to leak out that the U.S. Army was using atrocious methods to suppress Filipino rebels, President McKinley did not censure the army; he censored the news.

one laconic sentence the American President's interventionist diplomacy: "He who is not disposed to grant the means does not earnestly desire the end in view."[19]

Three weeks later, McKinley prepared to intensify still further
the diplomatic pressure on Spain. On July 16, America's newly appointed ambassador to Spain, General Stewart Woodford, was instructed to add a temporal condition to the original two demands.
The United States would give Spain only a "reasonable time" to secure peace before facing armed intervention. McKinley also asked
Woodford to find out whether European governments would come
to Spain's aid in the event of American intervention in Cuba. Well
versed in the diplomacy of war, the chancelleries of Europe saw
through McKinley's diplomacy at once. Visiting the Russian, British, French, and German embassies in Madrid, Woodford asked
each ambassador in turn what he thought of America's intention to
intervene in Cuba in the event that Spain failed to secure peace.
Each of them replied: What did the United States government intend to do to help Spain secure peace?[20]

While Ambassador Woodford was testing the European reaction
to a future war with Spain, the President was secretly laying the
groundwork for far-reaching wartime expansion in the Pacific.
Publicly, the President had already placed himself, as ambiguously
as he could manage it, in the Republican expansionist camp. On
June 16 he signed and submitted to the Senate a new treaty of annexation with the Hawaiian government, although he took pains to
assure the foes of expansion that Hawaiian annexation was not
meant to lead to further expansion. It was, he said, "not a change
but a consummation," exactly the opposite of what McKinley or
the expansionists intended it to be. Carl Schurz, for one, was not
convinced. At a White House dinner on July 1, he bluntly asked
the President how the annexation of Hawaii squared with his personal promise of "no jingo nonsense." McKinley was momentarily
taken aback. Hastily he disavowed any personal intentions. He
himself was not eager for annexation, he assured Schurz. He was
merely testing public opinion. Privately McKinley thought otherwise. As he later confided to his personal secretary: "We need Hawaii just as much and a good deal more than we did California. It
is manifest destiny." Since a two-thirds majority for ratification

was nowhere in sight, the Senate adjourned on July 24 without undermining destiny with a vote.[21]

Several weeks later McKinley privately conferred with his energetic assistant secretary of the navy on aspects of "manifest destiny" considerably more advanced than Hawaiian annexation. A decrepit Spanish fleet lay permanently anchored in the Bay of Manila, capital of Spain's Philippine colony. Would it not be useful, Roosevelt apparently suggested, to plan an attack on that fleet and even seize Manila should the United States ever intervene in Cuba to bring about peace? McKinley piously deplored the prospect of war, but he managed to encourage Roosevelt to pursue his Philippine assault preparations. Indeed, after hearing McKinley deploring war with Spain, Roosevelt promptly made plans to raise a regiment for the invasion of Cuba. McKinley never fooled anyone he did not wish to fool. Shortly after their meeting, Roosevelt suggested to the President that an aggressive naval officer, Commodore George Dewey, be made commander of the Asiatic Squadron over the heads of more senior officers. McKinley secured the necessary congressional approval. In October the squadron was placed on a war footing. The machinery of manifest destiny was now emplaced. All McKinley needed was a war with Spain.[22]

In the autumn of 1897, however, the Spanish threw a roadblock across McKinley's path to war. On October 4, the Liberal Party took over the reigns of government and pledged itself to a reversal of Spain's Cuban policy. On October 6, General Weyler was recalled. On October 26, the government announced plans to establish Canadian-style autonomy for Cuba and to put an end to the brutal neglect of the *reconcentrados.* On November 14, the new captain-general of Cuba initiated the policy of caring for the *reconcentrados* and reviving farming outside the urban fortifications. On November 25, the Spanish Queen Regent, Maria Cristina, formally proclaimed the new autonomy policy and publicly repudiated General Weyler. Desperately hoping to stave off American intervention, the Liberal government was determined to remove as far as possible any justification for it. Had McKinley wished to avert war he could, of course, have hailed Spain's new departure as a welcome sign of a Spanish change of heart and a personal triumph for his diplomacy. Instead McKinley kept studiously silent all through October and November while the press, anxious over American public opinion, assailed the Spanish reforms. Privately, however, the interventionists were downcast. As Roosevelt privately complained to a friend, intervention had suffered a setback. "At present, owing mainly to the change in the Spanish policy, it is not possible at the moment to do anything about Cuba."[23]

McKinley met these new difficulties adroitly. The first thing he did was add a new element to his war apparatus. On December 2, the President ordered the U.S. battleship *Maine* to the Florida Keys at the suggestion of Consul General Lee, who had reported, with his usual mendacity, that a dangerous anti-American conspiracy was brewing in the Cuban province of Matanzas. The ship's commander was instructed to proceed to Havana in the event of an anti-American disturbance. It was to do so, said McKinley, on receiving a coded signal from Lee, at whose disposal the President now placed the great warship. The President had "full confidence in [Lee's] judgment," the commander was informed. Exactly so. By putting a warship of the most provocative kind in the hands of an inveterate warmonger, McKinley had ingeniously arranged for a minor diplomatic official to provoke an anti-American incident in Cuba likely to inflame American passions, moot the whole question of the Spanish reforms, and leave the President no alternative save armed intervention to protect American lives and property. Like his plans for waging war in the Philippines, McKinley's scheme for exploiting the bellicose propensities of a minor diplomat was a secret known to very few.[24]

In his annual message to Congress, delivered on December 6, McKinley dealt more directly with the new Spanish obstacle to war. After noting as a "felicitous condition" of American politics, that the "spirit of patriotism is universal and ever increasing in fervor," the President devoted a third of his message to Cuba. Instead of emphasizing the concessions he had just won from Spain, he dwelt at length on the past record of Weyler's cruelties. Although he commented favorably, if skeptically, on the new Spanish reforms, the President significantly refrained from endorsing Spain's new scheme for Cuban autonomy. Having made reform in Cuba an essential condition for peace, he now refused to throw the vast influence of the United States behind it. Instead he instructed Ambassador Woodford that America's nonsupport of home rule in Cuba and the cruelty of the repudiated Weyler were the two chief points of his message. There was a third point of equal importance. In September Spain had been granted a "reasonable time" to achieve a settlement. Now with Spain initiating a complicated scheme for autonomous government, McKinley drastically shortened the deadline. Spain must achieve a peaceful settlement "in the very near future," he warned, or "it will be a duty imposed by our obligations to ourselves, to civilization and humanity, to intervene with force." With that McKinley sentenced Cuban autonomy to death. He had openly assured the rebels that if they fought on for a few more months Americans would step in and do their fighting for them. He had robbed those Cubans who dreaded American intervention of any hope that autonomy could stave it off. After McKinley refused the Spanish queen's request that America publicly endorse the new reforms, the Spanish government in January had to face up to the grim truth: The American President was deliberately subverting Spanish efforts to achieve a negotiated settlement. Despite the generally pacific tone of his annual message, McKinley on December 6, 1897, had let slip the dogs of war. With America's consul general openly working against autonomy in Havana, armed intervention in Cuba was now only a matter of time.[25]

The Democrats universally condemned McKinley's annual message—for its pacifism. The Democrats, by now, were a united, vociferous war party, for they were determined to sidetrack the dangerous reform hopes they had aroused in 1896. Retreat and retrenchment were the party's order of the day. In the South, the silverites were shelving their radical oratory as fast as they safely could. In the West, local Democratic bosses were shedding their troublesome Populist allies and subverting local schemes for fusion which they had so eagerly sought in 1896. Wherever reformers had invaded the party, the local bosses now strove to drive them out. In New York City, where "Bryanite" rebels challenged Richard Croker's Tammany machine in 1897, Bryan, a faithful servant of the Democratic organization, came to the rescue of Croker. In Illinois, the one genuine Democratic reformer of consequence, Peter Altgeld, would find himself virtually without a party as the Cook County machine retreated back to its precrisis ways. In the House of Representatives, too, the Democrats were determined not to represent too strenuously the reform hopes they had been temporarily forced to embody in their struggle against the Populists. The Democrats' House contingent chose for its minority leader Joseph Bailey of Texas, an old-line Bourbon Democrat whose cooperation with House Republicans cost at least one fusionist Populist his illusions about the Democratic Party. "When they kicked out Hill and Whitney and the goldbug gang that went to Chicago on their special trains," Representative Jerry Simpson of Kansas complained in the House on May 3, 1897, "we [fusionists] thought the party was going to be purified somewhat. But when I see the gentleman from Texas and a contingent of the Democratic Party in this House following up as a trailer behind the Republican party . . . I begin to lose faith in the earnestness of Democratic reform."[25]

For the fusionist Populists enlightenment had come a year too late. A fake reform party in 1896, the Democrats, determined to drive out reform and reformers, were becoming, as fast as they could manage it, a token opposition as well. Just as Republicans had agitated for war instead of opposing Cleveland's domestic policies, so now the Democrats clamored for intervention in Cuba instead of seriously opposing McKinley's. Had the Republican President controlled the Democracy he could scarcely have contrived matters better. Here was an entire national party vehemently demanding that he do today what he intended to do tomorrow while accusing him of being the earnest advocate of peace he was trying so hard to appear.

On January 12, 1898, however, McKinley's war apparatus slipped a gear. That day in Havana a number of Spanish Army officers attacked the offices of some Cuban newspapers, creating a brief rumpus in the streets. Although the fray lasted little more than an hour, Consul General Lee, as was his wont, reported that Havana was in the throes of a dangerous mob and that the situation was almost out of control. This was the moment McKinley had been waiting for. His agent in Cuba was now supposed to bring the *Maine* steaming provocatively into Havana to fish in its troubled waters. Unfortunately for McKinley's plans, Lee's nerve failed him in the pinch. Cabling lies to Washington was one thing; personally precipitating an international crisis, even war, was quite another.

The responsibility was too frightening for the old Confederate general to shoulder on his own. There was nothing for the President to do but send the *Maine* to Cuba himself. On January 24, after warning the Spanish ambassador that an anti-American outburst in Cuba would compel him to send in troops, the President ordered the warship to Havana to provoke an anti-American outburst. Publicly, McKinley assured the country that the *Maine* was merely paying a courtesy visit, but not many people were fooled. "A warship is a curious kind of oil on troubled waters," wrote Godkin in the New York *Evening Post,* "though the administration would have us believe the *Maine* to be about the most unctuously peaceful ship that ever sailed." That the *Maine* might trigger an anti-American incident was obvious. In London, the Spanish ambassador complained bitterly of McKinley's action to the British prime minister. In Havana, Lee himself was so rattled he vainly counseled delay. In Washington, the secretary of the navy, John Long, confided in his diary his intense fear "that the arrival of the ship may precipitate some crisis or riot." Mark Hanna put the matter with his usual bluntness. Sending the *Maine* to Havana, he said, is like "waving a match in an oil well for fun." [27]

The Cuban Junta was elated, the war press exultant. Senator Lodge expressed his delight in oddly prophetic words: "There may be an explosion any day in Cuba which would settle a great many things," he wrote an American diplomat in London. "We have got a battleship in the harbor of Havana, and our fleet, which overmatches anything the Spaniards have, is masked at the Dry Tortugas." Democrats, after their fashion, assailed McKinley's action as an empty gesture to appease Republican interventionists. With that explanation the Republican peace faction took what comfort it could get. [28]

The Spanish authorities, for their part, did their best to foil the American President. They received the *Maine* with an elaborate show of courtesy and strained every nerve to prevent an untoward outburst against the ship or its crewmen. McKinley, on his side, made matters as difficult as possible: He simply would not recall the *Maine.* Day after day for two weeks the menacing warship sat in the harbor of Havana, wearing out the flimsy pretext that it was paying a courtesy call and driving the Spanish frantic with fear. By

February 8, the Spanish government in Madrid was thoroughly alarmed. The sheer prolongation of the visit, Madrid wired Ambassador de Lome, "might, through some mischance, bring about a conflict. We are trying to avoid it at any cost, making heroic efforts to maintain ourselves in the severest rectitude." It was no fault of Spain's, however, that on the evening of February 15 the *Maine* exploded in Havana harbor, killing 252 of the 350 men aboard.[29]

It was not precisely the anti-American incident that McKinley had hoped for; nonetheless the shocking disaster was a stroke of good fortune for America's interventionists. Overnight it drastically shortened the road to war, for the *Maine* explosion wrought a profound change in American public sentiment. Not that it provoked a national clamor for war. After the initial shock and dismay the American people fell into a state of tense and sober expectancy. What restrained popular bellicosity was the fact, obvious to all, that whatever blew up the *Maine,* the Spanish government certainly had not: nothing could have been more contrary to its interests. When Hearst's reporters canvassed New Yorkers on the street, surprisingly few thought Spain to blame for the disaster. The public calm was deceptive, however. Although the explosion produced no clamor for war, it had made the great majority of Americans impatient for the first time to see matters settled in Cuba, by American intervention if necessary. Whoever blew up the *Maine,* as the war press insisted, the explosion was the bitter fruit of Spain's Cuba policy, its "culmination," as the Senate Foreign Relations Committee was to put it. With that sentiment the great majority of Americans agreed. The decisive question therefore was, had *anyone* blown up the *Maine?* It was possible, even probable, that an internal explosion had caused the disaster. The public could only await the report of a naval board of inquiry appointed by the President to ascertain the cause of the explosion.[30]

The naval board, at best, was a very poor guarantee of impartial inquiry. Ideally, given the international repercussions, the Spanish government or, perhaps, experts from some neutral nation should have had representation on a disinterested board of inquiry. A country that had been ready to go to war a few years before for the principle of international arbitration could well have invoked the same principle in regard to the *Maine.* From the first, however,

McKinley insisted on unilateral, *ex parte* proceedings. What Mc-
Kinley had arranged, in fact, was an *ex parte* proceeding within an
ex parte inquiry. High-ranking naval officers were being asked to
decide whether or not the U.S. Navy was to blame for destroying a
great battleship and killing 252 crewmen. They were to decide this
on the basis of the most ambiguous kind of evidence—from chunks
of twisted metal, from diagrams and descriptions provided by undersea divers picking their way through towering wreckage. That
navy officers would conclude from such evidence that the navy was
to blame for the worst disaster in American naval history was not
very likely from the start. Yet this was the only conclusion capable
of scotching interventionist sentiment and removing the *Maine* as a
factor in the Cuban equation. To allay suspicions that the President
had rigged matters to support intervention, White House spokesmen let it be known that McKinley, personally, thought the explosion accidental. On February 25, however, Commodore Dewey was
ordered to make preparations for the long-planned attack on Manila.[31]

The Senate interventionists now held all the trump cards. Beneath the surface calm, interventionist sentiment was running
strong in the country. After the navy's predictable report, it was
certain to become a torrent. Since inflammatory warmongering
was no longer necessary, the Senate interventionists decided it was
time to pose as calm, responsible statesmen. Like shipwrecked
mariners suddenly spying the yearned-for shore, they now proceeded to negotiate the last crucial miles with wary circumspection. On
February 23 leading interventionists took the floor to advise their
Senate colleagues to keep silent on the Cuba question while they
awaited the results of the naval inquiry. "Sobriety, steadiness, and
propriety of action," said Senator Morgan, were now the order of
the day. For five weeks after the *Maine* disaster agitation over
Cuba virtually ceased in the Senate. There were obvious reasons
for the new "sobriety." The interventionists simply could not afford
to cry up the *Maine*. Strictly speaking, its destruction was not a *casus belli*. To pretend that it was would undermine McKinley's efforts to present intervention as an act of compassion forced upon a
reluctant government by the inescapable dictates of humanity. To
make the *Maine* a pretext for war simply because it aroused stron-

ger passions than "humanity" did would make "humanity" itself look like a pretext. Seizing on two contrary reasons for waging war made both reasons suspect. Besides, as Democratic Senator Augustus Bacon of Georgia pointed out, agitation over the *Maine* would "obscure" the results of the naval inquiry; people might think it had been rigged.[32]

Despite the Senate's newfound gravity, the peace faction remained a force to be reckoned with. In early March a peace movement of "substantial citizens" gathered force and began protesting loudly against intervention in Cuba. McKinley took two quick steps to quash it. The peace faction contended, for one thing, that America was unprepared for war. McKinley met that objection easily. He called in Representative Joe Cannon of Illinois, chairman of the House Appropriations Committee, and told him to introduce a bill calling for $50 million for national defense. Still posing as a man of peace, McKinley directed Cannon not to associate his name with the measure. Cannon did as he was told. The national defense bill became law on March 9. That was the end of the preparedness argument. It also left the Spanish "stunned," Ambassador Woodford reported from Madrid.[33]

A week later McKinley delivered a more decisive blow to the peace movement. Senator Redfield Proctor of Vermont had made a quick visit to Havana and returned convinced that intervention was necessary. To those who knew him the conclusion was hardly surprising, since Proctor, a former secretary of war under Harrison, was "very ardent for the war," as Roosevelt remarked. He was also a staunch adherent of the Republican large policy. The public, however, did not know this. A quiet New England senator, he was widely regarded as an old-fashioned Republican untainted by the new jingoism. This false reputation made him especially useful for McKinley's purposes. On March 17, Proctor planned to deliver a speech in the Senate calmly describing the sufferings in Cuba and suggesting that America's armed intervention was the only possible solution. To give the speech maximum impact, McKinley pointedly invited Proctor to the White House on the morning of the scheduled address. For the further enlightenment of the press, Senator Frye took the unusual step of introducing Senator Proctor to his own colleagues as "a senator in whom the country has much confidence, and a conservative man." The speech had a devastating effect on the peace movement. Here was a "conservative" New Englander, a senator in whom the President reposed his trust, who felt there was no solution to the Cuban tragedy save America's armed intervention. Apprised by heavy hints that Proctor's speech was of the utmost importance, the press featured it prominently. Dwight Moody, the evangelist, read it aloud from beginning to end at Madison Square Garden. McKinley and the interventionists had pulled off a neat propaganda coup. A man who was "very ardent for the war" had called for war, and the "more intelligent classes," in Senator Lodge's phrase, were led to believe that a prudent advocate of peace had reluctantly changed his mind. That pretty much squashed the peace movement.[34]

A few days later the navy board of inquiry handed the President its fateful report. The *Maine,* it concluded, had been "destroyed by the explosion of a submarine mine," perpetrator unknown. Not surprisingly, the board's conclusion, though not dishonest, was unwarranted by the shaky evidence. Later inquirers have pretty much concluded that the *Maine's* destruction was due to an accidental internal explosion. With the *Maine* report in hand, McKinley's difficulties were at an end. He had only to bring his diplomacy with Spain to a crisis—never very difficult in dealing with a fifth-rate power—while satisfying the rapidly weakening peace faction that he was still trying to avert war if possible. On March 25, leading Senate Republican opponents of war—Aldrich, Platt, Hale, John Spooner of Wisconsin, William Allison of Iowa, and Mark Hanna—met with McKinley's flunky, Assistant Secretary of State William Day, to discuss the basis for a reasonable settlement. The antiwar senators agreed to the following U.S. demands, which the Spanish government received on March 29: First, Spain was to lay down its arms in Cuba immediately while negotiations between Spain and the rebels were conducted "through the friendly offices of the President of the United States"; secondly, Spain was to revoke at once the reconcentration order. The Spanish government was given two days to reply. The American ultimatum was harsh. To demand that the Spanish government cease fighting its own domestic rebels was tantamount to demanding that it yield up its sovereignty. That the antiwar senators agreed to those terms suggests how weak they now felt themselves to be. McKinley, however, was taking no chances that Spain might accede to his terms. Unknown to the antiwar senators, he attached a third, impossible, condition to the two demands he had allowed the peace faction to see. Ambassador Woodford was instructed to tell the Spanish government, informally, that in negotiating with the rebels the "friendly offices of the President of the United States" would be devoted to achieving "Cuban independence," which is to say, Spain's unconditional surrender. That was certain to secure Spain's rejection of the President's demand to negotiate a settlement.[35]

On March 31, the hard-pressed Spanish met McKinley halfway. They agreed to revoke reconcentration at once. They agreed to an immediate truce in Cuba, but only if "asked for by the insurgents," a stipulation put in to avoid utter humiliation. Understandably ignoring McKinley's demand that he negotiate between Spain and the rebels, the Spanish proposed instead that the new autonomist government in Cuba carry out the negotiations. In Madrid Ambassador Woodford thought peace was at hand. Had McKinley been seeking a peaceful solution, the Spanish concessions certainly provided the basis for one. Instead, McKinley rejected the offer and sat down to write the special message to Congress that would shortly precipitate war. With the official release of the *Maine* report on March 28, he now had overwhelming popular support for armed intervention; in the face of it even Wall Street's opposition was crumbling. The President's final dealings with Spain were merely a cruel farce. On April 5, Spain agreed to lay down its arms at the behest of the Pope—a desperate face-saving arrangement. "I believe that this means peace," reported Woodford, who still thought avoiding war was McKinley's objective. McKinley rejected that offer, too. He could not, he cabled the ambassador, "assume to influence the action of the American Congress." On April 9, notwithstanding McKinley's reply, the desperate Spanish government formally proclaimed an armistice in Cuba at the behest of the Pope. McKinley had now won virtually all his official demands: revocation of reconcentration and an end to hostilities. Few sovereign nations have ever made such concessions to a foreign power in peacetime over their own internal affairs. It availed Spain nothing.[35]

On April 11, the President delivered his war message to Congress. It began with one of the more notable deceptions in the annals of presidential messages. Tracing the course of his diplomacy down to March 31—thereby conveniently ignoring Spain's subsequent concessions—the President concluded quite falsely that he had "exhausted" all diplomatic means to secure peace: "The Executive is brought to the end of his effort." He therefore called for "the forcible intervention of the United States as a neutral to stop the war, according to the large dictates of humanity.... I ask the Congress to authorize and empower the President to take measures to secure a full and final termination of hostilities between the Government of Spain and the people of Cuba and to secure in the island the establishment of a stable government ... and to use the military and naval forces of the United States as may be necessary for these purposes." The issue was now up to Congress, the President having "exhausted every effort to relieve the intolerable condition of affairs" in Cuba. After saying all this, the President concluded his war message with the offhand remark that Spain had proclaimed some sort of armistice "the details of which have not yet been communicated to me."[37]

Thanks to McKinley's distorted presentation of his own diplomatic efforts, the Republican peace faction, as he intended, was left without so much as a straw to grasp. Its leaders could do nothing but grumble in hapless impotence. "If Congress had started this, I'd break my neck to stop it," Hanna glumly confided to friends, but it was the President who had forced intervention. There was nothing for Hanna to do but sit wrapped in gloom while Congress grappled with the insuperable problem of justifying intervention in terms that would put it within the orbit of international law. The result was prolonged squabbling in the Senate and the curious spectacle of interventionists taking the floor to refute the justifications offered by other interventionists. Democrats and several Republicans insisted that the only way to justify armed intervention was to recognize the guerrillas as the "Republic of Cuba." For the United States to set up a government for Cuba, said Senator Foraker, would be a "denial of independence." Other senators argued that the United States had no right to secure Cuban independence at all. The only justification for armed intervention, according to a number of senators, was the ground of humanity. Cuban independence, therefore, could not be, under international law, America's official war aim. To this contention, other interventionists replied that "the ground of humanity" no longer existed. As a justification it "has been taken practically from under our feet" by Spain's concessions. "We waited while the obnoxious orders of Weyler were in force," said Democratic Senator Stephen White of California, "and are now demanding war when the spirit of concession seems to be abroad." The chief result of the debate was that every legal argument for armed intervention lay smashed on the ground by the time Congress, on April 19, passed a joint resolution calling for armed intervention. The "Republic of Cuba" was not to be recognized; the guerrillas, having served their purpose, were to be brushed ruthlessly aside. On the other hand, by the terms of the resolution, the United States was forbidden from ever annexing Cuba. On April 20 the President signed the resolution. The war that so many had sought for so long was now but a few days away.[38]

The American people were jubilant. Pushed and prodded toward intervention for two and a half years, they now took the last mile at the gallop. Popular support for the war was more than overwhelming. It was joyful, exuberant, ecstatic. Americans greeted the war in a tumultuous holiday spirit, for in truth it was a holiday—a vacation from the years of suspicion, dissension, disillusion, and bitterness. Was the American Republic despoiled and corrupted? How could it be with America on the march, defending liberty, succoring the needy, and uprooting Old World villainy! Was the Republic in the grip of the money power? How could it be with the Wall Street peace faction so utterly routed! Like schoolboys tossing away their pencils on the last day of school, the American people cast aside the heavy burdens of liberty which they had taken up eight years before and which, for their pains, had gained them nothing and less. What was there to fret about? America was good! America was true! Cuba Libre! In that spirit, generous and giddy, righteous and irresponsible, the American people rallied to war against a fifth-rate power under the leadership of their ostensibly peace-loving President.

It was Henry Adams who put McKinley's role in its proper perspective. "At this distance," he wrote to Hays from Belgrade, "I see none of his tricks—real or assumed—I see only the steady development of a fixed intent, never swerving or hesitating even before the utterly staggering responsibility of war. . . . He has gone far beyond me and scared me not a little."[39]

5

"The Almighty Hand of God"

Before the war with Spain the Philippine Islands had not figured prominently in the plans of Republican expansionists. Unlike the American-run Hawaiian Islands, the Philippines were not a candidate, real or putative, for entry into the Union. Nor were they a mere coaling station ostensibly needed for America's enlarged navy or an offshore atoll arguably necessary for the safety of the nation. Lying some seven thousand miles from San Francisco, the Philippines form a vast archipelago. Its seven thousand islands extend across three thousand miles of the western Pacific. Its inhabitants then numbered some 6.5 million, a great many of them rude tribesmen, a large number of whom were headhunters. To seize the Philippine Islands from Spain would be an overt act of conquest. To possess the Philippine Islands would mean outright colonial rule, a subject race, and government by force. To seize and hold the Philippines would do violence to the Constitution, to republican principles, and to the deeply-held convictions of the American people. Moreover, it would make America a major power in distant Asia and lead to unprecedented "connections with European complications," as McKinley himself had put it. To conquer and rule Spain's Philippine colony threatened at one stroke to sunder solemn ties with the republican past, to reorder the political life of the country and leave all familiar havens astern. It would mean, as Andrew Carnegie was soon to protest, "a parting of the ways" for the American Republic. To conquer and rule the Philippines as an American colony was William McKinley's principal war aim. To press home all its fateful consequences was to be his principal postwar intent. When the President promised Lodge that he planned something "far-reaching" in foreign affairs, McKinley had spoken the truth. It was the last time he spoke truthfully on the subject.[1]

Of the audacity of his imperial designs, McKinley himself was acutely aware. Trusting no one to share his audacity, he disclosed his ultimate intentions to no one. Even at his death he was still disclaiming them. Responsibility for the new American Empire he would attribute to the "march of events," to the "Almighty hand of God," to the accidents of war, to popular demand, to "destiny," and to "duty." What he had done, he would insist at all times and places, he had done reluctantly—nay, unwillingly—bowing to forces, both profane and divine, far more potent than his own humble self. Behind this cascade of disclaimers, echoed and re-echoed by his party and its press, lay the force of an overwhelming political compulsion. McKinley understood quite well that Americans might accept, albeit uneasily, an accidental empire; an empire by design they would not have borne, not even in the giddy, war-feverish days of 1898. Like the buncombe artist who cranked the handle that operated the "Wizard" of Oz, so McKinley now cranked the handle of "destiny," set in motion the "march of events," and manipulated the "hand" of the "Almighty," which was no more than an empty glove.

McKinley's primary instrument was Commodore Dewey, still waiting in Hong Kong for the order to attack the Spanish fleet in Manila Bay and, if possible, seize the city. The order had not gone out with the signing of the intervention resolution. A bothersome technicality still stood in McKinley's way. Under the terms of the resolution, the United States was not at war with Spain. To attack a Spanish fleet eleven thousand miles from Cuba without a declaration of war would have looked ill for the cause of "humanity." To declare war against a country that had done us no injury, on the other hand, looked equally ill for humanity's American champions. McKinley, however, did not intend to let a technicality undermine America's Philippine "destiny." He escaped the dilemma in a manner that neatly prefigured his whole imperialist strategy, which consisted of presenting his intentions as if they had already been achieved. On April 25, the President asked Congress, not to declare war, but to declare that, since Spain had broken off diplomatic relations, a state of war already existed. McKinley did not even wait for Congress to declare that what he wanted had already happened. The day he delivered his request, the President approved the historic directive to Commodore Dewey: "War has commenced. . . . Proceed at once to the Philippine Islands. Commence operations at once." Speed was imperative; even a one-day head start for Dewey was imperative. All through the war McKinley feared that Spain would surrender before America's armed forces laid hands on her colonies, those "gifts from the gods" as he would later describe them.[2]

Dewey's victory made history but no martial glory has ever attached to it. The Asiatic Squadron reached Manila Bay on April 30. The next day, in about an hour's time, it destroyed the hapless hulks that passed for the Spanish fleet. The battle was no more perilous than target practice since Dewey's ships simply fired at will out of range of the Spanish guns. Glorious or not, the first step in McKinley's management of destiny had been successfully accomplished. Later on McKinley would arduously disavow any further intentions in the Philippines. "If old Dewey had just sailed away when he smashed that Spanish fleet," the President was fond of telling White House visitors, "what a lot of trouble he would have saved us." The truth was otherwise. The day after the battle, with only cabled rumors from Madrid to indicate that a battle had ever taken place, McKinley ordered an army expeditionary force to the Philippines. It was a remarkably bold decision. The situation in Manila was unknown. No blow had been struck as yet for Cuba Libre. Yet here was a President sending ten thousand much needed regular troops—the first American soldiers ever to leave the Western Hemisphere—eleven thousand miles from the cause of humanity. If McKinley wished "old Dewey had just sailed away" on May 1, he gave no sign of it on May 2.[3]

Nor did McKinley stop there. News of Dewey's victory sent the populace into a fit of ecstatic rejoicing. The American sky, it was said, turned red with fireworks from coast to coast. War fever and jingoism were sweeping all before it. Giddy already, the American people, on hearing of the victory, grew giddier still. The iron was hot and McKinley, a master of cautious maneuver when caution was needed, now showed he could strike, if required, with force and dispatch. He moved quickly on yet another expansionist front. Before Dewey's victory, his Hawaiian annexation treaty had languished hopelessly in the Senate. Overnight Dewey's victory gave it new life. It was now, claimed Republicans, a vital military measure. The United States needed Hawaiian bases to give aid to Dewey, the national hero of the hour. Pleading wartime exigency as a pretext, Republicans on May 4 took the unusual step of introducing a joint resolution of annexation in the House, thereby evading the Constitution's treaty-ratifying rule. Hawaii was to be annexed by simple majority vote. Behind the scenes as always, McKinley led the fight for annexation. Its advantages were clear. Annexation of Hawaii, as the Philadelphia *Press* had observed five years before, would "familiarize the public mind to the acceptance of other territory." McKinley wanted the public mind thus familiarized. Hawaiian annexation would provide a precedent for further overseas acquisitions. McKinley wanted that precedent. When Speaker Reed, hostile to all forms of expansion, bottled up the resolution in committee, McKinley threatened to annex Hawaii as a war measure under his authority as commander-in-chief. All the immense power of his office he pitted against the stubborn Speaker of the House, who was probably the first prominent Republican to realize that old-fashioned party stalwarts such as he had no place in McKinley's new order.[4]

With Hawaiian annexation safely launched in Congress, McKinley turned next to the Caribbean. On June 4 he asked the commanding general of the United States Army, Nelson Miles, to prepare for an invasion of Puerto Rico at the "earliest moment." Those "events" that "overrule human action" were marching swiftly to the presidential drill.[5]

For all the rejoicing over Dewey's victory, however, scarcely a single expansionist raised his voice, initially, for conquering or holding the Philippines. Whatever McKinley intended, neither public opinion nor party opinion was driving him. "The average man," admitted an expansionist magazine, "is somewhat mystified by the Philippine campaign." If so, the "average man" was in excellent company. The most important agents of McKinley's imperial design were equally mystified by the President's plans. McKinley's State Department fugleman, William Day, was now the secretary of state, but he too was kept in the dark. "Unfortunately," he remarked a few days after Dewey's victory, "there is nothing we can do but give these islands back to Spain." General Wesley Merritt, commander of the Philippine expedition, was equally mystified. He had no idea what the President wanted him to do when he reached the Philippines. Commodore Dewey, the hero of the hour, completely misread McKinley's intentions. He took it for granted that the President's Philippine policy would be the same as his Cuban policy: to oust the Spanish and create an independent republic. That McKinley hoped to annex the islands as an American colony in the midst of an anti-imperialist war was simply unthinkable to the commodore, an old-fashioned American by the new McKinley standards. It was unthinkable even to an expansionist like Day. That the President might contemplate such a venture, a Bostonian named William Endicott wrote to the secretary of the navy, was "a piece of hypocrisy too base to be conceived." The very audacity of McKinley's designs provided their best concealment; that McKinley felt compelled to leave so many highly placed people in the dark is, conversely, the measure of his audacity.[6]

The President's various agents were told only what they needed to know in order to further the President's designs. When the puzzled General Merritt asked the President to explain his Philippine mission, McKinley replied on May 19 that events in the Pacific "have rendered it necessary in the future prosecution of the measures adopted by this Government for the purpose of bringing about an honorable and durable peace with Spain to send an army of occupation to the Philippines for the twofold purpose of completing the reduction of the Spanish power in that quarter and of giving order and security to the islands while in the possession of the United States." That circumlocutory sentence contained in itself all the main elements in the tortuous rhetoric in which McKinley shrouded his imperialist policy. There was, first, the argument from a nonexistent necessity: A durable peace with Spain certainly did not require the United States to drive Spain from the Philippines. There was, second, the artfully dissembled intention: The U.S. Army was to keep "order" in the Philippines only "while in possession of the United States," implicitly a temporary affair, although after Merritt did his work McKinley would claim the islands by right of conquest. There was, third, McKinley's distinctive trick of presenting his wishes as though they were accomplished facts. What was the expeditionary force, General Merritt had asked. It was, said McKinley, an "army of occupation," exactly what it could not be until it had first succeeded as an army of conquest. Confounding fact and intention, purpose and necessity quickly became for McKinley and his spokesmen a sort of conspiratorial code. With it, McKinley's agents were simultaneously advised of his intentions, while the intentions themselves remained safely unavowed. Thus Secretary of State Day, the President's mouthpiece, would inform Ambassador Hay in London that the "outcome of our struggle with Spain may develop the need of extending and strengthening our interests in the Asiatic Continent," implying that McKinley intended to use the Philippines, one way or another, as a stepping-stone to intervention in China. Day would also inform Lodge in late June that the United States had a "destiny" in the Philippines, meaning that the President intended to seize something there. It was a vague assertion, but all that Senator Lodge needed to know to carry out his part in McKinley's plans.[7]

Commodore Dewey was not quite so manageable. He not only assumed that the President meant to liberate the Philippines, he almost ruined McKinley's scheme for annexing them. A number of Filipino rebels, led by Emilio Aguinaldo, had been exiled by Spain to Asia. Acting on his own initiative, the self-confident Dewey transported them in U.S. Navy ships to the Philippines to lead the fight against Spain. When news of Aguinaldo's arrival reached the White House on May 22, the President was furious. The hero of the hour was becoming an infernal nuisance. Two days later, McKinley wired Dewey a curt warning "not to have political alliances with the insurgents or any faction in the islands that would incur liability to maintain their cause in the future." The hero of the hour, wrapped in republican innocence, proved incorrigible. He encouraged Aguinaldo and his fourteen thousand troops to fight the Spanish Army. Indeed, it was Aguinaldo, far more than General Merritt, who "reduced the Spanish power in that quarter." When Aguinaldo, expecting America's friendship, proclaimed a Filipino

Republic in mid-June, Commodore Dewey seemed genuinely pleased. The Filipinos, he cabled Washington, were "more capable of self-government than the natives of Cuba and I am familiar with both races."[8]

Something had to be done to get around the commodore, and General Merritt was the obvious instrument. On June 15, Day wired firm instructions to the general which stand as the perfect example of McKinley's crafty pretense that the future was already past. Although American troops had not even reached the Philippines, General Merritt was advised that "in entering upon the occupation of the islands as a result of its military operations in that quarter [the United States] will do so in the exercise of the rights which the state of war confers and will expect from the inhabitants . . . that obedience which will be lawfully due from them." In other words, the Filipinos who were reducing the Spanish power owed "obedience" to a conquering army that had conquered nothing and would conquer nothing except the Filipinos themselves. Aguinaldo was to be crushed by force and Commodore Dewey, the overpraised hero of the hour, would discover belatedly that he had merely been McKinley's pawn.[9]

Although the President's "army of occupation" was still on the high seas, events elsewhere were moving more expeditiously. On June 10, Speaker Reed caved in to party and presidential pressure and released the Hawaiian annexation resolution to the House floor. Five days later "this important military measure," as it was now commonly described, passed the House by a vote of 209 to 91—"the first hole in the dike which let in the sea," as a Democratic legislator recalled. On June 22, the commander of the Caribbean expeditionary force, General William Shafter, after frantic urging from the President to "sail at once," finally managed to land his raw recruits on the Cuban beaches. Fortunately for them they met no defenders. Neither the Spanish government nor the Spanish Army had much of a will to fight; all they really cared about was offering just enough resistance to save face and then bow out as quickly as possible. On July 17, the Spanish troops in Santiago, Cuba, surrendered unconditionally. The next day Spain sued for peace. In response, McKinley promptly ordered the invasion of Puerto Rico. "On your landing," he instructed the army, "you hoist the American flag." This was an essential element in McKinley's strategy of the fait accompli. Speaking of the flag a few months later, the President would ask an Atlanta audience: "Who will withdraw it from the people over whom it floats?"[10]

First, of course, the flag had to be hoisted, and peace could not be staved off for long. McKinley did what he could to delay the inevitable. The Puerto Rican expedition was slow getting started; the bulk of the Philippine expeditionary force was not scheduled to arrive until late July, which left Aguinaldo's forces the main military power on the ground. A little more time was needed for the "gods" to bestow their "gifts." McKinley took it. He invited his cabinet on a Potomac cruise, on which, during a five-day river excursion, he discussed the pending armistice in commodious and leisurely fashion. Finally, on July 30, the President presented his truce terms. Spain was to cede Puerto Rico—captured on July 25—to the United States; it was also to recognize the United States' title to the city, bay, and harbor of Manila, acquired by right of future conquest. The final "disposition" of the rest of the Philippines was to be decided at a peace conference. For the harsh terms, McKinley blamed the American people. Public opinion, he told the French ambassador, was forcing him to "obtain some advantage from our great victories at Manila and for the sacrifices we have made in sending to the Philippines a large body of troops." The American electorate, who in fact were demanding nothing, were forcing the hand of a humble democratic leader who intended to defy in domestic affairs the most deep-seated sentiments of the American electorate.[11]

On August 7, Spain accepted most of McKinley's harsh terms but understandably demurred on the Philippines. How, asked the Spanish government, could the United States lay claim to Manila by right of conquest when the city was still in Spanish hands? Why did the disposition of the archipelago even enter into the discussion when the islands remained in law and in fact under Spanish rule?

Flatly rejecting Spain's conditional acceptance, McKinley on August 9 simply repeated his original terms. Logic is no help to the vanquished. Two days later Spain accepted McKinley's armistice terms without condition and on August 12 the President signed the protocol ending hostilities and formally proclaimed a truce. Two days later, after token resistance, Spanish troops surrendered the city of Manila to the U.S. Army, General Merritt's chief problem in the affray being to keep Aguinaldo's forces from entering the city. Coming after the truce, the capture of Manila was technically null and void, but international law is no help to the vanquished either.

The real battle over the Philippines was not fought in the islands. It was fought in America. Its weapon was a torrent of propaganda; its objective to weaken, by every possible argument—by sheer noise, if necessary—the electorate's traditional aversion to colonial empire and overseas dominion. It was the task of the press, as McKinley pointed out to a newspaper publisher, to make it "appear desirable" for America to retain the archipelago. The propaganda campaign to make Philippine annexation "appear desirable" proved extraordinarily intense. It began when the President, by his actions, by adroit hints to interested parties, by selective leaks to Republican publishers, began making it clear that something "far-reaching" was in the works in the far Pacific. Within weeks of Dewey's victory, the Republican press began the softening-up process with vague talk about "destiny" and the "inevitability of expansion."[12]

Reluctant acceptance of a fait accompli was the keynote of the propaganda campaign. "Much as we deplore the necessity for territorial acquisition, the people now believe that the United States owes it to civilization to accept the responsibilities imposed upon it by the fortunes of war." So wrote the administration newspaper, the Chicago *Times-Herald* in June, before American troops had even reached Manila Bay and before "the people" had given any sign whatever of craving "territorial acquisition." McKinley's trick of calling his plans accomplished facts characterized the expansionist rhetoric. The American people were invariably described as already demanding what the propagandists were trying to get them to accept. Readers of the *Times-Herald* could learn in June not only that the people "want the Philippines," but that they "may want [i.e., will get] the Carolines, the Ladrones, the Pelew and the Marianna groups" as well, although probably not one American in a hundred had ever heard of such places. Senator Foraker told an Ohio audience that the American people ought to "realize" that

they "want colonial possessions." They *wanted* them but apparently they still did not know it. The debasement of language by political mendacity was never more aptly illustrated than in the annex-
ationists' desperate pretense that imperialism was a popular
movement.[13]

Above all, the propagandists, again following McKinley, made
frantic efforts to deny any imperialist intentions. America's possession of the Philippines—still unachieved—was described from the
start as the "fortunes of war," which is to say, mere happenstance.
It was attributed to the workings of "destiny." It was deemed not
the design of men, but of "Providence." It was ascribed to "the natural outcome of forces constantly at work." Having happened
through destiny, happenstance, providence, or historical determin-
ism, America's control of the Philippines, so the propagandists insisted, brought distasteful but unavoidable "duty" in its train,
namely the duty to rule the islands. "Destiny," as McKinley liked
to say, "determines duty." Could the United States in good conscience "return" the archipelago to Spain and subject Filipinos to
its brutal imperial yoke? That the United States did not control the
Philippines and had nothing to return did not stand in the way of
the propagandists. The incessant pretense that the United States
had already captured the Philippines—"having broken down the
power in control of them," as Whitelaw Reid of the New York
Tribune put it—was expressly designed to make ultimate annexation by treaty seem mere recognition *de jure* of what had already
occurred through the fortunes of war.[14]

In the campaign to win popular acceptance of empire two important elements were missing. One was imperialism itself. A full-out
imperial creed, the candid laudation of empire, played an insignificant role in the propaganda for an American empire. McKinley
himself sternly repudiated the term "imperialism." That was the
sort of thing, he said, that only vile European powers practiced.
The arguments for America's first colonial venture were put on the
most narrow circumstantial grounds: the unintended consequences
of Dewey's naval victory and the inescapable "duty" it brought in
its train. If America was becoming an imperial power, it was an
empire purely by inadvertence. So the propagandists insisted. As
McKinley told an Omaha audience, "We must follow duty even if

desire opposes." If in the end Americans accepted the annexation of the Philippines, they did so without endorsing the imperial principle, indeed while still rejecting it, which was why straight-out imperialism would soon prove a dead-end for the Republican party.[15]

Americans might not have supported Philippine annexation at all were it not for the absence of a second element in the furious struggle for the public mind, namely the Democratic Party. Both in principle and in practice the Democrats were strongly antiexpansionist. They had been so before the war and they would be so again once the Philippines were safely annexed. But between June and December 1898, when the great propaganda fight was raging, the Democracy forgot its principles and lost its voice. While the Republican Party and its fuglemen were crying up duty and destiny in the Pacific, no Democrat of note said a word in protest. If, as William Endicott said, launching imperialism under cover of an anti-imperialist war was inconceivably base hypocrisy, the Democrats declined the opportunity to expose it. Republican expansionists had the political arena entirely to themselves. Had the Democrats marshaled their party strength against McKinley's designs, those designs would never have succeeded. Even without a Democratic opposition, the American people, with nothing to guide them save ceaseless expansionist propaganda, were painfully divided and confused about the Philippines. Even at war's end, with the American flag flying over Manila, there was no grass-roots demand for retaining the Philippines and no evidence that a majority even favored it. Even in October, when McKinley urged his emissaries in Paris to demand the entire archipelago, there was no popular mandate for such a policy. Nor was public faith in the Republican Party conspicuously strong. In the off-year elections that November, the Republicans, despite victory in a popular war and the nation's emergence from the economic depression, suffered losses in Congress. For the success of McKinley's imperial design the silent complicity of the Democrats proved decisive.[16]

To raise the banner of anti-imperialism once imperialism had been safely launched created a near perfect situation for the Democratic Party. Anti-imperialism, for one thing, was an eminently safe issue; making it "paramount," to quote the Democrats' 1900 platform, would lead the party safely out of the bogs of domestic affairs and the perils of domestic reform. Imperialism would change the question before the nation—from difficult ones to a manageable one. Moreover it was a harmony issue for the Democrats. Under the aegis of anti-imperialism the gold Democrats could—and would—return to the Democratic Party. Together again, the old-line Democracy and its former business partners could—and would—lay the ghost of reform to rest. These objectives Democratic leaders could not achieve, quite obviously, if they thwarted McKinley's plans at the outset. Imperialism could scarcely become the "paramount" issue of 1900 unless it was safely launched in 1898. Changing the question before the nation could not benefit the Democratic Party until McKinley had changed the question. William Jennings Bryan, faithful to his party's interests, perfectly embodied the Democrats' strategy: In 1899 he simultaneously denounced imperialism and urged Democratic senators to ratify the treaty that launched it.[17]

The party of White Supremacy had yet another reason for not opposing imperialism until the United States was an imperial power. What Republican-sponsored colonialism would mean to southern politics was scarcely lost on southern Democrats. That the once-great Republican Party, the historic party of Negro rights and political equality, was now claiming the right to govern lesser breeds without their consent gave the Democracy what it had hitherto never enjoyed: complete license from Republicans to treat southern Negroes as the McKinley administration intended to treat Filipinos. The Democrats quickly made the most of it. It is no coincidence that the legal disenfranchisement of black people—and poor whites—and the elaboration of segregation laws were carried out by southern Democrats in 1898 and the years immediately thereafter. If Republicans even wished to protest the final dismantling of their party's historic achievements they were now utterly compromised. Southern racist politics, as the Boston *Evening Transcript* sadly observed, is "now the policy of the administration of the very party which carried the country into and through a civil war to free the slave." On the very floor of the Senate, Tillman of South Carolina openly taunted the heirs to the party of Lincoln: "Republican leaders do not longer dare to call into question the justice or the necessity of limiting Negro suffrage in the

South. . . . The brotherhood of men exists no longer." Directly or indirectly McKinley's imperial design was to strengthen the powerful throughout the American commonwealth. That, in truth, was its ultimate purpose.[18]

On August 28, McKinley appointed the members of a five-man commission charged with conducting treaty negotiations with Spain in Paris. Not surprisingly, the commission was controlled by expansionists—Whitelaw Reid, Senator Frye, and William Day, whom John Hay replaced as Secretary of State. It is the measure of how far McKinley's imperial designs outstripped even the ambitions of Republican expansionists that the three expansionists on the commission intended, initially, to demand of Spain no more than the city of Manila as a coaling station for the U.S. Navy. With numerous Republican expansionists to choose from, McKinley could not find three who thought it wise or proper to take the precedent-shattering step of annexing a vast and remote archipelago. Like the American people in general, McKinley's handpicked emissaries had to be prodded toward empire and in the end expressly ordered to carry out the President's plans.[19]

It is not often that a President's diplomatic agents are treated as mere objects of propaganda, but such was the case with the peace commission. McKinley's formal instructions to the embarking members, dated September 16, might have appeared as a newspaper editorial. "Without any thought of complete or partial acquisition," McKinley told his representatives, "the presence and success of our arms at Manila imposes upon us obligations which we cannot disregard. The march of events rules and overrules human actions." To supplement his secular argument from chance, McKinley also invoked the Deity. "Without any desire or design on our part," he noted, America's military successes have "brought us new duties and responsibilities which we must meet and discharge as becomes a great nation on whose growth and career from the beginning the Ruler of Nations had plainly written the high command and pledge of civilization." The upshot was that he wanted the commission to demand all of Luzon at the least.[20]

Some weeks later, when negotiations began, McKinley deemed the time ripe to take the final step: He ordered his commissioners to demand the entire archipelago. Public opinion, he informed them, made any other alternative impossible. "It is my judgment," he cabled them on October 25, "that the well-considered opinion of the majority would be that duty requires we should take the archipelago." A majority that had not yet been heard from was dictating his present actions. McKinley's order brought consternation even to pliant William Day. Tool of the President though he was, Day could not square it with his conscience to demand the entire archipelago. In a rare display of independence he wired McKinley that such annexation ill-suited a nation "whose principle it is to rest its government on the consent of the governed." McKinley replied the next day with a sharp, impatient ultimatum: "Cession must be of the whole archipelago or none." Day's resistance collapsed in a trice.[21]

On October 31 the commission, under the President's express order, formally demanded the entire Philippines from Spain. Stunned, the Spanish negotiators balked. Once again Spain pointed out that the United States had no claim to the Philippines by right of conquest since it had not conquered them. Even Manila, captured after the armistice, by rights should be restored to Spain. The victor, however, was adamant. The vanquished were helpless. In the end the Spanish government, thoroughly humiliated, caved in to McKinley's demands. On December 8 the treaty of peace was signed. The United States by formal cession from Spain now possessed the Philippine Islands. The fait accompli that the President and Republican propagandists had been proclaiming for six months was now at last a fact.

All McKinley had to do now was secure Senate ratification of the treaty and crush the Filipino insurgents. The former was gained with a heavy dose of virtual bribery by the margin of a single vote. The latter was accomplished with machine guns and was to take three bloody years and more. The love of liberty for foreigners that had warmed the hearts of so many warmongering politicians disappeared in the "march of events." When the President asked Congress for funds to put down Aguinaldo's mischievous troublemakers (for that, of course, was how the administration described them) scarcely a senator from the anti-imperialist Democracy cast a dissenting vote. With the decline of the republican movement at home the "propaganda of republicanism" abroad ceased to stir

America's political leaders. The very politicians who had castigated Spain for trying to crush Cuban guerrillas now supported America's military efforts to crush Filipino guerrillas. And they watched without opposition as the party of White Supremacy robbed American citizens of the right to vote and enmeshed the South in an iron net of racist legislation.[22]

With matchless guile and unshakable aplomb, President McKinley had carried America across a great divide. He had ushered in a new age and it was an age of iron. Familiar landmarks were fast disappearing; venerated scruples were losing their authority. Men who had once stood at the center of events now trailed haplessly behind the President's van like wounded soldiers abandoned on the march. Andrew Carnegie, vehemently opposed to imperialism, found himself cast in the odd role of a professional agitator. Republicans who had been prominent when Lincoln was President now turned their backs in disgust on their once beloved party, which only tightened its internal discipline the more. In April 1899, the once powerful Speaker Reed—"Czar Reed" he had been called—resigned his House seat and retired from public life, broken and bitter at the age of fifty. "Why have we all changed," he asked, bewildered, in an article he never had the courage to publish. It was indeed a "parting of the ways" for the American Republic. A story that had begun eight years before with the revival of the republican cause had been brought to a close with the triumph of empire, "a vulgar commonplace empire," Senator Hoar called it, "founded upon physical force, controlling subject races and vassal states." A few years before—and how long ago it must already have seemed—Americans of every condition had been demanding republican reforms of one kind of another. Their demands had gone unmet, their hopes had come to naught. The ruling politicians whose power they had threatened now set to work ensuring that another such perilous outburst would never occur again.[23]

From the political crisis of the 1890s the two parties had made an escape that was not only narrow but lucky. Had Cuban émigrés not raised the flag of revolt the year 1898 would have found the parties still deeply mired in political troubles. They had made the most of the Cuban opportunity but the opportunity had been fortuitous. Even the war, however, could not restore the politics of precrisis days. The old Civil War loyalties were dead beyond hope of revival. The old no-issue politics could no longer be practiced with impunity. The near monopoly of public life that the two parties had once enjoyed seemed broken forever. Nonpartisan political associations, civic leagues, and the like were springing up in every city. Intraparty rebellions, once regarded as base treachery, were now commonplace events. The old, naive faith in mere industrial expansion was gone. All the old post–Civil War props of party power lay smashed like Humpty Dumpty. In the promising aftermath of the "splendid little war," the two party oligarchies now sought to replace them with more permanent foundations.

McKinley and the Republican Party leaders had no doubt what one prop, at least, would be. The transformation of the United States, already an imperial republic, into an active world power had been the party's goal since the onset of the political crisis. With jingoism rampant in the country, with American troops stationed five hundred miles from Hong Kong, the means for doing so for the first time lay at hand. To imperialists and anti-imperialists alike it was obvious that the annexation of the Philippines could give America a major voice in the affairs of China, the then-current cockpit of European greed and ambition. It was obvious, too, that any American intervention in China meant embroilment in European rivalries—"connections with European complications," as McKinley had rightly put it. Therein lay the advantage of intervening in Chinese affairs. A direct plunge into Europe was still politically impossible; entanglement with Europe violated a still-binding American tradition. That tradition, so crippling to any large foreign policy, McKinley and the Republican oligarchy were determined to breach. The United States could scarcely become an active power in the world if it never confronted the world's major powers. Foreign affairs could never overshadow domestic politics if it consisted, at most, of pulling and hauling among puny Caribbean republics. Since McKinley and his party dared not attempt a direct assault upon the tradition, China provided them with the means to outflank it. The European powers had exported their "complications" to Asia. All McKinley now had to do was export them from Asia to America. In truth, "complications" were the sole important commodity in the much discussed "China trade" which Republican propagandists held out as bait to American businessmen to disguise the fact that the United States had no interests, economic or otherwise, in the sordid affairs of Imperial China.

The task of making American intervention in China politically palatable President McKinley assigned to his new secretary of state, John Hay, as soon as the Philippines had been safely annexed. The result of Hay's cogitations was the famous "Open Door" policy, a policy, well-named, by which the Asian door to Europe was to be prized open. It was an ingenious scheme, carefully graduated to "familiarize the public mind" by degrees with the need to court difficulties several thousand miles from home. Hay took the first step in September 1899, with a circular note to Britain, Russia, France, Germany, Italy and Japan, informing them that America wanted its trading rights respected in their various Chinese spheres of influence. The note, by design, was entirely innocuous. The McKinley administration did not challenge the right of Europe's powers to carve out areas of influence in China. It merely asked them not to do what they were not even doing; no European power was infringing on America's Chinese trade, which in any event was so negligible that, as Speaker Reed had sarcastically remarked, its loss would have as much effect on the American economy as a store going bankrupt in Bangor, Maine. The innocuous assertion of America's commercial rights against the imperial designs of Old World villains proved a popular diplomatic move, perhaps because it reassured uneasy Americans that the country, despite all, remained hostile to imperialism.

Emboldened by the public response, McKinley and Hay took the next step. On July 3, 1900, Hay issued a second Open Door note to the powers. This one was far from innocuous. In nine months' time America's alleged interest in China had undergone an extraordinary expansion. The United States, Hay now proclaimed, was concerned with far more than its commercial rights. It now pledged itself to nothing less than the defense of China's "territorial and administrative integrity." A vast and prostrate empire, remote from our shores, remote from our concerns, had become by unilateral decree the protégé of the United States in the teeth of European greed. A more gratuitous, a less warranted, grasp at "European complications" can scarcely be imagined. That McKinley himself shared Europe's greed only made his China policy even more grotesquely cynical. When Hay first discussed the Open Door policy with McKinley, the President objected to one of Hay's original provisos, a formal disavowal of any American territorial ambition in China. "May we not want a slice," the President asked Hay, "if it is to be divided?" Thus, the self-appointed protector of China's "territorial integrity." The disavowal was never made.[24]

What McKinley had made was a vast, indeterminate, and utterly gratuitous commitment, one that would yoke the United States permanently to Asia, enable its leaders, hopefully, to entangle the country in international complications of every kind and degree. China, by fiat, was to become a sort of international bank for borrowing trouble. Such was McKinley's China policy, the perfect cynical epitome of the Republican large policy in general.

"In a few short months," McKinley proudly informed a visitor to the White House, "we have become a world power." It was true enough. The chancelleries of Europe, which a few years before had not deigned even to send embassies to Washington, now echoed with nervous talk of the growing "American peril." America's grand renunciation of "dominion and power," one of the nobler aspects of the American Republic's often murky history, was fast becoming, like so much else, a relic of the past. On the slender foundation of our alleged interests in Asia, McKinley and his party pressed for a two-ocean navy, for an Isthmian canal controlled exclusively by the United States, for a Caribbean Sea under American hegemony, and for protectorate rights over Cuba, whose independence, once so ardently cherished, was soon to become little more than a fiction. With America's "emergence as a world power," an oft-repeated cant phrase implying that it happened by itself, the first prop of the new political order was in place by the beginning of the twentieth century.[25]

As the party ostensibly devoted to the teachings of the fathers, the Democrats might have been expected to oppose the Republican large policy. Instead they endorsed it. The large policy, which is to say, the policy of supplanting domestic with foreign issues, served the interests of the Democratic oligarchy as well as its Republican counterpart. At their 1900 nominating convention, the Democrats took the opportunity of supporting America's new world role and its "expansion by peaceful and legitimate means." In accepting his renomination Bryan sounded the theme of missionary idealism which was to become the Democratic version of the Republican large policy. The candidate looked forward, he said, to the day when the United States became "the supreme moral factor in the world's progress and the accepted arbiter of the world's disputes." What a Pandora's box of "complications" that role would open up the American people were soon to discover. Democratic idealism (in contrast to Republican talk about overseas "trade") could scarcely disguise the fact that on the most fateful of national is- sues—the break with the renunciation of power and dominion—the major parties were indistinguishable. The electorate responded ac- cordingly. As Roosevelt, the Republican vice-presidential candi- date put it to Lodge during the 1900 elections, "There is not the slightest enthusiasm for Bryan but there is no enthusiasm for us."[26]

That bipartisan unity was but the outward sign of a deeper and more fundamental feature of the new political order: the deliberate effort to eliminate electoral competition as the decisive element in the two-party system. This was the second major prop of the new system of party politics that the ruling politicians began creating to replace the old, failed devices of the past. Electoral collusion—the mere pretense of two-party competition—had been practiced long before 1898. In New York City, Chicago, Detroit, Omaha, and other cities, state Republican leaders had rarely made serious ef- forts to win municipal elections from the Democrats. As Roosevelt had remarked back in 1884, Republican candidates in New York City were "figureheads simply put up for the purpose of being knocked down." When they showed signs of winning, Republican leaders, said Roosevelt, "betrayed" them. Such collusive arrange- ments, however, had been limited, local, often ad hoc exceptions to the rule of partisan competition for office. In the years after 1898 the collusive exception more and more became the rule as the Democratic Party, retrenching, ceased to offer serious electoral competition to Republicans outside their old southern and urban bastions. If the dominance of foreign affairs was to be the parties' functional equivalent of the no-issue politics of precrisis days, elec- toral collusion became the parties' functional equivalent of the old

Civil War party loyalties. Confining their vote-getting efforts chiefly to their traditional post–Civil War party bastions, the two parties actually succeeded in re-creating the post–Civil War voting patterns in the twentieth century. In hundreds of counties and dozens of states voters behaved more as their grandparents had done in 1870 than their parents had in 1890. The voting patterns were based no longer on the old passionate party attachments. They chiefly reflected the indisposition of voters to elect "figureheads simply put up for the purpose of being knocked down." Unchallenged in their respective bastions, party leaders scarcely had to appeal to the voters to control the politics of their communities or even of entire states. Increasingly elections became shams; increasingly, voters declined to vote.[27]

In the wake of the Democrats' retirement into a mere party of "outs," machine politics, supported by collusion, grew not only stronger but more extensive than ever. "The domain of the Machine," a foreign student of American politics wrote in 1902, "is daily growing larger. The Machine is gaining ground, especially in the West where it is invading districts which appeared to be free of it." If men opposed boss rule before, a few men by the turn of the century were coming to see it as the chief menace to the American Republic. In March 1900 Charles Francis Adams bluntly told a fellow anti-imperialist that he saw the danger to "republican principles" in the wrong place: "You see it externally in the Philippines; I see it internally in New York City and Pennsylavania—in Croker and Quay and Platt. . . . We cant about imperialism, and look for the 'man-on-horseback,' and all that nonsense. Our Emperor is here now in embryo; even we don't recognize him, and we scornfully call him a 'boss.' Just exactly as in Rome before the Caesars systematized [matters] a succession of Tweeds, and Crokers, and Quays had their day."[28]

In the immediate aftermath of the Spanish-American War the bosses indeed had their day. On the events of the preceding years they could look back with relief and satisfaction. A grave political crisis had been averted, a major threat to their power repulsed; the reform spirit seemed dead, the voters apathetic. The American Republic, torn from its old continental moorings, was now successfully launched on the broad sea of empire and dominion. "Unexampled political repose," as one newspaper put it, had been ushered in by the postwar years. Both party syndicates were stronger than ever. In the South, Achilles heel of the entire party system, disenfranchisement, racism, and segregation laws—a third major prop of the new order—promised to reduce southern farmers once more to a nullity and prevent any effective revival of the defeated Populist cause. After the 1900 elections the Democratic Party felt safe enough to discard the last vestiges of reform and began to proclaim itself once more the party of sound business principles. The triumphant Republican Party became so disciplined a ruling syndicate that people spoke of it in awe as the "national machine." As America entered the twentieth century, the leaders of the two major parties could well believe that they had at last solved the problem of ruling an unruly Republic and had at last placed their power on a secure and permanent foundation. If they did, they were mistaken and it would take a European war to rectify the mistake.[29]

PART II

6

"The People Are Through with Party Government"

In 1896 the leaders of the Republican Party had felt considerable trepidation when they forged their alliance with the major industrial and financial interests of the country. After the distractions of the Spanish-American War they had no fears whatever. The grand alliance appeared to be all that it had promised to be—the foundation of permanent Republican supremacy, the practical triumph of discipline, organization and wealth over the republican sentiments of the American people.

What the Republican oligarchy envisioned was an all-encompassing system of mutual aid. A handful of finance capitalists, preferably led by the prudent J. P. Morgan, were to take command of the national economy with the help of the party oligarchy. They would gain control of the nation's railroads, consolidate its industries into giant trusts, and monopolize control of capital under the aegis of the Republician party. The financiers, in turn, would use their immense wealth and influence to protect and enhance the oligarchy's power. Working in close personal consultation, the partners expected to divide between them the two chief spoils of the public world. The Republican oligarchy would rule the people; Morgan and his colleagues would manage the economy—with one eye to the needs and interests of the Republican leadership. To facilitate statesmanship among the capitalists Mark Hanna presided over an extragovernmental body known as the National Civic Federation, which was composed of leading financial and industrial magnates and a few safe, compliant trade union leaders, including Samuel Gompers. The Federation's chief task was to mediate labor disputes, encourage "conservative" trade unionism, and in general, as a labor member put it, "bring into closer and more harmonious relation those two apparently antagonistic forces," capital and labor, the most obvious point of strain in the Republicans' voting coalition.[1]

The new political order—it was sometimes called "the system of '96"—had some of the aspects of a bloodless coup. In the years after the Spanish-American War the national Republican Party became the most centralized, the most rigidly disciplined ruling party the American Republic has ever known. In the Senate, where the oligarchy convened, Republican senators took their orders from Aldrich, the "boss of the Senate," and a trio of his appointed lieutenants; they were known collectively as "the four." In the House of Representatives, Speaker Joe Cannon of Illinois could marshal virtually the entire voting strength of the party minions for every arbitrary ruling and every obstructionist tactic he deemed essential for the good of the party. All this display of party discipline was impressive enough, for a time, to the American electorate. The national Republican Party, still trailing wisps of its ancient glory, looked like a governing party, and its leaders generally comported themselves with statesmanlike gravity. As long as nobody asked them to do very much, no one could well dispute their claim that they alone provided the country with "responsible party government." Under their hegemony, America was fast becoming what Senator Lodge fatuously described as an "aristocratic republic." Firmly in control of the state party organizations, of most of the metropolitan press, of most of the political money in the country, with a jingo foreign policy to divert the electorate, the Republican oligarchy appeared to have nothing to fear, least of all from their token rivals, the Democrats, whose Congressional leaders were in all but open complicity with their Republican counterparts. By 1900 the national Republican machine had achieved the enviable position of serving the narrowest of interests—itself and its big business allies—while enjoying the support of a majority of those who bothered to vote. After the 1896 election fewer and fewer Americans bothered, which only made the oligarchy's task that much easier.[2]

Yet the system had a flaw and that flaw was radical. Instead of serving as the indestructible foundation of party power, the new economy of finance capitalism was in fact a foundation of quicksand. The aging hierarchs of the Republican Party still talked of the "manufacturing interest" and the "propertied classes." Such nineteenth-century terms, however, ill-suited the new economy they had helped to create, an economic system in which a few could control everything without proportionately owning much; in which bankers, not manufacturers, held the fate of industrial enterprise in their hands. The new finance capitalism was as fluid as water. A powerful financier might control a great economic asset one day only to discover on the next that a rival magnate had raided the stock market and wrested away his control. The new finance capitalists were utterly lawless. They bribed, they swindled, they defrauded; they ignored statute law, defied common law, betrayed fiduciary trusts. Worse, they were headlong, frenetic pursuers of monopoly, for competitive firms were useless to men incapable of running them and who would gain no further accession of economic power even if they could. The finance capitalists could not manage the economy; they could only prey upon it. They could not even manage themselves. The politically minded House of Morgan might wish to be discreet, might be reluctant to antagonize the public and make difficulties for the Republican oligarchy, but there were sharks in the waters of finance capitalism whom mighty Morgan could not control, against whom he felt compelled to do battle, inevitably with his rivals' weapons. It was virtually impossible for any finance capitalist to be more politic than the least politic among them. Hanna's vision of statesmanlike capitalists working in harness with the Republican oligarchy was only an old man's pipe dream.

In the failure of the new finance capitalists to serve the interests of their political allies, in the shocking spectacle of their lawless power lay the mainspring for a second national reform movement which was to provide the immediate background to America's entry into the First World War—the revolt of the American middle classes against political and economic oligarchy, a revolt known at the time and ever since as the progressive movement.

For almost three years after the Spanish-American War middle-class Americans—the "respectable classes" as the phrase then went—had watched with no outward signs of dismay the swift and unimpeded transformation of the American economy into huge industrial and railroad combinations controlled by a handful of New York bankers and financial manipulators. In March 1901, however, when a large number of once-independent steel firms disappeared into the bowels of a new billion-dollar corporation put together by J. P. Morgan, complacency turned to alarm and the alarm proved epidemic. From the sudden appearance of the U.S. Steel Corporation the complacent could draw no comfort whatever. Men who saw in free enterprise the national bulwark against socialism could find no solace in the virtual demise of free enterprise in the country's single most important industry. Men who had long admired America's "captains of industry" could find nothing to admire and much to fear in an industry captured by Wall Street financiers. Men who prided themselves on their conservative principles saw the Constitution itself falling prey to the new masters of capital. If the "community" did not restrain men who created corporations such as U.S. Steel, warned the president of Yale, "the alternative is an emperor in Washington within twenty-five years." Even the most ardent supporters of the established order looked upon U.S. Steel as a menace to order: The electorate, they feared, would rise up in revolt. "If a grasping and unrelenting monopoly is the outcome," the Philadelphia *Evening Telegraph* said of the formation of U.S. Steel, "there will be given an enormous impulse to the growing antagonism to the concentration of capital, which may lead to one of the greatest social and political upheavals that has been witnessed in modern history."[3]

Within eight months of the formation of U.S. Steel the complacent suffered yet another shock. On November 12, 1901, two rival groups of railway-banking magnates, James J. Hill and J. P. Morgan on one side, Edward Harriman and the Kuhn, Loeb banking house on the other, having grown tired of fighting each other, announced the creation of a vast holding company that gave the rivals

joint control of most of the railways of the West. With the formation of the Northern Securities Company every fear that U.S. Steel
had aroused was confirmed and magnified. Did a handful of monopolists run the economy? Two New York banking firms had just
bestowed upon themselves financial control of the arteries of commerce. Was a "grasping and unrelenting monopoly" the goal of
Wall Street interests? They seemed to have no other goal. Was
America governed by an elective government or by a plutocracy of
private men? A handful of monopolists clearly had more to say
about the economic life of the country than the national government itself. A wave of fury swept through the Middle West. Antitrust agitation revived across the country. Demands for the extirpa-
tion of monopoly were once more heard in America. The crust of
complacency was broken. Deaf ears were ready to listen, blind eyes
to see.[4]

In 1902 the magazine publisher S. S. McClure made a surprising
discovery: The middling sort of Americans who bought his magazine actually wanted, indeed were avid, to read about the evils of
monopoly, the lawless conduct of the very rich, and the deep corruption of politicians. Ida Tarbell's serialized account of the sordid
history of the Standard Oil Company delighted *McClure's* readers.
Lincoln Steffens's serialized report on the "Shame of the Cities"
proved equally compelling. Other magazines followed McClure's
lead and other writers followed Tarbell and Steffens. The heyday
of the "muckraker" had begun, a brief epoch that was both cause
and effect of the central political fact of the progressive era—the
rise of the American middle class, for decades a mere bourgeoisie,
to civic and political consciousness.

That very awakening was what the best of the muckrakers la-
bored to bring about. As an *Atlantic Monthly* writer was to complain in 1907, the muckrakers "expose in countless pages the sordid
and depressing rottenness of our politics; the hopeless apathy of our
good citizens; the remorseless corruption of our great financiers
and businessmen who were bribing our legislatures, swindling the
public with fraudulent stock schemes, adulterating our food, specu-
lating with trust funds, combining in great monopolies to oppress
and destroy small competitors." Again and again, Steffens, for one,
hammered away at his main theme: Corruption in America was *not*

the old dreary tale of grafting, small-time politicians—those perennial bêtes noires of middle-class America. The corruption, Steffens showed in city after city and state after state, invariably involved an alliance between machine politicians on one side and
respectable businessmen on the other, between the political dis-
pensers of corrupt privilege and businessmen avid for corrupt privilege. The solid pillars of the community were as lawless and corrupt in their own way as the politicians who served their interests.
Their alliance, Steffens argued in a 1906 work called *The Struggle
for Self-Government*, was the real reason why "oligarchy is the
typical form of the actual government of our states." This was "the
System," held together by corrupt privilege, that Americans had to
rise up and destroy, that the "good citizens" had to oppose if the
American people, in Steffens's words, ever hoped "to make government represent the common interest of a community of human be-
ings, instead of the special interests of one, the business class."[5]

What the muckrakers were trying to do was erase in a torrent of
sharp words nothing less than the most cherished political concep-
tion of the American middle class, its very picture of political reality itself, a picture in which politics and government were portrayed
as inherently evil and commerce and industry as inherently good.
To a remarkable extent they succeeded. After four years of exposé
journalism few Americans doubted the existence of "the System,"
or, as the alternative phrase had it, the "invisible government" of
Wall Street operators and political wirepullers. Prosperous businessmen decried the menace of finance capitalism and demanded
of Republican leaders "to be freed," in the words of a midwestern
meat packer, "of this modern oppression of commercial enslave-
ment." The very language of Populism was fast becoming the common parlance of people who ten years before had condemned the
Populists as "calamity howlers." As the municipal reformer Frederick Howe revealingly put it: "In 1896 the 'money monopoly'
seemed a heated Populist phrase. Within the past few years the
methods of banking have been laid bare. . . . A few score men practically control the available money of America. . . . The 'money
monopoly' has become a reality," a reality, that is, to the urbane,
the educated, and the affluent.[6]

Looking back on the progressive era from the dark days of wartime, the social critic Randolph Bourne decided that 1904 marked the year when "a whole people" awoke "into a modern day which they had far overslept. . . . They suddenly became acutely aware of the evils of the society in which they had slumbered and they snatched at one after the other idea, programme, movement, ideal, to uplift them out of the slough in which they had slept. The glory of those shining(!) figures—captains of industry—went out in a sulphuric gloom. . . . The American world tossed in a state of doubt of reawakened social conscience, of pragmatic efforts for the salvation of society." By the time the muckrakers had exhausted their subject, Republican politicians across the country found themselves face to face with an invasion of middle-class reformers—Committees of 40, Committees of 100, "New Idea" Republicans, "Lincoln-Roosevelt" Republicans—threatening their hegemony in the party.[7]

Never before had the party managers faced so massive an incursion of independent citizens into the political arena. Never before, in consequence, was their monopoly of political life—their ability to control nominations, to guard the avenues to renown, to control elected officials, to dictate the very issues to be discussed in the public arena—so severely challenged on so broad a front. From the point of view of the established party leaders the growing resolve of middle-class Americans to take an active part in public affairs posed a problem without precedent and without any visible solution: How were they to flush out of political life scores of thousands of influential citizens in a republic constituted precisely to enable the citizenry to participate in public life?

Republican leaders understood both the danger and its chief source. The letters of President Roosevelt were filled with complaints about the corporate magnates, not because they sought corrupt privilege, not because they built private monopolies, but because, quite simply, they were causing unrest and hurting their political partners. As Roosevelt said, they were "putting a heavy burden on us who stand against socialism, against anarchic disorder." Their illicit conduct, he complained, was creating "an unhealthy condition of excitement and irritation in the public mind"—Roosevelt's private description of the rising reform movement. Their "unwillingness to recognize their duty to the public," he told a Morgan partner in 1902, posed a greater danger to order than the labor radicals whom Wall Street professed to fear. Sharing Roosevelt's anxieties, Elihu Root, a New York corporation lawyer and a Republican Party statesman, exhorted his Wall Street friends to be "fair" and at least try to obey the law—they were setting a bad example for the ruled.[8]

In the eyes of Republican leaders the problem was not how to remedy the evils of the new finance capitalism. The problem was how to manage the discontent it aroused, particularly in the once-docile middle class. Two methods appeared possible. One was to curb the more irritating excesses of big business in hopes of placating the "good citizens" and restoring them to their former state of political torpor. The other method was to ignore reform sentiment entirely and wait until it waned out of sheer discouragement. "Stand pat," Mark Hanna had advised his party shortly before he died in 1904. Both methods were tried and both were to fail.

On the state level the failure of the policy of placating was epitomized in the brief New York political career of Charles Evans Hughes. It began in 1905 when rumors of a major insurance company scandal made its way into the pages of the press. Two of Wall Street's titans, Morgan and Harriman, had been vying, with every weapon at their command, for secret control of the $400 million assets of the Equitable Life Assurance Society. The rumors alone provoked a sharp public outcry. That money held in trust for "widows and orphans" might be the plaything of Wall Street speculators was more than even respectable New Yorkers could bear. Bowing to public pressure, the Republican governor appointed a commission to investigate the major insurance companies, and Hughes, an honorable forty-three-year-old lawyer, was chosen to conduct it. By the time he was finished in December 1905, the public, recalled Mark Sullivan, had been treated to a "tumbling cascade of sensations." Hughes demonstrated in meticulous detail how the great Wall Street operators had been using the policyholders' money to speculate in securities, to merge railways, to build their monopolies, to do, in short, with other people's money what other people hated them for doing with their own. He showed, too, how the insurance company directors had been cooking their books to disguise their betrayal of the public. He also showed that the three

major New York insurance companies spent $3 million a year—
also disguised by crooked bookkeeping—to bribe legislators and
political bosses around the country. Skillfully and remorselessly the
upright Hughes, a perfect specimen of the Republican "good citizen," laid bare for the first time the intricate workings of finance
capitalism—its reckless greed, its sordid chicanery, its insatiable
appetite for corrupt privilege, its incredibly branching tentacles of
influence that seemed to reach everywhere—the "invisible government" made visible.[9]

Life insurance is a sensitive matter. Further concessions had to
be made. As soon as the Hughes investigation ended, the New
York State legislature promptly enacted comprehensive legislation
to prevent another such Wall Street raid on the widows and or-
phans. Unfortunately for the state's party leaders, the concession
did not suffice. The good citizens were thoroughly aroused and
Hughes was their hero of the hour. Reluctantly, Republican bosses
made yet another concession. They nominated Hughes, a man
completely outside the organization, for the governorship, which is
to say, party leaders had lost full control of their most important
nomination. After Hughes won the election, Republican leaders
discovered they had lost control of the governorship as well.
Hughes cared nothing for the interests of the state machine. He
had a modest program of reform to enact, the very least that the
aroused voters of the state expected of him. At that point the Republican bosses decided they had made concessions enough to the
electorate. One disruption of machine politics was leading to another just a little too rapidly for safety. In order to block Hughes's
reforms, to embarrass his administration and so eliminate him
from public life, the Republican machine in the legislature threw
its full weight against the Republican governor. The machine succeeded only in puncturing its own fraudulent pretensions. Republican leaders habitually prated about "party loyalty" and "party regularity." Yet here were the party "regulars" turning treacherously
against their own party's administration. Republican leaders end-
lessly insisted that organization control of the people's elected legislators ensured "responsible party government." Yet here was the
machine's power being used, not to govern responsibly, but to protect the machine. Since Democrats in Albany joined Republicans

to defeat Hughes's legislative proposals, the public was treated to yet another long overdue revelation: Behind the hoopla of partisanship the leaders of the two parties worked together in collusive harmony. "The machine forces of both parties," as one progressive put it, "secretly united while ostensibly opposing each other."[10]

To placate the aroused good citizens the New York Republican machine had investigated a scandal, had enacted laws to prevent its recurrence, had even nominated an upright man for governor. In the end they placated nobody and had merely made everything worse. They had convinced the reform-minded that it was futile merely to switch back and forth between collusive party machines. They had convinced them, too, that only men independent of party organizations were to be trusted with office, that breaking machine control over nominations, in consequence, was a political reform of the most urgent kind, the quintessential progressive reform.

With far greater dramatic impact and far greater consequence the events in New York were duplicated on the national stage during Roosevelt's two terms in office. Prone to hysterical fears about Jacobin insurrections, Roosevelt viewed with equal displeasure, in his words, "the dull purblind folly of the very rich men" and the "unhealthy condition of excitement" it aroused in the people. Unfortunately he could do nothing about mitigating the former without drastically exacerbating the latter. In his first message to Congress, in December 1901, the recently installed President (McKinley had died of an assassin's bullet in September) addressed himself directly to the fears aroused by U.S. Steel and the Northern Securities Company. Great combinations of capital, he assured the American people, were natural and inevitable. To their continued existence the citizenry must submit. When it became clear that such apologetics had done no good, that public anger had not abated, Roosevelt decided to bring an antitrust suit against the Northern Securities Company. In part he did so because of public unrest, in greater part because he hoped the suit would encourage the "very rich men" to behave more discreetly in the future. The result was to typify the whole Roosevelt administration and privately exasperate Roosevelt. The American electorate ignored their President's preachments and ecstatically cheered his action. Three presidents in succession had failed to enforce the twelve-year-old Sherman Act. Here at last was a tribune of the plain people willing to unsheath the great weapon against the bloated magnates of Wall Street. By his suit, a President who kept insisting that business combinations were inevitable had with one stroke strengthened immeasurably the antitrust sentiment in the country. Bring "a thousand more suits at once," the Hartford *Times* cheerfully demanded.[11]

When Roosevelt, shifting ground, began distinguishing between "good" trusts (J. P. Morgan's) and "bad" trusts (Rockefeller's) the electorate continued to listen with exasperating selectivity. They cheered when the President denounced "predatory wealth" and scarcely heeded the inevitable Rooseveltian qualifier: Only "a few" of the wealthy were predatory. Similarly, the electorate cheered when Roosevelt attacked "malefactors of great wealth" and once again proved deaf to the qualifier: *"Certain* malefactors of great wealth" was the cautious phrase Roosevelt actually used. The citizenry heard what they wanted to hear and what they wanted to hear was a President who voiced republican sentiments. The first American President openly to defend the virtues of big business was adored by the voters as their fearless "trustbuster."

Roosevelt's dramatic efforts to extract a few exigent reforms from the Republican oligarchy in Congress further exacerbated the "unhealty condition . . . of the public mind." Occasional as they were, they virtually altered the whole country's perception of the national Republican Party. As with the Hughes affray in New York, men openly wondered what "party loyalty" and "responsible party government" meant when Republican leaders in Congress ignored or eviscerated the legislative proposals of an enormously popular Republican President. The admired discipline of the national Republican machine began to look considerably less than admirable. In the House it was the obstructive Speaker Cannon and his slavish followers; in the Senate it was Aldrich, his underlings, and his big business connections. Toward the end of Roosevelt's second term rank-and-file Republicans began speaking angrily of "Cannonism," of "Aldrichism," and of "Hannaism," the very terms attesting to the growing belief that the vaunted Republican Party, even on the national level, had become little more than a syndicate of personal fiefdoms, accountable to no one, not even to a Republican President, still less to the party rank and file.

Everywhere Americans turned, it seemed, they were finding the same dreary story repeated: rule by a few in the interests of few. To that rule they had no intention of submitting. By 1906 Roosevelt feared that the movement for reform was getting out of hand. He sincerely wished to see the American people governed by a liberal oligarchy; he did not want them governing themselves. In April 1906 Roosevelt assailed the exposé journalists collectively as John Bunyan's "raker of muck" in an effort to stem the tide of reform agitation. The effort proved futile; the term "muckraker" becoming, if anything, an honorific. By then the reform movement had reached the ominous stage when every concession it won—even a verbal concession—only sharpened its appetite for more. It was fast reaching that dangerous stage, too, when ambitious Republican politicians began to wonder which was more personally advantageous, adherence to reform or subservience to the party oligarchy. In 1906, for example, Senatory Albert Beveridge of Indiana, ambitious, brilliant, and regular, decided to cast his lot with the reformers. "You have no idea," he explained to a friend in November 1906, "how profound, intense and permanent the feeling among the American people is that this great reform movement shall go on." [12]

The movement was nowhere more intense nor more intensely republican than in the Republican states of the Middle West. There, farmers did not need the U.S. Steel Corporation to arouse them from complacency; they had never been particularly complacent. They did not need Steffens to tell them about the System: They had been misruled by Republican-*cum*-railway machines for years. The movement of midwestern businessmen and the small-town middle class into the ranks of reform did not create reform sentiment in the Middle West. What it did was give it a political strength it had not enjoyed since the days, long past, when farmers had comprised the great majority of the region's population. In the states of the Middle West and West, reform was not merely a diffuse demand for the "salvation of society." It was an open political rebellion, a rebellion that exploded in one state after another like a string of bursting firecrackers.

In 1900 the indomitable Robert La Follette, after years of wearying effort, finally overthrew the old Wisconsin Republican machine and won election as governor. During three successive terms he proceeded to enact the most comprehensive program of reform ever seen in American state history. In 1901 yet another insurgent Republican, Albert Cummins, defeated the Iowa Republican machine and won election as a reform governor. In 1902, Oregon voters, under the leadership of William U'Ren, forced passage of a legislative device known as the initiative and referendum. In the ensuing years, thus armed, they enacted progressive reforms in their state largely by direct popular vote. In 1906 a Republican named Coe Crawford ran on the La Follette reform program and won the governorship of South Dakota as an independent candidate. In Kansas and Nebraska reform-minded Republicans also gained ascendancy in the party and the state legislature. In California in 1907 Republican reformers, including Rudolph Spreckels, the sugar magnate, began organizing grass-roots League of Lincoln-Roosevelt Republican Clubs to combat the California Republican machine, the "corrupt but powerful few," as one of the movement's leaders put it. By 1910 they would sweep the machine out of power.[13]

Regarding party machines as the enemy of economic reform and the friend of corrupt privilege, the midwestern and western reformers made it their first order of business to improve the machinery of popular government through the statewide direct primary, home rule for cities, the initiative and referendum, and the recall of officeholders by petition. These standard progressive reforms, reforms aimed directly against machine politics, have often been regarded as futile by historians, but their intended targets did not, at the time, view them with such equanimity. Surveying the growing movement against oligarchy and privilege, Senator Lodge in November 1906 wrote in panic to his friend, the President: "We have got a terrible struggle before us to save the country from a movement which strikes at the very foundation of society and civilization." "The states just West of the Mississippi," he later reported to Roosevelt, "beginning in Minnesota and running down to Kansas are in a bad condition. The radicalism of La Follette and Cummins seems to be rampant in that region."[14]

Everywhere, but in the Middle West especially, respect for party "regularity" was vanishing like a puff of smoke. As Speaker Cannon's political lieutenant observed in 1908, he had never seen the public mind so "unsettled" in the region, "nor have I ever known a time when there was so little sentiment for the principles and policies of the political parties." That year virtually every midwestern Republican candidate for Congress had to pledge his opposition to "Cannonism," which is to say, to the arbitrary power and the obstructionist policies of the Republican Speaker of the House. "No one can forecast the possibilities of this growing progressive force," a Washington weekly observed in the summer of 1908 when Republican leaders at the national convention made their fateful decision to meet the "tidal wave of reformism" by openly defying it.[15]

The Republican oligarchy had compelling reasons for its decision. Roosevelt's strategy of scotching the reform movement by trying to remove a few major irritants had failed abysmally. Instead of calming the "respectable classes" he had succeeded only, in spite of himself, in making reform and insurgency more respectable. By "standing pat" the party leaders could scarcely fare worse. In truth, they no longer had an alternative. Faced with a growing intraparty rebellion that fed on every concession it won, the Republican Party managers had reached that critical stage where they could not carry out *any* legislative program without endangering their control of the party. Doing nothing, however, was still perilous to a party that had so long claimed to be the active governing party in the country. It was partly to disguise the fact that they were, in fact, paralyzed that Republican leaders decided not merely to "stand pat" but to make their defiance of the reform movement as active as they could manage it.

For such a brazen policy the party leaders in 1908 still felt themselves adequately equipped. Although the Republican rank and file was restive or openly rebellious and a half-dozen state machines had been smashed, the regular organization and its managers still dominated the national party, still controlled the party coffers and most of the party's representatives in Congress. After the 1908 election they were likely to control the presidency as well. William Howard Taft was Roosevelt's hand-picked successor (which went far to secure his election), but he was a soft, inept, and timorous man; Aldrich and his colleagues rightly expected to take him in hand once Roosevelt was safely retired. They did not even bother to wait until Roosevelt left office. In the winter of 1908–09, as a foretaste of what was to come, Republican leaders in Congress went out of their way to mock and humiliate their most popular President.[16]

For their major attack on the reform movement the Republican oligarchy chose its old speciality, the protective tariff, whose temporary reprieve in 1896 had not even survived the century. When Congress met in the spring of 1909 to consider tariff revision it faced the pressure of nine years of intense agitation for a reduction in the rates. The agitation had come not merely from the Democrats, but, far more important, from Republican businessmen, Republican manufacturers, and Republican farmers in the Middle West. The rates, last set in 1897, had become so prohibitively high that even the big protected manufacturers could well afford to see them reduced. In deference to popular sentiment, the 1908 Republican convention had pledged the party to tariff revision, but the party leaders, in writing the platform, had left a gaping loophole in the pledge. They carefully omitted to say in which direction they would revise it. The voters, understandably, expected downward revison; even Taft favored downward revision. By any conventional political reckoning the Republican Party seemed to have no reason whatever to do otherwise. That was exactly the reason they did otherwise. When the House tariff bill reached the Senate, Aldrich, the party's haughty manager of tariff legislation, sat down privately in his customary fashion to rewrite it completely. When he sent the bill to the Senate floor in April the country discovered that the tariff had not been reduced. In an astonishing act of brazen defiance, Aldrich and the party oligarchs had actually revised portions of it upward.

What the Republican leaders intended was clear enough. Entrenched in power for decades, regarding themselves as America's rightful rulers, they had decided to use the tariff to teach the electorate in general and the active reformers in particular just who held the reins of power in America and who knew best what was good for the country. The sheer arrogance of the deed, the naked party power needed to carry it off, were, hopefully, to deal a death blow to the national reform movement. Scorned and defied, the active reformers would abandon the political arena in disgust. Awed by the Republican leaders' self-assurance, impressed by their statesmanlike indifference to mere popular clamor, the "good citizens" would fall back into line and leave politics and government to the "professionals." The strategy had one fatal flaw. It depended entirely on a respect for party government and the disinterested wisdom of party leaders that was fast disappearing in America. Instead of overawing their enemies the Republican oligarchs played straight into their hands.[17]

By 1909 the Senate was no longer the exclusive headquarters of the state party bosses and their friends. As Republican machines in the Middle West were overthrown, insurgents, one by one, had begun to trickle into the upper chamber. Under the pressure of the reform movement, midwestern regulars, one by one, had begun to break away from Aldrich's rule. La Follette in 1906 was the first of the insurgents to arrive. By 1909, Cummins, Crawford, Joseph Bristow of Kansas, Moses Clapp of Minnesota, Jonathan Dolliver of Iowa, and Beveridge were ready to join him. The rebels were not merely men of nice scruple who chafed over party discipline. Nor were they Republicans like the late Senator Hoar, who split with the Senate leadership on one issue while plaintively demonstrating his "loyalty" on all others. Fresh from triumphs over state party machines, the Senate insurgents were determined, under La Follette's driving leadership, to smash machine rule in the Senate. Against them the usual instruments of party discipline were impotent. As ex-President Roosevelt observed to his son-in-law, "the Insurgent leaders represent not themselves but these big aggregations of voting units behind them," namely the aroused, rebellious, and politically active Republicans of their respective states. They spoke not for themselves, but for millions. They were men of power in their own right and they held that power precisely because, indeed only because, they were rebels against machine rule. They were as eager to use the tariff against Aldrich as he was to use it against them.[18]

Working in close concert, the insurgent senators—six comprised the hard core—set about mastering the immensely complicated details of the tariff, each insurgent taking responsibility for a section of the bill. They intended to storm the oligarchy at its strongest point: Senator Aldrich's unchallenged reputation as the high statesman of Republican tariffs. On that reputation the whole strategy of defiance depended. In two months the insurgents destroyed it, something the Democrats had not accomplished in twenty five years of allegedly trying. In one powerful speech after another, the insurgents took turns ripping apart the Aldrich tariff, schedule by schedule, provision by provision. Systematically they exposed its loopholes, its inequities, its false categories, its increases disguised as reductions, in short, all the wholesale tariff chicanery that had been hidden for years behind Aldrich's reputation as a responsible Republican leader. The boss of the Senate was stunned. Without a docile Senate to protect him, his famous hauteur deserted him. He blustered and fumed. Unable to answer his assailants, he accused them of party disloyalty, but the old anathema had lost its sting. The insurgents only mocked him from the floor: Who gave the senator from Rhode Island the right to speak for the Republican Party? The insurgents went even further: Who, they demanded, gave servile tools of the trusts and the interests the right to speak for the Republican Party?[19]

The insurgents could not block passage of the Aldrich bill, but the political victory was theirs. Republican leaders had set out to show the country who their rulers were; the insurgents had shown the country that their erstwhile rulers ruled by arrogance and bluff. Republican leaders had set out to show the country what responsible statesmen they were; the insurgents had shown what their statesmanship comprised: wholesale commerce in legislative privilege negotiated in a back room. The Republican oligarchy brought down upon its head a nationwide wave of rage and disgust. This time, ominously for the oligarchy, the disgust was mingled with contempt; the undoing of the boss of the Senate had been a particular delight to the American people.

To Aldrich, for one, it was all imcomprehensible, this radical alteration in the electorate's attitude. A handful of party rebels, instead of looking like a factious, stiff-necked minority, had managed to persuade millions of Americans that the party majority in the Senate was the stiff-necked faction, a self-serving, privilege-dispensing oligarchy. As the shaken boss of the Senate confided to

Lodge in June 1909, "we are dealing with a mental condition and that is the exact trouble with the situation." The "mental condition" was the republican spirit that Republican leaders thought they had safely buried in San Juan and Manila Bay. As for Lodge, he prayed for an upturn in the economy. "If prosperity fails to come," he reported to Roosevelt, "we shall find ourselves I fear, in deep water."[20]

Having vainly played self-confidence as their trump card, Republican leaders, for the first time in their history, lost their self-confidence entirely. In the winter of 1909–10 the party leaders, with Taft in their camp, decided on a desperate stratagem: an all-out national purge of every insurgent in the party, a war of political extermination. In January 1910, the Republican Congressional Campaign Committee announced that it would support "regulars" against insurgents in every Republican primary. President Taft cut off the reformers' patronage. At the White House plans were drawn up to put pressure on the Republican press, to establish "grass-roots" clubs of party regulars, to organize illegal party conventions wherever the regulars lost control of the legal party machinery. Fourteen states were to be the scene of the purge: Wisconsin, North Dakota, South Dakota, Iowa, Kansas, Nebraska, Illinois, Indiana, Ohio, California, Washington, New Hampshire, Pennsylvania, and New York—a list that suggests how widespread the Republican insurgency had grown. To finance the purge, Senator Aldrich drew upon his eastern financial connections to raise a huge war chest. All the power of the national party oligarchy, all the power and prestige of the presidency, all the skills of the state organization were to be deployed against a few score congressional candidates marked off for extinction by Republican leaders. In the Middle West in particular a campaign of wholesale abuse was unleashed against "the factious rats" and "socialist demagogues" who had dared speak for the electorate in defiance of the Republican oligarchy. Incapable of any constructive action, the desperate Republican leaders now demonstrated to the entire country how truly bankrupt they were, and this time there was no foreign adventure to disguise it. Here was the leadership of a once resourceful party incapable of any response to a national movement for reform save a campaign to destroy its Republican spokesmen.[21]

In the spring primaries, Republican voters showed how clearly they grasped the situation. At their hands, Taft and the party oligarchs suffered a complete and humiliating rout. Wherever regulars were pitted against insurgents, in almost every case the insurgents won. "The people," as a contemporary historian observed, "were through with Party government." In California, Washington, and North Dakota three more insurgents won seats in the Senate. In Maine, old Senator Hale saved himself from humiliation by retiring before he was retired. Aldrich, too, decided to retire before long. The oligarchy was not only losing its fight, it was losing its veteran personnel. In Michigan, an old-line machine Republican, Julius Caesar Burrows, lost to an insurgent in the first senatorial preference primary he had the misfortune to face, prompting a stand-pat Republican newspaper to ask the question of the hour: "When Michigan can be swept away by insurgency where can the rising tide be checked?" Within the space of five years the most centralized national party in American history had been split into two bitterly hostile camps. When Roosevelt, returning from an African safari, tried to appease both factions, he merely ran afoul of both of them. Hunting with the hounds and running with the hares—his old trick—was possible no longer.[22]

The November elections brought still further disaster to the Republican oligarchy. The Democrats not only gained control of the House of Representatives for the first time in sixteen years, they captured governorships in half a dozen eastern states. Losing to the opposition party is a temporary setback at most, but what the general elections revealed was something far more ominous to Republican leaders. The voters had rejected not Republicans in general, but "stand-pat" machine Republicans. Wherever progressive Republicans faced Democrats, in almost every case they won. With fine selectivity the electorate had delivered a rebuke not to a party label, but to a party organization and its minions. As Roosevelt rightly observed in 1910, the Republican oligarchy had become "a leadership which has no following." Its sole supporters, he told Lodge, were "the bulk of the big businessmen, the big professional politicians, the big lawyers who carry on their work in connection with leaders of high finance and the political machine, their representatives among the great papers and so forth." Ninety percent of the Republican rank and file, Roosevelt estimated, gave their erst-while party leaders no support at all. If the insurgents won them over—the last thing Roosevelt then wanted—"they get control of the organization."[23]

Senator La Follette, the acknowledged leader of the Republican insurgency, saw the opportunity quite as clearly as Roosevelt did. By now, after years of agitation and muckraking, the diffuse senti-ment for the "salvation of society" had been translated into a more or less coherent national program of republican reform. Politically, progressives called for more democratic national government through the direct elections of senators, direct election of delegates to national conventions, presidential preference primaries, and leg-islation to bar corporate influence in politics. Economically, they wanted strict federal regulation of railroads and railroad rates, to ensure that those who controlled the roads could no longer use them to create industrial monopolies. They wanted laws to protect the smaller entrepeneurs. They wanted the New York "money trust" eliminated through public control of banking and credit. They wanted corrupt privileges of all sorts—tax privileges, tariff privileges—eliminated. On these two basic goals, securing what they deemed to be both political and economic democracy, most progressives were in agreement, the moderates among them being those who hoped that moderate means would suffice to achieve them.

On the central issue of the age, however, the issue of industrial consolidation, the progressive movement was far from united. Fol-lowing Roosevelt, eastern progressives on the whole regarded in-dustrial concentration as inevitable and looked to strict government regulation of big business as the only feasible way to destroy pri-vate economic power. Following La Follette, western progressives on the whole regarded big business as an artificial menace to self-government, not merely aided but made possible by a whole system of special privilege. "Monopoly," as Frederick Howe put it in 1910, "is created by law. It is born of law-made privilege." La Follette and his followers wanted monopoly destroyed, not regulated, and industrial combinations, as far as possible, broken up. Had the pro-gressive movement been a party in control of the national govern-ment, it would have swiftly split apart over its deep disagreement on the question of the trusts. In 1911, however, the problem was yet in abeyance. Progressives in those halcyon days of the reform movement were little inclined to doctrinaire rigidity. However much they differed on the trust question, progressives saw themselves as comrades doing battle in a common cause. Steffens regarded La Follette's views on big business as "intelligent toryism," as he put it, but he and La Follette were personal friends as well as political allies, united in the great national effort to restore government to the people, to eliminate privilege, and to overthrow oligarchy. Though the progressives were not a party, their leaders by 1911 had become something very like a nationwide committee of correspondence. Steffens himself was the personal friend of such diverse progressive leaders as Judge Ben Lindsey of Denver, Louis Brandeis of Boston—"the people's lawyer," Howe of Toledo, Spreckels and William Kent of California, William U'Ren of Oregon, and George Record of New Jersey. La Follette and Brandeis were personal friends. A cross-hatching of friendships, exchanges of letters and mutual aid in numerous political battles had knit the progressive leaders into a genuine working coalition.[24]

In 1911, moreover, the common cause they shared had reduced itself to one overriding cause—the defeat of the Republican oligarchy. Whether they were moderate reformers of the eastern variety or radical republicans of the western sort, virtually every reformer was agreed that so long as the oligarchy controlled the national Republican Party there could be no reform at all. In order to cling to power, the oligarchy had shown itself, in Roosevelt's words, "cynically and contemptuously hostile" to even the mildest reforms. Now even the mildest reformers were ready to turn the tables. If they could not get from the oligarchy even moderate reforms, then that oligarchy was unfit to lead the Republican Party. This clear-cut perception, shared by the great majority of rank-and-file Republicans, shared even by moderate easterners, gave the Republican insurgency its national fighting strength when progressive leaders began laying plans to wrest the 1912 Republican presidential nomination from the party oligarchy in general and President Taft in particular. What had been utterly impossible a mere three years before had now become considerably more than possible, although it had never been accomplished since the emergence of organized political parties in America: the overthrow by genuine party rebels of the ruling magnates of a national party.[25]

At first La Follette was the insurgents' candidate for the Republican nomination. As the first Republican to raise the banner of rebellion in the states and the first one to dare raise it in the Senate, La Follette, more than any other single man, had been responsible for translating the national demand for reform into a national political movement. To further his candidacy the insurgents organized in January 1911 a virtual party-within-a-party, the National Progressive Republican League. Drawing on the scores of thousands of independent Republicans already in, or eager to enter, the political arena, the League began organizing with impressive rapidity a nationwide organization of state leagues outside regular party ranks. On October 16, 1911, the League held a triumphant three-day conference in Chicago and formally endorsed La Follette's candidacy. After the conference, there was no longer any doubt that the once-invincible Republican oligarchy was facing a fight for survival. Under the leadership of Senator La Follette, the last great republican of consequence in American history, the Republican Party seemed about to become, if not in 1912 then certainly by 1916, the party it had almost but not quite been in the days of Abraham Lincoln.[26]

At that point Colonel Roosevelt, who had grown increasingly radical in his public pronouncements, discreetly inserted himself into the political arena. By half-hints and pregnant nondenials, he let it be known to his followers that he just might be available to head the insurgency now that it looked like succeeding. His many supporters in La Follette's camp began working in secret to balk the senator's bid for delegate support. By December, they began deserting their candidate in droves. By February 1912, Roosevelt had captured the entire Republican insurgent movement; La Follette's candidacy was dead. What had proved its undoing, essentially, was precisely what had made it possible—the almost universal belief among reformers that the toppling of the Republican oligarchy was the one great task of the hour. Some progressives followed Roosevelt out of conviction. Others followed him in spite of conviction. It was simply impossible to deny that the popular ex-President was far more likely than La Follette to capture the Republican nomination. What happened after that they would worry about later.

On the face of it the Republican oligarchy seemed doomed to extinction. Outside their organizations they enjoyed virtually no popular support. What was more, they now discovered, even the finance capitalists were indifferent to their fate; some of them, including the Morgan forces, actually favored Roosevelt over Taft. This was a revelation of the greatest importance, one that is essential to any understanding of the role the Republican oligarchy was soon to play in the events leading up to America's entry into the European war.[27]

That oligarchy had based its power on an alliance with the most influential capitalists in the country. The alliance itself was now weak and for a quite simple reason. The Republican oligarchy, which was incapable of enacting reforms, was equally incapable of serving the interests of big business. By 1907 the finance capitalists had come to realize that passive political protection would no longer suffice. The whole structure of finance capitalism was jerry-built from top to bottom. Holding companies were illegal, trusts were illegal, banker control of industrial enterprise was illegal. Moreover the bankers' control of capital itself depended entirely on corrupt political privilege. With their prestige stripped away, with their economic power almost universally opposed, with their secret operations laid bare in numerous official investigations, Wall Street interests stewed in fear. As J. P. Morgan once privately confided, he had lived in dread of an antitrust suit ever since he first formed the U.S. Steel Corporation. What the finance capitalists needed now was statutory legitimacy. They needed new laws to protect them from the old laws, to protect them from the electorate, to protect them from the legislative demands of their smaller competitors. They needed laws to legalize their holding companies and, most of all, they needed laws to secure their control of capital, for that control was inherently shaky in an economy as rich as America's. Such comprehensive legislation the Republican oligarchy could not possibly provide, indeed would never be able to provide. Half the party would have risen in revolt. Even the most loyal party regulars west of the Alleghenies would have voted against the leadership. It would have been political suicide for them to do otherwise. Outside the East, fear and hatred of the money trust coursed too strongly to be openly defied. In order to control the national party Republican leaders were compelled to turn it into a do-nothing syndicate, a party useful to nobody, not even the "interests," a party with a grim future ahead of it as long as the oligarchy controlled it.[28]

Grim though the future might be, Republican Party leaders had no intention of relinquishing their power. Their immediate problem was renominating President Taft, who had lost his popular support precisely because he had thrown in with them.

If a presidential nomination were decided by the sentiments of a party's rank and file, Roosevelt would have won the nomination by a landslide. Of the 388 convention delegates chosen by popular vote, Taft won a mere 71, or less than 20 percent. If a presidential nomination were decided by money, Roosevelt again would have won. He had the preponderance of money on his side. If a presidential nomination were dictated by the party leaders' desire to win the general election, they would have nominated Roosevelt themselves. The Republican oligarchy, however, was fighting for its life. Compared to the prospect of losing power in the party, rank-and-file sentiment meant little—"even the Wall Street growlers," as Taft put it, meant little. Winning in November meant least of all. The oligarchy was determined to renominate Taft, a certain loser, solely to keep control of the party. "When we get back in four years," explained a machine senator from Indiana, "instead of the damned insurgents, we will have the machine."[29]

Working the party machinery for all it was worth, deploying the federal patronage, packing the party caucuses and the convention committees, Republican leaders, relying solely on organization and efficiency, secured by the narrowest of margins the renomination of Taft. In a Chicago auditorium near the convention hall twenty thousand members of the "respectable classes" stood by in rage as the convention machine rolled over their rebellion. When Roosevelt told them he would continue the struggle he was cheered as few American politicians have ever been cheered. And when he told them, "We stand at Armageddon and we battle for the Lord," the overblown utterance truly fit the superheated occasion. The movement for the "salvation of society" had become, at least for its active supporters, an evangelical crusade.

The November elections surprised nobody. Running as the candidate of a hastily organized Progressive Party, Roosevelt decisively outpolled Taft. Running as a reform candidate, the Democrats' Woodrow Wilson easily won the election. The Republican oligarchy had narrowly survived, but the national Republican machine was gone from American politics. Henceforth the party's leaders would be not the spokesmen of a disciplined national party, but merely its dominant faction, desperately clinging to power within it and meanly hopeful that the Democrats would prove still more unfit to govern than they. Lodge's "aristocratic republic" had lasted, in all, about fifteen years.

As for the reform movement in general, it emerged from the 1912 election with the political force of a national mandate. The voters had given the two avowed progressive candidates 70 percent of the total popular vote. They gave Eugene V. Debs, the Socialist candidate, about 900,000 votes. The candidate of the Republican Party, victor in eleven of the previous thirteen presidential elections, gained the electoral votes of just two states. Americans were elated with sanguine hopes. The privileged interests, the "money trust," and the "invisible government" seemed about to receive their death blow. Government of, by, and for the people was now to be restored to the American Republic. For all practical purposes, however, popular hopes were now in the hands of a President-elect whose conversion to reform was exactly twenty-five months old.

7

"A Man of High Ideals but No Principles"

War in Europe still lay in the unforeseeable future when President Wilson, in his Inaugural Address, called upon Americans to join him in "the high enterprise of the new day: to lift everything that concerns our life as a Nation to the light that shines from the hearthfire of every man's conscience and vision of the right." Foreign affairs had not seemed so remote in years nor domestic affairs so promising. In fact, except for the American people themselves, all the political elements that would bring America into a European war were already occupying the political arena.[1]

There was, first, the battered Republican oligarchy, paralyzed as long as domestic issues remained paramount and hungry for any chance opportunity to return safely to power. There was, for another, the major New York bankers, adrift in the wreckage of the national Republican machine, suffering from obloquy so severe that politicians feared to be seen in their company and determined to regain the security they had lost in the progressive upheaval. There was, in addition, the conservative leadership of the Democracy, a party still held together by the do-nothing principle and now compelled by an articulate national reform movement to do something that might pass for comprehensive reforms. Most decisively there was the singular figure of the new President himself, a man driven by vaunting ambition and haunted by a "nightmare," as he himself put it, that the American people, whose aspirations he did not share, would turn against him in their wrath and blight his own aspirations for personal greatness.

Thomas Woodrow Wilson had always yearned to become a "great statesman," a man, by his own strangely subjective definition, who is "conscious of great powers, whose mind is teeming and overflowing with great political plans and dreaming of great national triumphs." From his youth onward Wilson was obsessed with the subject of greatness. As a professor of political science, he dwelt often on the attributes of greatness, on the qualities of great men and the need for great leaders in a democratic age. As he once confided to his wife, he himself ached for the opportunity "to impel [the people] to great political achievements," achievements that, in Wilson's view, the ignoble masses were incapable even of desiring without strong leaders and strong governments to drive them. He looked upon his own writings not as scholarly efforts but as the means of "training" himself, in his words, for his self-imposed "task" of one day becoming a great American president. Such lofty ambition fades quickly enough even in ambitious young men. It fades even in men well launched in politics. What was remarkable about Woodrow Wilson was that his youthful ambition never faded at all. He still yearned to become a great president when he was already a middle-aged professor at Princeton destined, to all outward appearances, to achieve no greater eminence than a campus is likely to provide.[2]

In part, at least, what kept Wilson's ambition so strong was his keen awareness of "great powers" in himself. That he was born to greatness, that he stood far above his fellow men Professor Wilson of Princeton had no doubts whatever. Vain though he was, his self-esteem was well founded. Some of the qualities of great men were undoubtedly his. He had a driving imperious will that readily imposed itself on others, a will made steely by Wilson's conviction that those who blocked his path stood in the way of the light. He had, moreover, a mind that was ceaselessly active and astonishingly quick. In his years as President, White House visitors would come away amazed at Wilson's ability to sum up their own arguments more swiftly and cogently than they could themselves. He had, in addition, a still more remarkable facility with words. Striking phrases, elegant paragraphs, and sonorous perorations seemed to flow effortlessly from Wilson's lips. Indeed, when he thought of himself as a great man he chiefly saw himself as a great orator swaying the masses with the magic power of noble utterance. It would take many years before Wilson's contemporaries realized, in Senator La Follette's bitterly accurate judgment, that "with him, the rhetoric of a thing is the thing itself. . . . Words, phrases, felicity of expression and a blind egotism has been his stock in trade." The thought that his splendid gifts would go unused, that the great "task" would never be assigned him could make Wilson wretched with frustration and on occasion physically ill when he was already approaching his fiftieth year.[3]

Just what an American president would do to achieve greatness had posed something of a theoretical problem for Professor Wilson. Given his political views—views he publicly professed until 1910—there was exceedingly little an American president was permitted to do. An advocate of the principles of True Democracy, Wilson believed firmly in states' rights, laissez-faire, and minimal government (as well as White Supremacy, racial segregation, and the disenfranchisement of poor Southerners). Accordingly the chief domestic duty of an American president consisted in executing the laws, protecting property, and preventing the passage of new laws that interfered with the economy. If, as Wilson believed, the American people needed strong leaders to guide them, a president's only possible claim to greatness lay in persuading them to ask nothing of their government, a negative, obstructive greatness at best, although Wilson lauded Cleveland for achieving it.

Since the 1880s, the task of persuasion had been growing increasingly difficult in America. In consequence, Princeton's professor of political science had wholeheartedly welcomed the launching of the Republican "large policy" during the Spanish-American War. In his *History of the American People,* published in 1902, Wilson described the new policy as the single most heartening event in modern American history. By means of an active foreign policy the American people would gain what Wilson called a "unified will." It would divert them, in other words, from their new habit of "begging," in Wilson's words, for governmental help against the privileged, a "turning away from all the principles which have distinguished America," that Professor Wilson thoroughly deplored. An active foreign policy, in Wilson's view, would thereby protect American democracy itself from the ignorant masses, meaning all those Americans who did not share Professor Wilson's belief that democracy and the Democratic Party were one and the same thing. As Wilson wrote in 1901, the large policy had the virtue of being "an affair of strong government"—it strengthened the governors in their dealings with the governed.[4]

Wilson had still another reason for endorsing the Republican large policy. Quite simply, it would give future American presidents something large and glorious to do. According to Wilson the most important advantage of the Republican "plunge into international politics and into the administration of distant dependencies" was the "greatly increased power and opportunity for constructive statesmanship given the President" by that plunge. This was to be perhaps the most revealing statement Wilson ever made, for it invoked a standard of political judgment that foreshadowed his entire future career. It was not a standard he shared with his countrymen. Americans are not in the habit of judging a national policy by its personal advantage to their president. Nor are they in the habit of considering themselves and their country as mere instruments in a president's quest for glory. It is the last thing that would enter the mind of most Americans, whatever their political views. Yet that judgment, so antithetical to the entire republican tradition in America, came readily to Woodrow Wilson, who was to become the first American president to look upon the United States of America as a stepping-stone to personal greatness.[5]

Historians and biographers have often ascribed Wilson's singularities to his intense Presbyterian convictions and the "Scotch Covenanter's" blood in his veins. To these they have attributed, among other things, Wilson's tendency to regard himself as an instrument of Providence and to define personal greatness as some messianic act of salvation. The attribution, however, misses the main point. What lay at the core of Wilson's political character was neither Presbyterianism nor even Christianity. Strictly speaking it is anti-Christian and it is as old as politics itself. The decisive trait of Wilson's political character was vainglory: a hunger for glory so exclusively self-regarding, so indifferent to the concerns of

others, that it would lead him to betray in turn the national movement for reform, the great body of the American people, the fundamental liberties of the American Republic, and in the end the
hopes of a war-torn world. Had he not been a devout Presbyterian,
Wilson would still have been a vainglorious leader; had he not been
vainglorious, he would not have been Woodrow Wilson.

Such, at any rate, were the leading opinions and characteristics
of Professor Wilson when, in 1902, the trustees of Princeton named
him president of the University and Wilson, thus elevated, began
bidding for the support of would-be president-makers in the reactionary wing of the Democratic Party, which was once again directing its national affairs.

In theory, the Democratic Party was bitterly split between its
"Bryan" wing and its "Cleveland" wing, as the two party factions
had been known since the 1896 convention. The Bryanites, talking
for local rural consumption, railed against Wall Street, the railroads, and the Clevelandites. The Clevelandites, upholding True
Democracy, railed against "centralism," "socialism," "demagog-
uery," and the Bryanites. Since most of the Bryanites and Clevelandites owed their careers to state and local political machines, the
division between the factions was considerably more apparent than
real. Whenever the two "wings" came together as a national party,
they invariably composed their differences with a minimum of
strain. In 1904, when southern Bryanites no longer had Populism to
fear, they gladly returned to the safety of True Democracy by helping the Clevelandites nominate Alton B. Parker, a New York corporation lawyer, to run disastrously against President Roosevelt. In
1908, when it became apparent that the swing back to True Democracy had made rural southern and western voters restive, once
more the Clevelandites promptly obliged the Bryanites by nominating without opposition the party's balm to sore farmers, namely
Bryan himself.

In Congress, too, the bitter divisions had a way of disappearing
amicably. In the House, Democratic legislators marched in unison
to the leadership of their conservative minority leader, John Sharp
Williams of Mississippi, whose political views did not stop him
from grooming Champ Clark for the House leadership, although

Clark was an outspoken Missouri Bryanite. In the Senate, the ostensibly divided Democrats faithfully followed the lead of Senator Joe Bailey of Texas, a Bourbon Democrat who assailed Roosevelt for "exalting the General Government" and who considered the popular election of senators the death knell of the Republic.[6]

Even in their public professions the two wings of the party were not really far apart. Well aware that the national party was held together by the do-nothing principle, the Bryan wing rarely wandered far afield from the tenets of True Democracy. As with the free silver campaign of 1896 their reform proposals chiefly consisted of some simple panacea or other for the evils they decried. The party's House spokesman, Representative Williams, for example, took the radical Bryanite position by calling for the extermination of every trust and monopoly yet remained within the party creed by insisting that tariff reduction alone would secure that end. Skill at promising everything and proposing little was a talent much in request in Democratic circles.[7]

Dominated by what Roosevelt in 1911 rightly described as an "enormous mass of Bourbon reactionaries," the Democrats appeared to the electorate as a party that deplored all the evils the electorate deplored and all the remedies the electorate supported. Democrats opposed both trusts and any effective antitrust legislation. They decried both private monopoly and any governmental efforts to bring it to heel. Whatever reforms were in the air, a large proportion of Democrats could be relied upon to view them with alarm and predict upon their passage the downfall of the Republic. Pulitzer's New York *World*, the national house organ of the Democracy, perfectly mirrored the party's endemic duplicity. The *World* vigorously opposed the rapacity of trusts and stood for the enforcement of the Sherman Act; when Roosevelt brought a major antitrust suit, however, the newspaper complained that the Sherman Act gave presidents too much power. The *World* vigorously warned against the dangers of "plutocracy," but it opposed with equal vigor the "frenzy for regulation," the "undermining of business confidence," the appeal to "class hatred," and excessive "federal interference." Like the party for which it spoke, the *World* invariably grew alarmed about every effort to alleviate the ills it was ostensibly alarmed about. As the newspaper put it in 1907, the true Democrat was always one who feared "too much government rather than too little government." [8]

In that single proposition lay the Democrats' "dilemma," as the political analyst Herbert Croly rightly pointed out in 1910. The Democrats were extremely reluctant to scuttle the do-nothing principle merely to gain the presidency. The sudden emergence of finance capitalism, however, was simultaneously destroying the party creed's popular appeal, which was never very great, and its rationale, which was never very strong. Americans simply did not see themselves menaced by "too much government." The whole force of the reform movement was pushing in the other direction. What alarmed Americans was the menace of too much private power flourishing in the vacuum created precisely by "too little government." A national party that insisted elective government was inherently more dangerous than private power not only held small attraction for (northern) voters, it was exposing the hypocrisy of its vaunted conservative principles. What, after all, were Democratic conservatives trying to conserve: the purity of the republican tradition, as they claimed, or the existing corruption of republican institutions, which was what True Democracy came down to in practice? From 1901 to 1909 the Democracy was, literally, a reactionary party in headlong flight from the progressive movement. This was the reason the national reform movement, the national rebellion against oligarchy and the great debate on the great issues of the day, took place chiefly within the Republican Party. At its worst, the ruling party seemed a more promising vehicle for progressive reforms and free politics than an opposition party led by "Bourbon reactionaries" who dominated the party in Congress and controlled every important state organization from New York to Texas. [9]

The other horn of the Democrats' dilemma was that the prospect of perpetually losing presidential elections—and losing them badly—posed dangers almost as perilous as abandoning the party creed. It held within it the germs of intraparty rebellion, always a danger in a party that did nothing yet relied on the votes of those needing much, namely poor farmers and poor immigrants. What party leaders urgently needed was a sort of second Cleveland, an outstanding national figure firmly attached to the party creed and strong-willed enough to keep the national party safely attached to it despite the obvious temptation of trying to win elections. Consequently, after Alton Parker's disastrous showing in 1904, the "Cleveland" Democrats began shopping around for a fresh personality whom they might groom for the 1912 nomination (Bryan had already been allotted the 1908 nomination almost as soon as the 1904 elections were over) and, ipso facto, the titular leadership of the national party.

A few New York Democrats looked toward New Jersey. In February 1906, one George Harvey, publisher of *Harper's Weekly* and a man with close ties to the small clique of Wall Street operators still active in Democratic circles—August Belmont, Thomas Fortune Ryan, and William Whitney—publicly declared his support of Woodrow Wilson of Princeton for the presidency of the United States. The New York *World,* the *New York Times* and the Wall Street Democratic clique fell in quickly with Harvey's scheme. "A splendid suggestion," said the publisher of the *Times,* which spoke for the extreme reactionaries in the Democratic Party. From 1906 onward, Harvey, the conservative Democratic press, and other powerful elements in the Cleveland wing of the party began working publicly and privately to engineer Wilson's nomination.

Princeton's president was in every respect an attractive choice for party advancement, not least because, like Cleveland before him, he was new to party politics. Wilson's swift reorganization of the university had marked him as a genuine leader of men, despite all the years spent in the study and the library. His achievements as an educator had already gained him a fair share of fame. He was, moreover, not only a firm adherent of the party creed, he was a superbly eloquent one, and Democratic leaders were in dire need of a man who could make the do-nothing principle sound fresh and compelling once more.

Thus singled out for advancement, Wilson did what party leaders expected of him. Between 1906 and 1908 he confirmed in numerous speeches marked, as Roosevelt put it, by "skill, intelligence and good breeding," his unswerving adherence to the party creed. "Government supervision will in the long run enslave us," he assured conservative Democrats; Americans were "begging" for the government's help "because we have forgotten to take care of ourselves." He called upon America's leaders to resist the demands of the ignorant and the foolish. "The time has come," he advised them in December 1906, "for such sober counsel as will relieve government of the business of providence and restore it to its normal duties of justice and of impartial regulation." Wilson was particularly ingenious on the question of the trusts. While he deplored the misconduct of some big businessmen, he proclaimed it an "unprecedented" break with American tradition for the government to pass laws that dealt directly with corporations. Corporations, he argued, were mere legal fictions and consequently—although the reasoning is pure sophistry—should be immune to regulation by law. In a private "Credo" he composed for the benefit of his backers, Wilson went even further. Repeating the cant of big businessmen, he avowed that trusts were necessary because they were so efficient. Mindful that president-makers such as Harvey may propose nominees but that it is the state party bosses who dispose of nominations, Wilson gave them, too, their mead of reassurance. Boss rule, he admitted, was in some ways regrettable, but since it was inevitable it was futile to oppose it. Worse, it would be unwise for, according to Wilson, the American election system would be unworkable if nominations were not made by a few. Between 1906 and 1908 there was not a single item on the progressive agenda that the president of Princeton did not militantly oppose. As Walter Hines Page, influential editor of *World's Work* put it in 1907, Wilson was just the "right-minded man of a safe and conservative political faith" who would enable the Democratic Party to return to its "old doctrines and take on its old dignity." Four years later the egregious Page, who was soon to become the most disastrous ambassador in American history, once again called for Wilson's nomination, this time as the "Leader of the New Radicalism."[11]

In the four years, Page had not changed, Wilson had not changed, the "enormous mass of Bourbon reactionaries" had not vanished from the Democratic Party. What had changed essentially was the rhetoric and tactics of the conservative Democrats. By the end of 1909, it had become apparent that the national reform movement—then tearing the Republican Party apart—had become too powerful to be safely ignored. The stronger the movement grew the more dubious True Democracy sounded and the more suspect Democratic "conservatism" became. Progressivism, however, was a many-sided affair. It comprised both political reforms and economic reforms, state-level reforms and national reforms. By a judicious selection of issues—omitting most economic matters—it was not difficult to incorporate part of the progressive agenda into the Democratic creed without altering its essentials. A Cleveland Democrat could readily call for a purified, graft-free politics, for direct primary elections (they already existed in the South), for barring corporate wealth from politics (the Republican Party got most of the money), for tariff reduction (already part of the creed), and the like. In brief, the conservative leaders of the party, after 1908, began dropping the word "conservative" from their lexicon, ceased openly preaching laissez-faire doctrines, and began calling themselves "progressives," or, on occasion, "conservative progressives." By 1910 the ever-serviceable New York *World* proudly announced, on no foundation whatever, that the Democrats had become an entirely new party. Whereas before the paper wanted the party led by a man firm in the old party faith, it now called for a "sane progressive" leader. The superficiality of the new "progressive" Democracy is well-attested by the fact that the "conservative progressives'" preferred candidate for 1912 was still Woodrow Wilson, who, when last heard of in 1908, had opposed every progressive reform.

In the interim Wilson had suffered at the hands of Princeton's trustees some revealing defeats in his effort to turn Princeton into a tightly knit imitation Oxford devoted to training a well-bred elite of future national leaders. In the little world of Princeton affairs men took note of Wilson's petty vindictiveness, his blind willfulness, and what one of the trustees, none other than old Grover Cleveland, called his lack of "intellectual integrity," referring to Wilson's singular capacity to believe ardently in every self-serving sophistry he concocted. The final defeat, interestingly enough, Wilson's political backers turned into a political asset.[12]

The affair seemed unedifying enough. A wealthy alumnus had given the university a large gift to build new off-campus graduate school facilities. To Wilson the proposal was intolerable; an off-campus department would physically disrupt what he liked to call the "complete unity" of college life, that "unified will" which Woodrow Wilson considered the highest public good whether in a college or a free country. In the end Wilson lost his fight, lost his local reputation, and Princeton lost the gift.

Having powerful backers, however, is no small asset to a defeated man. Early in 1910 the *New York Times* approached Wilson with an interesting idea that had not occurred to Wilson himself. Would he mind if the newspaper treated his graduate school fight as a crusade for democracy against alumni money power? Wilson did not mind. He was, as one of his future cabinet members was to say, "a man of high ideals but no principles." On February 3, 1910, *Times* readers were duly informed that the president of Princeton was actually fighting on campus the great national fight for progressive democracy. Other "conservative progressive" papers echoed the line. The process of launching Wilson as a progressive Democrat had begun.[13]

A few months later Wilson's New York backers managed the next step in Wilson's advancement. They persuaded ex-Senator James Smith, a Cleveland Democrat and boss of the corrupt and collusive New Jersey Democracy, to nominate Wilson for governor. Since a boss-nominated progressive was by then a recognized contradiction in terms, Wilson blandly assured the state's voters that he owed his nomination to "the thoughtful Democrats of the State." That assertion, said a magazine writer, was "sublime audacity." It was also a typical example of Wilsonian spohistry. The Democratic bosses were undoubtedly thoughtful. Consequently, Wilson had every right to describe his nominators as "thoughtful Democrats." Wilson did not lie; he merely tried to deceive people.[14]

Winning the election, however, was not quite so simple. For years Republican reformers had been fighting the Republican state machine and agitating for a broad agenda of progressive reforms. On their support and the votes of independent Republicans Wilson's election depended. The price of their support was Wilson's uncompromising espousal of progressive reforms. Wilson, to his credit, resisted, but the Republican reformers had his career in their hands. Accordingly on September 30, 1910, Wilson made his first grudging break with the political beliefs of a lifetime; he publicly acknowledged that corporations must be regulated by state law. That vague pronouncement did not satisfy Republican reformers. They demanded next that Wilson formally subscribe to a checklist of reform measures which they submitted for his judgment. Wilson duly subscribed to them. Republican reformers continued to demand further proofs of Wilson's good faith. Exerting enormous pressure upon him even after his election, they forced a reluctant Wilson to break with boss Smith, a man he genuinely admired, and to support direct primary elections, a reform he had previously opposed. This was only the beginning. Ambition, expediency, and the national reform movement were relentlessly pushing Wilson into a position of profound moral falsity, compelling him to act in bad faith in order to prove his good faith, to turn against men he admired and praise men he despised, to espouse reforms he privately opposed and decry evils he thought no evils. This vain and ambitious man who yearned to "impel" the masses was being impelled by them and forced to pander to their foolish demands. From that false position Wilson was not to extricate himself until he brought America into the World War.

For the pangs of bad faith, however, there were more than ample compensations. Even before Wilson was elected governor, even before he had said or done anything worth mentioning, his Democratic backers were booming him across the country as the new progressive hero of the party, a "statesman," as the *New York Times* put it, eminently worthy of the 1912 presidential nomination. After enacting a few long-sought reforms in New Jersey (after which he dropped the matter, leaving New Jersey as corrupt as ever), Wilson in the spring of 1911 began touring the West and South delivering sonorous messages of moral uplift in a direct bid for party support. By the end of the year he was generally regarded as the likely choice of the national convention over his rival, Champ Clark, now Speaker of the House. Two serious obstacles, however, sprang up to hinder Wilson and complicate the plans of his backers.[15]

The first was Wilson's marked unpopularity with rural Democratic voters. His conversion from reaction to reform had been so sudden, so expedient, and so grudging it was understandably viewed with suspicion. Hearst, a Champ Clark backer, described Wilson in early 1912 as "a perfect jackrabbit of politics, perched on his little hillock of expediency." A Massachusetts Populist-turned-Democrat noted that Wilson's *History of the American People* was the "history of Woodrow Wilson's admiration for everything which the radical democracy now seeks to change; and a series of sneers and insults to every class of men who have sought to alleviate the injustices of capitalism." That conservative eastern Democrats had been promoting him for years only deepened rural suspicions further. George Harvey, in particular, became so embarrassing in his zeal for Wilson's nomination that Wilson was once again compelled to betray an ally. He politely told Harvey he no longer cared to be endorsed by *Harper's Weekly*. That makeshift scarcely sufficed. Not even the blessings of Bryan could persuade rural voters that Wilson was a genuine convert to reform. In January 1912, Bryan, for reasons of his own,* pronounced Wilson "the best modern example of Saul of Tarsus," but wherever Clark and Wilson contested a primary Clark usually won. The Speaker of the House swept party primaries in almost a score of states.[16]

The second obstacle was the opposition of Charles Murphy and his Tammany machine, which now controlled the entire New York State party. From long experience, Tammany knew what to expect of high-toned Democrats who professed to oppose boss rule: They would leave the other state machines alone and demonstrate their good faith by making Tammany a scapegoat. In a year in which the party was not nominating a loser but a candidate almost certain to become President, the Tammany machine was taking no chances. It intended to deliver its ninety votes (almost one-sixth the number needed for a majority) to Clark, a loyal party regular, and thereby secure protection in the upcoming Democratic administration, which was all Tammany cared about anyway.

The Democratic convention disposed of both Clark and Tammany by a simple, if drastic, expedient. It resolved by overwhelming vote not to nominate any candidate who had the support of Belmont, Ryan, J. P. Morgan, or their political "agent," meaning Boss Murphy's New York delegation. By that device Tammany's ninety votes were nullified; Clark, the intended recipient, was branded the

---

*Throughout the campaign for the Democratic nomination Bryan tried one way or another to produce a deadlocked convention in hopes of wangling the nomination himself. His efforts, which worked to Wilson's advantage, helped gain him his appointment as secretary of state.

Wall Street candidate and Wilson boomed forth as the true reformer by precisely those elements in the party that allegedly stood behind Clark. Although Tammany's votes gave Clark a majority of the delegates on the tenth ballot, for the first time since 1844 the Democratic candidate who received a majority did not automatically get the necessary two-thirds. The reactionary bosses of Illinois and Indiana, the Bourbon rulers of Virginia, North Carolina, Georgia, Alabama, and Florida, refused to give their votes to Clark, now the alleged candidate of the eastern reactionaries. Instead they threw them—and the nomination—to Wilson, whom eastern reactionaries had been grooming for half a dozen years.

Such was the party and such the man who were now to undertake "the high enterprise of the new day."

"It would be the irony of fate," Wilson remarked shortly before taking office, "if my administration had to deal chiefly with foreign affairs." Wilson's "fate," like McKinley's "destiny," had a human manager. Seven days after his inauguration the new President began a course of meddling in Mexican politics that would lead the United States to the brink of war by April 1914. To "deal chiefly with foreign affairs" was for Wilson the real enterprise of the new day, the only promising escape from the political dangers that confronted him from the moment he gained the presidency.[17]

The danger, quite simply, was that Wilson had no intention of fulfilling the expectations of the national reform movement or even of redeeming the reform pledges he had made as a candidate. Wilson was expected to lead the fight for drastic legislative intervention in the economy, intervention designed, as Wilson had promised, to extirpate the trusts, break Wall Street's control of capital, and liberate free enterprise from the tightening thrall of monopoly. Neither Wilson nor the Democrats in control of Congress shared these expectations. The new President had never been a reformer; he had merely been an office seeker in an age of reform. Privately Wilson regarded big business as beneficial and the national reform movement itself as a dangerous spasm of "ill-humors." Unfortunately for Wilson, the reform movement was too strong to be openly repudiated. Something had to be done to appease the reformers. The danger was that they were unlikely to remain appeased.[18]

Wilson planned to push through Congress a minimal program of unavoidable legislation touching on banking and big business. This, hopefully, would keep the progressives at bay until Wilson felt it politically safe to declare—as he would actually do in November 1914—that all remediable grievances had been remedied and the business of reform was at an end. Wilson's chief concern was that the enacted legislation *look* like progressive reform; that his banking legislation look as though designed to demolish the money trust; that his antitrust laws look like the comprehensive attack on monopoly that he and the Democrats had promised the voters in 1912.[19]

Wilson had no illusions about his strategy. At best it was a makeshift that could not, by itself, succeed. The reform movement was too powerful, its leaders too well armed with programs, principles, and shibboleths to be contented for long by mere shows of reform. The conservative press of both parties would duly praise Wilson's Federal Reserve Act as a milestone of reform legislation, but reform leaders in Congress would assail it for what it was—a "big bankers' bill," in Senator La Follette's words, that actually legalized the money trust it was supposed to dismember. The conservative press would praise Wilson's antitrust measures as the culmination of thirty years of antitrust agitation, but again reform leaders would not be deceived. "Almost a joke," La Follette would call them. "Not enough teeth to masticate successfully milk toast," Senator Cummins was to remark.[20]

As long as domestic affairs remained predominant, Wilson was on a collision course with the entire reform movement. He knew it, foresaw it, and dreaded it. The American people were going to turn against him, he confided to his friend and adviser Colonel E. M. House of Texas. His administration, he feared, would end in ignominious failure just as his administration of Princeton had done. That fear, he confessed to House, "hung over him sometimes like a nightmare." Unless he could divert the reform movement and distract the American people the nightmare would become a reality. Wilson was no Grover Cleveland: he had no wish to commit political suicide for the creed of True Democracy. The solution to his problem Wilson had arrived at long before he ever faced it, when he praised the domestic political advantages of the Republican "plunge into international politics." If he could make another such plunge and "impel" the nation to "great national triumphs" abroad, he could not only avert failure but reap glory as well. As soon as he took office, therefore, Wilson began trying to persuade the American people that the true spirit of reform was to be expressed not at home, but in a new altruistic foreign policy, a policy, in Wilson's words, of "service to mankind."[21]

Conditions in Mexico provided Wilson with his first pretext for "service." It was in his Mexican policy that Wilson revealed those singular qualities of character—the self-ennobling ambition, the contempt for the opinions of others, the bottomless self-deceit— that were to help him drag America into the trenches of France. Wilson's Mexican policy, too, revealed the extraordinary lengths Wilson was determined to go to inflict foreign complications on his unwilling countrymen.

The Mexican situation briefly was this: In 1910 Mexican rebels led by Francisco Madero had overthrown the thirty-five-year-old dictatorship of Porfirio Diaz. The Madero government, however, proved feeble and inept. Two weeks before Wilson's inaugural, General Victoriano Huerta, head of the Federalist Army, turned treacherously against Madero. In a swift palace *golpe* he deposed the fading hero of the 1910 revolution and began setting himself up as Mexico's new strong man. A few days later, probably with Huerta's complicity, certainly in his interest, Madero was murdered. Huerta's usurpation was not one of the more edifying political spectacles in Latin America but it was scarcely unique. For such eventualities a forthright diplomatic tradition had governed American foreign policy since the time of Jefferson. Every de facto government, however despicable, was routinely granted American diplomatic recognition. The practice was based on the prudent principle that the internal politics of other countries were no business of the United States. America does "not go abroad in search of monsters to destroy," as John Quincy Adams had put it on July 4, 1821.

Finding "monsters to destroy" being Wilson's intention, Huerta's brutal usurpation was too opportune to pass up. Accordingly, on March 11, 1913, the newly inaugurated President publicly announced a new principle of diplomatic recognition. The United

States, he told the American people, "can have no sympathy with those who seek to seize the power of government to advance their own personal interests or ambition." Henceforth, the political virtue of a foreign ruler was to be the new test of diplomatic recognition. Huerta, of course, failed the test. Nonrecognition of Huerta merely paved the way for a considerably more drastic act of "service." In the spring of 1913 Wilson decided it was his unavoidable duty to overthrow Huerta and establish a "constitutional government" in Mexico. Not for the last time would the President find himself with no choice but to do exactly what he wanted.[22]

Of their new President's perilous intentions the American people knew nothing. Wilson dared not profess them for, unlike their altruistic President, the American people cared far more about themselves than they did about Mexicans. Cautiously, Wilson tried to wean them from their unfortunate conviction that the foreign policy of the United States ought to serve the interests of the country. That conviction had severely shackled the Republican "large policy." As long as American foreign policy was determined by practical national interests, it was impossible to justify a policy large enough to overwhelm domestic affairs, to pacify the electorate, or to free President Wilson for "constructive statesmanship" abroad. On August 27, shortly after Huerta rejected Wilson's demand that he depose himself peacefully, the President went before a joint session of Congress to insinuate into the public arena the new altruistic principle underlying his undisclosed policy. The speech was to typify most of Wilson's foreign policy utterances: It said one thing while implying its opposite.

The President reassured the nation that he was not going to intervene in Mexico to protect either the interests of American investors or the fifty thousand Americans who lived there. Indeed, he said, Americans stayed in Mexico at their own risk. The United States government intended "to pay the most scrupulous regard to the sovereignty and independence of Mexico—that we take as a matter of course to which we are bound by every obligation of right and honor." A stronger promise of nonintervention could scarcely have been made, but there was a catch to it. According to Wilson, the United States had a duty to serve "the best aspirations" of the Mexican people and to do so, moreover, "without first thinking how we shall serve ourselves." America, according to Wilson, was to become the first nation in history to put the interests of other countries ahead of its own. Mankind (minus the American people) would henceforth be the object of our government's active concern and ministration.[23]

The public response to Wilson's address was far from encouraging to the President. His suave assertion of America's duty to help Mexicans sent no thrill of exaltation through the electorate. In truth, the perverse turn that events had taken during the Spanish-American War had inoculated most Americans against foreign adventures in the name of humanity. Having learned something about the domestic uses of war, Americans were a chastened people in 1913. What they greeted with an audible sigh of relief was Wilson's apparent promise to keep America out of Mexican affairs. The response might have daunted a lesser man, but therein lay Wilson's peculiar strengths as a political leader. Once convinced of the nobility of his own intentions—and the conviction always came easily—Wilson could act without scruple, defy men's reproaches, and ignore what to others was plain common sense. The most fanatical idealist does not cling to the principles of a lifetime more tenaciously than Wilson could pursue a noble aim he had just invented to suit his ambitions.[24]

In late October 1913, Wilson, whom historians describe as a President who hated war, decided he would have to use military force against the Mexican usurper. "A real crisis has arisen," Colonel House wrote in his diary on October 30, after speaking with the President. The "crisis" was Huerta's success in consolidating his power. The British government, for one thing, had extended him diplomatic recognition. The Mexican establishment was beginning to rally to his side. Huerta's enemies, the heirs of the Madero revolution, had raised the banner of revolt under Venustiano Carranza, "first chief" of the newly formed "Constitutionalist" movement, but they were still woefully weak. America's President, however, was "alert and unafraid," noted House. He "has in mind to declare war against Mexico." What choice, after all, did Wilson have? To a woman correspondent, the president confided his pious fears of the "terrible" events that were about to ensue. "No man can tell what will happen while we deal with a desperate brute like that traitor, Huerta. God save us from the worst!" Having decided to depose a foreign ruler Wilson now persuaded himself that the "brute's" refusal to go was forcing him to war.[25]

In a few days of hectic activity Wilson worked to clear away the major obstacles to armed intervention. To avoid international complications he curtly demanded that the European powers give him a free hand in Mexico. If they recognized the Huerta regime they would "make our task one of domination and force," he instructed Secretary Bryan to inform them. Except for Britain, the powers proved amenable. If the President of the United States wanted to set up his own government in Mexico, they had no wish to stand in his way. The British government, having already recognized Huerta, proved somewhat more recalcitrant, mostly, it seems, as a matter of pride.[26]

In Britain's resistance Wilson saw a chance to overcome the second major obstacle to armed intervention, namely American public opinion. Hoping to exploit both the old national anglophobia and the new reform spirit, the Wilson administration circulated to the press in late October a fabricated tale of sinister British oil interests working secretly in behalf of Huerta. A few days later, on October 27, Wilson, in a major address in Mobile, Alabama, linked the reform movement even more explicitly to his Mexican venture. Previously, he said, the United States had undertaken to keep the nations of the western hemisphere free of European imperialism. As the "friends and champions" of "true constitutional liberty," said Wilson, it was now America's duty to secure their "emancipation" from foreign capitalist domination as well. Huerta, already a brute and a usurper, had now become, in addition, the tool of the British money trust. This grave American duty, Wilson admonished the electorate, must not be shirked because no material American interests were being served. "It is a very perilous thing to determine the foreign policy of a nation in the terms of material interest." The peril, obviously, was that it hindered intervention. On November 1, Wilson warned both Huerta and the European powers that if the Mexican ruler did not soon depose himself it "would render it necessary for him to propose very serious practical measures to the Congress of the United States." In plain English, it would mean war.[27]

The "new day" was but eight months old and already Wilson had thrust America deeply, dangerously, and gratuitously into Mexican affairs. That something other than "service to mankind" lay behind Wilson's gratuitous meddling was scarcely lost on contemporary observers. As ex-President Taft inquired sardonically of Elihu Root in a letter of November 8, didn't Root think that "in the back of his head there is not a source of philosophical contentment that not the worst thing that could happen for his administration is a war?" On November 13, the British government agreed to let the American President do whatever he wanted to overthrow Huerta and set up a "constitutional" regime in Mexico, presumably in the name of Mexican "sovereignty and independence."[28]

At that point, however, Wilson stayed his hand. Mexicans are a patriotic people. They looked with no friendly eye on the American President's efforts to serve their "best aspirations." Wilson's flurry of threats and warnings had merely strengthened Huerta's hand at home. To overthrow him forcibly was clearly more than a good day's work. Wilson would have to send a major expedition into Mexico and this, for the moment, was more than Wilson dared to do. Like any other form of military aggression, "service to mankind," too, requires a popular pretext.

Searching for a pretext Wilson began to look with fresh eyes at the anti-Huerta forces of Carranza and his military ally, the bandit-rebel Pancho Villa. Previously Wilson had not regarded the Constitutionalists as fit instruments for fulfilling the "best aspirations" of the Mexican people. For one thing he thought them too radical. For another, Carranza was a stiff-necked patriot who refused to let Wilson meddle in Mexican affairs. Intervention being Wilson's object, the President had no desire to rid Mexico of Huerta in order to be excluded from Mexican affairs. The best pretext for intervening across a border, however, is chaos on the other side of that border. If Wilson could strengthen the Constitutionalists, a promising havoc would ensue in short order. In the winter of 1913–14, Wilson therefore changed his mind about Carranza's Constitutionalists. He decided that they did embrace the "best aspirations" of the Mexican people. On February 3, 1914, he lifted an arms embargo imposed by Taft, thereby enabling the Constitutionalist guerrillas to engage in full-scale civil war. The action stirred up a storm of severe criticism at home and abroad; to deliberately unleash bloody anarchy is an uncommonly ruthless act. The London *Spectator,* for one, described Wilson as a "Machiavelli in a mortarboard." The President, however, stood firm. The Constitutionalists, he announced, were fighting a noble fight to redress ancient wrongs. In the meantime, with a squadron of the U.S. Navy standing menacingly off the Gulf Coast port of Tampico, Wilson awaited his pretext for armed intervention. The "incident" Wilson chose to seize upon stands as one of the paltriest excuses a great power ever gave for using arms against a weak neighbor.[29]

The incident occurred on April 9, 1914, when a whaleboat of the U.S.S. *Dolphin* landed in Tampico to get gasoline, sublimely indifferent to the fact that the city was a war zone under siege by the Constitutionalists. Since the American sailors landed without the necessary permission, an officer standing by, following his orders, arrested them and brought them to his commanding officer. The officer advised the Americans of the port rules, had them politely escorted back to their boat, and let them load up on gasoline before returning to the ship. That was the incident in its entirety.[30]

Rightly fearful of American intentions, the commander of the city prudently made a "profuse apology" both to the local American consul and to Admiral Henry T. Mayo, commander of the U.S. squadron. Even General Huerta tendered an apology although, quite plainly, no apology was required. Admiral Mayo thought otherwise. Acting on his own initiative, but doubtless with a good grasp of his commander-in-chief's intentions, Mayo demanded that the arresting officer be punished and that the American flag be hoisted in Tampico and given a twenty-one-gun salute by way of atonement. Apprised the next day of the affair, Wilson declared at once that Admiral Mayo "could not have done otherwise." The arrest, as Wilson put it a few weeks later, was "a psychological moment" for intervention. It was "no great disaster like the sinking of the *Maine*," he admitted to a magazine writer, but in his view it was good enough. To Huerta he issued an ultimatum as harsh as it was absurd. If the general did not comply with Admiral Mayo's demand for a twenty-one-gun salute "the gravest consequences" would follow.[31]

For Wilson the very paltriness of the incident was precisely what made it so useful. What government on earth would yield to such a humiliating threat made in behalf of so unworthy a cause? What Wilson did not foresee was that the American people would substantially agree with Huerta. There, in truth, lay the weakness of Wilson's peculiar strengths. Blinded by a vainglorious ambition, contemptuous of any views save his own, Wilson had no very firm grasp of reality as it was seen and judged by his fellows. Reality for Wilson was his will and his words and his power to impose them on others.

The stubborn Huerta, at any rate, refused to be imposed upon. When he declined to furnish a twenty-one-gun salute, Wilson, on April 14, ordered the entire North American battlefleet to Tampico. The next day he ordered the warships of the Pacific fleet to Mexico's west coast. On April 15, too, the President called in the senior members of the House and Senate foreign affairs committees and informed them that Huerta's refusal to salute was part of a studied policy of insulting the United States government, thereby accusing Huerta of doing to him what he was doing to Huerta. He asked them, in addition, for congressional authority to seize the ports of Tampico and Vera Cruz and to initiate a total blockade of Mexico in the event that Huerta's refusal proved final. On April 19 Huerta's final refusal was made; his fate was now to be sealed by force of arms.

On April 20, President Wilson went before another solemn joint session of Congress to ask authority to compel Huerta to show respect for "the dignity and rights of this Government." "The incident cannot be regarded as a trivial one," Wilson noted with characteristic contempt for the common sense of others, "especially as two of the men arrested were taken from the boat itself—that is to say, from the territory of the United States." Even to Wilson that did not sound quite sufficient. Using force in the name of a punctilio of national "dignity" squared ill with the exalted ideal of "service to mankind." Undismayed, Wilson simply melded punctilio to service. The United States, he assured the nation's assembled representatives, was not merely standing on outward forms. "We seek to maintain the dignity and authority of the United States only because we wish to keep our great influence unimpaired for the uses of liberty." To a President devoted to "service," no incident could be too trivial to serve as a pretext for war. As Wilson put it to the newsmen that day: "I have no enthusiasm for war; but I have an enthusiasm for the dignity of the United States."[32]

That same evening Wilson called in his military advisers to draw up plans to seize Vera Cruz and Tampico, to blockade Mexico, and to send an expeditionary force to Mexico City. Incredibly, Wilson actually believed that such naked aggression could be successfully covered by a refusal to salute our flag. More astonishing yet was the incident that prompted Wilson to execute his war plans even before Congress had given him authority. In the small hours of the morning of April 21, the President received word that a German freighter was due to arrive the next morning in Vera Cruz with a supply of arms for the Huerta regime. This, to Wilson, went beyond all tolerable bounds. By telephone, according to his private secretary Joe Tumulty, he ordered the secretary of the navy to "send this message to Admiral Fletcher: 'Take Vera Cruz at once.'" He then turned to Tumulty and remarked, "We are now on the brink of war and there is no alternative." Apparently by ordering military supplies Huerta had defied the President of the United States so grossly that Wilson was compelled to invade his country at once.[33]

On April 21, a nation that had acclaimed Wilson's nonintervention in Mexico discovered that a thousand U.S. marines were trying to capture a Mexican seaport, were being fired on by Mexican troops, and were firing back; 126 Mexicans and 19 marines were to die in the skirmishing. In the fourteenth month of the "new day," the United States of America had gone well beyond the brink of war and Wilson, the self-appointed servant of the Mexican people, had become overnight the man most hated by the Mexican people. The whole country rose up in patriotic anger. Mexicans of every political persuasion swore to resist the American invaders. Carranza, leader of the anti-Huerta forces, denounced Wilson's intervention as strongly as did the Huertists. In doing so he marked himself as the next target of Wilsonian "service." When Carranza finally prevailed over Huerta a few months later (to go ahead of chronology), Wilson would once again alter his judgment of the "best aspirations" of the Mexican people. He decided that Carranza, who would not let him meddle, was unfit to govern Mexico and must be deposed in turn. Mexico's "best aspirations," he decided, were to be fulfilled by the brutish Pancho Villa, the only Mexican of note who was shrewd enough to praise Wilson's Vera Cruz attack. Having slyly offered himself as Wilson's willing tool, the murderous Villa at once became in Wilson's eyes a man of virtue. In all these twists and turns (by 1916 American troops would be chasing Villa halfway to Mexico City) Wilson adhered to one consistent principle. For him the "best aspirations" of foreigners would invariably be those that required American intervention, for it was by his wish to intervene that he judged their "best aspirations." Such was the stuff of "Wilsonian idealism," as historians have come to call it. What the best aspirations of the Mexican people actually were and how they might best be served were at bottom of no interest to Woodrow Wilson.

Unfortunately for Wilson's invasion plans, fury over the Vera Cruz attack was not confined to Mexico. The American people, too, rose up in opposition. A storm of cabled protests and pleas for peace rained in upon Wilson in the White House. Fear of war and opposition to war swept across the country in the fourth week of April 1914. The common sense of the citizenry had smashed through the picket line of pretexts, sophistries, and exalted ideals that Wilson had thrown up around his intervention. As Wyoming Representative Frank Mondell was to put it: "Smug and unctuous phrases and elaborate dissertations on the cardinal virtues and the blessings of constitutional government, were framed and fashioned in excuse of this indefensible interference with the sovereignty of an independent people." Halfway to full-scale war, Wilson was stopped in his tracks by the force of an aroused public opinion. When the envoys of Argentina, Brazil, and Chile offered to mediate the Mexican tangle, Wilson, trapped in a humiliating impasse, accepted their offer and shelved his war plans.[34]

A less self-exalted leader than Wilson might well have been chastened by the turn of events, but Wilson was beyond the reach of other men's reproaches. Had the Vera Cruz affray earned him the plaudits of a grateful nation, he could not have been more suavely complacent than he actually was in the aftermath of that fiasco. In the spring and summer of 1914, while leading progressives grew increasingly distressed over Wilson's failures as a reformer, the President devoted himself more intensely than ever to preaching the glories of an active, altruistic foreign policy. On May 11, at a ceremony in Brooklyn to commemorate the nineteen marines who died in Vera Cruz, Wilson noted that "a war of service is a thing in which it is a proud thing to die." On June 4, at Arlington Cemetery, he proclaimed it America's "duty" and "privilege" to "stand shoulder to shoulder to lift the burdens of mankind in the future and show the paths of freedom to all the world." On June 5, at the U.S. Naval Academy, he informed the assembled officers that "the idea of America is to serve humanity . . . is that not something to be proud of, that you know how to use force like men of conscience and like gentlemen, serving your fellow men and not trying to overcome them?" On Flag Day, June 15, he proclaimed that the American flag, his recent pretext for military aggression, "is henceforth to stand for self-possession, for dignity, for the assertion of the right of one nation to serve the other nations of the world." On July 4, in yet another foreign policy pronouncement, Wilson demonstrated his truly astonishing indifference to the real concerns of his fellow countrymen—to the debt-ridden farmer, the child laboring kind, and the sweated factory worker, whose relief by remedial legislation he was now openly opposing. To an audience at Philadelphia's Independence Hall, he declared that America was now rich enough and free enough to look abroad for great tasks to perform. The American people, he said, were too prosperous to care only about their "material interests." Our duty is to serve the world without regard for ourselves. "What other great people has devoted itself to this exalted ideal?"[35]

On July 31, in less self-exalted circles, La Follette and Brandeis met to discuss Wilson's all-but-declared retreat from reform. "It just breaks one's heart," Brandeis told La Follette, "to see him throw away chances for good things and swallow bad things with good labels, while the old Republican and the old Democratic devils chuckle." The next day, Europe erupted in war, a war the American people took for granted had nothing to do with them. They could scarcely suspect, it was too monstrous to suppose, that their President would view it as the opportunity of a lifetime, "the greatest, perhaps, that has ever come to any man," as Colonel House remarked to his vainglorious friend in the White House.[36]

8

"The Noblest Part That Has Ever Come to a Son of Man"

The central political fact about America's entry into the European war was that the American people wanted, above all else, to stay out of it. Aversion to joining in the carnage, the determination to remain neutral, was not the opinion of a mere majority, nor even of a large majority. It was virtually unanimous. Even after the sinking of the *Lusitania* in May 1915, opposition to entering the war, a bellicose Roosevelt ruefully estimated, remained the sentiment of 98 percent of the people. "The great bulk of Americans," an Englishman informed his countrymen in the fifteenth month of the war, "simply do not believe that the present conflict, whatever its upshot, touches their national security or endangers their power to hold fast to their own ideals of politics and society and ethics." To join the fighting, he noted, for "any cause less urgent than the existence or safety of the commonwealth seems to many millions of Americans a counsel of suicidal insanity." Even after Wilson broke off relations with Germany in February 1917, an overwhelming majority of Americans still opposed entering the war. Even when the United States had already been at war for some months a majority of Americans remained a sullen, silenced opposition, more profoundly alienated from their own government than any American majority has ever been before or since.[1]

Interventionists there were, but against that stone wall of near-unanimous opposition none dared profess their intentions in public. Straightforward war agitation would play no part in bringing America into the World War. Like water pent up by a mighty dam, the war agitation would be forced into oblique and covert channels. The crypto-interventionists* would cry up the need for a vast military establishment—in the name of preserving peace. They would cry down critics of the government's unneutral diplomacy—as enemies of true neutrality. They would heap unstinting praise on President Wilson for "keeping us out of war," when the great majority of Americans could not see, for all the world, what forces were supposedly pushing us into it.

As far as public opinion was concerned, the crypto-interventionists would labor under the severest of handicaps, for they could not persuade even a majority of Americans to take up a mere sentimental preference for the Allies—the Triple Entente of Britain, France, and Tsarist Russia. Armored by their historic contempt for the Old World, the great bulk of Americans refused to believe that the Kaiser and German "militarism" were the evil agencies solely responsible for the war—a central tenet of the crypto-interventionist propaganda. To most Americans the carnage in Europe was simply the corruption of the Old World nations bursting into ghastly fruition—the inevitable outcome of their ancient rivalries and their contemptible appetites for territory and pelf. They could see no special virtue in either side of the conflict. Even after two years of reading little save pro-Allied propaganda in their newspapers (disseminated to the countryside by the New York press and to the New York press by the scribes of Fleet Street) the majority of Americans scarcely progressed beyond the view that Germany was probably more detestable than Britain. In their general grasp of the war's meaning and origins the great majority of Americans were quite correct, although doubtless they had lit upon the truth more by tradition and general principles than by any rational sifting of the evidence.[2]

Only a few of their more thoughtful "betters" disagreed with the common verdict and concluded instead that the war's meaning and origin were fully explained by the official propaganda of the British

---

* The term rightly used by Woodrow Wilson's most judicious biographer, Arthur Link.

government. That Germany alone had started the war, that the Entente was fighting for "democracy" against "autocracy," that an Allied victory would put an end to "militarism" and secure "permanent peace" in the world were the views of a handful of anglophile extremists, chiefly literary gentlemen, college presidents, fashionable parsons, and upper-class inhabitants of the cities and towns of the eastern seaboard. Society matrons who fawned over Britain's hereditary aristocracy would be among the most ardent supporters of Britain's alleged fight for "democracy."[3]

There was only one place in America where the extreme anglophile views of a minute fraction of the American people enjoyed the support of an overwhelming majority—in the upper reaches of the Wilson administration. There, only one man of consequence, Secretary of State William Jennings Bryan, actually represented the near-unanimous sentiments of the American people, and his position would soon earn him the contempt and contumely of virtually every man of power in the country. The rest of Wilson's cabinet were fervently pro-Allied. The chief conduits of Wilson's foreign policy were fervently pro-Allied. Representing the United States at the Court of St. James's, Walter Hines Page suffered from anglophilia so purblind that his conduct would skirt the fringes of treason. The war was but a few weeks old when Page fatuously assured the State Department that he and the British Foreign Secretary, Sir Edward Grey, were "giving each other his full confidence" and that "he has told me every fact at every stage of this troublesome journey." And what had Sir Edward confided to America's emissary with a candor that any American chosen at random would have suspected at once? That the British were fighting, as Page duly reported in his September 10 dispatch, for "an end of militarism forever," a noble goal that required the defeat of Germany and the overthrow of its system of government. Such fawning gullibility would have earned for Page instant recall in any adminstration save Woodrow Wilson's.[4]

Far more important than Page in Wilson's pro-Allied cabal was the curious gray eminence, Colonel E. M. House. A wealthy, dapper little Texan with a passion for behind-the-scenes wirepulling, House had met Wilson in late 1911 and had become, in short order, his close personal friend and trusted colleague. "Mr. House,"

Wilson once informed an inquisitive reporter, "is my second personality. He is my independent self. His thoughts and mine are one." Silent, discreet, and suavely insinuating—one senator said of House that he "he can walk on dead leaves and make no more noise than a tiger"—the self-confident House was considerably more than a successful courtier. He did much to help Wilson overcome his peculiar personal defects as a political leader: the President's lofty indifference to practical details and the opinions of others and a consequent want of resourcefulness in devising practical schemes. Eager to exercise power by privately serving the powerful, House was both Wilson's chief source of information about the outside world and his chief supplier of practical plans. It was House—the President's "silent partner," as he was known in the press—who had actually chosen the members of Wilson's cabinet, and it was House whom Wilson would choose as his private emissary to the rulers of Europe, a role that enabled the President to reduce to a nullity his inconvenient secretary of state.[5]

The most important subscriber to the British view of the war was, of course, the President himself. When the fighting broke out, Wilson, as expected, had issued the usual proclamation of neutrality. On August 19 he went even further, offering a "word of warning" against Americans taking sides emotionally in the European conflict, perhaps because the only large body of partisan Americans were several million German-American partisans of Germany. "The United States," Wilson declared, "must be neutral in fact as well as in name. . . . We must be impartial in thought as well as in action, must put a curb upon our sentiments." From that prudent injunction, however, Wilson exempted himself. He was never impartial in "thought" and within two months of the war's onset he would not be impartial even in "action." From the start Wilson subscribed fully to the bromides of the British propaganda. "It does not seem clear now," he remarked in August to his factotum, Joe Tumulty (an Irish-American perhaps skeptical of British idealism), "but as this war grows in intensity it will soon resolve itself into a war between autocracy and democracy." That Germany and German "militarism" were solely responsible for the war was Wilson's apparently unshakable conviction. "He goes even further than I in his condemnation of Germany's part in the war," Colonel House recorded in his diary on August 30. Wilson even persuaded himself that Britain was serving America in the trenches of France. "England is fighting our fight," he told Tumulty in the autumn, "and you may well understand that I shall not, in the present state of the world's affairs, place obstacles in her way... when she is fighting for her life and the life of the world." In December, the ostensibly impartial President confided to a *New York Times* reporter in an understandably off-the-record interview that he hoped to see the war destroy the Austrian Empire and completely alter the German system of government, which is to say, he hoped for a crushing defeat of the Central Powers.[6]

Such views—and the diplomacy that followed in their trail—have often been attributed to Wilson's profound personal fondness for Britain, but the explanation is both trivial and lame. Whatever else Wilson was, he was neither a small man nor a silly one. That an uncurbable infatuation with a foreign power would prevent an American President of high intelligence, grave responsibilities, and driving ambition from seeing further into foreign affairs than a dithering society matron in Newport, Rhode Island, is highly unlikely even on its face. In October 1913, when it had suited his Mexican plans, Wilson had not scrupled to blackguard the British government and attempt to exploit American anglophobia. Nor did he have any compelling reason to credit the self-serving British doctrine of German "war guilt." On August 1, Colonel House himself had pointed out to the President, quite correctly, that Germany would be the first to attack because, with enemies on both flanks, she was forced to "strike quickly," out of prudent fear rather than a grand aggressive design. Neither did the President have any sound reason to regard the war as a conflict "between autocracy and democracy." An Allied victory, as House realistically pointed out to the President on August 22, would make tsarist Russia dominant in Central Europe—scarcely a defeat for "autocracy." If Wilson brushed those troublesome realities aside, if he professed to believe in British idealism and the overriding need for an Allied victory, it was chiefly because the skepticism proper to a statesman, a patriot, and a neutral would have crimped a certain grandiose ambition that began gripping the President as soon as the war erupted.[7]

In August the President was already confiding to his brother-in-law his belief that a permanent postwar settlement required the formation of what he called an "association of nations, all bound together for the protection of the integrity of each." The idea was by no means new to American leaders. Roosevelt had proposed just such a "world league for the peace of righteousness" in his 1910 Nobel Prize address, and he began calling for it again a few months after the outbreak of the war, chiefly to justify American intervention. That the President of the United States might be called upon at war's end to bring that "association" into being, that he might become the chief architect of a new pacific world order, seems to have become a serious prospect for Wilson before the war was many weeks old. By early September he was already giving out vague hints of glories to come. On September 4, in the course of declining a Democratic invitation to campaign for the party ticket, he noted that "the time has come for great things. These are days big with destiny for the United States." On September 28, when Wilson once again confided his fears that the American people would turn against him, House reassured the President that his forthcoming leadership in foreign affairs would forestall any such danger. Clearly, House understood how strongly rooted in dread of political failure at home was Wilson's ambition for "constructive statesmanship" abroad.[8]

In early October, with Wilson's consent, House began discussing with the British ambassador the prospect of Wilson's playing a role (as yet unspecified) in the peacemaking. Since the British were exceedingly wary of peace proposals, House assured them, via Page in London, that the President had no wish to force the Allies to the peace table before Germany was beaten and their war aims secured. The great conference over which Wilson hoped to preside, House informed Page, would deal solely with establishing an association of nations "guaranteeing the territorial integrity of every other nation." It would take place, wrote House, only after the "necessary territorial alignments [were] made" at an ordinary peace conference. The prospects were dazzling. By presiding over a great postwar conference, Wilson would become the first man in history to bring the world peace everlasting. "This," as House put it to the President, "is the part I think you are destined to play in this world tragedy and it is the noblest part that has ever come to a son of man." [9]

From autumn 1914 onward, the diplomacy of the United States would be conducted by Wilson and House not in the interests of America, not by the venerable traditions of the Republic, not by the nearly unanimous sentiments of the American people, not by the requirements of neutrality, not by the wish to avoid a horrendous war, but solely by the desire to secure by any means possible Wilson's opportunity to play "the noblest part that has ever come to a son of man." What burdens the American people might be forced to bear because of Wilson's grandiose ambitions, what damage might be inflicted upon a free republic when its citizens' deepest feelings were grossly flouted, were only of tactical concern to America's President. That "permanent peace"—which the world had never before enjoyed—might not be secured by an "association of nations"—which the world had never seen—was a proposition Wilson never honestly considered. "Association of nations" was to be for the President a magical catch phrase signifying an instrument of indisputable efficacy and a "service to mankind" of unsurpassed nobility. A mere catch phrase it would remain until 1918, for not until then did Wilson even begin to work out the practical details of, or resolve the endless perplexities involved in, the actual machinery of his "association of nations." Brought down to earth, subjected to realistic tests, set against a statesman's understanding of the shifting motives of men and of nations, its efficacy might be brought into question and its worthiness compromised. Wilson simply could not afford to think realistically about his "association of nations." For the burdens he was willing to inflict upon an unwilling America only a transcendent goal unsullied by the skeptical judgment of practical statecraft could possibly serve as adequate justification. In order to become a "great statesman," Wilson had, of necessity, to forfeit every quality that makes a statesman great. Self-deception, self-elation, and self-regard were the chief ingredients of Wilson's celebrated "idealism."

For some months Wilson's means for securing the "noblest part" for himself were discouragingly meager. America was neutral and seemed destined to remain so for the war's duration. As a neutral

leader Wilson could play a great role at a postwar general conference only by the grace and favor of the proponents of "permanent
peace," namely the Allies. He could win their favor only by helping
them win the war, and he could do that only by compromising
America's neutrality. On that score Wilson had no hesitation. To
secure the noblest part he was prepared, at the very least, to make
America's neutrality a false and biased neutrality, a perilous, ill-
disguised partiality whose "evils" George Washington had described with wonderful prevision in his Farewell Address. "It
leads," Washington had warned, and the warning is still read aloud
on his birthday in each house of Congress, "to concessions to the
favorite nation of privileges denied to others, which is apt to doubly
injure the Nation making the concessions—by unnecessarily parting with what ought to be retained—and by exciting jealousy, ill-
will and a disposition to retaliate in the parties from whom equal
privileges are withheld; And it gives to ambitious, corrupted or deluded citizens (who devote themselves to the favorite nation) facility to betray or sacrifice the interests of their own country, without
odium, sometimes even with popularity, gilding with a virtuous
sense of obligation . . . the base or foolish complacencies of ambition, corruption or infatuation." As will be seen, the politics of
America between 1914 and 1917 have never been more trenchantly
set forth.

A supplicant currying a belligerent's favor, Wilson first helped
the British at his country's expense by ensuring the success of Britain's grand strategy of naval warfare. From the start the British
hoped to use their peerless navy to blockade Germany, deny it raw
materials and foodstuffs, and thereby strangle its industrial economy and, as Winston Churchill candidly put it, "starve the whole
population—men, women and children, old and young, wounded
and sound—into submission"—an early example of what has since
been called "total war": that is, war in which little distinction is
made between combatants and noncombatants. Unfortunately for
Britain, its great navy was no longer capable of maintaining a
blockade in accordance with the requirements of international law.
The advent of the submarine made it impossible to station warships
outside the ports of an enemy to prevent all shipping from leaving
and entering. Britain's only alternative was to intercept on the high

seas neutral ships bound for Germany or nearby neutral ports and prevent them at long range from delivering their cargoes of food and raw materials. International law, however, forbade such a policy. The British, in short, could not carry out the planned strangulation of Germany without violating the acknowledged neutral rights of Americans. Unless the American government willingly surrendered those rights, the British could not render German submarines ineffective and thereby carry out their naval war of attrition. They could not starve German civilians without the American government's consent, and America could not give its consent without compromising its neutral status. To gain that consent, however, all the British had to do was tell America's President that they considered the starving of German civilians an important war measure. The "dictates of humanity," which Wilson would soon be championing against Germany, were not an issue where England was concerned. As Colonel House fatuously noted in his diary in early September, after the Austrian ambassador complained to him of Britain's illicit blockade, "He forgets to add that England is not exercising her power in an objectionable way, for it is controlled by a democracy."[10]

The chief hitch in Wilson's determination to help Britain set aside America's neutral rights was that he had not known at the war's outset that Britain wanted to do so. The State Department, in consequence, had formally requested the belligerents to abide by a 1909 codification of the rules of sea warfare known as the Declaration of London. Fearful of openly defying the United States, the British government announced in its August 20 Order in Council that it intended to adhere to the Declaration with certain "additions and modifications." The emendations, which virtually nullified the Declaration, authorized the British navy, in effect, to treat food as contraband of war and put the British in virtually complete control of neutral commerce between neutral nations.[11]

That the British had arrogated to themselves privileges forbidden both by the Declaration and by previous international law was obvious enough to State Department officials. The department duly set about working up a stern note of protest based on the understandable assumption that the United States, being genuinely neutral, had a duty to maintain its neutral rights and so avoid the charge of partiality. The resulting protest note was largely the work of one Robert Lansing, counselor to the State Department, a man who was to be torn for the next three years between devotion to the rules of neutrality and a somewhat greater devotion to keeping his job. When he sent the draft note to the President on September 26, Lansing, however, knew nothing of the peculiar requirements of Wilson's diplomacy; the "noblest part" was a secret known only to a few. The lengthy, well-argued note sharply condemned the British Order in Council. The United States, it declared, "cannot consent" to Britain's modification of the Declaration of London. It deemed three provisions of the order "wholly unacceptable" and rightly noted that two of them, taken together, would "make neutral trade between neutral ports dependent upon the pleasure of belligerents, and give to the latter the advantage of an established blockade without the necessity of maintaining it with an adequate naval force." The State Department pointed out, too, that foodstuffs were a legitimate article of neutral trade that belligerents had no right to seize even en route to an enemy's port. Nor did the State Department forget the danger that a neutral nation incurs when its failure to uphold its rights works to the advantage of one of the belligerents. "The United States cannot permit itself to be placed in a position where its neutrality and impartiality are doubtful or open to question."[12]

That danger, however, Wilson was willing to risk, for the note was never delivered. Meeting with Colonel House after reading it, Wilson decided to ask the British ambassador, Cecil Spring-Rice, what he thought America should do about British interference with America's neutral rights. When House showed Spring-Rice the protest note the next day, the Englishman predictably professed alarm. It would mean a crisis in Anglo-American relations, he warned, meaning that it would jeopardize the American President's peacemaking ambitions. That sealed the fate of the protest. The President ordered Lansing to withdraw it on the preposterous grounds that it would lead to war with England. Instead, House and the British ambassador sat down together to draft a brief substitute cable to Page.[13]

Sent on September 28, the fruit of that noteworthy collusion adroitly provided the British government with all the clues it needed regarding Wilson's willingness to collude with them. The cable, significantly, contained no legal contentions in regard to American rights nor did it even dispute the British policy of preventing American shippers from trading in foodstuffs. Instead it instructed Page to inform the British foreign secretary, Sir Edward Grey, "informally and confidentially" that "the President earnestly desires to avoid a formal protest," meaning that he had no wish to challenge the illegal basis of Britain's maritime war. Page was also instructed to say that the President was "greatly disturbed" by the Order in Council because it "will arouse a spirit of resentment among the American people." With that Wilson was virtually telling the British that the only obstacle to their naval war against German civilians was American public opinion. The implication was obvious enough: America's President would let the British violate America's neutral rights if they in turn would do so with prudent regard for the President's task of keeping the American people quiet. A belligerent was violating America's neutral rights and the upshot of doing so was America's President asking that belligerent, in effect, for a favor.[14]

In case the British were too dense to grasp the implications of the cable, Page in London on September 29 advised Grey that "there is no desire to press the case of people who traded deliberately and directly with Germany," namely shippers of American foodstuffs and cotton whose rights and whose continental markets now disappeared almost completely. Sir Edward was not dense. On October 9 he submitted to the American ambassador* the draft of a new Order in Council which authorized the British to do pretty much what the earlier Order allowed them, but which dropped the embarrassing pretense of adhering to the Declaration of London. On October 15, Page urged the President to acquiesce in the new British action on the plea that the war was a "world-clash of systems of government, a struggle to the extermination of English civilization or of Prussian military autocracy." On the same day the British ambassador, now certain that Wilson was safely in Britain's pock-

---

*In his memoirs, Grey wrote that Ambassador Page was "of the greatest value in warning us when we had to be careful or encouraging us when we could safely be firm" with the American government. Britain, in effect, had two ambassadors to the United States, one of them being the American ambassador to Britain.

et, wrote the President that it was essential for Britain to prevent war supplies (i.e., food) from reaching the German armed forces (i.e., women and children) even through neutral ports. Wilson found the letter, in his words, so "candid and sincere, and so earnest" he sent it on to Lansing. Lansing took the hint. The next day the counselor to the State Department duly instructed Page to inform the British government that the United States "is not disposed to place obstacles in the way of the accomplishment of the purposes which the British representatives have so frankly stated." The British, in short, could do what they pleased. Except for the occasional need to keep up a public pretense of neutrality, there were to be no further efforts to defend America's neutral rights against Britain. Henceforth all Wilson's diplomatic efforts as an ostensible neutral would go to defending to the death a dubious right of no practical value against Germany. As Grey understandably reported to Spring-Rice on October 24, "I am very sensible of the friendly spirit of the President."[15]

Emboldened by that "friendly spirit," the British government quickly tightened the noose around Germany with a still more radical violation of neutral rights. On November 3, Britain declared the entire North Sea a "military area" in which neutral ships sailed at their own risk due to British mines and the further risk of being treated there as "suspicious craft" by British patrols. By thus usurping the high seas for its military use, the British, citing "changed conditions of modern warfare" as a partial justification, intended to overcome the perils of searching neutral freighters on the high seas in the era of the submarine. Neutral merchantmen that did not wish to be blown up by British mines would have to put into British ports to get a pilot, at which time the British authorities could illegally search their cargoes and generally harass them at will. When neutral Norway, on November 6, invited the United States to join in a protest against Britain's unprecedented assault on neutral rights, the Wilson administration (which would soon be posing as the champion of all neutrals against Germany) curtly turned its fellow neutral down: "This government does not see its way at the present time to joining other governments in protesting to the British government against their announcement that ships entering the North Sea after November 5 do so at their own peril."

It would not be lost on Germany that Britain's naval war against German civilians was made possible by American consent.[16]

If Wilson felt a "virtuous sense of obligation" in thus serving a belligerent's interests at considerable expense to his country's neutrality, he had scarcely forgotten the twofold purpose that lay behind it. With war news dominating the headlines and the President himself "big with destiny," Wilson felt secure enough in mid-autumn 1914 to take a step he had been contemplating for some time. In a letter published in the *New York Times* on November 18, 1914, the President announced that the "high enterprise" of reform had come to an end. "The legislation of the past year and a half," he noted, had remedied all the people's just grievances. The era of reform, which Wilson now described as a period of "dangerous ill-humors" and "distempers," a terrible dozen years when "those who had power, whether in business or in politics, were almost universally looked upon with suspicion" was now thankfully at an end. The ruled, by presidential fiat, were now to cease bothering their rulers. The country, he said, would look back on the past twelve years "as if upon a bad dream." A truly revealing remark: Most reformers had regarded the previous twelve years as a time of awakening. As one of them, Herbert Croly, wrote in the *New Republic* in response to Wilson's pronouncement, the President had either "utterly misconceived the meaning and task of American progressivism" or had deceived himself into thinking there was no more to be done. If so, wrote Croly, "he should not be allowed to deceive progressive popular opinion." Wilson was not to resume the guise of reformer until 1916, when he had to do so to win re-election.[17]

Shortly after telling Americans they had no more to ask of their government Wilson took another step toward providing them with something they absolutely did not want from their government, namely a great role in the bloody affairs of Europe. In December, the President decided to send House on a secret mission to England to present the bill, as it were, for the services he had just rendered the British cause. In London, House and Grey discussed in friendly fashion how Wilson, as mediator, might negotiate a settlement between the belligerents. It would not be a routine cessation of hostilities. That, Wilson had no wish to "mediate." One reason he had sent House to London, in fact, was to circumvent Secretary Bryan's public efforts to bring the belligerents to the peace table at once. What House and Grey discussed was how the American President might negotiate "permanent peace" through Germany's surrender of Alsace and Lorraine and its payment of an indemnity to Belgium, followed by universal disarmament and the establishment of an association of nations, perhaps, as House wrote Wilson from London, through "a general convention of all neutral and belligerent nations of the world, at which you will be called upon to preside." Since permanent peace, thus defined, could not be achieved until the German army had been badly mauled and the Imperial government on the verge of collapse, House assured the British foreign secretary that he "held German militarism responsible for the war" and promised him, House noted in his diary, that "I had no intention of pushing the question of peace" until the Allies deemed the time was ripe. Since the prospect of America calling for early peace talks filled the British with dread, House's reassurances to Grey removed at once Britain's sole remaining fear of America and cost Wilson a powerful means of binding the British to his will. The surrender, however, was inherent in the diplomacy of the "noblest part." As long as America remained neutral, Wilson could fulfill his ambitions only through British gratitude and good will. He understandably felt debarred from exerting diplomatic pressure that might incur their ill will; the pressure would be self-defeating. The British might bow to his demands while the war was on, yet turn against him once the war was safely won. As long as America remained neutral, Wilson was condemned to be an impotent suppliant in the hope of becoming one day the world's puissant lawgiver. His entire position was in fact absurd. In his dealings with the Entente he had to make himself nothing in order, one day, to become everything, yet there was no guarantee that he would ever be anything at all. Good will and gratitude are not often decisive in the relations among nations. The weakness and absurdity of his position might have given even Wilson pause in his pursuit of the noblest part. Instead, in the seventh month of the war, it prompted him to pursue the prize by means considerably more drastic than supplication.[18]

Germany, which had hitherto given the United States government little to complain of, provided the opportunity. On February 4, 1915, the German Imperial Government announced that after February 18, German submarines would sink on sight the merchant ships of its enemies in the waters surrounding the British Isles, which Germany now declared a "war zone" in imitation of Britain's North Sea "military area." The German government made no pretense of obeying international law. To sink an unarmed, unresisting belligerent merchantman without first ascertaining by searching it that it carried contraband of war was a gross violation of a belligerent merchantman's rights. Instead, the German government rested its new policy on a belligerent's acknowledged right to retaliate by illicit means against the illicit measures of its enemies. The British government, as the German note of explanation pointed out, was violating neutral rights and international law in order to "strike . . . at the economic life of Germany and finally through starvation doom the entire population of Germany to destruction." Since the neutral nations had acquiesced in the "English procedure," Germany expected them, said the note, to acquiesce in Germany's retaliatory policy.[19]

The German proclamation sent no thrill of indignation through the American electorate. The lawless reprisals that nations at war visit upon each other are of no concern in themselves to nations at peace. The State Department itself agreed with the common opinion. The American government was under no obligation to protect the rights of a belligerent against the reprisals of its enemy; to do so, in fact, would be grossly unneutral. Moreover, since the administration had made no protest when the British sowed the North Sea with mines that destroyed *neutral* ships without warning (as many in fact as were to be sunk by German submarines in the next two years), it was scarcely in a position to protest against German submarines sinking *enemy* ships without warning. A few days after the German proclamation State Department officials duly informed the press that the American government would probably make no protest at all. Remarking on the similarity between the British "military area" and the new German "war zone," State Department officials, one newspaper reported, regarded the German proclamation as "a rather neat and clever diplomatic counterstroke."[20]

In one mooted area of international law, however, the new German submarine policy could be deemed a violation of neutral rights. A citizen of a neutral country traveling on a belligerent merchantman could claim under international law the right not to have his life endagered because an enemy warship failed to heed to rule of "visit and search" before sinking a belligerent ship carrying contraband of war. It occurred to almost no one, either inside or outside the State Department, that this ostensible neutral right to travel safely on a belligerent merchant ship was one that the government of the United States ought to enforce against Germany. Strictly as a matter of international law, no obligation to do so existed. Passengers on ships are commonly regarded as being under the jurisdiction of the flag under which they sail. They are also regarded as incurring the risks of their location. Sailing under a British flag was about to become dangerous, but the American government was under no obligation to reduce that danger. It could declare, either tacitly or openly, that Americans who chose to sail under a belligerent's flag did so at their own personal peril. Without obligation in law the government was equally without obligation as a matter of national interest, for the right was of no practical value. In a nation of 100 million people, only a few thousand had occasion to exercise it and even that handful could forgo its exercise without loss by the simple expedient of taking passage on a neutral ship.[21]

On the other hand, to undertake the defense of that right would have far-reaching consequences, all of them dangerous. It would mean, for one thing, that the neutral nation was debarring one belligerent from taking effective reprisal against the lawless policies of its enemy, thereby upholding international law at its expense, while ignoring it in favor of its enemy. It would mean, too, that the neutral was championing, in effect, the rights of a belligerent and putting a protective shield around its wartime commerce, for if a neutral citizen is to sail safely on a belligerent merchantman then any merchantmen he might sail on must enjoy that safety. Instead of neutral passengers incurring the risks of their location, the location would enjoy the safety of its potential neutral passengers. In short, a neutral nation undertaking to defend the right to travel safely on belligerent merchantmen would violate the most fundamental duty of a neutral, the obligation to be impartial. It would make itself a major party to war and an important influence on its outcome. Since the American government had no duty to defend that right and since the right of itself was of no material value, every consideration of national interest seemingly dictated that the government not take upon itself gratuitously the incalculable burdens of doing so. Little wonder then, that Lansing, who had already run afoul of the President for being exessively legalistic toward England, concluded that "in my opinion . . . the advisability of a sharp protest, or of any protest at all [is] open to question."[22]

Neither Lansing nor Bryan nor almost anyone else in America had any reason to suppose that President Wilson thought otherwise. Not being privy to the "noblest part," they assumed, understandably enough, that the President had acquiesced in Britain's violation of American rights out of a determination to keep the nation at peace without troubling overmuch about neutral rights. For the sake of peace, it was assumed, the President had allowed Britain to cut off our legitimate trade with Germany, had allowed it to sow the North Sea with deadly mines, had consented to Britain's altering international law in order to render German submarines less effective and its own blockade more effective. Now Germany, in reprisal against that policy, a policy that could not succeed without Wilson's consent, had announced its intention of setting aside international law in order to make its submarines effective in another way. Given these circumstances, the President was under considerable obligation not to protest against, but to acquiesce in, the German policy. Granting extensive privileges to England at Germany's expense had been risky enough. Then to turn around and deny similar privileges to Germany would be considerably more perilous. To make that denial in defense of a right of no practical value and one, moreover, that the government had no obligation to defend would constitute a virtual act of hostility against Germany. It would be an act so wanting in common prudence, so destructive of genuine neutrality, and so gratuitously dangerous to the peace of America that few had any reason to expect their President to do more than follow the advice of Cleveland's former secretary of war, D. M. Dickinson, who wrote to the State Department on February 6, urging the government to hold Germany accountable "if it attacks and destroys the property and lives of Americans under our flag." That the President might hold Germany accountable for American lives lost under a belligerent's flag did not occur to the ex-secretary of war. Why would a President who had shown in the previous months such a large-minded indifference to the technicalities of international law now wish to plunge the nation into an uncharted sea of troubles for the sake of a legal technicality? Why would a President who refused to defend the right of American ships to ply the North Sea without being blown up by mines choose to defend the right of a few travelers to sail in safety on belligerent ships laden with munitions? Wilson had recently warned fifty thousand Americans that they stayed in Mexico at their own personal risk. Why would he refuse to acknowledge that Americans who voluntarily traveled on British ships carrying contraband did so at their own personal risk rather than at the risk of an entire nation's peace and security?[23]

Except for the "noblest part," there was no reason whatever. On February 10, Wilson had the State Department send off to the German government a brief note which announced harshly and threateningly that the American government would go to extreme lengths to defend the right of Americans to sail anywhere in safety. It warned the German government that if its submarines failed to observe the rule of visit and search "and should destroy on the high seas an American vessel or the lives of American citizens, it would be difficult for the Government of the United States to view the act in any other light than as an indefensible violation of neutral rights. . . . The Government of the United States would be constrained to hold the Imperial German Government to a strict accountability for such acts of their naval authorities and to take any steps it might be necessary to take to safeguard American lives and property and to secure to American citizens the full enjoyment of their acknowledged rights on the high seas." The neutral United States was forbidding the German government, on pain of extreme consequences, to sink an enemy's merchantman without warning because an American might choose to be aboard. Quite deliberately and quite unnecessarily, Woodrow Wilson had pushed the United States onto a collision course with Germany. In England, old John Morley, a onetime British cabinet member, warned Andrew

Carnegie that Wilson's note would prove a "calamity" to the United States and to the world. And so it would prove to be.[24]

Diplomatic notes, however harsh, are always open to revision under the impact of events. It would take some months before even high-ranking administration officials realized that the President had every intention of committing the honor, the prestige, and the peace of the country to the defense of the dubious right—a "right of humanity" Wilson would soon be calling it—of a handful of Americans to sail in safety on Cunard liners laden with munitions of war. No other neutral nation saw fit to assert such a right. No other neutral nation, however, was in the hands of a leader so willing to sacrifice to his ambitions the enduring interests of his country and the honorable sentiments of his countrymen.[25]

9

"I Cannot Understand His Attitude"

For some time the intention behind Wilson's "strict accountability" note to Germany was a secret Wilson shared with no one. It was not until September 1915 that the President confided to Colonel House that he had long wished to see America take part in the European war. Wilson's willingness was readily understandable. What the American people regarded as "suicidal insanity" made perfect sense to their President in the light of the "noblest part." What did not make sense was neutrality.[1]

For six months Wilson had been forced to pursue his ambitions as a mere neutral because intervention had not seemed even a remote possiblity. Quite apart from the sentiments of the American people, whom Wilson expected to have to "impel to great political achievements," it was not clear until the winter of 1914–15 that the war was going to last long enough to give Wilson much room for maneuver. For the first six months, too, the only belligerent giving the United States trouble had been England, and England was Wilson's secret ally. The President simply had no alternative to playing the role of humble supplicant to a foreign power in the fragile hope of future consideration. Although he let Colonel House work in London on behalf of a postwar general conference, Wilson could scarcely have been sanguine about his prospects as long as America remained neutral. History, after all, records few examples of rulers radically altering international relations at the close of a titanic war solely by virtue of having stayed out of it. Quite the opposite is true. Only the leader of a nation roused and bloodied by combat, with a mighty, victorious army at his beck, is likely to preside effectively over the destinies of the world. That elementary fact, obvious enough to common sense, was equally obvious to Colonel House, to Sir Edward Grey, and most important to Wilson himself.

In the summer of 1915, for example, House made that very point to the British foreign secretary, and Grey agreed, in the latter's words, that if "you people . . . go to war, I believe it is certain that the influence of the United States on the larger aspects of the final conditions of peace will prevail, and I am very doubtful whether anything short of being actually involved in the war will stir your people sufficiently to make them exercise, or enable the President to exercise, on the terms of peace, all the influence that is possible." Shortly before America's entry into the war, Wilson himself told a peace delegation (Jane Addams recalled) that "as head of a nation participating in the war, the President of the United States would have a seat at the Peace Table, but that if he remained the representative of a neutral country, he could at best only 'call through a crack in the door.' "[2]

In Germany's submarine warfare against its enemies' shipping Wilson seized his chance—a slender chance but the only one he had—to force war upon the United States. All the reasons, seemingly so compelling, for not taking the stand he took on the right to travel safely added up for Wilson to one compelling reason for taking it. His position was grossly provocative, grossly partial to the Allies, and wholly gratuitous. It put the United States in absolute opposition to Germany's announced intentions. It created out of nothing a source of incalculable difficulties. It was certain to "excite jealously, ill-will and a disposition to retaliate" on Germany's part. Indeed it did so at once. As a U.S. consul in Germany reported on February 28, the note had produced in two weeks a "marked and unpleasant change" in popular attitudes toward America; cordiality had given way to "almost open hostility toward American citizens." Washington's farewell warning was Wilson's guide but the evils which the first President decried were the twenty-third

President's good. The "strict accountability" note was deliberately meant as a step toward war.[3]

The President, it must be said at once, had no "plan" for bringing America into the European conflict, in the sense of a predetermined series of steps leading to the desired end. No such planning was possible. Essentially, all Wilson could do was press Germany hard while blatantly favoring its enemies, act against its interests, provoke diplomatic confrontations, force a deterioration or rupture in German-American relations, and hope that Germany's disposition to retaliate might erupt, sooner or later, into action. Should that happen, and Wilson, of course, had no guarantee that it would ever happen, then Germany, not America's neutral and apparently peace-loving President, would be responsible for driving America into the European carnage.

The principle underlying Wilson's war course was simple enough. Whether a nation at war chooses to respect the vital rights of a neutral—chooses, that is, to keep it friendly—is always a matter of calculation. The unneutral actions of an ostensibly neutral nation can become so hurtful to one of the belligerents that its open enmity, on balance, will appear the lesser evil. In such a case, passion is certain to incline the scales toward bellicosity, for a false and hurtful neutrality, as Washington had warned, is peculiarly infuriating to a nation at war. Putting the principle into practice, however, was to prove an arduous task for Wilson, one that would require endless trimming and improvising—"infinite tact and Fabian strategy," as Randolph Bourne would aptly put it in the early months of the war. The reason, of course, was the overwhelmingly neutral and antiwar sentiments of the American people. Wilson intended, one way or another, to provoke Germany into providing him with a *casus belli*. It would have been fatal to Wilson's intentions, however, if the electorate divined his intention or seriously doubted his determination to keep the peace. He could bring America into the war only if a substantial number of citizens became convinced that Germany was forcing war on America.[4]

This requirement Wilson and House understood quite clearly. In August 1915, for example, House wrote to Lord Bryce, the famed British historian and diplomat, that the President could not carry the American people into war until he first convinced them that "he has done all that was humanly possible, with honor, to avoid it." Two months earlier, during the *Lusitania* crisis, Wilson himself slyly confided to Frank Cobb, editor of the New York *World,* that "I intend to handle this situation in such a manner that every American citizen will know that the United States Government has done everything it could to prevent war. Then, if war comes we shall have a united country." As the President said to Tumulty on the eve of the war: "From the very beginning I saw the end of this horrible thing, but I could not move faster than the great mass of our people would permit."* He then took from his pocket, Tumulty recalled, an old clipping from the Manchester *Guardian,* remarking as he did that it had correctly interpreted his policy, which was to lead Americans, said the *Guardian,* "by easy stages to the side of the Allies" and "convince the whole American people that no other course save war is possible."[5]

Given these compelling considerations, Wilson had, at one and the same time, to act provocatively toward Germany yet not appear to the general public outrageously provocative, provocative, that is, to the point of betraying a desire for war. Wilson enjoyed a certain amount of leeway here. Dying in the trenches of Europe seemed so monstrous—literally insane—to most Americans, that even severe critics of Wilson's diplomacy would find it hard to imagine that their President wanted war. Nothing in America's political experience as a nation had prepared Americans for Woodrow Wilson. Actions, however, will eventually betray their intentions and drawing a line between effective provocation and excessive provocation would require of Wilson a nicety of judgment of no mean order. Wilson's war course was to be rather like a walk on a tightrope. Should he relent toward Germany under the pressure of public

* The remark is a revealing specimen of Wilson's singular hypocrisy of utterance. In the first half of the sentence he suggests that America's entry into the war was a deplorable fatality he had merely foreseen a long time in advance. In the second half he describes it as a goal he would have achieved sooner had the American people not stood in his way. The full sentence only makes sense if the phrase "from the beginning I saw the end of this horrible thing" is translated as "from the beginning I tried to bring America into this war [but I could not move faster than the great mass of our people would permit]." The reason behind such transparent mendacity, I suspect, is that Wilson simply could not put into candid words what he was actually doing, namely maneuvering an unwilling nation into an unnecessary war. The demons of a guilty conscience, who were to cripple Wilson permanently in 1919 (see chapter 14), seem to have damaged Wilson's capacity to face reality some time before they drove him half mad.

opinion, he would topple over on one side. Should he be excessively belligerent, he would topple over on the other. The price of falling would indeed have been steep: A nation that wanted peace would have remained at peace, but its President would have been forced at the peace conference to "call through a crack in the door."

Given the depth and strength of antiwar sentiment, given the depth and strength of the venerable tradition of avoiding European entanglements, given that a frail "right to travel"—for which no American had the slightest wish to die—was to be Wilson's chief instrument of war provocation, the wonder is not that Wilson got his war, but that he even dared to seek it. It was to be the lasting misfortune of the American Republic that Woodrow Wilson had the courage to match his vainglory. That courage was in some respects, however, a bully's courage, for—as will be seen—Wilson's war course would enjoy the support of most of the wielders of corrupt power and influence in America—most of the Republican oligarchy, most of the chieftains of the Democracy, most of the big-city party press, most of the financiers of Wall Street, most of the very rich. In truth, the struggle to drag America into the European war was to be a virtual civil war between the powerful, the privileged, and the rich—for twenty-five years the targets of Populist and progressive reformers—and the overwhelming mass of the American people. Without the support of the powerful and the privileged Wilson would never have succeeded, but it was the President and the President alone who initiated the struggle and it was on February 10, 1915, that he did so with his "strict accountability" note to Germany.

Despite the bravado of their "war zone" proclamation, the Germans had exactly two submarines in British waters when their policy went into effect in late February. Nor did the Germans have a vast submarine fleet standing by. Germany's submarine warfare against its enemies' shipping had been launched in large measure as a domestic sop. It was meant to placate certain submarine enthusiasts in the German Admiralty and, in larger part, to appease the German populace, which had been whipped into a frenzy of anger and self-pity by Britain's announced starvation policy. The two factors were intimately connected; it was the extraordinary popularity of submarine warfare that gave the submarine enthusiasts their influence within the German Imperial government. The sop proved costly at once since its sole beneficiary was Britain.

On March 1, the British government announced that in reprisal against the German war zone, it intended to prohibit all neutral trade between neutral ports if the cargoes—foodstuffs, cotton, and other raw materials—were judged by Britain to be ultimately destined for Germany. With one eye, perhaps, on their high-minded friend in the White House, the British promised to starve German civilians by these new and more effective means "in strict observance of the dictates of humanity." Since the new British policy blatantly violated accepted rules of international law, President Wilson once more felt compelled to head off a State Department protest. The former professor, who once wrote that lying was permitted to great men, sent Bryan a draft note of his own which declared that the new British policy did not violate "any accepted principle of international law." At that, however, even the secretary of state demurred, although he himself cared little for the technicalities of international law and had no desire to borrow trouble for America on their behalf.[6]

Genuinely impartial toward the parties at war, taking it for granted that America's overriding interest was to remain at peace, Bryan shared none of the pious pretexts, the shaky rationalizations, and the strained anglophile sentiments of the Wilson cabal or of his cabinet colleagues in general. He was not aware, for one thing, that "democracy" was giving battle to "autocracy" in Europe. He saw, instead, two sets of belligerents engaged, for obscure reasons, in a deadly struggle between themselves, but who had no wish to harm or antagonize the United States. Bryan saw no reason why the United States government should harm or antagonize either set of belligerents and every reason to make genuine efforts to remain friendly toward both. The one-eyed moralizing of his administration colleagues played no part in Bryan's understanding of events and of the manifest interests of his country. To those who insisted that the Entente was fighting for "peace," Bryan pointed out that the Entente had rejected out of hand any suggestion of a negotiated settlement. To those who insisted that Germany's new submarine warfare was peculiarly immoral, Bryan pointed out that attempting to starve an entire nation's civilians through an illicit blockade was scarcely morally superior to killing a few civilians with an illicit torpedo. Bryan was neither a great man nor a strong man nor a profound man, but he had to be none of these to see events clearly. Common sense, realism, and moral sanity flowed as readily from Bryan's desire to keep the peace as sophistry, false moralizing, and gratuitous troublemaking would flow from the President's desire for war.

In his response to the new British blockade announcement, Bryan made one point to the President, but that point was crucial. The British starvation policy, which the United States had already condoned, and the German submarine policy, which the United States had already opposed, were inextricably linked, a point Bryan had been making ever since the "strict accountability" note had been sent. The more strenuously Britain sought to strangle civilian Germany the more stubbornly would the German government cling to its submarine policy, the greater would be the popular demand for it, the more difficult would it be for the German government to yield to the American President. It was imperative, Bryan pointed out to Wilson, that the United States demand and secure its right to trade in foodstuffs with neutrals. This was a right, he said, that America "cannot concede." If "strict accountability" meant anything—and the note hung like Damocles' sword over German-American relations—then the United States could not afford to acquiesce for a second time in Britain's still more drastically illegal methods of starving German noncombatants. Bryan's argument was both sensible and realistic. With Britain increasingly dependent on American munitions makers and intensely fearful of popular American demands for an arms embargo, it could scarcely afford to violate any American right that the United States government was determined to uphold. Indeed, as Edward Grey later admitted, the British would have lifted the blockade entirely rather than risk America's friendship. To Bryan's argument, however, Wilson merely replied: "The British are going to do it no matter what representations we make. . . . We cannot convince them or change them." Germany's intentions were a different matter. The note to Britain, which the U.S. government eventually sent on March 30, was largely pro forma; intended neither to convince nor to change, it naturally did neither.[7]

In was on March 28, while the U.S. government was completing its pseudo-protest to Britain, that the first American died as a result of submarine action. A small British liner, the *Falaba,* carrying munitions to Africa, had been hailed by a submarine in the war zone. Ordered to stop, it had attempted to escape, thought better of it, and hove to. The German submarine commander gave crew and passengers ten minutes to evacuate the ship. Spying an enemy warship approaching, however, the submarine commander fired his torpedo while the crew was still lowering the boats. One Leon C. Thrasher, an American, was among those who perished. The eastern press, which was invariably as pro-Allied as it dared to be, savagely condemned the sinking. The New York *World,* Wilson's press mouthpiece, called it "murder." The New York *Herald* deemed it "barbarism run wild." The press notwithstanding, the sinking was a legally tangled affair. The German submarine had not failed to give warning; on the other hand, it had not given the *Falaba*'s passengers ample time to escape. The apparent approach of a British warship and the *Falaba*'s abortive attempt to flee complicated the situation still further. If anything, the sinking of the *Falaba* presented a powerful case for warning Americans against traveling on belligerent merchant ships. Even when a German submarine did not attack without warning, it was clear that anything was likely to happen at sea when a nervous (or aggressive) merchant captain confronted an aggressive (or nervous) submarine commander.[8]

What was the American government going to do about Leon C. Thrasher? Having just condoned for a second time the British starvation policy and reaped the inevitable harvest of hostility in Germany (the Cologne *Gazette,* a hitherto moderate newspaper, termed the American note to Britain "*carte blanche* for the English war of starvation"), Wilson's determination to steer a provocatively anti-German course faced its first major test. The immediate obstacle before him was his secretary of state.[9]

On April 2, at Bryan's request, Lansing composed a legal memorandum on the sinking. According to Lansing, Thrasher's neutral rights had been violated because the submarine had not given ample time for evacuation. Legally, the United States could protest and demand an indemnity. On the other hand, Lansing rightly pointed out, if the U.S. government held Germany accountable for Thrasher's death "in fact it would be a denunciation of the German 'war zone' plan" and would commit the United States to demanding that Germany alter its submarine policy in its enemy's favor. Given America's condoning of Britain's starvation policy, the last point seemed to Bryan a particularly strong argument against holding Germany strictly accountable for Thrasher's death. Bryan advised the President to ask for a reparation but without condemning the German war zone in general, just as we had not condemned the British blockade in general. If, said Bryan, we assert "that the presence of an American on a British ship shall operate against attack, we would have to condemn the methods employed as improper in warfare." It was an enormous and dangerous commitment. It was also wholly unprecedented. Never before in the history of neutrality had a neutral attempted to defend a belligerent's shipping from attack by its enemies. What was worse, to Bryan, the commitment was unnecessary. Why, he politely suggested to the President, should the American government even undertake to protect Americans traveling voluntarily on British ships in the war zone. In Thrasher's death, he pointed out, "the doctrine of contributory negligence has some bearing. . . . Can an American, by embarking on a ship of the Allies at such a time and under such conditions impose upon his Government an obligation to secure indemnity in case he suffers with others on the ship?" The traveler took the risks voluntarily; must he risk the peace of an entire country as well?[10]

It was a question that Bryan would raise again and again and again, but he was talking to the President across an abyss. Sane arguments for avoiding unnecessary trouble have no appeal to a leader intent upon inviting them. On April 3, the President ordered the obliging Lansing to write a sharp note of protest. "We will insist," Wilson told Bryan, "that the lives of our citizens shall not be put in danger by acts which have no sanction whatever in the accepted law of nations." The result, two days later, was a vehement draft note that harshly condemned the *Falaba* sinking as "ruthless and brutal," and a "flagrant violation of international law and international morality." It demanded that Germany "disavow"—that is, admit the illegality of—the sinking and "take the steps necessary to prevent its repetition." In a covering note to Bryan, Lansing noted that "we cannot take the position that Thrasher should have kept out of the war zone. To do so would amount to an admission of Germany's right to perform lawless acts in that area." Insisting that Germany cease performing lawless acts against its public enemy would have "the most momentous consequences," Lansing conceded, but there was no alternative consistent with the "dignity" of the United States, which had granted without demur the right of the British to blow up *neutral* ships in the North Sea.[11]

To Bryan it must have seemed like the world turned upside down. To insist that Americans did not travel at their own risk on belligerent merchantmen meant undertaking to force Germany to alter a war policy in favor of its enemy, a gross, perilous, and gratuitous intervention in the war. Yet here was the President (speaking through Lansing) insisting that America was obliged to enforce the right to travel precisely *in order to* compel Germany to alter that policy in its enemy's favor. "The most momentous consequences" would admittedly follow. Why would the President wish to invite them? To Bryan Wilson calmly explained that it was simply a question of standing on "the firm ground of right."[12]

To the secretary of state, Wilson's actions were quite literally incomprehensible. "I cannot understand his attitude," he complained bitterly to his wife, who recalled how Bryan would return home each day from the State Department red-eyed, anguished, and frustrated. A less trusting, more strong-willed man than Bryan just might have been daring enough to throw Wilson off his course, but in the quiet fateful debate over the death of Leon Thrasher, a debate unknown to the press and the country, Bryan, to his credit, did his best.

Thoroughly alarmed over the draft note, Bryan on April 6 again confronted the President with what he considered the central question: "Whether an American citizen can, by putting his business above his regard for his country, assume for his advantage unnecessary risks and thus involve his country in international complications. Are the rights and obligations of citizenship so one-sided that the Government which represents all the people must bring the whole population into difficulty because a citizen, instead of regarding his country's interests, thinks only of himself?" Tactfully, Bryan put the blame on the reckless traveler, but his implication was plain enough: It was a President who put the interests of a few travelers above that of the whole country who was pursuing the reckless course.[13]

Receiving no answer from the President, Bryan doggedly tried again the next day. "I cannot help feeling," he wrote the President, "that it would be a sacrifice of the interests of all the people to allow one man acting purely for himself and his own interests, and without consulting his government, to involve the entire nation in difficulty when he has ample warning of the risks which he has assumed." This time, Bryan saw fit to play what he could rightly regard as his trump card. The State Department, he also advised the President, had learned that the British were permitting its merchant ships to arm. He asked the President to consider "the effects of such arming on the rules that govern the conduct of the submarine." Had Wilson wished to avoid war, Bryan's suggestion would indeed have been a trump card, for Britain's policy regarding her merchant ships vitiated even the legal foundation of Wilson's "strict accountability" note to Germany.[14]

On February 10, the British Admiralty had instructed British commercial vessels to ram submarines if escape proved impossible. Two weeks later, the Admiralty, which was also arming merchantmen, ordered them to fire at submarines on sight even if they had committed no hostile act. The British kept the instructions a secret (Bryan had found out something about them from several sources including the neutral government of The Netherlands), not for military reasons but for diplomatic ones. Had they made them public they could scarcely have expected even Woodrow Wilson to uphold with any severity, if at all, the implications of "strict accountability."[15]

The essential legal principle is simple enough. A purely private commercial vessel of a nation at war enjoyed certain immunities under traditional international rules. It could not be sunk by a belligerent warship until the warship had hailed the vessel, searched it, found contraband of war, and then provided for the safety of passengers and crew. This was the basis of Wilson's February note to Germany. A belligerent merchantman, however, enjoys its immunities under very stringent conditions. It cannot attempt to escape; it cannot take offensive action. If it does, it is subject to instant destruction. Moreover a commercial vessel carrying guns capable of destroying a ship of war does not enjoy the immunities of a commercial vessel. Since it can act like a ship of war it is regarded as a ship of war. An American travelling on a merchant ship so armed and so instructed could scarcely claim immunities that the merchantman had willingly forfeited.

The Admiralty instructions, moreover, made Wilson's insistence that German submarines follow the traditional rules of visit and search utterly unreasonable. If Germany acceded to Wilson's demands, a submarine would surface, hail a belligerent merchantman, and subject itself to swift destruction. As more than one angry member of Congress would point out when the whole issue exploded in Wilson's face in February 1916 (see Chapter 11), the President's demand that German submarines obey the traditional rules meant in practice that an armed British merchantman had all the privileges of a peaceful commercial vessel plus the added privilege of striking the first deadly blow in a naval engagement. As even Lansing would argue in early 1916, if the British armed their merchant ships "is there not strong reason why a submarine should *not* warn a vessel before launching an attack?"[16]

The arming of British merchantmen not only undercut Wilson's general legal case against Germany's submarine warfare, it destroyed his pretext for making it. The right to travel safely on belligerent merchantmen likely to be engaged in naval combat was nonexistent. Bryan's warning about Britain's armed merchantmen did nothing to dissuade Wilson from his course. International law for the President was merely a body of pretexts for doing what he wanted.

Again receiving no answer from Wilson (who found contradiction insufferable), Bryan returned the next day to his main contention. "What claim," he asked the President on April 8, "can this Government rightfully make for unintended loss which ordinary diligence would have avoided?" By now Bryan had the support of an ostensibly influential ally. On April 8, the United States Joint Neutrality Board, set up to advise the administration on international law, pointed out that the United States had no obligation to concern itself with new methods of warfare that did not touch America's vital interests. It was precisely not our duty to force Germany to use submarines against her enemies according to the old rules governing ordinary ships of war. To try to do what the Joint Neutrality Board advised against doing, at the possible risk of war, in the name of a few hundred Americans who preferred to sail on a Cunard liner instead of safe Dutch or Norwegian ship seemed to Bryan a position bordering on moral lunacy. Wilson continued to maintain aloof silence.[17]

Increasingly frantic, Bryan on April 9 cabled Ambassador Page about the arming of British merchantmen: "Important to know whether British merchant vessels have in fact armed to resist attack of submarines." Since the *Times* of London reported that a British merchantman had received a government bounty of $3,300 for ramming a submarine, Bryan again cabled Page on April 12 to confirm the report that the British Admiralty had instructed merchant ships to ram submarines. Page, who was as unlikely as any man to ferret out secrets adverse to Britain's interests, cabled back on April 13 that he knew of "no instructions" of any kind. The British government, Page added, was not offering a reward for sinking submarines; it had merely given one. Bryan was only allowed to know what the British press had already reported.[18]

With Lansing's draft note still pending and the President still in seclusion, Bryan tried again on April 19 to dissuade Wilson from his course. Thinking perhaps that the high-minded President had been unduly swayed by moral indignation over submarines, Bryan asked the President: "Why be shocked at the drowning of a few people if there is to be no objection to starving a nation?" This was more blunt than Bryan ordinarily dared to be, but neither the tone nor the substance of his arguments deterred Wilson. Breaking nearly three weeks of silence, the President, on April 22, submitted for Bryan's perusal his own draft of a protest note to Germany which insisted that Americans had an inalienable right to travel safely anywhere on any ship at any time and that Germany, in consequence, must use submarines in accordance with the rules governing ordinary battle cruisers. "My idea, as you will see," he wrote in a covering letter to Bryan, "is to put the whole note on very high grounds—not on the loss of this single man's life, but on the interests of mankind."[19]

To Bryan's central question, why should the American government obligate itself at great peril to protect a few Americans traveling unnecessarily on British ships, Wilson had now provided the answer. In preventing Germany from sinking enemy merchantmen without warning, the United States was fulfilling a humanitarian obligation to "mankind." If that meant in practice that an ostensibly neutral America was protecting a belligerent's munitions trade; if it meant in practice that a few heedless Americans could now embroil 100 million fellow citizens in a crisis with Germany; if it meant in practice that a nation situated three thousand miles from the fighting was now entagled by the mere thread of a legal technicality in the grinding mills of a titanic war, what was that compared to the President's lofy, self-imposed duty to secure "humanity" and "fair play," as he put it, in naval warfare.

Once more Bryan tried to persuade the President to alter his stand, this time with considerable force and eloquence. "The note which you propose, will, I fear, very much inflame the already hostile feeling against us in Germany, not entirely because of our protest against Germany's action in this case, but in part because of its contrast with our attitude toward the Allies. . . . If we admit the right of the submarine to attack merchantmen but condemn their particular act or class of acts as inhuman we will be embarrassed by the fact that we have not protested against Great Britain's defense of the right to prevent foods reaching non-combatant enemies. . . . I fear that denunciation of the one and silence as to the other will be construed by some as partiality. You do not make allowance for the fact that . . . the deceased knowingly took the risk of traveling on an enemy ship. I cannot see that he is differently situated from those who by remaining in a belligerent country assume risk of injury. Our people will, I believe, be slow to admit the right of a citizen to involve his country in war when by exercising ordinary care he could have avoided danger." In his grasp of popular opinion Bryan was undeniably right. He was right, too, in his grim conclusion: "Such a note as you propose is, under the conditions that now exist, likely to bring on a crisis."[20] Unfortunately for Bryan and his countrymen, he had utterly failed to avert it.

Bryan could claim but one hollow victory. Without altering his policy Wilson quietly decided not to make the *Falaba* sinking the occasion for declaring it. Nobody in America was calling for a note of protest, not even the pro-Allied press. The sinking itself was full of legal ambiguities. There was no need for haste. As long as Americans were not warned off belligerent merchantmen, as long as they continued to book passage on British liners laden with munitions of war, a far better occasion was certain to arise soon enough. As Ambassador Page remarked to a friend on May 2, "If a British liner full of American passengers be blown up, what will Uncle Sam do? That's what's going to happen." Wilson had no reason to force the issue. In his private debate with Bryan over the death of Thrasher he had already won a major victory for his war course. He had pitted his will against his secretary of state and he had won. After outlining a policy utterly repugnant to Bryan he had treated his secretary of state with silent, contemptuous indifference. Yet Bryan had not dared to make his own views public, to marshal his considerable support in the country, and to bring the issue of travel on belligerent ships to a head at a propitious moment. Had Congress been in session—it was not scheduled to convene until December—perhaps he might have made a stronger fight. In any case, by confining himself to private entreaties Bryan in April 1915 had wasted his only real chance of stopping Wilson. As far as the President was concerned, the secretary of state, whose views matched those of the vast majority of Americans, had ceased to matter, even as an obstacle to overcome.[21]

"What's going to happen" happened with stunning effect on the afternoon of May 7. At 2:10 P.M. in the war zone, a German submarine, without warning, fired a torpedo into the *Lusitania,* a Cunard liner carrying 1,257 passengers (including 159 Americans), 702 crew members, and 4,200 cases of rifle ammunition. In the remarkably brief span of eighteen minutes the mighty vessel sank. Among the 1,195 lives lost, 124 were American. It was the first—and it was to be the only—serious loss of American lives at the hands of the submarine. The pro-Allied American press, which grew indignant over trifles, understandably boiled over in fury. The *Lusitania* sinking was undoubtedly German war ruthlessness at its absolute worst. Theodore Roosevelt, who was already leading a corporal's guard of crypto-interventionists, denounced the sinking as "piracy on a vaster scale of murder than old-time pirates ever practiced." The entire country was thrown into a state of shock. The European war, which hitherto had seemed so remote, had suddenly reached out without warning and seized America by the throat. Yet to the dismay and surprise of the crypto-intervenionists there was scarcely a voice raised for war in the country. The sinking of a British liner, horrible and savage though it was, simply did not seem to the American people a just ground for war. On that score public opinion was virtually unanimous. Even the press, for all its editorial fury, did not clamor for war. Of a thousand editorials penned in the heat of the moment, less than 1 percent, a Washington correspondent reported, called for a war declaration. "Rotten spirit in the *Lusitania* matter," grumbled Roosevelt's friend, General Leonard Wood, "yellow spirit everywhere in spots."[22]

Within a few days of the sinking, as the initial shock began to wear off, public sentiment in the country began taking a turn that would soon give even Wilson pause on his road to war. Instead of being indignant over the sinking of the *Lusitania,* Americans began voicing sharp disapproval of the Americans who had chosen to travel on it. Even Wilson's vice president, Thomas Marshall, remarked that Americans boarding British liners should expect to take the consequences. No one had forced them to sail on the British liner. When the press reported on May 9 that the *Lusitania* carried a cargo of munitions, American indignation found yet another venue: the temerity of the British trying to protect their contraband of war with a shield of American travelers. To carry such a cargo on a passenger ship, declared Rear Admiral F. E. Chadwick, was an "outrage, one can call it no less." As Bryan pointed out to the President on May 9, "a ship carrying contraband should not rely upon passengers to protect her from attack—it would be like putting women and children in front of an army."[23]

The President made no reply. For three days after the sinking Wilson remained in seclusion while the returns from the country came in. According to Tumulty, the President considered the possibility of calling for war but decided that public opinion was not ready for it. "I am not sure," he told his faithful factotum shortly after the sinking, "whether the present emotionalism of the country would last long enough to sustain any action I would suggest to Congress," meaning a war declaration. Wilson apparently found it easier to seek war than to pronounce the word "war." "When we move against Germany we must be certain that the whole country not only moves with us but is willing to go forward to the end with enthusiasm." The President knew, or thought he knew, how to persuade the people to "go forward to the end." With the horrific spectacle of the *Lusitania* sinking providing the impetus, he would demand, as he told the German ambassador, nothing less than "total abolition of the submarine war." In the name of "right" and "humanity" he would make the demand absolute and give Germany no alternative except humiliating surrender to his fiat or, what was considerably more likely, defiance of his fiat. Should the latter happen he would then be compelled to break off diplomatic relations and worse, in due course, would likely ensue.[24]

With that strategy Colonel House in London heartily concurred. Rightly convinced that Germany would never abandon the submarine at the order of America's President, certain that such an order would make war "inevitable," as he wrote in his diary, House cabled the President on May 9 urging him to order Germany to abandon the submarine. "America has come to the parting of the ways, when she must determine whether she stands for civilized or uncivilized warfare. We can no longer remain neutral spectators." According to House, the President had to defend "civilized warfare" at the clear risk of war, "because our actions in this crisis will determine the part we will play when peace is made, and how far we may influence a settlement for the lasting good of humanity." America's youth might have to die in faraway battle so that Wilson could have more "influence" at a peace conference. "If war follows it will not be a new war," House pointed out reassuringly, forgetting the main point, that it would certainly be a "new war" for America, "but an endeavor to end more speedily an old one." As that remarkable cable indicates, in the little world of the Wilson cabal, the grave issues of war and peace were discussed without the slightest reference to the interests of America or its people.* Wilson found the cable so praiseworthy he read it aloud to his cabinet, which greeted it with marked approval. Most of Wilson's cabinet was eager for war.[25]

---

* Another example of this was the exchange between Wilson and Lansing in late August 1915. On August 24, Lansing told the President that he ought to welcome "a state of war" with Germany because it would increase "our usefulness in the restoration of peace." Wilson replied at once that Lansing's view "runs along very much the same lines as my own thoughts." Within the Wilson cabal the United States of America was merely an instrument for furthering the President's ambitions. See *U.S. Foreign Relations, The Lansing Papers,* vol. 1, pp. 470–471.

Before sending the fateful note to Germany the President took care to fortify his image as a man devoted to peace and to rally the people around his soon-to-be-announced stand for "right," which he hoped might bring war. On May 10, in the course of a routine speech in Philadelphia on America as "the hope of the world," Wilson slipped in an oblique reference to the three-day-old *Lusitania* sinking. "There is such a thing as a man being too proud to fight. There is such a thing as a nation being so right that it does not need to convince others by force that it is right." Being "too proud to fight" cost Wilson some severe heckling in the Republican press, but in fact his remark was a master stroke. In the months ahead even the bitterest critics of Wilson's diplomacy could not bring themselves to conclude that a President who had uttered such words at such a time could possibly want war. In fact, Wilson's distinction between "fighting" and being "right" was utterly specious, if not in a barroom then certainly in diplomacy.[26]

The *Lusitania* note, which Bryan signed, he told Wilson, "with a heavy heart," was sent to Germany on May 13. The claims it made for Americans' right to travel (Wilson's first explicit public reference to the right) were sweeping. So, too, were the corresponding demands it made upon Germany. "The lives of non-combatants, whether they be neutral citizens or citizens of one of the nations at war, cannot lawfully or rightfully be put in jeopardy by the capture or destruction of an unarmed merchantman." In observing that rule, the note pointed out significantly, it was not sufficient to allow those aboard a merchantman to escape in lifeboats. That, too, violated the right to travel. Since a submarine had no room to take aboard a merchantman's passengers, "Manifestly submarines cannot be used against merchantmen, as the last few weeks have shown, without an inevitable violation of many sacred principles of justice and humanity." Germany must not only cease sinking enemy ships without warning, it must cease using submarines against enemy shipping entirely. America's concern in securing "justice and humanity" arose first from American citizens' "indisputable rights in taking their ships and traveling wherever their legitimate business calls them upon the high seas" and secondly, on the duty of the American government to "sustain them in the exercise of their rights." Germany was to admit the illegality of the *Lusitania* sinking, make reparation, and "take immediate steps to prevent the recurrence of anything so obviously subversive of the principles of warfare." The note ended with a threat: "The Imperial German Government will not expect the Government of the United States to omit any word or any act necessary to the performance of its sacred duty of maintaining the rights of the United States and its citizens and of safeguarding their free exercise and enjoyment." Germany would have to abandon the submarine or face the prospect of war with the United States over a "sacred duty" which, a mere three months before, scarcely a single American, ignorant or expert, even knew existed.[27]

That Germany would bow to the President's sweeping and unprecedented demand Wilson had no more reason to expect than did House, or, for that matter the elated British government, whose press organ hailed Wilson's note, understandably, as "the greatest event of this war." Engaged in a life-and-death struggle, a belligerent, even in the friendliest atmosphere, would have found it difficult and humiliating to surrender a major weapon of war on the demand of a foreign power. Wilson, however, had already poisoned the atmosphere so thoroughly that the difficulty and the humiliation were multiplied immeasurably. He had shown gross partiality to the British; he had condoned their starvation policy; he had surrendered America's neutral rights to Germany's enemies. How could he expect the German government to surrender to its enemies' friend and to do so, moreover, in the name of a neutral right of no consequence? The German government dreaded the prospect of war with America, but as Wilson well knew, the hostility he had aroused among the German people, their clamorous demand that submarine war continue, made it politically dangerous for the German government to accede absolutely to so sweeping a fiat. As for the logic of Wilson's position, the President could scarcely expect the German government to be persuaded by a legal argument that had failed to convince his own secretary of state.[28]

The truth is, Wilson not only did not expect Germany to bow to his demands, he did not want Germany to bow to his demands. This is one reason why Wilson looked with a jaundiced eye on popular approval of his note, for the grounds of that approval were not at all propitious. Americans at large were chiefly relieved that the President had not sent a war ultimatum. As the President remarked to a woman correspondent, popular trust in his peace-keeping efforts were touching, but "I may have to sacrifice it all any day, if my conscience leads one way and the popular verdict the other." More important, it was the reason why the President rejected out of hand every sensible suggestion for averting the impending crisis.[29]

Desperate to forestall an imminent rupture with Germany, Bryan urged two such proposals on the President. One was to make it easier diplomatically for Germany to accede to the President's demands. Since Wilson ostensibly was defending "humanity" in warfare, there seemed no reason why the President would object to doing so. "We unsparingly denounce the retaliatory methods employed by [Germany]," Bryan wrote the President on May 13, "without condemning the announced purpose of the Allies to starve the non-combatants of Germany and without complaining of the conduct of Great Britain in relying on passengers, including men, women and children of the United States, to give immunity to vessels carrying munitions of war." Under those conditions Germany could not bow to our demands unless the United States, at least, sent an immediate "protest against the objectionable conduct of the Allies." It was, said Bryan, "the only way, as I see it, to prevent irreparable injury" to German-American relations. Lansing, too, agreed with Bryan that a protest should be dispatched to Britain. Four days later, Bryan, after talking to the Austrian ambassador, again urged the President to send a stern note of protest to Britain. "It will give Germany an excuse [to accede] and I think she is looking for something that will serve as an excuse." At rebutting sensible arguments with empty sophistry, however, Wilson was a practiced hand. On May 20 he curtly rejected Bryan's suggestion that a protest note be sent to Britain.* "We cannot afford even to seem to be trying to make it easier for Germany to accede to our demands

---

* Wilson's determination to make it as hard as possible for Germany to accede to his demands is underscored by the fact that the President was under strong economic pressure at the time to defend America's neutral rights against Britain. The South's politically influential cotton interests were particularly incensed over Britain's cutting off their European markets. To get the South off his back, Wilson tacitly allowed the British to cut off America's European cotton market completely in return for Britain's offer to buy American cotton and so keep up the price. When Germany made the same offer, Wilson rejected it indignantly. It was a "palpable bribe," he told Lansing. However the only difference between the two offers was that the British were bribing us to surrender our rights while the Germans were trying to bribe us to enforce them. See Link, *Wilson,* vol. 3, pp. 604–612.

by turning in similar fashion to England concerning matters which we have already told Germany are none of her business." Wilson was risking war, ostensibly, to secure "justice and humanity" in naval warfare, but if "justice and humanity" were to be served by a German accession at the price of no war, then "justice and humanity" would have to be sacrificed, sacrificed to a concocted punctilio, for quite obviously Wilson's argument was no argument at all. It was simply one pretext for not averting a crisis piled on top of a pretext for forcing one.[30]

Bryan's second suggestion for avoiding "irreparable injury" was even easier to handle for a President standing on "the firm ground of right." If, as the President insisted, Americans were entitled to travel safely to Europe on British ships, the simple way to secure their safety, Bryan suggested, was to prohibit British passenger ships from carrying munitions. "I have no doubt," he wrote the President on May 17, "Germany would be willing to so change the rules in regard to submarines as to exempt from danger all passenger ships that did not carry munitions." In that way Americans could travel safely on British liners—what more could the President properly demand?—and the American government would not have to risk war by ordering Germany to give up the submarine. "A person would have to be very much biased in favor of the Allies," as Bryan aptly put it to the President, "to insist that ammunition intended for one of the belligerents should be safe-guarded in transit by the lives of American citizens."[31]

Bryan found strong support for his proposal from the American ambassador to Germany, James Gerard, a former Tammany Hall judge who, like most ordinary Americans, found it impossible to understand why anyone would want "to enter this awful war," as he put it to Colonel House, "to enforce a right which is of no practical use." There was, he reported from Berlin, a strong segment of the German government willing to guarantee the safety of Americans "who insist in traveling on British ships" if the United States government, in turn, would guarantee that such passenger ships sailed unarmed and carried no war contraband. This was a sensible solution, Gerard cabled Washington, "if you do not desire to go to extremities." It took Gerard several weeks to realize that going to "extremities" was exactly what Wilson wanted. Until he did, the

American ambassador, with considerable pertinacity and candor, bombarded Washington with his compromise proposal. By effecting such a compromise with Germany, Gerard wrote on his fourth try, America would have secured "a reasonable solution" to the whole problem of travel. "The safety of American passengers desiring to cross the ocean even on English ships is provided for. Anyway why should we enter a great war because some American wants to cross on a ship where he can have a private bathroom? ... On land no American sitting on an ammunition wagon could prevent its being fired on on its way to the front and England made land rules applicable to the sea when she set the example of declaring part of the open sea war territory; nor can English passenger ships sailing with orders to ram submarines and often armed be put quite in the category of altogether peaceful merchantmen."[32]

Here was yet another voice of common sense raised within the Wilson administration, and it suffered a predictable fate. Wilson instructed Lansing to order Gerard to cease talking compromise with Germany. "The President," Gerard was told, "is determined not to surrender or compromise in any way the rights of the United States or of its citizens as neutrals." So much for securing, as a practical matter, safe passage for Americans traveling on belligerent liners. About the actual safety of American travelers Wilson cared nothing.[33]

It was neither Bryan nor Gerard but the German government that forestalled temporarily a rupture of diplomatic relations. On May 28, Germany sent what it termed a preliminary note calling attention to certain factual allegations about the *Lusitania*—some true, some false—and inviting the American government to review them before Germany made a "final statement of its position with regard to the demands made in connection with the sinking of the *Lusitania*." Dealing with a mere preliminary reply, Wilson could make no decisive statement in response. He did, however, make short shrift of the German note. There were no mitigating facts to investigate, the President insisted in his draft note of reply. In its demands upon Germany the United States was "contending for nothing less high and sacred than the rights of humanity." The demands enunciated on May 13 still stood unaltered. Wilson did, however, take the occasion to close one loophole left open in his earlier note. At that time, as a concession to Bryan, he had confined America's travel rights to "unarmed" merchantmen. Scores of British merchantmen were now furnished with arms. The solution was simple. In Wilson's reply to Germany's preliminary note the word "unarmed" was changed to "unresisting." Americans now had the "sacred" right to travel safely on armed belligerent merchantmen, too.[34]

Secretary Bryan, weary and humiliated by his long futile struggle with the President, was in a state bordering on nervous collapse. Regarded by the people at large as a man peculiarly devoted to peace, he was now scarcely more than a name attached to diplomatic notes which he bitterly opposed. After the June 1 cabinet meeting, a meeting in which Bryan hotly accused his colleagues of taking sides with the Allies, the secretary of state took his stand in the last ditch. He told Wilson flatly that he could not, in good conscience, sign the new note. Four days later, after the President curtly rejected once again all of Bryan's suggestions for averting crisis and keeping the peace, Bryan took his courage and his political life in his hands and decided to resign. It was a harrowing decision for Bryan, for he was well aware of the reception awaiting him. The administration, the big city press, and the leading politicians of both parties would assail him from every side. Politically, the country was no longer what it had been a mere five weeks before. Since Wilson had taken his public stand on the right to travel, the lines of battle in America's fateful civil war over war had already begun to take shape.

Among the vast majority of Americans the perilous implications of Wilson's diplomacy were slowly sinking in. The prospect of serious trouble, perhaps even war, over the dubious right of a few heedless Americans to travel on belligerent ships was beginning to alarm the people at large. Previously they had taken peace for granted. They could take it for granted no longer. Peace sentiment—antiwar sentiment—was becoming active and vocal.* As early as June 4, two powerful Virginia Democrats, Senator Thomas

* It was always far more vocal in the South, West, and Midwest than in the East. This sectional difference was due in large measure to the fact that in those sections plain people could still make themselves heard. In the East, antiwar elements were almost as strong numerically as elsewhere, but the commonality in the East, as always, had a far weaker voice in public affairs than their fellow citizens elsewhere.

Martin, the boss of the state, and Representative Hal Flood, chair-man of the House Foreign Affairs Committee, wrote to Bryan warning him that the administration was pushing the *Lusitania* af-fair far beyond what the electorate would tolerate. That was only a harbinger. By early July active antiwar sentiment, almost entirely spontaneous, would become a force to be reckoned with.[35]

What alarmed the many, however, brought hope to a few. All those who thought they had anything to gain from war (see next chapter) saw in Wilson's diplomacy the chance—a quite unexpect-ed chance—to begin actively pushing the country toward war with Germany. In the wake of Wilson's public stand on the right to trav-el, a small determined crypto-interventionist faction began to crys-tallize outside as well as inside the administration. Since the fac-tion was recruited almost entirely from among the powerful, the rich, and the influential (and their inevitable clients, protégés, and fuglemen), it was they who, by definition, had primary access to the organs of opinion. They were determined to destroy Bryan be-fore he could marshal the vast majority against the President's promising diplomacy. It was an understandably frightened ex-sec-retary of state who came before the cabinet on June 8 to bid fare-well to his colleagues. "I go out into the dark," said Bryan. "The President has the prestige and the power on his side." Then Bryan's voice cracked and he abruptly remarked: "I have many friends who would die for me." Far fewer, however, than he supposed.[36]

When Bryan's resignation was publicly announced, the former secretary of state was not merely attacked; he was crucified. "Nev-er," recalled Oswald Garrison Villard, publisher of the New York *Evening Post,* "did a greater storm of abuse and vituperation burst upon a public man." Had Bryan stood accused of betraying mili-tary secrets in wartime he could not have been assailed with greater fury. Wilson's house organ, the New York *World,* cried down Bryan's resignation as "an act of unspeakable treachery." Another Democratic newspaper, the Louisville *Courier-Journal,* proclaimed that "men have been shot and beheaded, been hanged, drawn and quartered for treason less serious." From one end of the country to the other, the major metropolitan dailies (with a few exceptions in Dallas, Akron, Pittsburgh, and Chattanooga) were virtually unani-mous in their frenzied determination to depict William Jennings

Bryan, who thought the right to travel not worth a war, as one of
the darkest villains of American history, or, at the very least, as one
of its most despicable cowards. While the "hurricane of abuse," as
the secretary of the treasury, William McAdoo called it, pelted
down on Bryan's head, the "Commoner," returning to his native
Nebraska, found himself shunned by the Democrats of Omaha.[37]

Despite the crucifying of Bryan, however, the antiwar sentiments
of the American people were still able to make themselves heard
and heard vociferously in the summer of 1915. Had they not been
heard, had they not been strong, had they not been virtually unanimous, there is little reason to doubt that the United States would
have been at war with Germany in 1915. Diplomatically the stage
was set. On July 8, the German government, after secretly instructing its submarines not to sink large enemy liners without warning,
gave its defiant reply to Wilson's *Lusitania* demands. It insisted
that its submarine policy was justified reprisal against the British
starvation policy and that British Admiralty instructions had
"obliterated" the distinction between merchantmen and warships.
It contended that since the British had treated the North Sea as
though it were land, the neutral right to travel safely no longer existed. "The Imperial German Government is unable to admit that
American citizens can protect an enemy ship through the mere fact
of their presence on board." Germany suggested a compromise to
ensure Americans safe passage through the war zone, but as Lansing, now secretary of state, pointed out to Ambassador Gerard, it
refused to concede that America was right "in principle."[38]

The next logical step in Wilson's diplomacy was obvious. Having
demanded with utmost rigor that Germany abandon its submarine
warfare, what was required now was to put the demand in the form
of an ultimatum: Accede within a given span of time or face some
kind of reprisal, a rupture of diplomatic relations being the most
feasible. Unfortunately for Wilson, the moment to strike hard had
already passed in July. Antiwar sentiment, growing in vocal force
for weeks, was galvanized and intensified by the German note.
From every quarter the electorate began demanding that the President pursue the *Lusitania* affair no further. From Indiana, a congressman warned the administration that the people of his district
were not only opposed to war, but were "very much afraid that the

Administration is going to pursue Germany until we become involved with her." Their solution to the diplomatic crisis, he said, was simple: "To thunder with the free seas. Stay out of the war zone, then there will be no Americans sent to the bottom of the ocean." An Ohio congressman warned Lansing: "Under no circumstance now in sight will Congress vote for war." Ex-Senator Beveridge called Wilson's stand on travel "absolutely indefensible." The eminent Catholic prelate Cardinal Gibbon spoke for millions when he remarked in the *New York Times* that "it seems like asking too much to expect the country to stand up and fight just because a few travelers are overdaring." Even within the administration there were rumblings of antiwar sentiment. On July 16, the solicitor of the State Department, a Texan named Cone Johnson, wrote to Lansing a long, closely reasoned, and impassioned argument for compromise on the right to travel, a compromise that would prohibit British liners, in Johnson's words, from carrying "mixed cargoes of babies and bullets."[39]

The public onslaught shook Lansing's resolve. On July 14 he obliquely suggested to Wilson that diplomatic retreat might be prudent. "As I read the state of mind of the vast majority of the people, it is that they do not want war, that no war spirit exists." The next day, Lansing tried again to persuade Wilson to modify his stand. "Is it possible," he delicately asked the President, "to be firm and at the same time compromise?" If he pushed Germany too hard, Lansing pointed out, the "public consequences" could be dangerous.[40]

Wilson would admit no compromise and make no retreat. The public outcry persuaded him, however, that an ultimatum was now out of the question. In his July 21 reply to Germany the most Wilson could do was make his note as harsh and as hostile as possible. All Germany's various arguments he vehemently rejected. "The Government of the United States . . . cannot consent to abate any essential or fundamental right of its people because of a mere alteration of circumstance," referring to the nature of the submarine, the British starvation policy, the British North Sea military area, and indeed all the "mere" actualities of the real world in which diplomacy is conducted. "The rights of neutrals in time of war are based upon principle not upon expediency and the principles are immutable," except when they hampered Germany's enemies. As for proposed arrangements for ensuring safe passage for American travelers, they were, according to Wilson, utterly unacceptable. "The very agreement would, by implication, subject other vessels to illegal attack." To the question posed by Bryan, by Cone Johnson, by Ambassador Gerard and others, namely, why should the American government do more, at most, than secure safe passage for Americans in the war zone, Wilson's answer was, quite simply, that he was not concerned about actual American lives, but with defending the "immutable" laws of humanity. The note concluded with a threat that sent a wave of fear and anger through Germany. If a German submarine violated an American's travel rights, the United States government would regard it as a "deliberately unfriendly" act. Whatever else Wilson was, there can be no doubt he was implacably determined. When he wrote those ominous words, Americans in every walk of life were expressing their opposition to waging war in defense of the right to travel. Yet here was Wilson, undeterred, solemnly declaring that the violation of that right by a German submarine virtually constituted a *casus belli*. Even at its most clear and intense, the antiwar sentiments of the American people could do no more with Woodrow Wilson than temporarily impede his war course.[41]

Wilson's failure to rupture relations with Germany angered and disappointed the British government. Sir Edward Grey bluntly warned Colonel House (who was now back in America) that Wilsons's failure might well cost the President his "influence in the future." Colonel House hastened to make amends for his friend. On August 4, he wrote to Ambassador Page to explain the difficulties under which the President was laboring. Wilson could not have been more truculent over the *Lusitania,* House pointed out, because "ninety percent of our people do not want the President to involve us in war." Had he pushed the *Lusitania* crisis further than he had, "his influence would have been broken and he would not be able to steer the nation, as he now is, in the way which in the end will be best for all. He sees the situation just as you see it and as I do, but he must necessarily heed the rocks."[42]

The "rocks," which is to say, the American people, were still jutting out of the diplomatic waters when a German submarine on

August 19 sunk the British liner *Arabic* with the loss of two American lives. For several days the United States teetered on the brink of war. The German government, thoroughly alarmed, managed to frustrate the American President by two timely concessions. On September 1, the German government, ignoring Wilson's rejection of compromise, publicly pledged itself never to sink large enemy passenger liners without warning and provision for the safety of passengers and crew. Some weeks later the German government, still facing the threat of war, publicly admitted that the German submarine commander had violated secret Admiralty instructions in effect since June. Such being the case, Germany formally disavowed the commander's action in attacking the *Arabic*. With Germany conciliatory and the American people opposed to war there was nothing for Wilson to do but watch the *Arabic* crisis evaporate in his hands. It was an understandably irritated President who complained to Colonel House in September that popular opposition to war was keeping him "in bonds."⁴³

10

*"Never Before Were
More Lies Told"*

If the interests of the country or even the desire to win elections had shaped the policy of Republican Party leaders, Wilson's diplomacy would have provided a political target impossible to miss. Impeaching it would not even have required an alteration in the Republicans' customary policies and pretensions. As the party of vigorous nationalism, Republicans could have assailed the Democratic President for his lame submission to the British, whose arrogance was becoming increasingly insufferable to Americans. As the party of experienced statesmen, they could have mocked Wilson's priggish fight for "fair play" in a remote foreign war. As the party of practical, business-minded leaders, they could have held up to derision the legal pedantry of an ex-professor in the White House who was risking war "to enforce a right of no practical use." An alarmed and puzzled electorate—as alarmed and puzzled as the former secretary of state, the American ambassador to Germany, and the solicitor of the State Department—would have welcomed such Republican opposition as a man lost in a forest welcomes the sight of a familiar landmark. The leaders of the Republican Party provided no such opposition and offered the electorate no recognizable landmarks. Instead they supported Wilson's diplomacy and worked to strengthen his hand in every possible way.

Their reason was obvious. Wilson's diplomacy opened up the

prospect of war, and war was what the Republican oligarchy wanted and needed. Behind that desire lay a single overriding ambition: the restoration of themselves as the governing council of an "aristocratic republic," which meant, in practice, the restoration of the halcyon days of 1900. Without a war prospects were dim for the Republican oligarchy. The electorate of 1915 was not the electorate of 1900. The "respectable classes" had broken away from the oligarchy's control; faith in "party government" had been shattered like Humpty Dumpty. Although Wilson's legislation had momentarily blunted the progressive rebellion and Roosevelt's fading Progressive Party had taken thousands of active citizens out of Republican Party politics, both conditions, though welcome, provided only a respite. Worse yet, America's industrial workers, once the mainstay of the Republican Party's voting strength, were showing a disturbing want of gratitude for their officially vaunted "American" wages. In 1915 their discontent was publicly substantiated by an official arm of Congress itself. The United States Commission on Industrial Relations, after dealing harshly with Rockefeller, Morgan, and Carnegie during sensational hearings in January and February 1915, reported in August that industrial wages were not only low, but were kept artificially low by the lawless greed of the industrial magnates. "The workers of the nation, through compulsory and oppressive methods, legal and illegal, are denied the full product of their toil. . . . Citizens numbering millions smart under a sense of injustice and oppression. The extent and depth of industrial unrest can hardly be exaggerated." If nothing else, the years of reform agitation, reform promises, and reform investigations had virtually eliminated from the public life of the country the two mainstays of oligarchic rule in America: the apathy of the well off and the mean gratitude of the ill treated. All the official myths had toppled. There was an unruly ferment in the political atmosphere. To Frederick Howe, for one, the years between 1912 and 1915 were the freshest, the most liberated, the most exhilarating time he had ever known.[1]

The Republican oligarchy was not exhilarated. The party's leaders understood quite clearly that the only real chance for a restoration of their old hegemony lay in a radical transformation of the American people themselves. "It isn't merely a willingness to fight

that is required," said Elihu Root, referring to party efforts to incite bellicose jingoism among the electorate, "it is a change in the
whole attitude of the people toward government." Americans must
be taught, said Root's protégé, Henry Stimson, secretary of war
under Taft, to think more of their duties toward the government
and less of what they can "get." A drilled and disciplined electorate, submissive toward its rulers, expecting nothing of its government, was the civic condition the Republican Party needed and
sought. Nothing in the domestic politics of the United States could
possibly bring it about. Only the cataclysm of a major foreign war
could undo the deep damage of the preceding ten years. Out of
power the Republican oligarchy had few, if any, scruples. Imperial
Germany was not decadent Spain, the right to travel was not a battle cry on a par with "Cuba Libre," the trenches of France were
not ninety miles from our shores. It is a measure of how desperate
the Republican oligarchy had grown under the impact of defeat
that once Wilson opened up the prospect of war Republican leaders
were prepared, in the face of overwhelming public sentiment, to
muster all their political power to bring war about.[2]

The Republican oligarchs' resolve to push for war was strengthened by support they had not enjoyed in 1898—the major Wall
Street capitalists, the futile peace faction in the days of "Cuba
Libre." Contemporary Americans believed that Wall Street interests wanted war because only an Allied victory would redeem their
holdings in Allied securities. However, since they avidly supported
Wilson's war course several months before they invested in British
government securities, the true explanation lies elsewhere. In fact
their motives were far deeper, far stronger, and far more comprehensive than mere concern for repayment of loans. What they
wanted, in essence, was what the Republican oligarchy wanted: the
restoration of their former place in the councils of government, the
restoration of their lost prestige, and the recovery of their lost political security. In the days of McKinley they had been open partners in rule; within a dozen years they had become mere privileged
clients of government, dependent on unreliable politicians and
hated by the public at large. As Bourne shrewdly observed in his
wartime writings, the financial and industrial magnates had not
been hurt financially by the reform era. What they had lost was

their place, their legitimacy, and their "glory." They wanted war, said Bourne, because they saw in war the opportunity to become the great captains of an industrial war machine and partners, once again, in the governance of the country. At least one farsighted spokesman for corporate interests admitted as much almost openly. "Industrial mobilization" for war, said George Perkins in December 1915, would establish "an attitude of understanding and co-operation in the aims of government and business" whereas "not long ago conditions were such that a statesman wouldn't dare be seen talking to a man of industry." With their prestige restored, with their partnership with government reestablished, with the citizenry drilled and submissive, the monopoly capitalists would be able, through a great foreign war, to put an end to all republican opposition to their existence and their privileges.* "Investigated, prosecuted and muckraked," as the wealthy reformer Amos Pinchot put it, Wall Street interests "needed a change in Federal politics as never before in their history." That is why they too joined the Republican oligarchy in the active pursuit of war for "democracy against autocracy." As Bourne put it with bitter truthfulness in June 1917, "Hearts that had felt only ugly contempt for democratic strivings at home beat in tune with the struggle for freedom abroad." Such were the corrupt and reactionary ambitions that Wilson's diplomacy had ushered back into the political arena in the third year of the "new day." Washington had foreseen it all 120 years before. Wilson's diplomatic "partiality" had indeed given to "ambitious, corrupted or deluded citizens (who devote themselves to the favored nation) facility to betray, or sacrifice the interests of their own country, without odium, sometimes even with popularity, gilding with a virtuous sense of obligation . . . the base or foolish complacencies of ambition, corruption or infatuation."[3]

Despite their great power and influence the crypto-interventionists faced a formidable task. On the direct issues of foreign policy,

* Indirect confirmation for this view comes from the active refusal of the Rockefeller family to join in or support in any way the crypto-interventionist activities of the other Wall Street magnates. Having survived the very worst of the reform era—muckraking attacks, harsh investigations, a President's condemnation, and a successful antitrust suit—the Rockefellers were far more secure economically and politically than most Wall Street capitalists. It was just this want of security that turned Wall Street interests into interventionists. See Amos Pinchot, *History of the Progressive Party, 1912–1916,* 1958, p. 217.

the Republican oligarchy could do little except give its unswerving support to the Democratic President. Wilson's war course was a walk on a tightrope. There was no way for Republicans to urge him forward without pushing him off. Given the nearly unanimous public opposition to war, straightforward warmongering was out of the question. It would have brought not war, but political disaster to the agitators. Even straightforward jingo nationalism was out of the question. The Republican oligarchy could not demand, in their usual fashion, that Wilson stand up more belligerently for America's interests. Since genuine neutrality was America's interest, the interests of the United States formed the one standard of political judgment that every crypto-interventionist tried desperately to evade. Nor could the oligarchy effectively demand that the Democratic President stand up more strongly for America's neutral rights. The demand invariably invited the retort—often from Republicans beholden to German-American votes—that the President stand up at last against Britain. Since it worked in favor of genuine neutrality, straightforward jingo nationalism actually imperiled the war course. Neither could Republicans demand vociferously that Wilson take stronger measures in defense of the right to travel. They understood quite clearly that Wilson was already pushing that pretext to its limits. In August 1915, the bellicose Roosevelt complained privately that "the Republican politicians have been afraid to assail" Wilson, but Lodge, Root, Philander Knox, and other Republican foreign policy leaders were far shrewder than the frenzied ex-President. They knew there was only one way to war: through the devious, vulnerable diplomacy that Wilson had personally concocted.[4]

That diplomacy had to be defended not criticized, and Republican leaders duly rallied to its defense. Was the President partial to the Allies? No, insisted Senator Lodge, reverting to the "humanitarianism" of his Cuba days. The "human rights" Wilson asserted against Germany were "more important than American dollars" lost through the British blockade. That happened to be the official line of the Wilson administration. Eastern Republican newspapers even insisted, quite falsely, that Britain was doing to neutral commerce only what the great Lincoln had done in the Civil War. That, too, was the administration's official line. Was Wilson's diplomacy leading toward war? Republican interventionists, like their Democratic counterparts, insisted that Wilson's diplomacy alone was keeping America out of it. Was Wilson's interpretation of international law unsound? "In the matter of international law I am ready to follow our State Department pretty closely," said Lodge's son-in-law, Augustus Gardner of Massachusetts, who came as close to being an open interventionist as any man in Congress.[5]

Republican leaders did more than defend Wilson's diplomacy. Invoking the repressive virtues of wartime, they proclaimed it the "patriotic duty" of every "loyal" American to "stand by" the President, as if America were already at war and the enemy at the gates. "I will not criticize his attitude in the European matter," declared old Joe Cannon. "It is not a time for partisanship." Although Republicans mercilessly attacked Wilson's Mexican policy, "in the European matter" they mercilessly assailed his critics. "In the European matter," by Republican fiat, the Democratic President stood above reproach. Wilson's great and growing power in the country, the celebrated force of his autocratic will, were largely the gifts of the Republican oligarchy. When Republican leaders pulled the props out from under Wilson in 1919, his power, seemingly so awesome, was to collapse in a matter of months.[6]

As long as Americans remained almost universally opposed to war, however, even the most vigorous support of Wilson's diplomacy could not bring about war, for public opinion severely hampered that diplomacy. From the President on down the question every crypto-interventionist faced was how to weaken and nullify that opposition. If straightforward war agitation was impossible, if even straightforward jingoism was ruled out, some other kind of propaganda was needed. The crypto-interventionists found their answer in the relatively safe issue of national defense, to which they gave the enticing name of "preparedness"—"a word," as Senator James Vardaman of Mississippi was to say on the eve of war, "that will stand as a colossal blood-stained monument marking the turning point in the life of this Government." Under the pretext of calling for a stronger military defense in the interests of *peace,* the interventionists in the Republican oligarchy, their counterparts on Wall Street and in Congress, and the administration turned "preparedness" into a frenzied crusade, an organized national movement to arouse war hysteria, to incite fear and hatred of Germany, to cry up "national honor," to cow into silence those who spoke for the citizenry, and to confuse with alarmist predictions of foreign invasion, with lurid pictures of a "defenseless America," with ceaseless talk of warships and "citizen armies," the all-too-plain issues of war and peace.[7]

The preparedness movement had nothing to do with the nation's defenses. It was crypto-war agitation intended, as Roosevelt frankly put it to a British correspondent, "to get my fellow countrymen into the proper mental attitude" for war without actually calling for it openly. The American people, Roosevelt explained, were too timid and pacifistic to tolerate frank talk of intervention. The goal of the movement was put even more graphically by Robert Bacon, a former assistant secretary of state and a Republican leader of the preparedness agitation. "In America," Bacon explained to a Frenchman, "there are 50,000 people who understand the necessity of the United States entering the war immediately on your side. But there are 100,000,000 Americans who have not even thought of it. Our task is to see that the figures are reversed."[8]

Reactionary in its leaders, reactionary in its ultimate goals, the preparedness movement was almost explicitly an organized anti-reform movement, a counterrevolt of the powerful and the privileged "to undo," as California's reform governor Hiram Johnson put it, "the progressive achievements of the past decade." At the movement's peak in 1916, when it had behind it the power, prestige, and eloquence of President Wilson himself, preparedness advocates scarcely bothered to conceal their ultimate political goals. What America needed, they said, was not merely military preparedness but "moral preparedness." This was to be achieved through universal military training, through "patriotic education," through military drill in the public schools. They called for a new militarized polity—a "Prussianized" America, antipreparedness spokesmen called it—that would forge a "national soul" and overcome "domestic shortcomings and discord." "Moral preparedness" would undo the damage resulting from "the dissolution of party ties" and the "shock that has been given to the party system of government." It would bring the blessings of "complete internal peace." Through universal military training (a virtual code word for war since peacetime conscription had not the slightest chance of being enacted by Congress) Americans would be taught a new "religion of vital patriotism—that is, of consecration to the State." Through proper education and military training, a population of selfish cowards—which was how preparedness agitators commonly described their fellow countrymen—would learn "not to sit supinely under insult, injury and violation of right and law," meaning the right to travel on belligerent merchantmen; learn not to sing disgraceful songs such as the all-too-popular "I Didn't Raise My Boy to Be a Soldier"; learn that opposition to war meant "national loss of self-respect"; learn through the "discipline of the camp" and the schoolhouse drill period "what it means to be an American"; learn, last but not least, that "we have a part to play in the redemption of humanity and the future organization of the world." Openly appealing to every reactionary element in the country, to every businessman frightened of industrial unrest, to every machine politician hoping to revamp his machine, to every infatuated upper class anglophile, the preparedness propaganda held forth the promise of a new nation, conceived in "preparedness" (meaning war), whose citizenry, radically transformed, would ask for nothing from their government save the chance to serve its international goals. "No policy of preparedness can be complete without a strong sense of international duty."[9]

Such appeals came later. Until the *Lusitania* crisis there was no preparedness movement at all, merely a few futile voices raised for improved national defense. Roosevelt had spoken for preparedness as early as late 1914, but by then the ex-President had lost most of his influence in the country. The Republican oligarchy despised him; his progressive supporters had drifted away; his passion for war was so ill-concealed that all Roosevelt won for his pains, as he ruefully observed to a friend in June 1915, was a reputation for being "a truculent and blood-thirsty person." Other preparedness voices were even more feeble. The Navy League, led by retired admirals and steel company magnates, was ready to inform whoever cared to listen that the U.S. Navy, third largest in the world, was virtually a piece of junk. In New York City, future headquarters of the preparedness movement, leading Republicans such as Stimson,

Bacon, and Joseph Choate led a propreparedness "patriotic society" known as the National Security League. Destined to become
the chief nongovernmental engine of the movement, it was beneath
anyone's notice before May 1915. What enfeebled these preliminary efforts was the sheer want of a strong motive. Republican
leaders in the National Security League were chiefly preparing the
ground for a 1916 campaign issue, industrial leaders were lobbying
for a little extra business, and the retired admirals were doing their
usual big navy song-and-dance. It was Wilson's *Lusitania* diplomacy, his extraordinary demand that Germany abandon submarine
warfare against Britain, that supplied the necessary motive—the
prospect of war. Overnight the President's action turned an incon-
sequential lobby into a crypto-interventionist crusade.[10]

The first theme of the agitation was a frenzied propaganda of
bogies and alarms. Germany, according to the "prepareders," was
bent on world domination. Germany, at war's end, would turn next
on America. Dire peril lay ahead. "Wake up, America! " cried the
agitators. The Hun was on the march; America lay supine. Our
navy was worthless, our army a nullity, our coastal defenses mere
toys. The public air suddenly rang with talk of "landing parties"
and "surprise attacks." Amphibious landings across three thousand
miles of ocean suddenly became a commonplace military feat,
which men wholly ignorant of military matters described with fac-
titious precision. James Beck, for example, a former assistant U.S.
attorney general and a leading Republican interventionist, solemnly assured Philadelphians that it would take Germany exactly sixteen days to land precisely 387,000 men on our shores. No absurdity was too great for the crypto-interventionists to propose. In the
summer of 1915 Americans learned for the first time that they
were virtually doomed by 1921 to become "another Belgium," as if
nothing were more plausible than a comparison between a tiny
country abutting Germany and a nation of 100 million a broad
ocean away. No absurdity of the preparedness agitation, however,
was too great for the American press to swallow. Big city newspapers took up the preparedness line with obliging fervor. In vain did
reputable military men point out the fatuity of the alarmist talk
and the military ignorance of the alarmists. When a genuine mili-

tary expert stands in the way of political propaganda, the party press can make itself remarkably deaf to eminent generals.[11]

While the press made Hunnish designs and American weakness the daily fare of millions of readers, a platoon of eager scribblers turned the propaganda into book-length treatises: *Are We Americans Cowards or Fools?; America and the German Peril; The Game of Empires: A Warning to the United States* (preface by Roosevelt); *Are We Ready?* (preface by General Wood); *The Conquest of America: USA, AD 1921.* In *America Fallen: A Sequel to the European War,* the author, an editor of *Scientific American,* described how a German armada would capture Philadelphia and Washington and force a hapless United States to pay a $20 billion indemnity to retrieve them. Like so many other preparedness effusions, it was bought up and distributed free by the Navy League. In *Defenseless America,* Hudson Maxim, brother of the Maxim gun's inventor, provided an enterprising New York film company with subject matter for a sensational movie, *The Battle Cry of Peace.* Opening in New York City on September 9, 1915, the movie showed in alluring detail a sinister, Hunnish-looking enemy laying waste to New York. True to the crypto-interventionist pretense that they were trying only to preserve peace, the movie was advertised in the press as "A Call to Arms—Against War." Day after day, week after week, for months the deluge of alarmist propaganda poured over the country from New York City. "Not a mail pouch is opened in a second-class post office," said a Texas member of Congress, "that does not carry hundreds of letters, circulars, magazines and newspapers urging us to hurry up our preparations before the bogie man gets us."[12]

By midsummer the crypto-intervenionists, taking advantage of the feminist movement, began recruiting their own wives and daughters for the preparedness cause. On July 10, for example, the Navy League created a "woman's section" of "prominent women" who were to organize "patriotic national defense pageants" to help America avert the fate of Belgium. The late Mark Hanna's old outfit, the National Civic Federation, organized its own "Movement for National Preparedness" with yet another "women's section" of "prominent women." J. P. Morgan's daughter served as treasurer. The National Special Aid Society of 597 Fifth Avenue boasted a membership of female prepareders that included, according to the press, "Mrs. William Alexander, Mrs. T. J. Oakley Rhinelander, Mrs. John Jacob Astor, and other women of prominence."[13]

To spread the gospel of preparedness among "prominent men," General Leonard Wood, with the Wilson administration's permission, organized in May a private "businessman's" military training camp at Plattsburgh, New York. In August the press wallowed in patriotic and snobbish ecstasy over the spectacle of 1,007 "men of affairs," including society-page yachtsmen and polo players, Morgan partners and leading Republican interventionists humbly shouldering arms and listening to General Wood describe the social benefits of putting wage workers into uniform.[14]

In that summer of diplomatic crisis and manufactured hysteria, the U.S. Navy threw its weight, too, behind the new discovery that America lay defenseless against transoceanic invasion. The result was a vast "war game" carried out from Maine to Florida, in which half the Atlantic Fleet was asked to repel an "enemy" armada consisting of the other half. In October, readers of the daily press learned that the "enemy" had beaten the "American" navy hands down. America was defenseless indeed. The New York National Guard, for its part, offered a modicum of comfort. In September it demonstrated in a New York park its ability to recapture New York from foreign invaders. The guardsmen's display of prowess in the park, said the visiting governor of Massachusetts, David Walsh, was certain to awaken "an intensely patriotic spirit among the people."[15]

Yet for all the noise and the shouting, for all the shows, pageants, and "prominent women," the preparedness movement made few converts to preparedness. Confined chiefly to lower Manhattan and upper Fifth Avenue, the handiwork of stand-pat Republicans and corporate "patriots for profit" (as the movement's Wall Street adherents were widely known), the movement utterly lacked popular support. That Germany had either the will or the means to invade America at the close of a supremely exhausting war was, as an Ohio legislator put it, "the most preposterous proposition that was ever exploited." Most Americans agreed. The preparedness agitators, however, scarcely expected to convince Americans that Germany was soon to invade us. Their propaganda had quite other aims in mind. Under the pretense of discussing national defense, they were trying, first, to label Germany as America's endemic enemy, and the Allies, by implication, as America's first line of defense. Far more important, the crypto-interventionists were trying to change the question before the nation. Men who tried to discuss the issues of war and peace were to be compelled in the preparedness frenzy to discuss questions of national defense instead. Men who criticized Wilson's diplomacy—Bryan most conspicuously—found themselves forced to defend *unpreparedness* and suffer ready defamation for trying. Audiences at *The Battle Cry of Peace,* for example, learned who was responsible for the destruction of New York and the humiliation of America. Its opening scene showed a "radical pacifist" unwittingly conspiring with a foreign spy to keep America defenseless. Who then was inviting war and invasion? The crypto-interventionists of course knew the answer: It was all those cowards, dupes, and traitors, all those "peace-at-any-price men" who criticized Wilson's diplomacy and who dared to suggest that the right to travel on belligerent merchantmen was an insane reason for war. The preparedness agitation was not meant to persuade but to slander. It did not change public opinion, it poisoned the atmosphere in which opinions were discussed.[16]

That, in truth, was its principal purpose. The crypto-interventionist faction understood quite well that Wilson's diplomacy was indefensible in a free and open debate. Obviously it was false to neutrality, obviously it rested on flimsy legal pretexts, mocked common sense, and disserved the interests of the country. To bring America into the war, truth had to be defamed, honest critics silenced, and free speech suppressed. The crypto-interventionists were equal to the task. "Preparedness" had as many heads as the Hydra. In the summer of the *Lusitania* crisis, the preparedness agitators added a second theme to their original cry for military defense against Teutonic invasion. They discovered "Americanism" and portentously warned the country that America was not a nation at all but merely a weak, disunited hodge-podge of unreliable immigrants.

The discovery was quite sudden. Until the *Lusitania* crisis the powerful and the privileged had not regarded the country's huge immigrant population as a serious problem. The immigrants' fidelity to faithless party machines was a bulwark of the party system, their gratitude for mean wages the chief support of the industrial order. Unfortunately, the foreign-born and their children posed a conspicuous obstacle to war. Irish-Americans were bitterly anti-British, Jewish Americans hated tsarist Russia, Swedish-Americans and German-Americans were strongly pro-German. Overnight, in consequence, the diverse origins of the American people ceased to be an official boast and became instead an official menace.

In the eyes of the crypto-interventionists, the German-Americans formed by far the most dangerous element. With 8.25 million first-generation Americans among them, the German-Americans were not only the largest immigrant group, they were also the most politically powerful. Prosperous, self-possessed, and civic-minded, their fidelity to the Republic proven in their own eyes by their ancestral sacrifices for the Union cause, German-Americans (unlike some other ethnic groups) had no fear of speaking their minds or of holding their elected representatives to account. Animated by their sympathy for Germany, they ceaselessly assailed Wilson's diplomacy, exposed his partiality to Britain, declaimed against his one-sided defense of neutral rights, accused him openly of putting British interests ahead of American interests, all of which, to the discomfort of the interventionists, had the misfortune of being true. Confined to the German-American press, such attacks might not have mattered greatly, but there were scores of legislators directly beholden to German-American votes. When Congress convened in December, "standing by" the President "in the European matter" seemed likely to suffer a setback, and once breached, that flimsy bipartisan dike was all too likely to let in a torrent.

It was the resourceful Roosevelt who first grasped that the danger was in fact an opportunity. Throughout the *Lusitania* summer the ex-President gave speeches not only assailing "ultra-pacifists," "poltroons," and "mollycoddles"—his usual targets—but the "disloyalty" of what he was pleased to call "hyphenated Americans." The charge was base slander. It was not the duty of Americans to believe that Britain was fighting for "democracy," that Wilson's want of neutrality was true neutrality, or that the right to travel safely on belligerent munitions ships was worth a war to defend. Roosevelt's stratagem, which the entire crypto-interventionist faction quickly took up, was obvious enough. If opposition to war and Wilson's diplomacy could be branded the handiwork of foreigners, then native Americans, hopefully, might be less inclined to oppose them. If that opposition could be tarred as "un-American," then more Americans, hopefully, might abide by the new crypto-interventionist dictum that "standing by" Wilson was the duty of every true patriot. If Americans could not be united for war, hopefully they might be induced to turn in hatred against each other. In their determination to drag America into the European war, the crypto-interventionists found no tactic too base to try.[17]

At the White House, the President did more than merely watch these helpful developments. That open criticism was a hindrance to his diplomacy and free speech itself a menace to his ambitions no one knew better than Wilson. From the start he gave the preparedness movement every encouragement save that of his own eloquent endorsement. The reason for that precaution was political: The reformers in the country were almost universally opposed to a military buildup. They saw in preparedness not so much a movement for war (which still seemed remote to most reformers) as a movement led by their inveterate political enemies to defeat reform. "War preparations and emphasis upon militarism," as Frederick Howe put it, "is national suicide to all the things I am interested in." Espousing preparedness, he said, was like "taking poison into the system." To lead the preparedness movement too openly was more than Wilson thought prudent. His reform flank was his weak flank. To protect it Wilson intended, when the time was ripe, to yield, with a hint of reluctance, to the ostensibly overwhelming popular demand for preparedness.[18]

Unfortunately, without the President's support, a New York pamphlet agitation had only the feeblest prospect of resembling the putative voice of the people. The movement needed official encouragement and this Wilson provided through the press. On May 21, for example, at the height of the *Lusitania* crisis, the White House issued a statement calling for an enlarged navy. Only after that did major New York financiers publicly announce their financial support of the Navy League. On July 17, Wilson's secretary of war, Lindley Garrison, announced plans for a 410,000-man "Army of Defense" as a "precautionary measure." On July 21, the day Wilson's third *Lusitania* note was dispatched to Germany, the White House issued two more highly encouraging preparedness statements. The President, said one, favored "proper training of the citizens of the United States to arms." The administration, said the other, was busily at work drawing up a "reasonable program of national defense." "Reasonable" preparedness was to be Wilson's shrewdly chosen middle ground between the so-called frenzied demands of the New York agitators and the antipreparedness views of the "peace-at-any-price" men, whom Speaker Clark duly attacked in the press in the course of crying up preparedness. Since preparedness had nothing to do with national defense, the whole point of Wilson's "reasonable program" was precisely to isolate the foes of preparedness as "peace-at-any-price" extremists. As Colonel House put it to the President on August 8, the great virtue of the preparedness movement was that it would "lessen" Bryan's antiwar influence in the country.[19]

Throughout the *Lusitania* summer, Wilson's press outlet, the New York *World*, encouraged the preparedness agitators with inspired stories from the White House: The President favored a navy second to none; the President was personally drawing up military defense plans; the President intended to make national defense the main theme of his December message to Congress. At the Governors' Conference in August, Secretary of the Navy Josephus Daniels interrupted the usual discussion of state-level affairs by calling for a greatly enlarged navy. At the end of the conference, a half dozen governors, taking the obvious cue from the White House, rose up to urge their fellow governors to return home and organize "a propaganda for preparedness." In the crypto-interventionist agitation to get Americans into "the proper mental attitude" for war, the hand of the President was everywhere; only his powerful voice had yet to be heard.[20]

Like his fellow proponents of war, Wilson, too, was determined to defame the foreign-born in order to silence all who dared speak for the overwhelming majority of Americans. Fortune, on July 23, put the weapon for doing so in the President's hands. On that day a

Secret Service agent, in the course of shadowing a German diplomatic official on the New York "El,"* made off with his briefcase. The contents proved extremely interesting. They showed that the German government was giving money to support a number of German-American newspapers and lobbyists. As an effort to counteract the torrent of pro-Allied propaganda in the American press the German subventions were a feeble affair. Moreover, there was nothing illegal about them. The only crime involved in the whole business was the original theft of the briefcase. Nonetheless it provided Wilson with a perfect opportunity for discrediting his critics. Properly handled by an obliging press, the possibilities were limitless. If criticizing the President for being pro-British was paid German propaganda, then anyone who did so would be open to instant defamation. Such a critic was not neutral at all but a "pro-German," and if "pro-German" he was possibly a paid "conspirator" or at the very least a dupe of the Kaiser. On August 10 Colonel House urged the President to publish the documents at once. "It may in my opinion lead to war," said Wilson's optimistic friend. At the very least, said House, "it will strengthen your hand enormously and will weaken such agitators as Mr. Bryan and Hoke Smith," the latter a Georgia senator who spoke for the cotton interests and criticized the British blockade. Wilson agreed to supply the documents to the *World*, but under the strict proviso that the editors not disclose that it came from the President. Aside from the diplomatic indelicacy of admitting a theft, Wilson felt it best not to be seen leading the crypto-interventionist assault on German-Americans which was now about to commence.[21]

On Sunday, August 15, the *World* spread across its front page the first of its five-installment report on Germany's "elaborate scheme to control and influence the press of the United States." Editors who took their war news and opinions directly from England professed horror at Germany's nefarious designs. On August 16, the *World*, determined to portray the subventions as a limitless plot, branded them a "Conspiracy Against the United States." Other New York newspapers took up the cry. The *Sun* called the

---

* In May, at Wilson's direction, the German Embassy was wiretapped and German officials and their friends put under twenty-four-hour surveillance. See Charles Tansill, *America Enters the War*, 1938, pp. 355–356.

subventions "sowing the seeds of treason." The *Herald* divined in them "a plot to ruin America." The *Evening Sun* likened Germany's propaganda efforts to "political assassination," the assassination by just criticism of President Wilson. The *Evening World* called it a "conspiracy on a colossal scale."[22]

Having laid down the proposition that German-American criticism of Wilson's diplomacy was the vile fruit of a vast foreign conspiracy, the party press quickly demonstrated its political utility. On August 18, the *World* reported that petitions from southern cotton growers asking the President to stand up to the British would have to be regarded as the work of "pro-Germans," which now meant paid agents of the Kaiser. The war faction took up the stratagem at once. In early September, for example, a German-American newspaper editor was barred from the Union League Club of Chicago for calling Wilson's foreign policy pro-British. For stating what was fairly obvious to everyone he was charged with being "un-American." Plaintively the editor asked why criticizing Wilson was "un-American" when former President Roosevelt did it all the time. The answer to that was simple. Roosevelt stood for war and Wilson stood for neutrality.[23]

For outspoken native Americans there was no safety either. In a vicious organized whispering campaign launched in August, Georgia's Senator Smith was accused of being on the German government payroll. The senator had dared to assert in public that the British blockade violated international law. When Bryan criticized Wilson's views on preparedness, the entire party press savagely assailed the former secretary of state for being "un-American." Stunned by the charge, Bryan asked in a press statement, "When did it become unpatriotic for a citizen to differ from a President?" The answer to that was simple, too. Ever since the powerful and the privileged had united behind Wilson to drag an unwilling people into an unnecessary war.[24]

In the darkening political atmosphere truth was being stood on its head, for Wilson's critics were invariably accused of doing what Wilson himself was guilty of doing. Was the President favoring the Allies? Only a "pro-German" tool of the Kaiser would say so. "Hyphenated Americans," said the *World,* only "sought to injure President Wilson because of his unswerving neutrality." Was the

President sacrificing America's interests for the sake of a belligerent? Only virtual traitors would say so. When German-Americans in New York, angry but undaunted, cheered a non-German speaker who accused Wilson of betraying the American people, the *World* announced that such "disloyalty" was the greatest threat to America since secession. "Even the treason of the copperhead did not extend to promoting the military interests of a European power against the United States." As an anti-preparedness writer put it in 1916: "Perhaps never before were more lies told, more truth suppressed, more insincerity shown" than in the frantic agitation for war carried out under the aegis of "preparedness."[25]

Determined to break the "bonds" of American antiwar sentiment, Wilson decided in early October that it was politically safe to take public charge of the crypto-war agitation. On October 6, the President, in an address before the Civilian Advisory Board of the Navy, came out strongly for a military buildup; overwhelming public sentiment (which was nonexistent) had persuaded him: "I think the whole Nation is convinced that we ought to be prepared, not for war, but for defense, and very adequately prepared." America needed a mighty military establishment, said Wilson, to "command the respect of the world" and safeguard America's "mission." Local politicians, previously leery of anti-preparedness sentiment, immediately took heart. In the wake of Wilson's speech, seventy-five mayors appointed citizens' committees to organize preparedness propaganda—"Mayor's Committee for Defense," they were called. On October 12, the Ohio and Massachusetts legislatures appointed committees to study the establishment of military training in the public schools.[26]

Nor did the President neglect the new repressive theme of "Americanism." Five days after his preparedness speech Wilson, in an address to the Daughters of the American Revolution, called upon "loyal" Americans to assail all "disloyal" critics of his foreign policy. "Hazing," Wilson slyly pointed out, was an old college custom and an excellent one for adults to practice. And who was to be "hazed" by the "loyal" at Wilson's behest? "Everybody," said the President, "who is not to the very core of his heart an American." In detecting the disloyal "heart," Wilson advised the D.A.R., there was one acid test to apply: "Is it America first or is it not?" A President who put both the interests of a belligerent and his own ambitions ahead of the good of America, was calling for vigilante action against anyone who dared say so—in the name of "America first."[27]

On November 4, the President, in a major address, made a still more urgent appeal for preparedness and vigilante "Americanism." The United States, he said, must arm itself not for "attack," not for "aggression," and "not for the satisfaction of any political or international ambition, but merely to make sure of our own security." He called for a greatly enlarged navy and a reserve military force of 400,000 "citizen-soldiers" who would be "asked to enlist"—a Wilsonian euphemism for conscription—for three years of brief annual training with the regular army. To dissociate himself from the Republican alarmists, Wilson assured the country that we were "not threatened from any quarter." At the same time he wanted to speak "in terms of the deepest solemnity of the urgency and necessity of preparing ourselves to guard and protect the rights and privileges of our people, our sacred heritage of the fathers." Unfortunately, warned the President, "voices have been raised in America" which disagreed, voices "which spoke alien sympathies." He called upon "the Nation" to "rebuke" all such people and drown out their voices "in the deep unison of a common, unhesitating national feeling." Having once again invited the war faction to browbeat his critics, Wilson concluded, "Let us lift our eyes to the great tracts of life yet to be conquered in the interests of a righteous peace."[28]

Ugly and repressive though the atmosphere was growing, "great tracts of life" in America remained stubbornly unconquered by Wilson and the war party. The President's speech aroused a storm of opposition around the country. In mass meetings and angry editorials, reformers of every kind thundered their opposition to preparedness. Farm organizations, almost unanimously, registered their adamant opposition to a military buildup. A reform publication, the *Public,* reported that Wilson's progressive supporters "are asking themselves if this is the parting of the ways." As Representative Claude Kitchin of North Carolina put it to Bryan: "It seems that the war goblins and jingoes have caught him. The present attitude of the President, so surprising and disappointing, has worried me more than anything in my political life."[29]

The public outcry drove home a painful truth to Wilson. Despite the "hazing" and "rebukes," despite the risk, as Senator La Follette said, of being denounced "as a fool, a coward or a traitor," liberty in America still menaced the President's ambitions. Too many Americans were still unafraid to speak in behalf of the great majority of the American people. Wilson felt forced to take sterner measures. What those measures should be Wilson outlined on December 7, 1915, in his annual message to Congress, one of the most astonishing speeches ever delivered by an American President. Its sole theme, as the *World* had rightly reported, was preparedness, which now embraced, according to the President, not merely "military efficiency and security" but "industrial and vocational education" as well. Once again Wilson took pains to assure progressives that he had in mind "no thought of any immediate or particular danger arising out of our relations with other nations. We are at peace with all the nations of the world." The real danger to America was not military but political, not external but internal. "The gravest threats against our national peace and safety have been *uttered* within our own borders. There are citizens of the United States, I blush to admit, born under other flags . . . who have poured the poison of disloyalty into the very arteries of our national life." Yet the government, said the President, stood by helpless to deal with those threatening the nation's security from within. He wanted Congress to pass legislation to enable him to "close down over them at once." On December 7, 1915, one hundred fifteen years after the infamous Sedition Act had helped destroy the Federalist Party forever, Woodrow Wilson was suggesting (in vain) that Congress make criticism of his foreign policy a criminal act.[30]

To this had the logic of Wilson's ambitions driven him: The right to travel safely on belligerent merchantmen—his pretext for war— had become the "sacred heritage of the fathers," and freedom of speech—which hindered his ambitions—had become a national menace. Whom the gods would destroy—and they were to destroy Wilson in 1919—they first make mad.

Despite the contrived furor over "defenseless America" and the "hyphenate menace," America's relations with Germany appeared more peaceful in the autumn of 1915 than they had for many months. Germany's September 1 pledge not to sink enemy passenger lines without warning proved immensely gratifying to the American people. Oswald Villard's New York *Evening Post,* one of the few genuinely neutral papers in the East, spoke for millions when it hailed the pledge as a "tremendous moral victory won by the President." Bryan, whom the administration was bent on destroying, wired his congratulations to Wilson and Lansing for their "successful settlement of the submarine controversy." Overnight public alarm over Wilson's diplomacy gave way to pride and relief. America's President, however, felt otherwise. To Wilson, the German pledge, unsolicited, unwanted, and indeed rejected in advance, proved a major setback for his war plans. The German government had hoped it would be. That Wilson was seeking a pretext for intervention German leaders understood clearly enough. "America," as the Kaiser put it in a memorandum explaining why he agreed to the September 1 pledge, "must be prevented from participating in the war against us as an active enemy." That Wilson was a hostile neutral was of course manifest by then.[31]

What endangered Wilson's ambitions was that the American people agreed implicitly (and not for the last time) with the German Imperial government. Since British passenger liners were in fact major munitions carriers, the Germans believed they had made a major concession to the American President. So did the American people. The German government believed that Wilson was now obligated to secure a comparable concession from Britain. So did the American people. After the submarine pledge Americans began demanding that the President vindicate at long last American neutral rights against Britain. Impartiality is the first duty of a neutral and the American people remained resolutely neutral in their outlook, which was why Wilson and the war party were doing everything in their power to slander and discredit those who spoke for genuine neutrality. Given his ambitions, however, Wilson simply could not enforce any neutral right against Britain. Submarine warfare and the British blockade were inseparably linked, a point Bryan had made from the start and which the German government continued to make. Were it politically feasible, Germany's civil government (which was but one faction of Germany's ruling elite) would have abandoned the submarine entirely at the American President's insistence. Given Wilson's failure to vindicate a single American right against Britain, it was politically impossible to do so. If Wilson loosened the British blockade, however, he would sharply reduce the intense pressure on the German government to use the submarine without restriction. Genuine neutrality would cost Wilson his pretext for war over unrestricted submarine warfare. Moreover it would forfeit Britain's good will. If he failed to favor the British, as the British continually warned him, he would lose his place at the peace conference even as a neutral. One way or the other, genuine neutrality would cost Wilson the "noblest part." In spite of popular demands that he stand up to the British, Wilson was determined to give Germany no satisfaction in return for their submarine pledge. As a concession to American opinion he was forced on October 21 to send a protest note to Britain, but House privately assured the British ambassador that it was merely a public sop. It was sent, as Spring-Rice duly reported to the British foreign secretary, "to make a good showing before Congress meets." It was treated in the spirit in which it was sent.[32]

For Wilson a pro-forma protest was merely a stopgap. It would not take long before Americans realized that his fake protest to Britain had been as ineffectual as his previous fake protests had been. Inevitably, as the German government warned, the Germans would remove the restrictions on the submarine. The German government was neither willing nor able to maintain a military concession to the American President when its enemies made none. Yet what was likely to happen when Germany resumed unrestricted submarine warfare? There would be no mass drownings of American travelers to incite war fever; few Americans now cared to travel on belligerent passenger ships. There would be no popular demand for war. Far from it. As matters stood, Americans would probably sympathize with Germany's refusal to restrict the submarine when the British persisted in doing as they pleased.

Such was the calamitous prospect facing Wilson in the autumn of 1915. Since he had no intention of loosening the British blockade, he knew better than anyone that unrestricted submarine warfare would one day be resumed. "Deliberately unfriendly acts" would occur. When they did, he would call for a declaration of war or a rupture of diplomatic relations leading shortly to war. Suppose the American people refused to fight? Suppose they rose up in wrath, not against Germany, but against their own government? The prospect might have shattered the resolve of a Bonaparte. The prospect was to haunt Wilson himself up to and even beyond America's entry into the World War. What it did not do was weaken Wilson's resolve to bring America, one way or another, into that war. Instead it prompted him to make two fresh diplomatic starts intended to ensure as far as possible a war that the American people might be willing to tolerate. One was a frantic effort to revive the faded *Lusitania* crisis. The other was a remarkable plot to open up a second, or nonsubmarine, road to war.

The plot was prompted by the bait of postwar "influence" that the British foreign secretary perpetually dangled before Wilson via a private correspondence with Colonel House. The bait itself was scarcely subtle. Grey simply told House that the British favored whatever House had already told him the American President favored. On August 10, for example, Grey had suggested to House that "some League of Nations" would be a "pearl of great price" in the establishment of permanent peace and the enforcement of universal postwar disarmament, which were already cheerfully agreed upon as Allied "war aims." On September 22, Grey asked House if Wilson himself would "propose that there should be a League of Nations" in the ultimate settlement. In maundering about universal disarmament and a League of Nations, Grey had little more in mind than keeping Wilson wed to the Allied cause. In expatiating on Wilson's postwar "influence" he chiefly wanted to keep the American President dependent on British good will. For results so favorable to British interests a little clumsy pandering was a small price to pay. Much to Grey's dismay, however, the baiter found himself baited.[33]

In the aftermath of Germany's unwanted submarine pledge, Wilson decided to take Grey at this word. After reading the foreign secretary's September 22 letter, Wilson remarked pointedly to House that he favored mediation to end the war on the basis of universal disarmament. At the time a number of Americans, resolutely neutral and antiwar, were also calling for American mediation to bring about a negotiated settlement. The kind of mediation they had in mind was not at all what Wilson wanted. To make sure that House did not misread his intentions and devise some *neutral* proposal for a negotiated settlement, Wilson decided to tell his intimate adviser for the first time that he actually favored armed intervention. "He had never been sure," he told House, "that we ought not to take part in the conflict."[34]

The quick-witted House needed no further cues from the President. To help Wilson "take part in the conflict," House quickly worked out a truly singular proposal for Wilsonian "mediation" in the European war. The "plan," as House fondly called it, was a plot to concoct under the pretense of mediation a more convincing *casus belli* for Wilson than the enforcement of the right to travel seemed likely to supply. In its preliminary form the plan provided for Wilson to call for peace talks when the Allies secretly told him to do so. The basis of the talks would be the belligerents' willingness to agree to universal postwar disarmament. Should Germany refuse to disarm its military establishment—which meant the overthrow of its ruling class and the monarchy as well—the President of the United States would have a truly lofty reason for going to war. The United States could declare war on Germany as the enemy of universal peace itself. "America could say," as House noted in his diary, " 'We have come to help in a war to end war.' " The great advantage of the scheme, as House later explained to the British foreign secretary, was that Americans were an idealistic people. They were much more likely to support intervention in the name of peace everlasting than over the enforcement of the right to travel on belligerent ships.[35]

On October 8 Wilson and his "second self" met at the White House to discuss the elaborate trap House had prepared against Germany. What made the plan urgent, House pointed out to the President, was that "I thought we had lost our opportunity to break with Germany" over the submarine. America was in grave danger of never getting into the war. The President, said House, must "do something decisive now—something that would either end the war in a way to abolish militarism or that would bring us in with the Allies to help them do it." Since abolishing "militarism" was by now an established synonym for defeating Germany and overthrowing its government, House was proposing that Wilson "do something decisive" that would either defeat Germany or defeat Germany. Even among themselves apparently, House and Wilson spoke in code. The Allies, by secret prior agreement, would give Wilson the signal to offer mediation on the "high grounds" of universal disarmament. "If the Central Powers accepted," House assured the President, "we would then have accomplished a master stroke of diplomacy," as indeed they would have; they would have brought about the millennium. "If the Central Powers refused to acquiesce we could then push our insistence to a point where diplomatic relations would first be broken off and later the whole force of our Government—and perhaps the force of every neutral— might be brought against them."[36]

Formally the plot was equivocal. Either Germany would or would not "acquiesce." In fact House's assurance that the German Imperial government just might consent to political suicide was mere false piety. House clearly felt it would be easier for the high-minded Wilson to enter a conspiracy for war if he could pretend that the conspiracy just might conceivably bring about universal disarmament. The bare possibility justified the conspiracy but Wilson, in fact, neither expected nor sought such an unlikely result. In the end he would agree to offer peace terms so favorable to Germany's enemies that the German government could not conceivably acquiesce. Germany's refusal, of course, was the spring of the trap, the elaborately concocted pretext for employing "the whole force of our Government." House scarcely even pretended to Wilson that his "plan" for abolishing militarism by "mediation" was anything but a war plot. As he reminded the President, it was imperative for America to "abolish militarism" because Germany was bent on world domination and it would be "our turn next."

With hopes high, the enthusiastic House addressed himself next to persuading the British to enter the plot. He foresaw no difficulty there. After all, the President of the United States was offering up the lives and treasure of the American people "practically to ensure victory to the Allies," as House put it in his diary. On October 17, with Wilson's approval, House sent off a letter to the British foreign secretary outlining the plot. In it House laid particular stress on the Allies' control of the trap's mechanism and timing, for the

Allies dreaded a negotiated settlement. The President, he assured Grey, would call for peace talks only when "you consider the time is propitious." As for the crux of the plot, "if the Central Powers were still obstinate, it would probably be necessary for us to join the Allies and force the issue." What belligerent had ever received so handsome an offer from a neutral government?[37]

Much to House's puzzlement and chagrin, however, Sir Edward Grey proved far from enthusiastic about the "plan." In their eagerness to wage war on "high grounds," House and the President had overlooked the gaping flaw in their ingenious plot. They were asking the British to place absolute faith in Wilson's ability to carry an unwilling nation into war over a mere abortive mediation proposal. The risk of misplacing their faith was greater than the British cared to take. The sticking point was civilian war morale. Expecting a long, costly war of attrition and fearful of popular "defeatism," the British government was severely discouraging all talk of a negotiated settlement. The American plan, however, required Britain to agree publicly to peace talks and therein lay the danger. It would mean bringing the whole machinery of war propaganda to a halt. It would evoke, inevitably, all the sternly suppressed sentiment for a negotiated end to the war. If Wilson failed to bring America into the conflict—and Spring-Rice advised his government that Wilson could never bring if off—the British war effort might be damaged irrevocably. The British government simply could not afford to take chances with civilian morale. They were in much the same position that the German government stood in regard to popular demands for unrestricted submarine warfare. Never having fought a mass war before, every belligerent government was intensely fearful of mass disaffection. Tempting though Wilson's offer was in some ways, the British had no wish to gamble everything on a foreign leader who had failed to rupture relations with Germany over the sinking of the *Lusitania*.[38]

The two war conspirators were crestfallen over Grey's wary reply, but Wilson was not one to give up easily. In November he decided to send House to Europe to allay Allied suspicions and press for a formal agreement to the plan. House, said Wilson, was to "let the Allies know how our minds are running" and make it clear, as House in turn put it to the President, "that we considered their cause our cause and that we had no intention of permitting a military autocracy to dominate the world if our strength could prevent it." House was to go to London and beg the British, in effect, for yet another favor, the favor of letting Wilson go to war on its side under one pretext—peace everlasting—instead of the alternative—the right to travel on belligerent merchantmen. House, for one, never grasped the fatuity of his position. The more he insisted to the Allies that America would go to war one way or the other, the less reason the Allies had to favor Wilson with a risky pretext tailored to his domestic political requirements.[39]

Wilson, at any rate, was more farseeing than House. Like the British, he had no intention of gambling his war entirely on a foreign government's cooperation. Unlike House, he did not think the "opportunity" to break with Germany over the submarine had been irrevocably lost. He could ill afford to dispense with the submarine pretext. The urgent task was to make that pretext as convincing a *casus belli* as possible. The President's diplomatic means were now meager. All he had left to work with was a loose end from the *Lusitania* sinking, now a half year in the past and, as far as Americans were concerned, a crisis amicably settled by the German pledge not to sink enemy passenger ships without warning. In foreign relations, however, nothing is easier than borrowing trouble.

On November 2, the Wilson administration curled the diplomatic loose end into a diplomatic trap. That day at a meeting with the German ambassador, Count Johann von Bernstorff, Lansing demanded that Germany admit "very soon" that the sinking of the *Lusitania* was illegal, formally "disavow it," and make reparation through the payment of legal indemnity. The German ambassador was stunned. The *Lusitania* crisis he thought had been settled. The German government, he told Lansing, could not possibly make such an admission. Sinking belligerent merchantment without warning was Germany's justified reprisal against England's illicit "starvation war." That was the position the German government had taken from the start. To admit its illegality meant renouncing forever the effective use of a justified weapon of reprisal. This the

German government would not do precisely because it could not possibly guarantee that the submarine would stay half-sheathed indefinitely. If the stalemated war continued to drag on, if the Allies did not consent to a negotiated settlement, if Wilson's failure to loosen the blockade made the pinch of hunger felt in Germany, no power in the country would be strong enough to withstand public and naval pressure to resume unrestricted submarine warfare. Were it to be resumed after being disavowed, Germany would be a self-condemned criminal state and America's President would have his pretext for war.[40]

That was precisely why Wilson revived the *Lusitania* crisis six months after the sinking. By refusing to vindicate America's rights against Britain he intended to force Germany to resume unrestricted submarine warfare; by first compelling Germany to call that warfare illegal he would hopefully secure his *casus belli*. Wilson's demand was a war trap and Germany was determined to elude it. As Colonel House was to cable Wilson from Geneva: "The civil Government believe that if the blockade continues they may be forced to yield to the navy; consequently they are unwilling to admit illegality of their undersea warfare. They will yield anything but this."[41]

Wilson was equally adamant. From November to February the President struggled to drag Germany into his trap. For three months the German government wriggled desperately to stay out of it. The illegality of all-out submarine warfare Germany would not admit. Anything short of that admission Wilson refused to accept. Week after week Lansing and the President privately bombarded Bernstorff with ominous threats. He was advised, in Wilson's words, that "the matter of the *Lusitania* is just as important and just as acute now as it was the day the news of her sinking arrived." He was told that German failure to admit illegality would be taken by America's President as a "repudiation of the assurances" Germany had given in the *Arabic* sinking. He was warned that a "crisis" was brewing and threatened with a rupture of diplomatic relations. When the negotiations appeared deadlocked, Lansing advised the German ambassador quite untruthfully that "American public opinion is becoming more bitter" and that Germany

cannot procrastinate much longer without "the gravest consequences."[42]

Under Wilson's unremitting pressure the German government
grudgingly gave ground. They offered a formal apology and promised to make reparation. An admission of illegality they refused to
give. As long as they refused, the "crisis" (of which most Americans were scarcely aware) continued. Frantically the German ambassador pleaded with House to work out a compromise. Wilson,
he said, was pushing Germany to the wall. He was forcing her to
make concessions without giving anything in return. For all the
President's talk about neutral rights on the seas, the illicit British
blockade was tighter than ever. To the weary and frightened Count
Bernstorff, Wilson's determination to rake up "the past" and cause
"friction" seemed grossly unfair and unwarranted. How could the
German ambassador realize that Wilson was fighting desperately
himself for the chance to bring peace everlasting to suffering humanity? The negotiations narrowed down to a deadly squabble
over words. Did the German assumption of "liability" in the sinking equal an admission of "illegality"? If so, the trap was set; if
not, the trap was eluded—weighty matters for Wilson to decide.[43]

It was in the midst of this tense struggle—a struggle between a
government still trying to avoid war with America and an American President determined to secure a war that Americans would
tolerate—that Wilson was suddenly reminded that he no longer enjoyed an entirely free hand. On December 21, Lansing was shocked
by a visit from Senator William Stone of Missouri, Democratic
chairman of the Foreign Relations Committee. As Lansing reported to the President, Stone bluntly told him that "we are bearing too
heavily on the Teutonic Allies and we're not pressing Great Britain
as strongly as we should in insisting upon observance of our trade
rights." Lansing gave Stone the administration's stock reply. "Loss
of life seemed to me," Lansing told the Missouri senator, "to require more drastic treatment than loss of property." What shocked
Lansing was Stone's retort. German babies, he said, were "dying
because Great Britain would not allow us to send them condensed
milk." The secretary of state professed himself "disturbed" over
this intrusion of moral sanity from the legislative branch; from the
executive branch it had virtually vanished with the departure of

Bryan. "This seems to me a serious matter," Lansing wrote to the President. "This is indeed not a little disturbing," Wilson wrote back in reply. As Woodrow Wilson well knew, it was on the willingness of the people's elected representatives to betray those who had elected them to Congress that the success of his war course depended.[44]

11

"We Do Not Covet Peace at the Cost of Honor"

When Congress convened in December 1915, Wilson rightly took it for granted that the electorate's antiwar sentiments would be weakly voiced by its elected representatives. The Republican hierarchy's support of Wilson's foreign policy guaranteed that half the Republican opposition in Congress would defend any harsh measures he took against Germany and any partiality he showed to the Allies. The dominant antireform factions of the President's own party— the southern Bourbons and the big city machines—were even more willing than their Republican counterparts to rise above the opinions of the voters. In the summer and autumn of 1915 southern party leaders had obliged the President by turning harshly against Bryan, their onetime champion, for daring to say, rather mildly, that Americans ought not to travel on belligerent merchantmen and that Germany wanted no war with America. Transcending the cotton interests of the South, southern Democrats assailed Georgia's Senator Smith, chief southern spokesman for cotton, for his "treasonable, treacherous attacks ... on the President of the United States." The big city Democratic machines were equally steadfast. Rising above the anti-British sentiments of their Irish-American supporters, they stood faithfully behind the President's pro-British foreign policy. Anglophobia, their old stock in trade, they conveniently shelved just when it would have served the cause of genuine neutrality. Nativism, their stock bogie when it was non-existent, they conveniently overlooked just when a real assault on "hyphenates" begged for a rejoinder from Democrats who had thrived for so long on immigrant votes. As a Wyoming Republican tartly remarked in the House of Representatives, the Democrats in Congress did not have to represent their constituents. "You can tell them you are following your President."[1]

By the time Congress convened the Democratic Party had already made its own signal contribution to the crypto-war propaganda. While Republican interventionists cried up preparedness and "national honor" (meaning the enforcement of the right to travel), Democrats who favored war heaped fulsome praise on Wilson for trying desperately to avert it. This bizarre interpretation of Wilson's diplomacy had one important fact to lend it some credence: Germany's conciliation of Wilson in September, which is to say, Germany's effort to keep America out of the war. According to the Democrats, Wilson's intense efforts to enforce a useless technical right, so far from borrowing trouble, was the sole barrier between America and war. With his "iron nerves," his "unshakable poise," and his invincible "integrity" the President, by his very effort to prevent Germany from using its submarines effectively against its enemies, had "kept us out of war." By the winter of 1915–1916, "he kept us out of war" had become the catch phrase of every Democrat who wanted America forced into it. "Wilson has kept you at peace," cried Senator John Sharp Williams of Mississippi, the leading Democratic interventionist in the Senate. "He has kept peace with honor." In the 1916 presidential elections, "he kept us out of war" was to become the official Democratic campaign slogan, although in truth the most feeble of Presidents could have kept America out of war and only a President of uncommon ability, boldness and vaunting ambition could possibly have gotten us into it.[2]

The Democratic slogan was aptly chosen, nonetheless, for it summed up succinctly what the electorate had to believe if America was to be brought successfully into the European carnage. It implied that a President who had gratuitously put America on a collision course with a belligerent was straining every nerve to avert an almost inevitable collision. It implied, too, that Wilson's stand on the right to travel was a matter of course and Germany's unrestricted use of the submarine against its enemies' shipping an act of hostility toward the United States. To Ambassador Gerard's unanswerable question: "Why should we enter a great war because some American wants to cross on a ship where he can have a private bathroom?" the Democrats' slogan provided not an answer, but a shrewd and necessary evasion. Perhaps most simply, the Democrats' slogan implied that the roots of any future war with Germany lay in anything and everything *except* the foreign policy of President Wilson. By the winter of 1915–1916 the political arena was flooded with crypto-interventionist lies and distortions and "he kept us out of war" was perhaps the most effective lie of all.

Not everyone was deceived, for common sense is not so easily confounded. On January 5, 1916, Wesley Jones of Washington took the floor of the Senate to point out that the President's actions were not responsible for peace and to suggest, albeit delicately, that his intentions might be other than pacific. "The President," said Senator Jones, "has been highly commended for keeping us out of the war in Europe. I want to give him all the praise he deserves, but it has not been a question of keeping us out of this struggle. The people have not wanted to get into it. The question has been not to lead us into it, and I beseech the President now to be careful, to proceed slowly, to make no harsh or arbitrary demands, to keep in view the rights of 99,999,000 people at home rather than of the 1,000 reckless, inconsiderate and unpatriotic citizens who insist on going abroad in belligerent ships and that he do not lead us into a position that means trouble or humiliation." The American traveler on a belligerent ship, said Senator Jones, "is entitled to no consideration whatever, and for this country to become embroiled in this trouble on his account would be a colossal crime against humanity."[3]

Unfortunately for the peace of the country, Senator Jones was a member of a congressional minority, an ill-sorted collection of insurgent Republicans, progressive reformers, and rural Democrats, for the most part, who genuinely believed that American intervention in the European war was suicidally insane and that defending the rights of a few travelers an outrageous reason for borrowing trouble. For the first two months of the congressional session, however, the antiwar minority in Congress made only sporadic efforts to break through the bipartisan cordon surrounding and protecting the President "in the European matter." As long as Germany restricted its submarine warfare, it was impossible in the poisoned political atmosphere to mount an effective attack on Wilson's submarine diplomacy or his European policy in general. Nevertheless, Wilson was understandably "disturbed" that he still had strong vocal critics in Congress, for his war course depended on the American people's enjoying virtually no voice whatever in the councils of government.

The mere presence of a sizable antiwar minority in Congress had an inhibiting effect on the legislative branch. Much to Wilson's disappointment, his congressional understrappers proved conspicuously passive in their support of the President. Wilson had expected the party minions of both parties to turn the national legislature into a powerful organ of crypto-war propaganda. He had expected them to raise up a hue and cry over the *Lusitania* and join him in demanding a German disavowal of the several-months-old sinking. He had expected them, too, to enact a "spy bill" to enable him to "close down" on dangerous utterances. On the floor of the House and Senate, however, the prowar majority did nothing. They neither agitated for preparedness nor denounced the "hyphenate menace." Not once did a legislator so much as mention the *Lusitania*. In the "European matter," Congress, so often a cave of winds, remained mute for two months, the silence sporadically broken by critics of Wilson's diplomacy and opponents of a military buildup.

Behind the silence lay an elementary fact of congressional politics. The prowar legislators simply could not say in the free political space of a congressional chamber what they said with impunity outside it. The crypto-war propaganda consisted chiefly of lies and distortions. Wilson's supporters triumphed over his critics chiefly by slandering their character, impugning their patriotism, and drowning them out "in the deep unison of a common, unhesitating" contempt for the "national feeling." The free and formal atmosphere of parliamentary debate, however, placed the crypto-interventionist majority at a severe disadvantage. Outside Congress they could defend the British blockade, for example, by praising the idealism of the Allies. To do so inside Congress was grossly unneutral—"not discreet," as one Ohio Republican admonished a pro-British colleague. Outside Congress, the interventionists could shout "America first" at a critic of Wilson's partiality to Britain. Inside Congress that lying retort invited the all-too-obvious rejoinder that those who shouted "America first" really meant "England first." Outside Congress, the prowar faction could call Wilson's defense of safe travel a sacred obligation of "national honor" and defame skeptics as "peace-at-any-price men." On the floor of a legislative chamber, however, it was not so easy to answer a legislator who asked—as blind Senator Thomas Gore of Oklahoma asked in early January—why a "single citizen should be allowed to run the risk of drenching this Nation in blood merely in order that he may travel upon a belligerent rather than a neutral vessel." And of course it was forbidden to impugn the motives of a fellow legislator. Wilson's policy in "the European matter" simply did not bear up under calm scrutiny in a free political atmosphere. The President's legislative understrappers prudently preferred not to discuss it at all.[4]

What was true of Wilson's foreign policy was equally true of the crypto-war agitation in general. Outside Congress it was easy enough to sound the alarm about German invasions of New York. Inside Congress, however, antipreparedness legislators readily mocked such preposterous bogies and had no trouble deriding the dubious "patriotism of the Dupont Powder Company" and all the other profiteers for preparedness. Outside Congress it was easy enough to impugn the patriotism of "hyphenated Americans." However, when Augustus Gardner did so on the floor of the House in early January his fellow Republicans soundly rebuked him for using "intemperate and reckless" language and for trying to "fan the flame of racial hatred." The political atmosphere inside Congress and outside it were as distinctive as two different countries. Whatever prowar legislators did outside the legislative chambers, in Congress assembled they dared do no more than give the President as free a hand as possible until he succeeded in making war seem "inevitable" to the American people. Until then they preferred keeping Congress out of European affairs entirely.[5]

In mid-February 1916, however, a momentous blunder by Wilson thrust the issues of war and peace into the unwilling hands of

Congress. For a few tense days America was to totter on the brink of peace.

The ultimate source of the blunder was Wilson's secretary of state and his personal conviction that going to war was a legal question to be settled by a well-argued legal brief. Secretary Lansing had no doubt that German violation of an American citizen's right to travel safely on the commercial vessels of her public enemy constituted a just and exigent ground for war. Privately he welcomed war with Germany, but Lansing's mind, though by no means judicious, was incurably juridical. From his point of view the case for intervention had to be legally airtight and in the autumn of 1915 America's legal case for war with Germany was rapidly losing its technical validity. The problem for Lansing, as for Bryan before him, was Britain's arming of its merchant ships and the use of those arms to sink submarines that rose to the surface, in deference to Wilson's demands, to give the required warning.

America's "lenient attitude" toward the British, as Lansing put it, had largely created the problem. At the war's outbreak, the British had insisted that their commercial vessels had the right to carry so-called defensive arms without losing their status as peaceful, private commercial vessels. That right, at best, was legally dubious, "very questionable" as the U.S. Joint Neutrality Board put it. For one thing the right was obsolete, being based on a trading ship's need to fight off capture by pirates, long since banished from the high seas. For another, it was difficult to distinguish in practice between a "defensive" and an "offensive" weapon. In principle if the weapon was powerful enough to attack an enemy ship of war successfully, then a belligerent merchantman so armed ceased to be a mere commercial vessel. It became, in the eyes of the law, a ship of war, technically an auxiliary cruiser of the belligerent's navy, which that belligerent's public enemy had the right to sink on sight. Traditionally the United States had taken a markedly stringent view of armed commercial ships, considering these incongruous vessels to have a martial character and to forfeit, in great degree, the immunities enjoyed in wartime by unarmed belligerent trading ships. Sharing America's traditional viewpoint, the Netherlands, for one, banned all armed belligerent merchantmen from its ports for the duration of the war. The Wilson administration had been much more obliging. On September 19, 1914, the State Department issued a circular accepting the British claim that merchantmen armed for "the sole purpose of defense" did not acquire "the character of a ship of war." The circular then proceeded to define a purely defensive weapon by certain factual criteria, chiefly its small caliber and its location. Well aware that allowing armed merchantmen free use of our ports looked less than stringently neutral, the American government persuaded the British to agree, informally, to dismantle their guns before entering our harbors.[6]

What had been "very questionable" in September 1914 had become for Lansing legally disastrous one year later. First and most important, the advent of the submarine as a commerce destroyer made the original State Department definition of "defensive" completely outmoded. The small-caliber gun that merchantmen could not use successfully against an ordinary battle cruiser could destroy a fragile submarine with one shot. British merchantmen not only could, they were doing so even before German submarines committed a hostile act. Under international law armed merchantmen capable of such aggressive action were ships of war subject to instant destruction. To deepen Lansing's legal qualms, the British, in September 1915, broke their "gentlemen's agreement" with America and ceased bothering to dismantle their guns before sailing into American harbors. America's neutral territory was being used by ships engaged in naval combat, a grave transgression of neutrality. On September 12, in consequence, a troubled Lansing wrote a memorandum to the President advising him that the United States had to issue a new circular redefining a defensive weapon. "Changed conditions" required it, said Lansing, "because an armament, which under previous conditions was clearly defensive may now be employed for offensive operations against so small and unarmored a craft as a submarine." Moreover, reported Lansing, armed British merchantmen were in fact taking the offensive against submarines. The use of such ships, so armed and so acting, "makes it difficult to demand that a submarine shall give warning and so expose itself to the heavy guns carried by some of the British passenger vessels."[7]

To Lansing this was the heart of the legal problem. As he put it somewhat more bluntly to Colonel House: "If we are to hold the

Germans responsible for sinking ships without warning, we must also insist that merchantmen be unarmed." The American government simply could not demand that German submarines give warning and then allow armed British ships to sink them when they did. The British, Lansing told House, cannot "have their cake and eat it too." As long as armed British merchantmen plied the seas the United States could not justly hold Germany "strictly accountable" for sinking belligerent ships without warning should an American be aboard. Lansing did not want Wilson to abandon his stand on the right to travel. It would have meant abandoning the war course. What he felt America needed was an airtight legal case. Unless Britain's merchant ships were disarmed Wilson's "firm ground of right" had ceased to exist.[8]

In reply to Lansing's memorandum the President agreed in principle that a new State Department circular was proper but he counseled delay and never raised the subject again. For three months neither did Lansing. At the end of December, however, Lansing's legal qualms took on a new urgency. On December 30, he received from the German government documentary proof of Britain's original order instructing merchantmen to attack submarines whenever possible. For the Germans the documents were partly a ploy in their struggle with Wilson over the *Lusitania* apology. Determined not to admit the illegality of unrestricted submarine warfare, Germany now argued that merchantmen armed for and instructed to attack made it impossible to concede that sinking merchantmen without warning violated international law. Germany's contention, as Lansing knew, had considerable validity. Hoping to undermine it, Lansing on January 2, 1916, once again raised the question of armed merchantmen with the President. He suggested that the United States bluntly inform the Allies that due to "the unreasonableness of requiring a submarine to run the danger of being almost certainly destroyed by giving warning to a vessel carrying an armament . . . merchant vessels should refrain from mounting guns large enough to sink a submarine, and that, if they do, they become vessels of war and liable to treatment as such by both belligerents and neutrals." Since the President was determined to compel Germany to admit the illegality of unrestricted submarine warfare, Lansing himself was prepared to help him do so by dealing quite harshly with the British. "Unless the Entente Allies positively agree not to arm any of their merchant vessels and notify the Central Powers to that effect, is there not strong reason why a submarine should not warn a vessel before launching an attack?" Lansing, in short, was ready to threaten Britain with abandoning America's opposition to German submarine warfare if it did not disarm its merchant ships.[9]

Receiving no reply from Wilson, Lansing on January 7 made a somewhat milder suggestion to the President. He proposed that the United States suggest a friendly "modus vivendi" to the Allies. The United States would privately ask them to disarm their ships on the grounds that adherence to cruiser rules "could hardly be required justly of a submarine if the observation of the rule compels the submarine to expose itself to almost certain destruction." Once the Allies agreed to disarm, the United States would then turn to Germany and compel them to pledge never to sink any belligerent merchantmen without warning. Such a pledge was a major goal of Wilson's submarine diplomacy, just as avoiding it was the chief object of German dealings with the American government.[10]

On January 10, Wilson wrote to Lansing that "this seems to me reasonable and thoroughly worth trying." On January 18, Lansing sent off to each of the Allied emissaries in Washington the administration's proposal for a modus vivendi. It repeated all the arguments that Lansing had been making in private: that arming merchantmen at best was a "dubious legal right"; that since the advent of the submarine "any armament, therefore, on a merchant vessel would seem to have the character of an offensive armament"; that it was not "just or reasonable" to demand, under such conditions, that Germany obey the traditional cruiser rules; that if the Allies agreed to disarm their merchantmen the United States would in turn try to compel Germany to pledge public obedience to those rules; that the United States—by way of a threat—was "seriously considering" a public declaration that armed merchantmen were "auxiliary cruisers" subject, as far as America was concerned, to legal attack without warning.[11]

On the face of it Wilson had done something he had never done before and was never to do again. He had taken a position that was sensible, fair-minded, fully in accord with international law, *and* favorable to Germany. Helping Germany, however, was the last thing Wilson had in mind. He had accepted Lansing's suggestion, as he apologetically explained to Colonel House a few weeks later, because he took it for granted that the Allies would accept the proposal and that Germany, desperate to avoid a submarine pledge, would almost certainly reject it. He hoped to maneuver Germany into a position of publicly spurning a fair-minded American proposal which the fair-minded Allies had publicly accepted. The rejection, for one thing, would underscore for the American people the lawlessness of the German government, a demonstration useful in itself when unrestricted submarine warfare resumed. More important, it would enable Wilson to relieve a situation at once unfavorable to Britain and dangerous to his war course. Anti-Allied sentiment had been growing by leaps and bounds in America and Britain's indifference to America's October note of protest had only made matters worse. Wilson was faced once again with intense and mounting demands that he begin to assert America's neutral rights against the British blockaders, a demand that all the frantic crypto-interventionists cries about "America First" and "pro-German" conspiracies had been unable to blunt. Germany's rejection of the modus vivendi would hopefully stifle anti-Allied sentiment and revive antagonism toward Germany. If Germany, by chance, should accept the proposal, Britain lost nothing. As long as Germany adhered to the pledge, Britain's munitions traffic would be safe. As far as Wilson could see, the British had everything to gain and nothing to lose by agreeing to disarm their merchantmen. Their acceptance seemed certain. In that Wilson was mistaken, and the mistake was soon to set off a political explosion that almost blew Wilson off his war course.[12]

The British government, unfortunately for Wilson, saw nothing to gain and much to lose from the American modus vivendi. For one thing, agreeing to disarm its merchantmen would have provoked a furious outcry in England; once again, as with the House "plan," Wilson had failed to take into account public sentiment in a nation at war. The scheme suffered from the endemic weakness of Wilson's peculiar strength: a blind egotist's inability to imagine any viewpoint save his own. Even if British leaders braved the outcry, they could scarcely share Wilson's certainty that Germany would reject its half of the bargain. It took intimate knowledge of negotiating with Germany to appreciate how obstinately it resisted a public pledge to obey cruiser rules. Moreover, the British government did not seriously fear, by then, that America's President would puncture holes in its blockade of Germany. Wilson's proposal seemed wholly unnecessary if not downright suspicious. On January 26, the administration learned from Ambassador Page that far from approving the proposal, the British foreign secretary considered it "a great calamity." The next day a furious British ambassador confronted the American secretary of state with a stinging cable from Sir Edward Grey. The American proposal, said Grey, was "incredible. . . . I cannot adequately express [my] disappointment and dismay." Spring-Rice expressed it for him. To Lansing's face he vehemently accused the President of treacherously plotting to restore harmony between America and Germany. By now, the British ambassador viewed any American action inconvenient to Britain as an ally's gross breach of faith, an understandable view in the circumstances.[13]

For Wilson far worse was shortly to follow. On February 8 the German government, taking advantage of the modus vivendi proposal to the Allies, put Wilson and the war party to the severest test they had yet to face. On that day, Germany announced that, commencing February 29, the armed merchantmen of Germany's enemies would be treated as auxiliary cruisers enjoying no immunity from sudden attack. In a supporting memorandum the Germans pointedly defended their decision with the same arguments the American secretary of state had made in his January 18 modus vivendi proposal. Both the people at large and the State Department took the news calmly, just as they had done one year before when Germany made its first announcement of submarine warfare against enemy shipping. Since the President said nothing and instead went cruising on Chesapeake Bay, the conclusion seemed obvious: The United States would take no issue with the new German policy of sinking armed enemy merchantmen without warning. There seemed no reason on earth why we should. We ourselves had said on January 18 that in relation to the submarine the arms carried by British merchantmen "have the character of an offensive weapon." We had admitted that it was not "just or reasonable" to expect German submarines to give warning and be exposed to "almost certain destruction by the guns on board a merchant vessel." We ourselves were "seriously considering" calling armed British trading ships auxiliary cruisers.

State Department officials made it clear, the *World* reported on February 13, "that the position of the Central Powers in regard to armed merchantmen is considered well-taken." The only action the administration contemplated, the *World* reported, was to warn American citizens "that they will take passage aboard armed merchantships at their own risk, and be entitled to no more protection from the United States than if they had embarked upon a belligerent warship. Officials today seemed not to be able to conceive that any issue could arise in the future" from the new German submarine policy. As for the British charge that it would be unneutral for America to abrogate its merchantmen's right to arm defensively, "high officials of the government" simply denied the contention. Suspecting nothing, the *World's* editorial for February 15 summed up forcefully what it—and State Department officials—took to be the President's position. Two weeks later members of Congress who agreed with that *World* editorial would be denounced by the *World* as pro-German conspirators. The editorial noted as a point of international law that the right to arm defensively existed solely "for purposes of defense against privateers and pirates" and did not apply to enemy ships of war. "Nobody ever held that a merchantman could attack anything without becoming a ship of war or possibly a pirate, thus losing its character and immunity as a merchantman." The British contention that America was proposing to change international law in wartime was baseless. It was the British who were asking for a "departure" in international law, namely the unheard-of right of its merchantmen to carry guns capable of destroying an enemy ship of war while enjoying all the privileges of a peaceful commercial vessel. "There is no reason, however, why the United States should support the British departure, or why, if it is to be insisted upon, individual Americans should risk life and property upon so-called merchantmen which in fact are ships of war."[14]

In the Wilson administration there was only one person of consequence who disagreed with the administration's position and that was the President himself. Germany's February 8 proclamation,

quite simply, posed a deadly threat to Wilson's war. If he acquiesced in the new German policy, if he agreed, that is, with the State
Department, both his routes to war would be permanently sealed
off. For one thing House's mediation plot would be instantly abort-
ed. The British, angry with Wilson even before the German announcement, would write him off as a completely untrustworthy
neutral if he recognized Germany's right to sink armed merchantmen without warning. Worse yet, Wilson would risk losing the submarine as his alternative *casus belli.* By allowing the Germans to
sink armed British merchantmen on sight he would remove a serious cause of friction between America and Germany, reducing
rather than exacerbating its "jealousy, ill-will and a disposition to
retaliate." He would be helping the German civil government alleviate popular demands—increasingly pressing—for resumption of
unrestricted submarine warfare, on which Wilson's hopes for intervention depended. Even were it resumed, his acquiescence in the
new German policy regarding armed ships would have fatally
weakened the America people's already feeble willingness to go to
war over the right to travel. This was true not as a matter of international law, but as a matter of practical politics. Acquiescence
meant, indeed automatically entailed, warning Americans that
they traveled on armed ships at their own risk. Such a warning,
once made, could only strengthen popular demands that Americans
be warned off all belligerent ships, a demand still voiced in the Senate and one so sensible and popular that it had taken the massed
power of two party hierarchies, the press, and the administration to
blunt it. Acquiescence meant, too, that German submarines and
armed British merchantmen would be locked in ceaseless combat in
the war zone. The American press would be filled daily with reports of such naval engagements. The sheer impact of events would
strengthen immeasurably the popular impulse to wash our hands of
the whole vexing business of submarines, merchantmen, and travel
rights and to wish a plague on both belligerents' houses. That impulse had been the governing sentiment in America since the outbreak of the European war. Anything that strengthened it would be
absolutely fatal to Wilson's designs. In short, if Wilson acquiesced
in the German submarine policy, if he publicly supported his own
apparent position on armed ships, the United States would never
get into the war in order to "end war."

To avert that worldwide, if hypothetical, calamity, Wilson had to make a complete turnabout in public. And he did. On February 15, the very day *World* readers were told of the propriety of the German position and the falsity of British counterclaims, Secretary of State Lansing, eating his own words and impeaching his own understanding, issued a statement to the press taking the very opposite view. The right of the British to outfit their merchantmen with defensive arms, said Lansing, was an "established rule" of international law. The mere fact that those arms were now "offensively superior" to the submarine made no difference whatever. The fact that a submarine's obedience to cruiser rules subjected them to instant destruction also made no difference whatever. Under the "rule" Britain's offensively armed merchant ships enjoyed all the immunities of unarmed, peaceful commercial vessels. The United States could not, at the risk of its neutrality, change that "rule" in wartime. An American citizen, accordingly, had the absolute right to travel safely not only on unarmed ships but on armed ships capable of attacking and destroying submarines. Since the government was obligated to maintain its citizens' rights, reports that Americans would be warned against traveling on armed belligerent merchantmen were denied. "There is no present intention to warn Americans to refrain from traveling on belligerent merchantmen armed with guns solely for defensive purposes." And what constituted a solely defensive gun? A gun the State Department had defined as such in its September 9, 1914, circular. According to the announcement, the United States could not alter its own departmental definition without transgressing against neutrality. In short, the moment Germany had taken Wilson's own position, Wilson had switched to the British position. Hearing of the administration's announcement, John Bassett Moore, a former counselor of the State Department, wondered, as he later recalled, "whether there was any limit to our credulity and subserviency."[15]

The weakness of Wilson's position in mid-February can scarcely be exaggerated. Politically, his reputation as a peace-loving leader had reached a low ebb even before his volte-face. During an eight-day speaking tour from January 27 to February 3, the President, desperate to persuade Americans that the right to travel constituted worthy grounds for war, had been crying up "national honor," insisting that violators of international law "touch the very vital in-

terests and honor of the United States," and warning audiences in
city after city that they might be called upon "at any time" to go to
war "if it is necessary that I should maintain your honor." By the
time Wilson had returned to Washington, opponents of war began
to suspect openly that the peace-loving Wilson might be secretly
coveting war, suicidally insane though it seemed to them. Now with
Wilson's astonishing turnabout, the suspicions multiplied tenfold,
for as a matter of international law the President's stand was utterly untenable. That an armed belligerent ship capable of destroying
a ship of war with one shot retained all the immunities of a peaceful, private commercial vessel was a principle unknown to international law. It was not "the established rule," but, as the State Department's own legal experts had indicated a few days before, a
"departure" from the rule. The administration's basic contention,
that it could not change a rule of war in wartime, was utterly specious, as Lansing himself well knew. The right to arm defensively
was the rule, although a "doubtful" one at best. What constituted a
defensive weapon, however, was a matter of fact. For six months
Lansing had contended that "changed conditions" made our original definition obsolete. For six months Lansing had been asking not
for a change in the "rule," but for a change in a State Department
circular that would make our definition of a defensive weapon con-
form more closely to the rule. It had not occurred to Lansing, or to
Wilson for that matter, that the rules of neutrality forbade the
American government from rewriting its own harbor rules in the
interests of a more impartial neutrality. Such was now the government's claim. Neither had it occurred to Lansing that the rules of
neutrality forbade the sovereign United States from calling an offensively armed belligerent ship an auxiliary cruiser. This, too, was
now the government's claim. Nor had it occurred to Lansing that
the rules of neutrality obliged the sovereign United States to prevent a belligerent from sinking an offensively armed merchant ship
of its public enemy. This, too, was now the government's claim. In
the hands of the Wilson administration, the alleged rules of neutrality had become a maddening series of dubious obligations and
prohibitions designed to *prevent* a neutral country from maintaining its peace and neutrality.

What made matters far worse was public knowledge of Lansing's modus vivendi proposal. Shaken and embarrassed, administration spokesmen tried frantically to explain it away. It was merely a friendly suggestion, they insisted. It was not the government's official position on international law. It could not be cited against the administration to prove, in the popular parlance, that Wilson had "flopped." It was impossible, nonetheless, to persuade people that Lansing's earlier opinions meant nothing. The secretary of state himself had said that the United States was "seriously considering" calling armed British ships that used our harbors auxiliary cruisers. How come, a month later, the secretary of state was insisting that the sovereign United States had no such right to define the status of belligerent ships using our harbors? The secretary of state had called the right to arm merchantmen even for defense "a doubtful legal right" at best. Why was the administration so determined to enforce it now, just when it created an immediate perilous crisis with Germany? The secretary of state had said it was not "just or reasonable" to demand German adherence to cruiser rules. Why was the adminstration, ostensibly neutral, making unjust and unreasonable demands on one of the belligerents?[16]

Of all the questions raised by Wilson's volte-face, the hardest to answer was the one most often raised and most dangerous to Wilson's ambitions. Why did the United States not simply wash its hands of the whole business? If the United States could not, so Wilson claimed, call armed British merchantmen auxiliary cruisers and if it could not, so Wilson had admitted, justly demand that German submarines give warning to such ships, why did the government not simply tell Americans not to travel on armed belligerent ships? As Senator Porter McCumber, a North Dakota Republican, put it: "I confess I cannot see anything fair in the proposition that while a submarine—which may easily be sunk by a single shot from one of these defense guns—must give notice before it fires at the armed merchant vessel, the armed merchant vessel need not give notice that it purposes to fire at the submarine." Since we cannot compel the British to disarm, said Senator McCumber, "it logically follows that Congress or the President may with entire propriety" prohibit Americans from traveling on armed merchant ships. Surely "national honor" did not oblige the United States to defend with force of arms any so-called "right" to travel safely on armed belligerent ships capable of sinking enemy submarines on sight. Before February 15, 1916, nobody had ever known of such an alleged right. Before February 15, 1916, even the staunchest Senate defender of the right to travel had explicitly specified travel on unarmed ships. No one had as much as mentioned on the Senate floor any right to travel safely on armed ones. If we cannot call an armed British merchantman a ship of war, said Senator Norris, "we do have the acknowledged right to see that any such vessel leaving an American port should not carry passengers." What could be more simple, more just, and more genuinely neutral than keeping American travelers off armed belligerent ships? What better way to maintain the peace of the country and avert a wholly unnecessary collision with Germany?[17]

On February 17 an obscure Texas legislator named Jeff McLemore assured himself a place in history by introducing a resolution that, upon passage, would have registered the nonbinding opinion of the House of Representatives that the President ought to "warn all American citizens . . . to refrain from traveling on any and all ships [that] mount guns . . . and that in case Americans do travel on such armed belligerent ships that they do so at their own risk." Obscure members of Congress submit hundreds of resolutions to the House every session, but this was no ordinary resolution to be pigeonholed in committee and promptly forgotten. Americans by an overwhelming majority wanted American travelers kept off armed belligerent ships. With the new German submarine policy about to commence, they expected the government to do something at once to keep them off those ships. In New York, perhaps the least antiwar city in the country, a Republican member of Congress soon reported that letters were running 10 to 1 in favor of a travel warning. In Massachusetts, perhaps the most anglophobic state in the Union, a member of Congress reported receiving a large number of pro-travel-warning letters. Due to Wilson's turnabout, the common sense of the American people, thwarted for so long, seemed on the verge of erupting in the halls of Congress itself.[18]

With the pressure mounting in Congress and the country, the three Democratic legislators most directly concerned with a travel warning decided to consult the President on the matter. On the afternoon of February 21, Senator Stone, chairman of the Foreign Relations Committee, Representative Hal Flood, chairman of the Foreign Affairs Committee, and Senator T. J. Kern of Indiana, Senate Majority Leader, met with Woodrow Wilson at the White House. It was a rare event in itself. By 1916 the President had become a singularly remote and even mysterious figure, shunning as far as possible all personal contacts outside his small official family. The meeting by all accounts (and no single account is authoritative) was dramatic. Senator Stone, the only opponent of war among the three visitors, got to the heart of the matter at once. He asked the President bluntly what he would do if an American lost his life aboard an armed British merchantman sunk without warning by a German submarine. In his reply Wilson demonstrated once again his remarkable ability to stand as firmly on a flimsy pretext as the great Lincoln stood on the solemn obligation to preserve the American Union. Given his vulnerable position and given the temper of the country, to hesitate was to lose. Wilson did not hesitate. The result of such a sinking, he reportedly told Stone, would be "a breach of diplomatic relations; that the breach of diplomatic relations would probably be followed by a state of war." He was duty-bound to go to any lengths to defend the right of Americans to travel safely on armed belligerent merchantmen. In that case, asked Stone, should not Americans be warned not to travel on such ships? Once again Wilson did not hesitate. He absolutely opposed giving any such warning. He claimed it would interfere with his diplomatic negotiations, although the modus vivendi proposal was dead, killed by the very fact that he had taken Britain's side. Wilson claimed even more dubiously that a travel warning would even make war more likely. Knowing that a travel warning was immensely popular, Wilson urged his three visitors to prevent, at all costs, a floor vote on the warning resolution. Senator Stone, reportedly, was thunderstruck. "Mr. President, I have followed you in your domestic policies, but—by God! I shall not follow you into war with Germany."[19]

When accounts of the meeting began filtering through Congress the next day the House of Representatives was thrown into turmoil. Congress, Lansing wrote in his diary, was "seething" with war talk. In every cloakroom and corridor, members of Congress discussed in

anger or fear news of the President's position. "Veteran legislators," reported the *New York Times*, said that "not for many years
had they seen a situation so dramatic and sensational." The *World*
said the House was in "panic." Opponents of war were outraged.
What the secretary of state had called a "doubtful legal right," the
President had now elevated into a right worth defending by a major
war. In the space of five days the right to travel on armed ships,
hitherto unmentioned anywhere, had become so precious that the
President did not want Congress even to discuss the common opinion that Americans ought not to travel on them.[20]

Why should the President oppose a travel warning at all? As
Senator La Follette put it, the President "certainly did not regard
it as an abject relinquishment of the sacred rights of American citizens to order them to abandon their property and seek the shelter
of their home country in order to avoid the responsibility for protecting them in their rights in Mexico. . . . It was a small sacrifice
on the part of the few to preserve the peace of the nation. But how
much less sacrifice it requires for our citizens to refrain from travel
on armed belligerent ships." To many opponents of war in the
House Wilson's opposition to a travel warning meant only one
thing. "The President," as Claude Kitchin put it to a friend, "is
anxious for war with Germany." Representative Mondell of Wyoming, Wilson's sharpest critic in the House, put the case with his
usual cogency. "When anyone fully informed contends that an
American citizen has a right which shall not be denied, curtailed or
abridged, to travel on a ship armed to fight, purposed to fight, proposing to fight and bound into regions of war at the present time
and under present conditions I am compelled to believe that the one
so proposing and so insisting is either playing politics with the national honor, or is disposed to embroil the nation in war."[21]

Of the deeper implications of Wilson's position not all the proponents of a travel warning were fully aware. Many merely wished to
avert any imminent trouble with Germany over the sinking of an
armed British ship. Others felt that far more was at stake. To Senator Gore the real purpose of a congressional travel warning was to
"check," as he put it, the President's "headlong" descent into war.
One way or another opponents of war saw in a travel warning a
blow struck for peace and neutrality. So did the crypto-interven-

tionists. They opposed it to a man. Advocates of a travel warning in Congress had behind them the remote power of the electorate. The crypto-interventionists had behind them the proximate organized power of the national political establishment: the President, the press, and most party chieftains. The civil war over war had entered Congress itself.[22]

For two feverish days antiwar Democrats and progressive Republicans met in excited conferences to plan ways to wrest a travel resolution from the House Foreign Affairs Committee. For two days, Wilson's congressional lieutenants—Speaker Clark, Hal Flood, and other leaders of the House Democratic party machine—worked to keep it bottled up in committee. Despite the mildness of a mere House recommendation on travel, despite the popularity of such a recommendation, despite the urgency of such a recommendation, the struggle proved to be no contest. A majority of Democratic legislators were ready, despite their constituents, to "stand by" the President and go to war, if necessary, to vindicate the right of Americans to travel safely on armed British ships. So, too, were half the Republicans in the House. Senator Lodge, who served as the Republican oligarchy's minister of foreign affairs, had laid down the oligarchy's line on armed merchantmen a few days after Wilson's volte-face. In a perfect display of partisan bipartisanship, Lodge, on the Senate floor, had vehemently denounced the administration's modus vivendi proposal and proclaimed it "incredible" to dare abrogate Britain's unalienable right to arm its merchantmen—which is to say, he agreed entirely with Wilson, as a Democratic senator promptly pointed out. Republican support of Wilson in the Foreign Affairs Committee and in the House at large was probably decisive. By the end of the February 23 session, Hal Flood was able to assure an anxious Wilson via telephone that no travel warning resolution stood the remotest chance of coming to a vote. Legislatively speaking, the issue was dead; the President's foreign policy was safe. The next day the "panic" in the House was over. Legislators who favored war had been saved from the prospect of having to "stand by" the President with their vote. It was that prospect which had caused the panic in the first place.[23]

No one knew better than Wilson what the House of Representatives had done by its refusal to do anything. It had demonstrated—

in fact, for the first time—that not even overwhelming public sentiment could compel a majority of House members to hamper him in
any way regardless of how dubious the position he took, regardless
of how questionable his motives had become, regardless of how
modest, how sensible, and how reasonable a popular gesture of dissent might be. With the political ground once again firm under his
feet, Wilson immediately launched a counterattack against a travel
warning. On the evening of February 24, he issued to the press a
letter he wrote to Senator Stone in which he defended his position
with sheer jingo bombast. He promised, as usual, to "do everything
in my power to keep the United States out of war." However, his
"power" to do so was limited, as usual, by scruples and duties that
made trouble with Germany inevitable. "I cannot consent to any
abridgment of the rights of American citizens in any respect. . . . To forbid our people to exercise their rights for fear we
might be called upon to vindicate them would be a deep humiliation. . . . Once accept a single abatement of right and many other
humiliations would certainly follow and the whole fine fabric of international law might crumble under our hands. . . . What we are
contending for in this matter is of the very essence of the things
that have made America a sovereign nation." By failing to uphold
the right to travel safely on armed British ships, America, said the
President, would be "conceding her own impotency as a nation."[24]

Representative Mondell called the President's statement "mock
heroism." It was also mock nationalism, for it turned the normal
meaning of national sovereignty completely on its head. By Wilson's own argument America was compelled to defend the right to
travel on armed merchantmen because it did not enjoy the sovereign power to issue a new State Department circular regarding belligerent ships using our own harbors. The United States did not
even have the sovereign power to forbid armed belligerent ships
using our harbors from carrying American passengers. What Wilson was "contending for," in fact, was our "impotency as a nation"
to maintain an impartial neutrality by independent actions of our
own, in other words, by putting "America first." The party press,
by an overwhelming majority, however, lauded the President for
his patriotic assertion that American sovereignty consisted of external obligations and prohibitions that America had not the right to

alter in its own interest. The *New York Times*, equally avid for Wilson and war, gravely opined that "no nobler utterance by tongue or pen has come from the President. . . . We do not covet peace at the cost of honor."[25]

Set in motion by Wilson's inverted nationalism, the well-oiled machinery of defamation moved into high gear. The *World*, forgetting that it and the State Department had held the opposite view ten days before, now denounced the advocates of a travel warning as enemies of their own country. Its advocacy now meant only one thing: "Germany has invaded Congress." The *New York Times* denounced the McLemore resolution as nothing less than "a conspiracy against the President. . . . An unspeakably base thing, it is despicable beyond the power of denunciation." With their usual frenzied mendacity, the interventionists quickly distorted the issue of armed merchantmen beyond recognition. The real issue, said a Philadelphia newspaper, was not a travel warning, but whether Congress stood for "America First or Germany Over All." The real issue, said the *World*, was "America First or Deutschland Über Alles." Mississippi's Senator Williams agreed: The real issue, he told his Senate colleagues, was "America First or Deutschland Über Alles." Wilson, by fiat, had become "America." Opposition to him even in Congress had now become "conspiracy." His congressional critics had become "Germans," virtual traitors giving "actual aid and comfort to the nation we are at controversy with," as a Kentucky Democrat put it in the course of rebuking legislators whose whole point was that no genuine grounds for a controversy existed. By now the crypto-war propaganda had been welded into a virtually self-contained system of slanderous lies.[26]

To ensure that no rational rejoinder would issue from the Senate, the upper chamber on February 25 took an unusual step to silence its small but redoubtable antiwar minority. Faced with a travel warning introduced that day by Senator Gore, the Senate voted to go into continuous legislative session, a parliamentary device by which each succeeding day was deemed to be February 25, thereby preventing antiwar senators from introducing the travel question into the business of the "day," which was to last until March 2. "Every effort was made to prevent discussion" of armed merchantmen, said a Republican senator shortly after the gag was removed.

Determined to protect a vulnerable President from public opinion and those elected officials who still gave it voice, the war party in Congress had thrown up a cordon of silence around Wilson while the party press prated noisily about "Germans" in Congress, "conspiracy" against the President, and "America First."[27]

There the matter might have rested were it not for Wilson himself. Tacitly, at least, Congress had declared itself unwilling to make a suggestion, or even discuss a suggestion, regarding travel on armed British merchantmen. Tacitly, it had declared it improper for Congress to express a popular opinion in the European matter which ran counter to the President's. With the "pro-German insurrection," as it was called, so easily put down in Congress, Wilson, with characteristic boldness, decided to go one step further. On February 29, Wilson sent a letter to Edward Pou, acting chairman of the House Rules Committee, asking him to arrange for "an early vote on the resolutions with regard to travel on armed merchantmen which have recently been so much talked about." He was making this unusual request, Wilson explained, because "the report that there are divided counsels in Congress in regard to the foreign policy of the government is being made industrious use of in foreign capitals." He wanted "all doubts and conjectures . . . swept away" by a vote. He made a similar request to Senator Stone.[28]

"Divided counsels in Congress" were not to be borne; unanimity of opinion was essential. But how does a parliamentary body demonstrate unanimity by a vote that could not possibly be unanimous? There was only one way to do so: by voting its opinion that it had no right to an opinion—the unanimity of silence. This was well understood by everyone in Congress. What Wilson wanted, said an angry Senator La Follette, was "nothing less than a complete denial of any intent or purpose to express an opinion or offer advice." The President, said La Follette, wanted Congress to "unconditionally surrender all right to voice the popular will," to grant him "unprecedented" and unconstitutional "one-man power" over foreign policy while Congress "was to keep silent in all that pertains to foreign affairs."[29]

On the face of it the Senate should have risen up in fury against Wilson's arrogant presumption. A strong voice in foreign affairs had been the Senate's jealously guarded prerogative since the founding of the Republic. In the past, when it chose to assert its power, the Senate had not scrupled to entrench upon even the rightful diplomatic prerogatives of a President. It would soon do so again—at the expense of Woodrow Wilson. On the face of it, Senator Lodge should have led the revolt against Wilson's unprecedented claims, for no senator was more zealous than Lodge in asserting the Senate's prerogatives in foreign affairs. He had done so in the past and he would do so again—at the expense of Woodrow Wilson. For the present, however, the war party in Congress could ill afford constitutional scruples. Extraordinary as Wilson's claims were, they perfectly suited the war party's extraordinary needs. To bring America into the war the popular will had to go unvoiced in Congress; congressional criticism of Wilson's policies had to be branded as improper "interference" with a President. To bring a people who opposed war into war, Wilson had to be given exactly what he asked for—complete and unhampered control over foreign affairs. Such being the need of the hour, the war party in Congress, led by Lodge himself, agreed at once to declare that Congress had no right to a voice in the European matter.

The parliamentary procedure for doing so was to vote not on the merits of a travel resolution—McLemore's in the House, Gore's in the Senate—but on a motion to table it, a vote, that is, which registered the required opinion that Congress considered itself without right to an opinion. The motion to table had the additional merit of permitting no prior debate. On March 2, the Senate, in an extraordinary act of voluntary self-abasement, agreed to turn itself temporarily into an impotent self-gagged body.

On March 3, the day of the vote, Senator Gore, convinced that Wilson wanted war, tried to "check" him by a parliamentary trick. Just prior to the vote he amended his own resolution so that it became the exact reverse of the original. As a result the Senate actually voted without debate to table not a resolution advising the President to warn Americans off armed belligerent ships, but one that declared that the loss of an American life on such a ship sunk without warning would, in the Senate's opinion, "constitute a just and sufficient cause of war." Most senators voted as if the resolution stood in its original form. All that Gore accomplished, aside from a momentary confusion, was to lose a few votes against tabling. A number of antiwar senators, Gore included, voted to table the resolution as it actually read. The final vote was 68 to table, 14 against, the 14 including such leading opponents of war as Senator La Follette, Senator Norris, and Senator Jones, who remarked shortly after the vote that "we have decided nothing today except that the Senate can be gagged absolutely." Senator Cummins denounced the whole tabling procedure as "the most indefensible and outrageous suppression of the right of debate and the opportunity of intelligent consideration I have ever seen."[30]

If opponents of war were angry, the crypto-interventionists were elated. According to the *New York Times,* the vote demonstrated that there were only fourteen "Germans" in the Senate, a "sorry lot," and that "there is still an America, instinct with national patriotism, hot to resent and prevent the sacrifice of the least tittle of American rights, calm and majestically strong in upholding the President who is striving in stormy times to maintain peace but with no diminution of national right, no stain upon national honor." Like the other interventionists, the *Times* did not include among "the least tittle of American rights" any American right whose assertion would have helped maintain peace—our neutral right to trade in foodstuffs with Germany and European neutrals, our right to regulate the conduct and define the status of belligerent ships using our ports. Even the "national patriotism" of the interventionists was fraudulent.[31]

With the allegedly proud Senate voting to gag itself, the vote in the House, although closer, was a foregone conclusion. For two days Democrats who welcomed war rose up in their usual fashion to praise Wilson for keeping "peace with honor" and to insist that it was the patriotic duty of every member of Congress not to "interfere" with the President in his "supreme struggle to maintain the honor, the dignity and the prestige of this nation." The issue, as Hal Flood put it, was simply whether Congress "shall stand with our President or with a Foreign Government." If war should come as a result of standing by a President who was trying to keep out of war, "were it not a thousand times better," said a West Virginia Democrat, "that we should all die in the trenches and national honor live than that we should all live to see the honor of this Nation ignominiously die?" The right to travel safely on armed belligerent merchantmen had come a long way since the days—a mere three weeks before—when nobody knew it existed.[32]

In rebuttal, Mondell derided the Democrats' "buncombe appeals for loyalty to the President when the question is . . . shall we be loyal to our convictions and to our country," thereby flouting the new crypto-war dictum that Wilson was America incarnate whenever he took a step toward war. Henry Cooper of Wisconsin, a progressive Republican who led the floor opposition to tabling, bitterly assailed Wilson's pretense that he was bound by inescapable, ironclad obligation. The President, said Cooper, claimed in his own words that he had "no choice" but to hold Germany to "strict account" in sinking an armed belligerent merchantman. " 'Strict account!' How is the President going to hold a belligerent nation to 'strict account' in the midst of war except by handing passports to its representatives and employing force. . . . 'No choice!' Protect the foolhardy people at any hazard! 'No choice!' There is but one thing to do when Americans thus risk their lives on armed belligerent merchant ships. Enforce their rights!" Toward the close of his impassioned speech Cooper asked: "Must we stand by the President no matter what he may do or demand?"[33]

The answer was a resounding yes. On March 7, the House tabled the McLemore resolution by a vote of 276 to 142. Democrats voted 181 to 33 to "stand by" the President. The Republicans decided the issue by casting 95 ballots with Wilson to table; 104 Republicans voted against tabling.

The significance of the vote was far-reaching. If, as Senator Gore said, a travel warning would have checked Wilson's descent into war, then Congress had voted overwhelmingly against checking that descent. If, as Senator La Follette said, Congress had voted to "unconditionally surrender all right to voice the popular will," then the American people had lost their only effective check against Wilson's policies, namely Congress itself. Domestically, the vote advanced the war party's cause on every front. For months, prowar spokesmen had been insisting that "loyalty" to the President was the paramount duty of a patriot, that criticizing Wilson in the European matter was "un-American" and "pro-German," that a President who was patently borrowing trouble was striving nobly to keep America out of trouble, that subservience to Britain proved devotion to "America first." Until Congress voted, those propositions had been put forth by agitators, the party press, and individual politicians. Now, for the first time, by formal vote, the Congress of the United States had lent its immense authority to the crypto-war propaganda.

After the vote a number of nervous legislators insisted for the benefit of their constitutents that they had voted to table McLemore's resolution because of the irresistible power of the President. That was the cant of the hour. The truth was otherwise. When Congress rallied around Wilson, he was weaker and more vulnerable than he had been since the outbreak of the European war. Far from bowing to the President's power, Congress had restored his power and increased it greatly, while refurbishing his tarnished reputation and saving him, in point of fact, from certain defeat in the forthcoming election. At a moment of dire peril for Wilson and his war course, Congress, dominated by the war party, had rescued both. That was the true significance of the vote to table a travel-warning resolution. As Senator Norris put it to a friend on March 8: "We are now in much greater danger of being involved [in the European war] than we were a week ago."[34]

12

"A Hopelessly False Position"

With the defeat of the McLemore resolution, Wilson had good reason to suppose that war would be imminent. As the month of March began, each of his alternate routes to "permanent peace"—the low road of the submarine and the high road of "mediation"—appeared unobstructed.

On February 22, the day Washington's historic warning against partiality to a "favored nation" was read aloud in Congress, the British foreign secretary formally agreed to the House "plan" for America's contingent entry into the war on the side of the Allies if Germany rejected peace terms favorable to its enemies. The secret understanding, known as the House-Grey Memorandum, was put in writing by Sir Edward himself. According to the agreement, "President Wilson was ready, on hearing from France and England that the moment was opportune, to propose that a Conference should be summoned to put an end to the war. Should the Allies accept this proposal, and should Germany refuse it, the United States would probably enter the war against Germany." Should Germany agree to negotiate when its enemies thought it "opportune" for themselves, Wilson would help "secure peace on terms not unfavorable to the Allies." These included, at Grey's insistence, the "transfer of Alsace and Lorraine to France." If the Conference "failed to secure peace the United States would leave the Conference as a belligerent on the side of the Allies, if Germany was unreasonable."[1]

Since only a crushing military defeat would possibly persuade Germany to "transfer" two of its provinces to France, the chance of Germany proving "reasonable" was nil. Colonel House did not doubt for a moment that Germany would reject the proposed terms. That was the point of proposing them. A fraudulent peace conference—fitting climax to eighteen months of fraudulent neutrality—was to provide the pretext for "intervention based upon the highest human motives," as House put it to the President shortly before reaching the agreement.[2]

Although the British cabinet had not yet approved—a cautionary point made in the Memorandum itself—House sailed for America convinced that he and Grey had reached an iron-clad agreement. On March 6, one day after landing in New York, the President's private emissary rushed to the White House to deliver in person a full report of his diplomatic triumph. A delighted Wilson quickly gave his assent to the agreement. There is no reason to suppose that his motives were peaceful except in the Wilsonian sense that entering the war meant ending war. Not even Wilson could seriously believe that Germany would accept the terms of the Memorandum although doubtless he thought that the terms, although *unacceptable,* were nonetheless "reasonable." After all, was it not manifestly "unreasonable" for Germany to retain two provinces wrested from France in an earlier war? After Germany rejected Wilson's "reasonable" proposal, the American people would presumably see for themselves the wickedness of German militarism and the imperative need for America to "abolish" it. That demonstration, not a negotiated settlement, was the political point of Wilson's mediation.*

---

* Those who argue—Wilson's distinguished biographer Arthur Link for one—that Wilson, unlike House, expected to end the war peacefully through the House "plan" must assume that Wilson intended to go to the conference, renege on a written pledge to the Allies, whom he favored, and offer peace terms acceptable to Imperial Germany, whom he assuredly disfavored. Nothing in Wilson's professed convictions, ambitions, or actions even remotely suggests that he harbored any such intention, an intention that, if carried out, would have preserved Imperial Germany, would have failed to "abolish militarism," and would have made "permanent peace" in Wilson's view impossible. To maintain the orthodox fiction that Wilson was vainly trying to keep America out of war, Wilson's apologists have been forced to turn him into (a) a trifler who cared little about world peace; (b) a hopeless incompetent who could not see that his betrayals of neutrality were leading the country into war; (c) a

Overwhelmed by the extraordinary favor they intended to confer on the Allies, the favor of total victory in a titanic war, Wilson and House both expected an imminent call for their fake mediation. What America's two enthusiasts for "permanent peace" still could not grasp was that they were not conferring but begging a favor—the favor of going to war for the "highest human motives" rather than over the technical right to travel safely on belligerent merchant ships. The Allies had no reason whatever to bestow such a favor. Sir Edward had drawn up the Memorandum merely to keep America's President well affected. After Wilson's turnabout on armed ships, the British could scarcely afford to spurn the President's importunate emissary, an overconfident fool in all his dealings with the British. Unaware that he had been graciously duped, House assured the British ambassador that America, in due course, would intervene in the war. Privately, House, always optimistic, expected the United States to be at war within a month.[3]

While Wilson and House waited impatiently for the signal to "mediate," the German government, undeterred by Wilson's stand on armed ships, resumed submarine warfare in the war zone after a five-month lapse. Popular demands for resumption had been growing increasingly clamorous in Germany for months, and the demand was fortified by an increasingly reckless animosity toward America. Even in Germany's moderate ruling circles, ill will toward America had risen sharply since Wilson's turnabout on armed ships. As Ambassador Gerard informed House on February 29, Wilson's bombastic letter to Senator Stone had "convinced" the German Chancellor, Bethmann-Hollweg, that "America had a secret understanding with England"—a remarkably astute guess—and that peaceful relations between America and Germany could never be arranged. Moreover, the German civil government's hope that Wilson would loosen the British blockade—its chief intramural argument for restricting submarine warfare—was beginning to wear thin. Wilson had accomplished nothing and the starvation blockade, constantly perfected by the British, was now a genuine menace to the civilian population. Politically, Germany's subma-

man who passionately desired to bring peace to mankind but who (d) made every effort, nonetheless, to prevent himself from achieving that ambition and who (e) miraculously *failed* in his titanic effort to prevent himself from achieving his own ambition.

rine zealots were growing correspondingly stronger and their strength was apparent in March. On March 13, German submarine commanders were instructed not only to attack armed belligerent merchantmen without warning but to attack without warning any unarmed belligerent freighters encountered in the war zone. Still hoping to avoid a fatal clash with the United States, the Germans continued to adhere to their original pledge: submarine commanders were forbidden to attack without warning any belligerent passenger ships anywhere, whether or not they were armed. German hopes quickly proved vain.[4]

On March 24, a German submarine commander, prowling in the English Channel, spied through his periscope a somewhat ambiguous-looking enemy steamer. Possibly a small passenger ship, it lacked, as he noted in his log, the usual passenger ship markings. Painted black, with a bridge resembling that of a warship, it was sailing outside the routes prescribed by the British Admiralty for passenger vessels. The German commander, probably eager for a score, decided it was an enemy mine layer and sent a torpedo into its hull. Although damaged the ship was towed safely to port. Unfortunately it was not a mine layer. It was the unarmed French Channel steamer *Sussex,* bound for Dieppe with 325 passengers including 25 Americans, four of whom were injured in the attack. As a sensational outrage the *Sussex* affray was scarcely in the *Lusitania*'s class. It became clear soon enough that a mistake had been made. To Americans who thought as did the senator from Washington that it was a "colossal crime against humanity" for America to go to war for the sake of a few heedless travelers, the attack was a further argument for warning Americans that they sailed at their own risk on belligerent ships in the war zone. Had Wilson wished to avoid a major crisis he could have demanded—and he certainly would have gotten—a German disavowal of the sinking and a legal indemnity for the four injured Americans.

Wilson had no wish to avoid a major crisis. He was intent upon precipitating one. With his hand greatly strengthened by Congress, with the war party now dominating the political arena,Wilson decided to do what public opinion had prevented him from doing in the summer of 1915: send Germany an ultimatum demanding that it cease submarine warfare altogether on pain of an immediate rup-

ture in diplomatic relations. It was a decision of uncommon boldness. Sending an ultimatum to a major power is an inherently dangerous act, for yielding to an ultimatum is an inherently
humiliating one. Circumstances made any American ultimatum
humiliating in the extreme. America was a prosperous neutral,
Germany a nation engaged in a supremely exhausting war. The
rights Wilson proposed to defend to the limit did not even touch
our vital interests; their observance, however, seriously affected
Germany's ability to fight. Germany had everything at stake,
America nothing, a circumstance that was infuriating as well as
humiliating. Nor was there in Germany any reserve of good will
toward America or any faith in Wilson's neutrality to cushion the
blow. Wilson had little reason to expect a German accession to his
demands. Through the dispatch of a harsh ultimatum all too likely
to be rejected, a nation thoroughly opposed to war was to be forced
up to, and very likely beyond, the brink of war.

That prospect even Wilson found a little daunting. Would the
American people tolerate an ultimatum to Germany? Of that Wilson could hardly be sure. If they did, would they be willing to
"stand by" the President in the ensuing complications? Of that
Wilson could not be sure either. Powerful though the war party had
become, the overwhelming majority of Americans could not be ignored with impunity. If nothing else, they would have to do the
fighting. For some time Wilson held back from taking the fatal
step. As the President was to put it some weeks after the *Sussex* attack in a speech before the National Press Club, "You can imagine
the strain upon the feelings of a man who is trying to interpret the
spirit of the country when he feels that that spirit cannot have its
way beyond a certain point." Antiwar sentiment in America inspired Wilson with self-pity.[5]

For several days after the *Sussex* attack, Wilson waited for de-
finitive proof that a torpedo rather than a marine mine had been
responsible for the damage. Letting Germany temporize over circumstantial details had given American peace sentiment a chance
to assert itself during the *Lusitania* crisis. This time Wilson was
taking no chances. Until April 5, when U.S. naval experts supplied
the proof Wilson needed, the President gave no hint of his plans to
anyone, not to Lansing who urged him to send an ultimatum, nor

even to House, who urged him to sever diplomatic relations at once. With the proof in hand, Wilson instructed the secretary of state to draft an ultimatum to Germany. War over the submarine was imminent, the President told his intimate adviser. It was time to try the alternate—and preferred—route to war. At the President's request, House cabled the British foreign secretary on April 6, asking him to put their agreement into effect at once. The reason for the President's request, House explained to Grey, was that "we are not so sure of the support of the American people upon the submarine issue, while we are convinced that they would respond to the higher and nobler issue of stopping the war." The request to favor America's President with his personal choice of war pretexts received from Grey an answer so readily understandable the wonder is how House and Wilson could have expected any other. Sir Edward rejected it out of hand.[6]

There was no alternative now but the "submarine issue." On April 7, the day Wilson received the ill tidings from London, the President went into seclusion for three days to draft the fateful ultimatum that would hopefully produce a breach of relations with Germany followed by war in due course. Diplomatically speaking, there was nothing difficult about forcing a break with Germany. As Colonel House pointed out to the President, all he had to do to make a rupture certain was to demand outright that Germany cease using the submarine altogether, a demand the German government was automatically bound to reject. Wilson's difficulty was political: The American people might reject it as well. As the President explained to House, if he explicitly demanded total cessation of submarine warfare, Germany's rejection of his ultimatum might not persuade Congress to declare war. Such a demand was too harsh, too sweeping, and too provocative to gain even congressional support. Wilson was operating at the outer limits of the politically tolerable. A degree of ambiguity in his demands was a political necessity. Wilson's long walk on a tightrope had now come down to the precise wording of an ultimatum that would provoke a diplomatic rupture with Germany without provoking a political eruption at home. It was indeed a "strain upon the feelings" of a President when he was trying to figure out how far he dared go against the sentiments of his countrymen.[7]

After completing the ultimatum on April 10, Wilson still hesitated before sending it. Understandably anxious, he tried his best to gauge the political reaction to his plan without, however, revealing it. Wilson did not want the antiwar faction in Congress to know of the ultimatum until it was sent, although he had promised antiwar Democrats during the travel-warning fight that he would inform them in advance when he contemplated any action that might lead to a rupture with Germany. That vow Wilson intended to break because he could not afford to keep it. Given a chance to protest in advance, the opponents of war might well stop him in his tracks. Once the ultimatum was sent, however, the interventionists would be able to invoke the national duty of "standing by" the President and drown out his critics with the by-now-standard slanders against "peace-at-any-price" men and "pro-German conspirators."

To sound out his cabinet members, Wilson read them his draft note to Germany on the pretense that it was merely a possibility he was putting forward for discussion. Cabinet members were cautioned to tell nobody about it. Speaking on April 13 at a Jefferson Day dinner, Wilson proclaimed to a throng of Democratic Party notables that "the interests of America are coincident with the interests of mankind." By now even the dimmest party fugleman could grasp that the President was referring to the sacred rights of neutral travelers and German submarine warfare. What the President wanted to know was, did the Democrats assembled at the dinner have the "courage" to go to war to defend "the interests of humanity"? The audience cheered and shouted "Yes!" On April 18 Wilson finally sent his ultimatum to Germany.[8]

It was a harsh and hostile note, framed even in its opening remarks to infuriate its recipients. The United States, wrote Wilson, would accept no disavowal of the *Sussex* attack for the attack was merely "one of the most terrible examples of the inhumanity of submarine warfare." The other examples Wilson cited were the sinkings of the *Lusitania* and the *Arabic* the previous year. That Germany had pledged since then not to sink munitions-carrying passenger ships without warning Wilson did not even deign to notice. As far as the American President was concerned, Germany had made no concession, for no concession or compromise was possible. As used against enemy commerce, said Wilson, the submarine produced "constant gross and palpable violations of the accepted law of nations." America had been "patient" but our patience was at an end. "The use of the submarine for the destruction of an enemy's commerce is, of necessity, because of the very character of the vessels employed and the very methods of attack which their employment of course involves, utterly incompatible with the principles of humanity, the long-established and incontrovertible rights of neutrals and the sacred immunities of non-combatants." Clearly Wilson was demanding as emphatically as possible the complete cessation of submarine warfare. If the German government took it that way a diplomatic break was certain. Wilson, however, still had to "heed the rocks." Mindful of American public opinion, the President did not make that demand explicit in the formal conclusion of his ultimatum, which read: "Unless the Imperial Government should now immediately declare and effect an abandonment of its present methods of submarine warfare against passenger and freight-carrying vessels, the Government of the United States can have no choice but to sever diplomatic relations with the German Empire altogether." Beyond the ambiguous phrase "present methods" Wilson had not dared to go. How much, if anything, Germany would yield nobody could possibly foretell. America now stood on the brink of war.[9]

Before a joint session of Congress the following day, Wilson explained to the country that he had taken the drastic step of an ultimatum with great reluctance. After assailing the "wanton" nature of submarine warfare and giving the gist of his note to Germany, the President insisted, as usual, that he had had no choice. "By the force of circumstances," said Wilson, America had become "the responsible spokesman for the rights of humanity" (except when Norway asked America to champion the right of neutrals not to be sunk by British mines in the North Sea). There could be no shirking our duty to humanity, dangerous though its discharge might be. As always under Wilson, neutral America lay haplessly ensnared in a net of inescapable obligations that perpetually imperiled our peace and neutrality.[10]

In the bastions of "America First," Wilson's grim call to international duty received a predictably warm welcome. The Senate strongly approved the ultimatum. The metropolitan press favored it overwhelmingly. Overseas, French and English newspapers were ecstatic; they expected America to be at war within days. Only the American people remained unenthusiastic. As the *Journal of Commerce* ruefully admitted on April 20, the American people simply "do not want war with Germany." Within days of Wilson's address the Senate received thousands of telegrams protesting against war. Wilson's ultimatum incensed many members of Congress. No less a party regular than the Republican minority leader, Representative James Mann of Illinois, publicly accused Wilson of seeking war. Henry Ford, the antiwar carmaker, pronounced Wilson's speech "political bunk." Yet the public expression of antiwar sentiment was far weaker in April 1916 than it had been in the days of the *Lusitania* crisis. Then, the crypto-war propaganda had not yet enveloped the political arena. By now it had taken its toll on the force and clarity of popular opposition to war. Americans were growing reluctant to voice "disloyal" and "un-American" opinions in a moment of crisis. Sullen submission to an odious fate, so marked in the American people after the United States entered the war, was already beginning to infect the country. The war party was winning the civil war over war.[11]

While the world waited tensely for Germany's reply, Wilson, though forced to leave his ultimatum ambiguous, did what he could to goad Germany into defiance. On April 21, the administration informed the German ambassador that the United States wanted Germany to abandon all submarine activity pending a resolution of the crisis, a demand so arbitrary and hostile that a German chancellor who acceded to it would not have remained in office for a day. When Germany asked for a clearer definition of "present methods of submarine warfare" and a more explicit American statement concerning cruiser rules, Wilson promulgated rulings equally arbitrary and hostile. On April 27, for Germany's benefit, the administration published for the first time the official U.S. government position on armed belligerent ships. It was an act of provocation in itself. For all Wilson's cant about the "immutable" rules of war, he and Lansing had concocted a novel rule that was not only unfair to Germany but an affront to common sense. According to the new American rule, a belligerent merchantman could carry *offensive* arms and still retain all the immunities of a peaceful unarmed private commercial vessel. Its weapons were offensive only if used for an "aggressive purpose." A submarine could attack such a ship only after it obtained "conclusive evidence" of that purpose, which is to say, only after it was first attacked and quite possibly sunk. The next day, Lansing informed the Germans that the rule requiring a ship of war to provide for the safety of a merchant-man's passengers and crew was not fulfilled by putting them in "an open boat." Clearly, adherence to cruiser rules meant the total cessation of submarine warfare, an impossible demand, as Wilson well knew. Formally, Wilson had been forced to leave the Germans a narrow out; informally he was trying to convince them there was none.[12]

If Wilson hoped to goad Germany's leaders into angry defiance he certainly succeeded in infuriating them. In the margin of the Kaiser's copy of Wilson's ultimatum the much-despised German emperor hit off with angry precision the maddening hyposcrisy of America's President. Circling the word "humanity" in the American note, the Kaiser scribbled the comment: " 'Humanity' in Wilson's head means unlimited possibilities for real or hypothetical citizens of U.S.A. to cruise about on hostile & armed merchant-men whenever they like in the zone of war." On the other hand, Britain's starvation war against German civilians "is absolutely *not* 'inhuman' in Wilson's eyes & quite right. . . . Either starve at England's bidding or war with America! That is, in name of Wilson's 'Humanity.'" Angry, humiliated, and backed against the wall, Germany's leaders nonetheless decided for the second and last time to keep America out of the war. On May 3, the German government handed to Ambassador Gerard its conciliatory reply to the American ultimatum, known to history, somewhat misleadingly, as the "Sussex Pledge."[13]

After rejecting Wilson's extreme demand for total cessation of submarine warfare, Germany announced as a "further concession" to the United States that henceforth no enemy merchant ship, armed or unarmed, would be "sunk without warning, and without saving human lives, unless these ships attempt to escape or offer resistance." With that, the German government had been forced into the trap it had tried so hard to elude—a public pledge to the United States to keep submarine warfare severely restricted. It had even conceded to armed British merchantmen the right to take the first deadly shot. The German government, however, was determined to leave itself an exit from the trap. The German pledge, the note made emphatically clear, was entirely conditional. "Neutrals cannot expect that Germany, forced to fight for her existence, shall, for the sake of neutral interest, restrict the use of an effective weapon if her enemy is permitted to continue to apply at will methods of warfare violating the rules of international law." To demand Germany's adherence to neutral rights at sea without making similar demands upon Germany's enemies, the note pointed out quite correctly, was "incompatible with the character of neutrality." Germany would therefore abide by its pledge on condition that "the United States will now demand and insist that the British government shall forthwith observe the rules of international law." Should the United States fail to secure its neutral rights against Germany's enemies, "the German government would then be facing a new situation, in which it must reserve itself complete liberty of decision." In plain language, unless Wilson stood up to the British, Germany would consider itself free of the pledge it had made.[14]

Under the humiliating pressure of an ultimatum Germany had made a major military concession to the United States. The condition it placed on that concession was eminently reasonable and in truth unanswerable. For Wilson to demand the observance of American neutral rights at one belligerent's expense while failing to do so to the advantage of that belligerent's enemy was truly "incompatible with the character of neutrality." Wilson, however, was by no means pleased with the "Sussex Pledge." The obvious obstacle was Germany's attached condition. If Wilson accepted it he would have no grounds for war when unrestricted submarine warfare resumed. All his efforts to elevate a technical right of no practical use into a "dictate of humanity," a touchstone of "national honor," and the test of America's sovereignty would have been utterly in vain. Having sought a rupture in diplomatic relations, Wilson was tempted at first to reject the German note entirely. At any rate Colonel House seems to have thought so, for he advised Wilson curtly that the German concession provided "no adequate excuse for a break." It was politically impossible to reject it. Wilson agreed, but only in part. To the German condition, so fatal to his war, he could not possibly accede.[15]

On May 8, Wilson sent to Germany a sharp, unfriendly note accepting the German concession and curtly warning the German government that the United States expected a "scrupulous execution" of its pledge. The German condition Wilson rejected out of hand. America's neutral rights were "absolute, not relative." They could not be made "contingent" upon America's relation with another belligerent. As far as the United States was concerned, the German pledge was absolute and to that pledge, come what might, Wilson would hold the German government. If Britain continued to blockade Germany at the expense of America's neutral rights that was no business of Germany's although its entire civilian population might starve.[16]

Possibly Wilson's argument was technically correct. If so, it was correct only in the narrowest sense for it was utterly false to neutrality. No President who cared for the peace of his country would ever have claimed the right to hold one belligerent to international law while letting its enemy enjoy the advantage of ignoring it. Wilson's reason for doing so was obvious enough. Having failed to provoke a rupture he had settled for the next best thing. By stripping the German pledge of its conditional nature, America was now virtually honorbound to break with Germany when it "violated" its pledge to the United States and resumed unrestricted submarine warfare. That resumption was inevitable since Wilson had no intention of securing America's neutral rights against England.

With Wilson's note of acceptance the *Sussex* crisis came to an end. Once again Democrats could exultantly proclaim that Wilson had "kept us out of war." In fact, a fatal conflict with Germany was now only a matter of time. "It begins to look as if war with Germany is inevitable," Wilson remarked to his secretary, Tumulty, in June, as if he himself had had nothing to do with it.[17]

In the spring of the *Sussex* crisis constitutional necessity interrupted the civil war over war. In 1916 the American people were once again called upon to elect a President. The crypto-interventionists, a bipartisan faction, were once again compelled to resume their expected partisan roles. It was an awkward situation both for Wilson and for the leaders of the Republican Party, the ostensible opposition. The Republicans could scarcely campaign on a platform of "standing by" a Democratic President: It would have made the election an open farce. Opposition of some kind was required and there was no doubt what kind would make a Republican victory certain. Republican leaders had only to nominate a candidate who stood convincingly for peace. Let him campaign with full party backing on a policy of genuine neutrality; let him contrast that policy with Wilson's partiality to Britain; let him point out to the electorate that such partiality endangered our neutrality and invited embroilment in the European war. The Republican candidate who offered that opposition would have won the presidency in a landslide. The Democratic Party was weak in the country. Wilson himself was widely disliked or distrusted despite his bipartisan support. Millions of "hyphenated Americans," seething with hatred of the President, would have rallied to the Republican banner, including even Irish-American voters, the mainstay of the Democracy in the Northeast. The British army's suppression of the Dublin Easter Rebellion on April 24 had alienated the Irish still further from their pro-British President. Native Americans, too, resented Britain's apparent domination of the Wilson administration. By May the electorate was so incensed over the British blockade that the British ambassador, in alarm, warned his government on May 26 that "any step taken against British action will be hailed with enthusiasm" by Americans, who still understood, despite all the slanders of the war party, that the first duty of a neutral is impartiality. Moreover, a moderate Republican candidate advocating genuine, peace-preserving neutrality would have won back to the party the most important body of voters in the campaign—the millions of progressive Republicans who had voted for Roosevelt over Taft in 1912. Wilson had alienated them as well. They distrusted his foreign policy and resented his support for preparedness. They had discovered, too, that the President, for all his progressive talk, had revealed himself to be an old-line states' rights Democrat opposed to every measure concerning what reform circles now referred to as "social justice."[18]

For Republican leaders, however, running an antiwar candidate on a platform of genuine neutrality presented a fatal difficulty. They would win the election but lose the war. To endorse antiwar sentiment in America, to assert that Wilson's foreign policy rather than German villainy endangered the peace, would destroy all chance of dragging America into an "inevitable" conflict. Once pry loose the lid on American public opinion and there was no calculating the force of the eruption. So far from winning the presidency at so steep a price certain Republican leaders, Lodge and Root in particular, urged Republicans to go before the country as an all but open war party. They wanted to attack Wilson for not espousing universal peacetime conscription, for showing partiality to *Germany,* for weakly defending the "rights of humanity," for not backing his threats with force, and in general for "humiliating" the country with his allegedly timid and pacifist policies. Neither Lodge nor Root thought such a campaign would win the election. Indeed it would have been so radically repellent to the electorate the Republican candidate who followed it would be committing political suicide in public. The trouble with following the urgings of Lodge and Root, however, did not lie in losing the 1916 presidential election. It would have brought disaster incomparably more serious. At best the eastern Republican leaders formed the dominant faction in a perilously divided party. On war and war-related issues, the party split was even deeper than it had been over reform. West of the Alleghenies the great majority of Republican Party members, regulars as well as reformers, opposed partiality to Britain and any drastic defense of the right to travel safely on belligerent merchantmen. In the House vote on the McLemore resolution, Republican legislators from Illinois, Minnesota, Wisconsin, Iowa, North Dakota, South Dakota, Kansas, and Nebraska had voted 51 to 1 against tabling the resolution. Had the eastern oligarchs gone to the national convention determined to force through a crypto-interventionist candidate and a bellicose party platform they would have destroyed the Republican Party altogether.[19]

Between their fear of losing the war and their fear of sundering the party, the Republican oligarchy adopted a two-step compromise strategy. At the national convention in Chicago the oligarchy, for the sake of party unity, nominated a man free of any interventionist taint and put through a moderate platform which actually called for "honest neutrality." They then turned around during the ensuing campaign and virtually forced their chosen candidate to take an unpopular, bellicose line.

The oligarchy's chosen nominee—he had no serious rivals—was Charles Evans Hughes, Supreme Court justice since 1910 and the perfect "available man" for national convention purposes. Remembered as mildly progressive, Hughes, as a member of the Court, had taken no part in the bitter intraparty struggles of 1912 nor had he uttered a single public word about the European matter. Respected and above all untainted, Hughes enjoyed enormous initial advantages over the President, whom Americans by a considerable margin were strongly inclined to be rid of. Among the Republican nominee's assets was Roosevelt's well-known dislike of him. The former President, returning to the Republican fold after killing off his dying Progressive Party, was so desperately truculent that anyone he publicly disapproved of enjoyed a virtual certificate of pacific intentions. Nor was Hughes an interventionist in 1916. In a private interview with Oswald Villard, the New York publisher, he sharply attacked Wilson for, in his own words, "maneuvering the country into a position where war may be a necessity."[20]

Had Hughes said that plainly and clearly in public, Wilson's chances for reelection would have been nil. Unfortunately for Hughes, the Republican oligarchy did not want their candidate telling the electorate home truths that imperiled the war. They wanted Wilson attacked as a pacifist, not as a warhawk disguised, and their demands could not be disregarded. If Hughes defied the oligarchy the party organization would knife his candidacy and the results would be fatal: No nonincumbent candidate for the presidency ever won the office over his own party's opposition. On the other hand, if Hughes did the oligarchy's bidding he would obviously lose votes, but presumably with their backing he would have regular Republican votes to spare, a point Colonel House himself made to the President. That was the logic of Hughes's situation, although he struggled against it for a time. Initially Hughes tried his best to find some middle ground between the Republican oligarchy and the American electorate, to straddle, as it were, the civil war over war.[21]

Using the crypto-interventionist slogan "America First," Hughes tried to give it its honest, as opposed to its interventionist, meaning by calling for "firm and unflinching maintenance of *all* the rights of American citizens." That implied rebuke to Wilson's fraudulent,

war-inviting neutrality was not to the oligarchy's liking. To keep
them loyal to his candidacy, Hughes felt compelled to vitiate his
campaign theme entirely by absurdly insisting on several occasions
that Wilson was anti-British and cared more for property than human life. It was an obvious lie and Hughes knew it was a lie. Worse
yet, it was a vote-repelling lie. During the election campaign
Americans were vehemently demanding retaliatory measures
against Britain. To escape his dilemma Hughes tried to play down
war issues as much as possible, but Republican leaders would not
let him escape so easily. They unleashed Roosevelt, their newly appointed foreign policy spokesman, against their own candidate.
Throughout the campaign Roosevelt stumped for—in fact
against—the Republican candidate by fulminating against Wilson's "mean timidity" and his "course of dishonor" against Germany; by making it clear, in short, that whatever Hughes said he
was—and he insisted over and over that he was a man of peace—he
was shackled to a party that was all but openly in favor of war. Every time Roosevelt delivered one of his intemperate attacks on
"mollycoddles," "poltroons," and "ultra-pacifists" the Republican
National Committee was flooded with protests while Hughes privately stewed in frustrated rage.[22]

For some time, however, Wilson took little advantage of the favor Republican leaders were bestowing on him. Though considerably more determined to win reelection than Republicans were to
elect Hughes, Wilson was as loath as they to encourage antiwar or
to appease anti-British sentiment in the country. So too was his
party. To the many millions of Americans who suspected that the
Democratic President was doing something other than keeping
them out of war, the Democratic convention held few attractions
since it chiefly celebrated the President's allegedly incomparable
efforts to "keep us out of war." At Wilson's personal behest, the
Democrats at the convention made it clear that though they opposed war they did so only under the usual war-inviting conditions.
The Democrats were for peace but only "with honor," meaning
that they were willing to wage war over the right to travel on belligerent merchant ships. The party platform, written by Wilson,
praised "Our President who has preserved the vital interests of our
government and its citizens and kept us out of war," meaning that

the right to travel had now become a "vital interest" although it affected about a thousand Americans and even them scarcely at all. According to the convention's keynote speaker, the Democrats wanted "no jingoistic war" but they were ready to fight "when Reason primes the rifle," the electorate being asked to choose between a jingo Republican war and a high-minded Wilsonian war, when of course they preferred neither. During the campaign Wilson was so reluctant to pose as a "peace" candidate that he himself seldom claimed that he had "kept us out of war." He continued to impugn the loyalty of "hyphenated Americans" and he resisted as best he could the almost overwhelming popular demand for retaliation against the British blockade.[23]

Temporarily split by election-year formalities yet determined to give public opinion in America as little encouragement as possible, the war party was doing its best under trying conditions to keep itself, its policies, and its system of lies intact.

Wilson placed his own hopes for reelection on grounds other than peace. His only chance for victory lay in winning the support of millions of independent progressive Republicans who were now virtually partyless. They wanted peace and they wanted further reforms, which in themselves seemed to betoken peace. The President, who had declared the "bad dream" of reform at an end in 1914 and who had opposed every reform measure since then, decided he had no choice but to become a progressive reformer once again. In the winter of 1915 Wilson had opposed as "class legislation" federally backed credits for farmers. In 1916 he switched and supported it—it became law on July 17. Previously he had opposed on states' rights grounds federal child-labor legislation. He now switched and supported it—it became law on September 1. Under intense pressure from reformers Wilson supported the first genuinely graduated income tax in American history to finance the costs of preparedness. He pushed through legislation that mandated the eight-hour workday on the nation's railroads—it became law on September 3. He claimed in his first formal campaign speech that he was now the champion of "social justice," which is to say, of everything he had opposed six months before.[24]

Wilson's 1916 reforms were an impressive, if expedient, performance. Yet despite the reforms, despite Hughes's compromised campaign, despite the vote-repelling rant of Roosevelt, a clear majority of the voters were still inclined as of late September to get rid of Woodrow Wilson. The President's reversion to reform had helped him greatly, but the paramount issue in the country was peace. Given a choice—inherently an unhappy one—between a fresh challenger submissive to a bellicose party and a President who "kept us out of war" by perpetually inviting it, voters preferred to trust the challenger. Faced with the prospect of defeat, Wilson on September 30 at last brought himself to take the step that was to put victory within his grasp—he turned on his Republican allies. In the course of a campaign speech Wilson asserted that "the certain prospect of the success of the Republican party is that we shall be drawn in one form or another into the embroilments of the European war." In short, Wilson did to his Republican supporters what they refused to allow done to him: He accused them of wanting war.[25]

To the American people Wilson's remark represented far more than a partisan campaign slur. For one thing it was the first straightforward antiwar statement Wilson had made since the *Lusitania* crisis, the first, that is, that he had not hedged round with exiguous qualifications and "no choice" obligations that invariably spelled trouble. More important, he had offered the electorate a piece of the truth, and the American people were starving for any morsel of truth, so long had they been fed on a diet of lies. For more than a year the citizenry had seen legal technicalities magnified into "national honor," heard partiality described as "unswerving neutrality," national impotence called "national patriotism," subvervience to Britain lauded as "America First." The lies had done much to silence, but they had done little to convince, the vast majority of Americans. Millions of Americans knew in their bones that they were being led by men who secretly craved war. Now at last someone of consequence had confirmed that private knowledge and upheld in part their own common sense. In 1916 the American people were more prosperous economically and more impoverished politically than they had ever been before in their history. The effect of Wilson's remark was startling; across the country it was greeted with overwhelming, electrifying approval, although it came from a man voters deeply distrusted. That alone suggests how hungry for truth and how grateful for elementary respect a free people had grown under the contemptuous, unrelenting mendacity of their "ambitious, corrupted or deluded" leaders.[26]

That Wilson had not attacked the Republicans as the war party from the start suggests how reluctant he was to break into the war party's system of lies. Once he made the breach, however, the Democrats followed it up, within limits, with considerable verve and efficiency. As Colonel House put it to Wilson on October 5, "would it not be well to take some of Roosevelt's most violent utterances and assume that he is voicing Hughes?" To kill Hughes with Roosevelt became the Democrats' closing campaign theme. Roosevelt, quite obviously, was a warmonger; Roosevelt spoke for a bellicose Republican leadership. Who then was the Republican candidate? The answer, said the Democrats, was obvious: He was a man in "complete accord with Roosevelt," a warmonger thinly disguised. For Hughes it was a painful accusation and a bitterly ironic one, for Roosevelt detested him, wanted him to lose, and thought his very nomination proof that America was "yellow." To the Democrats' accusation, however, Hughes had no adequate reply. Struggle and squirm though he tried, he dared not repudiate Roosevelt. Approving Roosevelt's violent speeches was one of the Republican oligarchy's ground rules, and Hughes feared to breach them. Unless party leaders got out every regular Republican vote on election day, he no longer had a chance to win. Indeed, the more he had curried their favor at the cost of votes the more urgently he needed their favor. With his once formidable lead melting away, the hapless Hughes was reduced in the final days of the campaign to crying up the virtues of the protective tariff, the only safe issue Republican leaders allowed him. As Wilson himself rightly observed, Hughes was "in a hopelessly false position."[27]

While Hughes spread the Republican gospel of 1884, the Democrats hammered away at the Hughes-is-Roosevelt theme to the end. On election eve, in one last appeal to the voters, the Democrats put an advertisement in every major newspaper in the country eloquently summing up their campaign stratagem:

> "You are Working;
> —*not Fighting!*
> Alive and Happy:

—not Cannon Fodder!
Wilson and Peace with Honor?
or
Hughes with Roosevelt and War?"[28]

To the electorate, however, the choice was not quite so clear-cut. Although Republican leaders had grown strident over the European matter, their views did not really differ from the President's. Given unhappy alternatives, voters chiefly expressed their discontent by voting against the party they usually supported. In the East, Irish-Americans and other ethnic voters deserted the Democratic candidate in droves. In the Middle West, Republican farmers and progressives deserted the Republican candidate in droves. The result of the balloting was one of the closest presidential elections in American history. Until the California votes were tabulated the day after the election, the outcome remained in doubt. By the slender margin of 3,773 votes, Wilson carried the normally Republican state and with it the election. Contemporaries cited Hughes's preference for California's stand-pat Republicans over the dominant progressive Republicans for his loss of the state and the presidency. If so, it was the perfect epitome of his entire campaign. Running strongly in the Middle West and West, where Democrats usually fared poorly, Wilson had actually eked out his victory by capturing the antiwar reform wing of the national Republican Party, whom Republican leaders had spurned throughout the campaign. Wilson's reelection has often been regarded as a great personal triumph, but it was nothing of the kind. Had the Republican oligarchy allowed its candidate to campaign as he wished, Wilson would have gone down to a decisive, humiliating defeat. His reelection was the gift of a Republican oligarchy that preferred to see a Democrat lead the country into war rather than risk having no war at all. Hughes was not the only candidate "in a hopelessly false position."

13

"The National Conscience Is Clear"

A few weeks after the November elections, Ambassador Page called in an American war correspondent for a confidential interview. "He had certain knowledge," the reporter later recalled, "that [Germany] intended to declare unlimited submarine warfare. Wilson could make only one answer—war. 'We'll be in it before spring,' said Page." The ambassador's information was accurate and quite well known to the President. All was not well at the White House, however. In the autumn of 1916 Wilson's personal faith in his war to "end war" had begun to weaken. It was a difficulty he could not have foreseen, and it was to give rise to the oddest episode in his long quest for the "noblest part." For twenty months Wilson had been maneuvering America toward war without any troublesome misgivings. Insulated by a carapace of catch phrases—"service to mankind," "democracy against autocracy," "German militarism," "immutable law," "the dictates of humanity," "permanent peace," "association of nations"—the President had disregarded everything save the noble vision of himself delivering mankind from the scourge of war. In the autumn, doubt and anxiety assailed him. His nerves grew frayed; his head ached; his stomach burned with dyspepsia. What caused the alteration was reality's rude intrusion into Wilson's private crazyhouse of ambition and blind egotism. While he was betraying the American people in the interests of the Allies, the Allies, he discovered, were betraying him.[1]

The discovery was painful, but not even Wilson could shut his eyes to it. Personal affronts he deeply resented, and the Allies had personally affronted him. No matter how hard House begged and cajoled them, they refused to put the House-Grey Memorandum into effect. To Wilson and House only one explanation seemed possible: The Allies were harboring war aims far more ambitious and far less conducive to "permanent peace" than the "not unfavorable" terms laid down in the Memorandum. If so, then helping the Entente destroy "militarism" at America's expense was not quite the supreme service to mankind that Wilson had persuaded himself it was. The President was maneuvering his country into an unpopular, unnecessary, immeasurably costly war that was losing, even in his own eyes, its former unblemished justification, namely the certainty that an Allied victory would "end war" forever.[2]

The situation cried out for the obvious solution—avert war with Germany. The means of doing so still lay at hand. All Wilson had to do was disengage himself from "the European matter." The President was under no compulsion whatever to dictate or influence a postwar European settlement. Far from it. He was reluctant even to admit in public that he harbored any such ambition. The outcome of the European war, as Wilson himself acknowledged, would have no effect on American interests one way or the other. Nor was Wilson under any compulsion to hold Germany unilaterally to the terms of the "Sussex Pledge," conditional on Germany's part in any case. The British blockade had not been loosened. Not a single American right had been restored by the Allies. Moreover, the British, taking full advantage of Wilson's stand on armed merchantmen, were vigorously sinking submarines that obeyed the Wilsonian rules of submarine warfare. Had the President reverted to "honest neutrality" he would have had the entire body of the American people behind him. Neutrality was all Americans ever wanted of Wilson from the start. The war party would have disintegrated in a trice. Without Wilson to lead them, the crypto-interventionists were helpless.[3]

There was one insuperable drawback to genuine neutrality: It meant sacrificing the "noblest part," and that Wilson could not bring himself to do. He had already invested too much in its pursuit. It was the sole justification for all he had done since the outbreak of the European war: for making America's neutrality a mockery, for betraying the interests of his countrymen, for poisoning the political atmosphere. Without his ambition, the man who longed to be "a great statesman" would have had to admit to himself that his statesmanship had been destructive, disgraceful, and fatuously naive. Wilson had trapped himself cruelly. The more he had done to further his ambition, the more tightly ambition held him in thrall. In 1919 Wilson was to say that if he did not believe he was doing God's work he would go insane. He might have said as much in the autumn of 1916. Neutrality and disengagement were ruled out. What then was to be done?

It is the measure of Wilson's blind egotism that he perceived the situation facing America entirely in personal terms. It was not America's plight that concerned him but the qualms of an uneasy conscience. He no longer felt fully justified inflicting a war on the American people. The answer, therefore, was to do something that made him feel justified again. On November 14, the President first broached his plan of action to House. He felt obliged, he told House, to make a public bid for peace before the inevitable break with Germany. He was going to try to avert war over the submarine by attempting to stop the European war itself, a gratuitously difficult way of accomplishing what honest neutrality would have readily achieved.[4]

Knowing Wilson and his self-deceptions, House assumed, quite correctly, that Wilson had no real wish to avoid war with Germany. It is not very difficult to avoid a war when 90 percent of one's people do not want it and the chief grounds for the war is the enforcement, unilaterally, of a belligerent's conditional pledge to restrict its mode of fighting its own public enemies. House supposed that the President intended a mere public gesture designed to persuade the American people that their President was exhausting all means of averting his "inevitable" war. That had been Wilson's pretense from the start. House strongly advised Wilson against making the gesture. Instead of preparing the people for war over the submarine, House pointed out to the President, it would make them even *less* willing to fight than they already were. The Allies were determined to win a war of exhaustion, a strategy made possible by American-supplied munitions, American bank loans, the American-protected blockade, and the fair certainty that America would intervene when all-out submarine warfare resumed. It was Germany that wanted a negotiated settlement. The German government had been vainly asking Wilson since May—and as recently as mid-October—to initiate peace talks. The German desire for a settlement was unfortunately genuine. Temporarily Germany held the upper hand on the battlefield; a negotiated settlement would inevitably come out in its favor. Unless Germany got a negotiated settlement, however, danger and even disaster loomed ahead. Germany could not win a war of attrition, and Germany's military leaders had no intention of fighting one. Unless the civil government could secure a prompt settlement, the alternative was all-out submarine warfare and war with the United States, a prospect dreaded by both the civil government and the Kaiser himself. Clearly if Wilson made a peace move the Allies would reject it and the Germans would accept it. Then, said House, the American people would never go to war over the submarine "for the reason that Germany, having consented to peace parleys, would be thought more or less justified in employing unrestricted submarine warfare." The American people had an unfortunate propensity for sharing Germany's viewpoint, not out of any sympathy for Germany but through their clear understanding that holding one belligerent to international law while letting its enemy do as it pleased was "incompatible with the character of neutrality." Had Wilson wished to keep America out of the war, he would not have found much substance in Colonel House's argument. Determined to wage war over the submarine, however, Wilson found it genuinely worrisome. He did not want to try to avert war at the cost of losing his war. For several days after talking with House the President did nothing, while the German government, increasingly impatient, waited for Wilson's reply to their latest, month-old peace feeler.[5]

If Colonel House thought he had disposed of Wilson's peace move, however, he soon discovered his mistake. House, in fact, had entirely misread Wilson's intentions. The President had something in mind other than a propaganda gesture. It was not the American people he wished to placate, it was the qualms of conscience. Wilson did not want to avert war with Germany, but he did want to persuade himself that he had *tried*—an altogether different objective, as his actions were soon to make clear.

Wilson's powers of self-persuasion were redoubtable, but the task facing him was by no means easy. It was difficult getting around the awkward fact that the wrong country wanted a negotiated peace. That the German desire for a settlement was not a whit more virtuous than the Allied determination to fight on made little difference to most Americans. The German desire meant peace for the United States, the Allied determination spelled trouble. For that very reason anti-British sentiment had already reached alarming proportions in America, the electorate perceiving, despite the war party's propaganda, that it was Britain, not Germany, which was pushing America toward war. Public opinion, as Wilson himself pointed out to House that November, was as "hot against Great Britain as it was at first against Germany." Put Britain publicly in the wrong, as House had rightly observed, and it would prove impossible to bring America into the war when Germany unleashed its submarines. Any peace move Wilson made, therefore, had to meet at least one essential condition: the onus for prolonging the war must not fall upon the Allies, who were determined to prolong it. Calling for a peace conference was clearly out of the question. That was exactly what Germany wanted and the Allies dreaded. Consequently it was precisely what Wilson would not do. On November 29 the American emissary in Berlin was instructed to tell the German government that the American President would not initiate peace talks because Germany was deporting Belgians to work in German war factories, a typical Wilsonian mixture of moralizing and mendacity.[6]

By then Wilson had drafted what he called a "peace note," which seemed to meet the demands of conscience without undue risk to ambition. Drafted by the President on November 25, the note would request each of the belligerents to state its peace terms preparatory to a conference in which their respective terms would be discussed. One advantage of Wilson's request was that it lightened the moral burden on the Allies while increasing the burden on Germany. The German government had never specified its war aims because the country was hopelessly divided. The conservative parties had conqueror's ambitions; the Social Democrats, whose support for the war was indispensable, favored moderate goals. Any public disclosure of war aims would seriously embarrass the German government. Despite this advantage, House viewed Wilson's preliminary draft with dismay. The President, it seemed, might be harboring plans to compel Germany to offer moderate terms which he would then force the Allies to accept. It was imperative, House advised the President, that he do no such thing. Being dependent on America, the Allies could be forced to a conference table but, as House pointed out, they would never forgive Wilson for doing so. Moreover the Germans "don't care how you come out." Wilson, in a word, would have no voice in the settlement. War with Germany would be averted, the European war would be ended, millions of lives would be saved, but the price, House advised Wilson, would be prohibitive. He would lose "the biggest opportunity for service that was ever given to man." The Allies must not feel themselves under any American pressure to come to terms with Germany. Again Wilson found his adviser's argument a strong one. At House's suggestion, the President made clear in a second draft of his "peace note" that he was neither offering his personal mediation nor personally demanding peace negotiations. The Allies, who had every reason to sabotage peace talks, were to feel free to state what peace terms they pleased.[7]

Even thus weakened, the note posed dangers to the Allies and therefore to Wilson's war. House again advised the President not to send it and Wilson reluctantly agreed to hold it back. As he remarked to Lansing on December 1, he did not want to do anything rash. For several days more, the President continued to procrastinate while he fretted over the perils of his "peace note." On December 8 Wilson weakened it still further by eliminating the suggestion that the belligerents confer on their war aims once they had disclosed them to the American President. The suggestion was clearly dangerous. The Germans might answer the call for a conference, ignore Wilson's request for a disclosure of their war aims, and still leave the Allies looking in the wrong. Wilson's venture in peacemaking was becoming farcical before it even began. A peace move so formulated that the belligerents opposed to a settlement would neither bear the onus for rejecting one nor feel any American pressure to accept one was doomed before it was made. Unfortunately for the United States, Wilson's peace venture only had to satisfy Wilson.[8]

In the meantime events were moving rapidly in the major war capitals. In London on December 5, Lloyd George took over the premiership as head of a coalition government avowedly determined to fight on until Germany was vanquished. In Berlin Chancellor Bethmann gave up hope that the American President would ever initiate peace talks. After six months of German urging Wilson had failed to do anything. The situation was growing more desperate by the day. With time running out fast on the Sussex Pledge, a break with America was imminent. Only a negotiated settlement could avert the fatal clash that German civil leaders had been struggling to avoid since Wilson had sent his first *Lusitania* note in May 1915. The German chancellor decided he had only one recourse left: He would propose peace talks himself. On December 12, accordingly, the Germans dropped a diplomatic bombshell on Wilson and the world. They informed the American President that Germany was ready "to enter immediately upon peace negotiations" and requested him to make the offer known to the Allies. On December 16, Wilson duly transmitted the German offer with the curt reminder that it was not to be "construed in any way as an attempt at mediation" by the United States. America in no way endorsed, supported, or sympathized with the German proposal. The Allies were to feel free to treat it as they pleased.[9]

The German offer, which shocked and surprised the world, was both an embarrassment and a spur to Wilson. The embarrassment was obvious. If one of the belligerents wanted the European war settled, what had the President who "kept us out of war" been doing in the interests of peace? Clearly nothing, for Germany had acted on its own. It was imperative now that Wilson do something himself in the name of peace. The German proposal, moreover, removed the chief fear staying Wilson's hand, namely that his own peace move would make Germany look good and the Allies look bad and thereby ruin everything. That the Allies would reject the German offer was certain. If that damaged the Allies in American eyes, then the damage was done, or would be as soon as the Allies replied. By merely asking the belligerents to state their war aims,

Wilson's note, as he himself observed to Lansing, would "inject new elements into the debate now going on among the nations at war." It might possibly put the Allies in a better light; it would certainly put the Germans in a worse one. If they demanded territorial gains, they would be open to condemnation; if they refused to state their war aims, they would be open to the charge of untrustworthiness.[10]

Prompted by expedience as well as conscience, Wilson on December 18 finally sent his much revised "peace note" to each of the parties to war. The note simply asked them to state "their respective views as to the terms upon which the war might be concluded." It emphatically disavowed any other intention. "The President is not proposing peace; he is not even offering mediation. He is merely proposing that soundings be taken." It was a woefully feeble peace effort, one that suggested nothing, foreshadowed nothing, insisted upon nothing. The United States was in a powerful position to end the European war, but the note made no use of that power. What peacemaking potential it had rested chiefly on the Allies' fear that Wilson just might be serious, which is to say, that he just might, at long last, put the interests of America ahead of his own ambitions. That fear the secretary of state dispelled at once. He privately assured the French and British ambassadors that Wilson was in no way trying to force peace upon the Entente, which was certainly true.* The Allies breathed a collective sigh of relief. Knowing that it was they who stood in the way of any negotiated settlement, they concluded at once that Wilson's note was a sham sent chiefly to prepare the American people for armed intervention. They decided, accordingly, that it was safe to state war aims so extreme that they would destroy all chance of a negotiated settlement and thereby force America into the war. Wilson did nothing to hinder or discourage them.[11]

Germany's initial response was hardly more promising. The

---

* According to Wilson's biographer, Arthur Link, Lansing's communications with the Allies were entirely unknown to Wilson and constituted a deliberate attempt to "sabotage" his peace efforts. See Arthur Link, *Wilson,* vol. 5, pp. 223, 249. Link's assertion is scarcely tenable. That Lansing, a docile subordinate, would take upon himself so momentous an act of betrayal is difficult to credit on its face. More to the point, his assurances to the Allies were in complete accord with Wilson's fears and House's warnings. Had the President wished to put pressure on the Allies, they would have felt it soon enough, all Lansing's alleged "sabotage" notwithstanding.

German government declined to state its peace terms and merely repeated its earlier request for "the speedy assembly, on neutral ground, of delegates of the warring states." Four days later, on December 30, the Allies jointly rejected the German proposal and denounced it as a "maneuver of war," a propaganda ploy to gain American sympathy.[12]

Objectively, Wilson's diplomatic bid to end the European war was an abysmal, self-sabotaged failure, but Wilson himself was undisturbed. After sending his note to the belligerents the President sat back for a month and let matters drift. His qualms of conscience were dying down rapidly. Wilson even managed to persuade himself by January that the chief obstacle to a negotiated peace was the country that had been seeking one for the past eight months. It was Germany's failure to "confide in me," Wilson told House, that made a negotiated settlement impossible. The Allies' uncompromising terms, on the other hand, he airily dismissed as mere "bluff." It was the Germans, according to Wilson, who had to give ground, but when they appeared to do so it did them no good anyway. On January 15 when the Germans, in a last-ditch effort to avert war, proposed moderate terms in a second reply to Wilson's note, the President did not even bother to inform the Allies, although they opened up prospects for a negotiated settlement. He regarded the offer as a mere German ruse to gain the good will of Americans and thereby forestall war with the United States. That Wilson could not possibly allow. "I do not want to walk into a trap," he told Colonel House, "and give them immunity for the next year" for unrestricted submarine warfare. The remark perfectly epitomized Wilson's mock venture in peacemaking. He would do anything to avert war with Germany except risk losing his war with Germany.[13]

While the dismal returns from his "peace note" were coming in Wilson decided to make an altogether different sort of bid for world peace. The goal of Wilson's new effort was not merely to stop the European war—that was clearly too dangerous to try—but to stop the war by establishing the millennium, which posed no dangers at all. The method Wilson chose was a speech he had worked on for weeks. Delivered before the Senate on January 22, it was to become one of the most celebrated addresses in American history. In it, Wilson described with uncommon eloquence his own terms for a lasting European settlement. It was to be a "peace without victory," a peace "between equals." It would encompass universal disarmament, establish "government by the consent of the governed," and provide for the self-determination of European nationalities (which meant the dissolution of the Austrian Empire). It would be crowned by a "concert of powers," including the United States, to ensure that the peace would be permanent. This was the shimmering vision Wilson now offered the world. Presumably on reading about it in their newspapers the European masses would rise up and demand that their rulers rush forward to embrace the American President's millennial vision. So Wilson, who could believe anything, apparently believed. Of course they did nothing of the sort. Raging mass wars, fueled by every device of mass propaganda, are not brought to a halt by the visionary utterances of a neutral bystander. Wilson's famous "peace without victory" speech is sometimes regarded as a prime example of Wilson's exalted impracticality, but Wilson's speech had nothing to do with practical statecraft. Its object was self-justification. The President had tried to end the European war by grandly offering the world a splendid prize for laying down its arms. If the world did not rise to Wilson's vision, if the European war raged on, if America were drawn into it, was that any fault of the President's? If the world was less noble than Wilson, was Woodrow Wilson to blame? Averting war with Germany had gotten lost in the President's self-ennobling bid for peace; Wilson's famed speech, in fact, was a statement of his war aims. The President's conscience and his ambition, however, were once again in harmony. It had taken two months of flummery to accomplish and it was achieved just in time.[14]

On January 10, with German hopes for a negotiated peace reduced to the merest flicker, German military leaders finally persuaded a reluctant, rattled Kaiser Wilhelm to gamble the future of his country on submarine warfare conducted without restriction of any kind. German submarines were to sink on sight every merchantman found in the war zone, neutral as well as belligerent. According to the German Admiralty, only through an absolute blockade could German submarines deliver the swift fatal blow to the enemy on which the whole immense gamble depended. The German high command no longer seriously cared about keeping America neutral. The price had become too high, for it was Wilson's protection of the British munitions traffic and his support of the British blockade that made possible the Allies' deadly war of attrition. Given America's hostile neutrality, America's active enmity seemed, on balance, less dangerous, especially if the blockade proved as swiftly effective as the German Admiralty claimed it would be. Against these purely military calculations, the German chancellor could say little in rebuttal. The American President had let him down at every turn. For two years Wilson had done everything to help the belligerents who wanted America dragged into the war and everything to undermine the German civil leaders who had struggled to keep America out. The end result was inevitable, but it was Wilson, not Germany, who had made it so. On January 31, Germany sent out its fatal announcement that unrestricted submarine warfare would commence on the following day.

The announcement came sooner than expected; it was thought that Germany would wait until the weather grew warmer. It was no real surprise, however. Wilson had known the Sussex Pledge would be broken from the moment he forced Germany to make it. Having reaped exactly what he sowed, Wilson was nonetheless morally outraged. Germany had played him false; Germany, which had urged him to inititate peace talks since May 1916, had foiled his noble effort to end the war by establishing the millennium. Germany, he told Colonel House on February 1, was "a madman that should be curbed." Two days later, Wilson went before a joint session of Congress to announce that he had broken off relations with Germany. As always he spoke more in sorrow than in anger but his rueful reluctance was somewhat belied by the strained argument Wilson felt compelled to marshal to justify the rupture. To the Congress assembled he cited Germany's conditional May 4 Sussex vow; cited his own May 8 note rejecting Germany's stipulated condition; noted further that Germany had made no reply to his note. Consequently, said Wilson, as if he were in civil court arguing a breach of contract case, Germany, by its silence, had accepted the American contention that its pledge was absolute. Since the German government had now violated its absolute pledge, "this Government has no alternative . . . but to take the course which in its Note of 18th of April, 1916, it announced that it would take," namely to sever all relations with Germany. On hearing the news Congress burst into thunderous applause. Wilson cautioned his enthusiastic listeners, however, that until Germany committed "overt acts" against American ships and citizens he would not call on them to declare war. Politically, Wilson could do no more for the moment. Despite the vehement denunciations of Germany in the press, support for an immediate war declaration was virtually non-existent.[15]

With the rupture of relations Wilson's peacemaking venture came to an end, but "the national conscience is clear," as Wilson's confidant and mouthpiece, Frank Cobb of the *World,* put it in his Sunday editorial: "In all the records of history there will be found no other example of a great and powerful nation exerting such effort and making such sacrifices to keep the peace as America has done. . . . If all our efforts have come to naught . . . let us at least thank God that we shall enter the war on the right side."[16]

For Wilson the war "to end war" was now clearly in view. He had only to sit back, it seemed, and wait for German submarines to give him no choice. With understandable optimism, the President, on February 6, informed his bellicose cabinet that he was "passionately" resolved to avoid any act of hostility toward Germany or to commit even the smallest breach in punctilious neutrality. "If we are to have war," said Wilson, "we must go in with our hands clean." With Germany planning to sink neutral ships on sight, Wilson decided not to make an issue of American travelers killed on belligerent vessels. The exalted "human right" to travel safely on belligerent merchantmen had never seemed very important to most Americans. Since it was only Wilson's pretext for conflict with Germany, the President preferred to make the sinking of an American freighter, rather than the death of an American traveler, the "overt act" that necessitated war. Having served its purpose, the "sacred" right to safe travel was quietly shelved by the President who had been exalting it for so long. In the meantime the administration secretly busied itself drafting legislation to raise a mass conscript army for combat in France. Wilson intended to fight a precedent-shattering land war in Europe in order to vindicate, ostensibly, our citizens' rights on the seas. If the disparity between cause and effect was gross, the "national conscience" was clear. Without a great army on the European battlefield, America's President could scarcely hope to dictate the postwar settlement and bring everlasting peace to the world.[17]

It soon became apparent, however, that not even with German submarines completely unleashed would Wilson enjoy the moral luxury of both "clean hands" *and* a war. A simple untoward fact quickly withered Wilson's optimism: American freighters bound for England were afraid to leave port. Left to their own devices, they had no more wish to be sunk by a German torpedo in the "war zone" than to be sunk by a British mine in the North Sea "military area." Day after day Wilson waited impatiently for the "overt act" that meant war; day after day America's Atlantic ports grew increasingly clogged with freighters understandably reluctant to provide one.

Worse yet, the American people by a large majority viewed the spectacle with indifference and perhaps even with relief. If the timidity of the "war traffickers," as the phrase then went, kept America out of difficulty, the great bulk of the American people were content with that windfall. For two years England had been blockading Germany. Now Germany was blockading England. Neither blockade threatened the safety of America; neither was an act of deliberate hostility toward America. If German methods were more brutal than British methods, in either case only the private commercial rights of a few were involved. Most Americans were unconcerned about their pecuniary losses. For two years their national leaders had insisted that the defense of mere commercial rights against England was contemptible compared to the "sacred" defense of "human rights" against Germany. The American people had learned the lesson well. To their chief mentor's dismay, however, they were now applying it to the wrong country, for in February 1917 Wilson could scarcely afford to regard with lofty disdain the militant defense of America's oceanic commerce with a belligerent.[18]

For Wilson the entire situation was intolerable. If American freighters refused to enter the war zone, German submarines would be unable to sink them. There would be no "overt act," no war to "end war," no "noblest part" at the peace conference. To get American ships into the war zone was a matter of some urgency for the President. Nor was that Wilson's only problem. In a sense it was not even the main one. Popular indifference to the shipping situation was, if anything, even more intolerable. If the American people remained convinced that American commerce with a belligerent was the private affair of "war traffickers," grave trouble lay in store for the President.

By now the large antiwar majority in America was virtually impotent to block Wilson's war course. Eventually some American ships, drawn by the lure of high profits, would leave their home ports. Eventually one of them would be sunk. The President would ask Congress for a declaration of war and Congress would enthusiastically oblige. Short of a spontaneous national insurrection there was nothing the American people could do to alter that inevitable sequence of events. Nevertheless, it was they who would have to do the fighting. It was they who would have to be persuaded, once war was declared, that German submarine attacks on American freighters justified a mass conscript army, total mobilization of the national economy, and the dispatch of an armed host to the blood-soaked battlefields of Europe. That prospect was so alien to all American experience, so contrary to all American tradition, that it was to remain beyond the imagining of most Americans until the reality itself burst in upon them. That millions of Americans, even in wartime, might resist conscription and prevent the dispatch of an expeditionary army was a possibility that filled Wilson with dread. To protect his future war from popular dissent the administration was already drafting an "espionage" bill that Wilson was shortly to use in the severest assault on political liberty ever launched by an American President. In short, if Americans were going to fight the massive land war Wilson intended to wage, it was not only imperative that he get American freighters sunk it was equally imperative to convince Americans that the sinkings were a *casus belli* sufficiently provocative to justify reprisal on an unprecedented scale.

On February 17, a mere eleven days after vowing "passionately" to act peacefully and punctiliously, Wilson disclosed to a number of

Senate Democrats his bold solution to the dual problem facing him: getting American freighters in the war zone to be sunk and persuading the electorate that the sinkings constituted an act of war against America itself. The President intended to arm American freighters with U.S. Navy guns, man them with U.S. Navy gun crews, and authorize them to attack submarines in the war zone. By putting America's private commerce with a belligerent under official military protection, Wilson meant to declare as emphatically as possible that such commerce, so far from being a private affair, involved a government obligation so binding that the sinking of an American freighter could only be regarded as an act of war against the United States itself. The chief purpose of Wilson's plan—"armed neutrality," he called it—was to persuade the American people that what they stubbornly regarded as private was inescapably public—which is to say, its chief purpose was domestic war propaganda. To make the propaganda more persuasive, Wilson intended to go before Congress to ask for specific legislative authority to outfit freighters with navy guns and gun crews. Technically, the President did not need new legislation to do so. What Wilson wanted was an overwhelming display of congressional support designed to further impress upon a skeptical citizenry that challenging the German blockade of England by force was a solemn obligation of the American government.[19]

Unfortunately for Wilson, "armed neutrality" put him on the horns of a dilemma. Wilson needed it, in essence, to make the American people more willing to tolerate a major land war in Europe. On the other hand, he was still posing as a peace-loving President determined to avoid war until war was brutally thrust upon him. The two policies were in flat contradiction, for there was nothing pacific about Wilson's "armed neutrality" scheme.

Had the President intended only to arm freighters trading in noncontraband with England he had strong justification for doing so, given Germany's submarine declaration. Wilson, however, was determined to put navy guns on American ships carrying munitions to England. The President had neither the obligation nor the warrant to arm such ships. The very opposite was true. Neutral ships carrying contraband to a belligerent sail for their own private profit and assume their own private risks; they are legally subject to cap-

ture and destruction. For the neutral America to protect by force a
private munitions trade with a belligerent was far worse than a
gross breach of neutrality. It constituted an act of war in itself.
Worse yet, it was a wholly gratuitous act. So far from assuming a
time-honored obligation Wilson hoped to evade a time-honored obligation, the obligation President Washington recognized in 1793
when he publicly proclaimed that Americans shipping contraband
of war to belligerents "will not receive the protection of the United
States." Even Wilson's secretary of the navy, Josephus Daniels,
warned the President that if he armed ships carrying war contraband and authorized them to attack submarines he would be violating Germany's acknowledged right to seize and destroy them.[20]

To all such legal considerations the President turned a deaf ear.
International law was "sacred" to Wilson only if it led to war with
Germany. If he armed all freighters except those carrying contraband of war—a policy actually urged by two antiwar senators,
Stone and Norris—it would defeat the whole purpose of arming
freighters. The Germans, who still hoped to escape war with America,* would likely let the armed, noncontraband carriers pass
through and sink the munitions freighters on sight. When they did
Wilson would not even have grounds for war, since by declining to
arm munitions freighters he would have admitted that they sailed
at their own risk. Not to arm munitions ships threatened peace, and
Wilson was bent on war.

Therein lay the difficulty. "Armed neutrality" blatantly betrayed that determination. How was an allegedly peace-loving
President going to justify challenging the German blockade at the
certain risk of war when for two years he had not challenged the
British blockade at the risk of nothing? How was he to explain to
the American people why the dubious rights of munitions traders
required government protection of the most perilous kind when
those Americans who wanted the government to defend the acknowledged rights of food shippers he had virtually accused of
treason? Wilson did not even have an expedient argument for

---

* When the German government, acting through the Swiss minister, offered to make arrangements for American ships sailing in the war zone, Wilson slammed shut that escape
hatch from war by insisting that he would discuss nothing with Germany until it stopped
submarine warfare and reverted to the Sussex Pledge.

"armed neutrality." He could scarcely claim that armed American freighters would be safe from unlawful attack when armed British freighters were being sunk daily. How, in short, was he going to keep up the pretense that war was being forced upon him when arming freighters carrying munitions to a belligerent constituted a bellicose, unwarranted action that not only invited war but could manifestly accomplish nothing else? Wilson was well aware of the difficulty. On February 23, when his impatient cabinet urged him to begin arming ships, Wilson had to caution them that "the country is not willing that we should take any risks of war."[21]

It was the British government, always aware of Wilson's political needs, that solved the President's domestic problems at a stroke on the very day the President and his cabinet were discussing the political pitfalls of armed neutrality. Had British agents been privy to the discussion they could not have timed their move more accurately. At the meeting one cabinet member had suggested that Americans would more willingly accept the arming of freighters if the administration were to launch a propaganda campaign to arouse popular hatred of Germany. He suggested that the President broadcast to the country reports that German officials were stripping American consuls' wives naked and subjecting them to indignities. The suggestion was crude but the point was well taken. Fortunately for Wilson the British possessed a propaganda weapon immeasurably more potent than tales of lascivious Germans—the now celebrated Zimmermann telegram.[22]

On January 16 the German foreign minister, Arthur Zimmermann, had cabled the German ambassador in Mexico coded instructions for a countermove against America should America declare war on Germany. British agents had intercepted and deciphered it. On February 5, the British Foreign Office had the telegram in its hands. On February 23, the British handed it to Ambassador Page, who relayed it at once to Washington. The famous cable read as follows: "We intend to begin unrestricted submarine warfare on the first of February. We shall endeavor in spite of this to keep the United States neutral. In the event of this not succeeding, we make Mexico a proposal of alliance on the following basis: make war together, make peace together, generous financial support, and an understanding on our part that Mexico is to reconquer the lost territory in Texas, New Mexico, and Arizona." The German ambassador was to make the offer to President Carranza (whom Wilson had humiliated but failed to overthrow) "as soon as the outbreak of war with the United States is certain."[23]

There was nothing villainous about Zimmermann's instructions. A war stratagem aimed against America that was contingent on America's waging war against Germany was scarcely a shocking proposal. Wage a war and you will get a war. The stratagem itself was as old as organized warfare. In 1915 the Allies had induced Italy to attack Austria by secretly offering similar territorial inducements. As ex-Senator Joe Bailey of Texas was shortly to put it to a friend, Germany "had done no more than we might have expected," considering the profound antagonism toward America that Wilson's meddling in Mexico had aroused below the Rio Grande. So much was obvious. It was equally obvious that Zimmermann's Mexican maneuver was perfectly designed to wound American sensibilities—the popular faith in America's continental security; popular hatred of the Old World's cynical machinations; the popular conviction that no nation on earth could seriously intend harm to an innocent America. More important than the actual content of the cable was the fact that the war party dominated the press and the political arena. Given the Zimmermann telegram by Wilson, the war party was not going to point out to the American people that you get a war when you go to war. On the contrary, they were certain to raise up a national hue and cry over deep-dyed Teutonic villainy, "pretending," as Bailey was to put it, "that we have discovered some great plot on the part of Germany and . . . inflaming the popular mind with appeals both to fear and honor." Properly handled, the telegram's potency was great. "As soon as I saw it," Lodge said to Roosevelt, "I felt it would arouse the country more than anything else that has happened."[24]

So, too, did Wilson. After reading the telegram the President expressed "much indignation," recalled Frank Polk, a high-ranking State Department official, but not enough to conceal his immense gratification. He immediately ordered Ambassador Page in London to thank the British foreign secretary for supplying information "of such inestimable value," and to tender his personal appreciation of "so marked an act of friendliness on the part of the

British government." If Wilson's gratitude was fatuously fulsome—Britain's act obviously had nothing to do with "friendliness"—it was because he was deeply and genuinely gratified. The British government had delivered into his hands exactly what he needed to blow open the first major breach in popular opposition to war, a document, as Lodge put it, "of almost unlimited use in forcing the situation." Wilson was so filled with "indignation" over the Zimmermann telegram that Polk had to dissuade him from releasing it to the press at once before it was even authenticated.[25]

With the Zimmermann cable in hand, Wilson had no reason to delay his call for "armed neutrality." On Monday, February 26, the President went before Congress to ask for legislative authority to arm American freighters and challenge the German blockade of England by force. Doubtless Wilson would have done so even without the Zimmermann note but he was fortunate, nonetheless, to have it on hand, for his speech to Congress was one long, transparent non sequitur. Germany, Wilson reminded his legislative audience, had not yet committed the "overt act" that meant war. "Our commerce has suffered, is suffering, rather in apprehension than in fact, rather because so many of our ships are timidly keeping to their home ports than because American ships have been sunk." Having delivered a stinging rebuke to America's ship captains, the President then outlined his solution to the deplorable situation created by their cowardice, namely Germany's want of an opportunity to sink them. In order to preserve the peace of the country it was imperative, said Wilson, for the United States to arm American freighters with navy guns and crews so that they might be able to sail through the war zone and actively prevent an "overt act" against them. Mindful that he had never before championed commercial rights and interests, had indeed been high-mindedly disdaining them since the days of "the brute" Huerta, Wilson assured Congress that far more than mere "material interests" was involved in arming American freighters carrying munitions to a belligerent. It was rather a matter of arming them to vindicate "fundamental rights . . . those rights of humanity without which there is no civilization." Selling munitions to belligerents had now joined the ranks of sacred human rights. The main purpose of armed neutrality was nonetheless to keep America at peace. Of that Congress could rest assured. "I am not now proposing or contemplating war or any steps that may lead to it."[26]

As soon as the President finished his speech Senator La Follette threw up his hands in despair. That Wilson was going to use "armed neutrality" to push America into the war he understood at once. Nobody else in Congress was fooled either. Every legislator who wanted war enthusiastically supported armed neutrality for peace; almost every legislator who wanted peace bitterly opposed it. Whether the American people would have been fooled is exceedingly doubtful, but the Zimmermann telegram was shortly to moot the question. That was part of its "inestimable value."

On February 27 Wilson introduced into Congress an armed neutrality bill, drafted by himself, authorizing him not only to arm American freighters but "to employ such other instrumentalities and methods . . . to protect such vessels and the citizens of the United States in their lawful and peaceful pursuits on the high seas." Under the proposed legislation Wilson could, if he chose, use American battleships to protect American traffic in munitions and start a war at sea at once. That Congress would approve the measure swiftly and overwhelmingly Wilson had no reason to doubt. Congress was avid for war. One cloud only loomed up on the President's horizon: the formidable figure of Senator La Follette himself. Like a battle-scarred lion rudely awakened from his slumbers, an aroused La Follette, grim and angry, was determined to give battle to Wilson and stop him, if possible, in his tracks. As in the days of the tariff fight against Aldrich, the Wisconsin senator quickly rounded up insurgent Republican members of the dwindling peace faction—Norris, Cummins, Gronna of North Dakota, Works of California—for a concerted assault on the armed ship bill. With the 64th Congress scheduled to expire at noon, March 4, La Follette's immediate objective was to block a final vote on the measure. More important, La Follette was fighting for time—time to expose the perils and shams of armed neutrality, time to marshal the antiwar sentiments of the American people. Then let Wilson call the new Congress into special session if he dared. In the long roster of American senators, few, if any, could match La Follette's fighting courage and tenacity. It was a man of heroic stature who was now about to stand up with a handful of allies to challenge the President and the legions of the war party.[27]

On February 28 Wilson first got wind of the danger. On the following day the House was scheduled to vote on the armed ship bill. The moment was clearly at hand to let loose the Zimmermann telegram. It was not likely to stop the indomitable La Follette but it was certain to push his forthcoming Senate struggle to the margin of events. Accordingly, at 6 P.M. on February 28, in time for the next morning's editions, Wilson released the cable to the editorial minions of the war party through the Associated Press. The press knew what to do with it. On the morning of March 1 Americans woke to read about a truly stupendous and sensational revelation, the laying bare of "The Prussian Invasion Plot," the infamous Teutonic scheme to knife America in the back. The press threw itself into a hysterical rage. What more proof did purblind Americans need of Germany's limitless hostility toward America, what more evidence of its bottomless villainy than this plot to enlist Mexico in a war against us after we entered war against Germany? Lest people doubt their newspapers, the war party in the House that day amplified and reamplified the hysterical press clamor. One after another, legislators vied with each other in denunciations of Germany's unparalleled wickedness and in calls for reprisal and revenge. That any revenge would have to take place in advance of the act to be avenged was a chronological anomaly the war party drowned out in its own thunderous din. After venting its spleen against Germany, the House voted 403 to 13 in favor of America's solemn obligation to defend with armed force those "rights of humanity without which there is no civilization," namely the nonexistent right to trade safely in munitions with a belligerent.[28]

Wounding in itself to American sensibilities, distorted beyond recognition by a prowar press, the Zimmermann telegram genuinely shocked and angered the American people. For the first time since the European war began, it became safe to call openly for war and intervention. Overnight the political atmosphere, radically altered, was charged with war clamor as the crypto-interventionists began discarding their masks. Although popular anger was shortly to fade, one effect of the Zimmermann note was irrevocable. It persuaded a sizable minority of Americans, chiefly in the East, that war with Germany was inevitable and even desirable. For the first time the war party, which held most of the organized power in the country, actually enjoyed, in addition, a modicum of popular support. Their enemy in the long civil war over war was no longer the great body of the American people but merely a large numerical majority whose last spokesmen of consequence were vainly struggling to be heard from the floor of the United States Senate.

For more than twenty-four hours La Follette's band of antiwar senators—eleven in all—took turns tearing apart Wilson's armed neutrality bill. What purpose could it serve, antiwar senators insisted, except to set "privately owned vessels loose on the ocean" to sink and be sunk and cause war? What obligation did the American government have to protect contraband commerce with a belligerent when the great Washington had expressly refused to provide it? Why should the United States challenge one belligerent's blockade when it had never challenged the blockade of its enemy? Why, if the United States was willing to wage war to protect private commercial rights, hadn't the government declared war on England long before? What was the moral difference between a German torpedo and a British marine mine? Savagely assailed by the press, the antiwar senators struck back at the hypocrisy of their fellow senators who were now openly calling for war yet supporting armed neutrality on the grounds that Wilson— "this President who abhors war" as one prowar senator put it— would use it only to keep peace.

When the hour of noon struck on March 4, the antiwar senators still held the floor. The armed ship bill had been blocked, but the bill's death was a mere technicality. La Follette's band had accomplished nothing, for Wilson and the war party had achieved their major goals. The antiwar senators' arguments, persuasive enough in a calm atmosphere, were lost in the Zimmermann uproar. Even without a formal Senate vote, Congress had expressed with the utmost passion its determination to challenge the German blockade by force. Goaded in part by Wilson's rebuke to their courage, American ship captains, one by one, were heading unarmed into the war zone. Angered by the Zimmermann cable, millions of Americans were no longer indifferent to their fate. Antiwar sentiment in America, still the sentiment of a large majority, was losing its strength and conviction. The war party was now ready for a final propaganda assault on the enemy's wavering lines.

It was Wilson who initiated the attack. On the afternoon of March 4 the President relased to the press a scathing statement virtually accusing La Follette and his colleagues of treason to their country. "A little group of willful men, representing no opinion but their own, have rendered the great Government of the United States helpless and contemptible." The statement was itself an extraordinary act, for never before had a President singled out members of the Senate for such savage public denunciation. Wilson's purport was unmistakable: "This President who abhors war" wanted the nation's chief antiwar spokesmen politically destroyed. The war party duly swung into action. On March 5 the press turned from denouncing Germany to savaging the "willful men," Benedict Arnolds and Judas Iscariots who represented "no opinion" but that of a popular majority. Between March 5 and 6 the legislatures of seven states—Ohio, Washington, Arkansas, Idaho, Kentucky, Oklahoma, and Tennessee—voted resolutions condemning the "willful" eleven, doubtless to "encourage the others," for none of these states was conspicuous for pro-war sentiment.[29]

Picking up the tempo, Wilson on March 9 formally called Congress into special session for April 16. The administration also let it be known that it intended to arm American freighters even without congressional authority. Again Wilson's signal to the war party was clear. "This President who abhors war" no longer thought it necessary to keep up the old pretense of vainly striving to avoid war. Democrats no longer had to pretend that they wanted peace when they "stood by" the President against the opponents of war. Full mobilization of war propaganda now began in earnest. In New York City the Federation of Churches publicly announced its intention both to "mobilize its Christian strength behind President Wilson" and call for a holy war against Germany. On Sunday, March 11, "War Sunday," churchmen in every American city urged their parishioners to join the President in the great forthcoming struggle against European autocracy. On Monday, March 12, Samuel Gompers's American Federation of Labor swore fealty to the President and voted its support for war against Germany. As yet no "overt act" had been committed, but that was a mere formality. It was not because of American shipping that the war party and its minions wanted to wage war in France. Nor was it because a majority of Americans now wanted war that the war party was straining every nerve to arouse war fever in the country.[30]

Ironically, during the two weeks following the release of the Zimmermann telegram the war party found itself not gaining, but losing ground. By mid-March, anger over the Zimmermann revelations had cooled down considerably. The angry calls for war and reprisal, heard round the country on March 1, were no longer heard at all from the public at large. Plainly, Americans were finding in the "Prussian Invasion Plot" considerably less than had first met their eye in the screaming banner headlines of the moment. Plainly, too, the crusading zeal of bellicose parsons had little power to persuade the commonality. Nor were many Americans impressed by the flowering of "democratic" idealism among old guard Republicans, by Elihu Root's assurance, for example, that in fighting Germany, "we shall be fighting over again the battle of American democracy along with the democracy of England, the democracy of France, the democracy of Italy . . . fighting for the principle of free self-government against the principle of old-time autocracy and military power."[31]

Despite the best efforts of the President, the press, the political parties, and the "patriotic societies," the antiwar sentiment of a vast continental nation was slowly but surely reasserting itself. Not even the sinking of four American freighters between March 12 and March 18 seriously arrested that tidal movement of dissent. The convinced had been convinced without an "overt act." The unconvinced were proving unconvinceable. On March 20, the President decided that the war propaganda had probably achieved its maximum effect. An irreducible majority of Americans remained opposed to war. If Wilson delayed his call for intervention much longer their numbers were likely to grow larger, rather than smaller. The President, as Colonel House explained to an Englishman, was "anxious about danger of cooling down of public feeling." Accordingly, on March 21, the President issued a new proclamation calling Congress into special session on April 2, fourteen days earlier than originally scheduled. They were to hear the President speak on "grave matters of national policy." What that meant everybody knew.[32]

On March 31 Wilson sat down to write his war message. He seems to have taken few pains with it. It was not a grave state paper he intended to deliver to Congress, not a detailed account of events leading up to the present crisis, not a statesmanlike weighing of interests and consequences, not a searching discussion of alternatives pondered and rejected. There was not sufficient merit in Wilson's war to permit more than he intended to provide: a propagandist's appeal for war—glib, vapid, and meretricious; a speech notable for one famous phrase still remembered for its hollow ring.

On the evening of April 2, Wilson rode to Capitol Hill escorted by a troop of United States cavalry. On Capitol Hill itself detachments of the U.S. Army ringed the legislative halls. Within, a swarm of Secret Servicemen, local police, and Post Office inspectors stood ready to foil any attempted assassination as the President addressed the excited, happy legislative assemblage. Wilson began by dwelling at length on the horrors of German submarine warfare. It was "throwing to the winds all scruples of humanity. . . . The present German submarine warfare against commerce is a warfare against mankind. It is a war against all nations." Armed neutrality, although as yet untried, was "impracticable," said the President. It "is likely only to produce what it was meant to prevent; it is practically certain to draw us into the war," but without the advantages of formal belligerency. That, of course, was exactly what the "willful" ones had said in the first place. Having thus disposed of armed neutrality, Wilson then called on Congress to declare that Germany was already at war with America and that the country "formally accept the status of belligerent which has thus been thrust upon it."[33]

After swearing his "sincere friendship" for the German people, and the "utmost practicable cooperation" with Germany's enemies, the President went on to concoct for the occasion a higher historical necessity for joining the Entente and sending Germany to defeat. Peace and freedom in the world, said the former professor of political science, enunciating a new pseudo-law of history, is inevitably and inherently menaced by "the existence of autocratic governments," for they alone can secretly plot war without the "knowledge or approval" of their people. Imperial Germany demonstrated this natural antipathy toward democracy, said the President, by setting "criminal intrigues everywhere afoot against our national unity of counsel," a statement looking back to twenty months of ascribing criticism of Wilson to the Kaiser's gold and forward to the day soon to come when Wilson's critics would have twenty-year prison terms hanging over their heads. It was clear, therefore, said the President, that Imperial Germany was the "natural foe to liberty" and must be defeated and overthrown. The United States stood ready to "spend the whole force of the nation to check and nullify its pretensions and its power." In doing so, said the President, reaching his peroration, America would be fighting "for the rights of nations great and small and the privilege of men everywhere to choose their own way of life and of obedience. The world must be made safe for democracy. . . . America is privileged to spend her blood and her might for the principles that gave her birth."[34]

When the President finished his brief address, everyone in the packed chamber of the House rose to his feet, clapping, shouting, and enthusiastically waving small American flags. There was one conspicuous exception: Senator Robert Marion La Follette, who stood with his arms grimly folded and a sardonic, mirthless smile on his face. If the rest of the peace faction was prudently bowing to the inevitable, not so the senator from Wisconsin. If it was too late to avert war, it was not too late for La Follette to expose the lies and false dealings by which a sovereign people were now being pushed into the bloodiest war in history.[35]

At 4 P.M. on April 4, Senator La Follette took the floor of the upper chamber to deliver one of the bravest speeches ever made in the United States Senate. The speech, a long one, began slowly with a close discussion of armed neutrality, the now-forgotten cause célèbre of the previous month. The President, La Follette pointed out, had been utterly wrong about the arming of American freighters. He had now admitted as much himself. Yet with what confidence had he held up to scorn those who had dared say he was wrong. Two days ago the President again came before Congress equally confident of his judgment. Was he, asked La Follette, perhaps equally wrong again? "Let us with the earnestness and single-

ness of purpose which the momentous nature of the question involves be calm enough and brave enough to examine further the
President's address of April 2." Then, with a cold and noble fury,
La Follette proceeded to tear to shreds, pretense by pretense, distortion by distortion, the glib propagandist's appeal for war that
the President of the United States had seen fit to put before an ostensibly free people.

The President had emphasized, said La Follette, Germany's
broken submarine "promise." The diplomatic record showed otherwise. "The promise, so-called, of the German government was conditional upon England's being brought to obedience of international law in her naval warfare." Nobody would contend that this had
been done. "Was it quite fair to lay before the country a statement
which implies that Germany had made an unconditional promise
which she had dishonestly violated? . . . The public mind should be
calm, not inflamed" by its President. The President had dwelt long
on Germany's violation of international law. "Would it not be well
to say also that it was England, not Germany, who refused to obey
the Declaration of London? . . . Keep that in mind. Would it not
have been fair to say, and to keep in mind, that Germany offered to
abide by those principles and England refused?" The President had
said that German submarine warfare against commerce was "a
war against all nations," but "is it not a little peculiar that if Germany's warfare is against all nations the United States is the only
nation that regards it necessary to declare war on that account?"
Does that fact not suggest in itself that "Germany's conduct under
the circumstances does not merit from any nation which is determined to preserve its neutrality a declaration of war?"

The President had said he was a "sincere friend" of the German
people. How, asked La Follette, did he now propose to demonstrate
his friendship? He had told us: by "the utmost practicable cooperation" with Germany's enemies. "Practicable cooperation with England and her allies in starving to death the old men and women, the
children, the sick and the maimed of Germany." Let us, said La
Follette, mocking Wilson's own phrase, "throw pretense to the
winds." The President wanted the United States to wage war on
the side of the "hereditary enemies of Germany." When we did so,
their purpose would "become our purpose." Did the President think

that when the war was over Great Britain would be unable "to bend us to her purposes and compel compliance with her demands?"

The President, of course, professed higher goals. The President said this was a war "for democracy, for the right of those who submit to authority to have a voice in their own government." That, said La Follette, was indeed an "exalted sentiment." In accordance with it, the President looked forward to the overthrow of German autocracy. Why not the dissolution of the British Empire? "The President has not suggested that we make our support of Great Britain conditional to her granting home rule to Ireland, or Egypt or India." Russia's tsar had been overthrown two weeks ago, "but it will hardly be contended that if Russia was still an autocratic Government, we would not be asked to enter this alliance with her just the same." Indeed, a President who told the people of Germany they could have peace only by "giving up their Government" had a very strange notion of self-government. The President made "a profession of democracy that is linked in action with the most brutal and domineering use of autocratic power. Are the people of this country being so well represented in this war movement that we need to go abroad to give other people control of their governments? . . . It ill becomes us to offer as an excuse for our entry into the war the unsupported claim that this war was forced upon the German people by their government 'without their previous knowledge or approval.' Who has registered the knowledge or approval of the American people of the course this Congress is called upon to take in declaring war upon Germany? . . . The espionage bills, the conscription bills and other forcible military measures which we understand are being ground out of the war machine in this country is the complete proof that those responsible for this war fear that it has no popular support." So much for Wilson's "profession of democracy" and his devotion to government by the consent of the governed.

Leaving Wilson's war message where it lay, Senator La Follette then turned to Wilson's diplomatic record of false neutrality. It was not Germany, La Follette noted, who first disregarded the rules of international law. It was England. It was not Germany who refused to accede to our protests. It was England. It was not Germany who first sank neutral ships without warning. It was England, when she sowed the entire North Sea with submarine mines. Yet what did the Wilson administration do in the face of that act "unheard of before in the history of the world?" It "agreed to the lawless act of Great Britain. . . . The present administration has never uttered a word of protest. . . . The only reason why we have not suffered the sacrifice of just as many ships and just as many lives from the violation of our rights by the war zone and submarine mines of Great Britain as we have through the unlawful acts of Germany in making her war zone in violation of our neutral rights is simply because we have submitted to Great Britain's dictation." Having "acquiesced in England's action without protest, it is proposed that we now go to war with Germany for identically the same action on her part." Worse yet, it was proposed that we do so by the President in utter disregard for his own "moral responsibility for the position in which Germany has been placed by our collusion and cooperation with Great Britain. By suppressing the rule with regard to neutral rights in Great Britain's case, we have been actively aiding her in starving the civil population of Germany. We have helped to drive Germany into a corner, her back to the wall, to fight with what weapons she can lay hands on . . ."

Because of Wilson's policy of "collusion and cooperation" with one of the belligerents, America's neutral rights were no longer a just ground for war. "We from early in the war threw our neutrality to the winds by permitting England to make a mockery of it to her advantage against her chief enemy." That had been the President's policy. He had claimed the right as a neutral to enforce the rules of war against one belligerent and not against its enemy. He made that claim formally and explicitly, noted La Follette, in his May 8, 1916, *Sussex* note to Germany when he insisted that Britain's violation of America's neutral rights was no concern of its enemy. That note "misstates the law; it asserts a principle that can not be maintained for one moment with a decent regard for equal rights between nations with whom we are dealing upon a basis of equality." The President had no right to make such an assertion, for no neutral enjoys such a right. "There can be no greater viola-

tion of our neutrality than the requirement that one of two belligerents shall adhere to the settled principles of law and that the other
shall have the advantage of not doing so." Because of Wilson's
false neutrality, America had lost the character of a neutral; America could no longer claim absolute neutral rights. Because of Wilson's violation of neutrality, our neutral rights were no longer absolute but "relative." Yet the President who worked in "collusion"
for two years with one of the belligerents now was asking Congress
to declare war against its enemy in defense of the very neutral
rights he himself had wantonly compromised. Such were the false
and dishonest grounds of the President's proposal for hurling
America "into the bottomless pit of the European conflict."

As La Follette spoke, senators one by one left their seats and
headed for the cloakroom. It was not a pleasant speech for most
senators to hear, but La Follette was not really speaking to his fellow senators. In a sense he was not even speaking to the American
people. More than anything else, he was speaking for the record on
which he hoped one day they might act. "There is always lodged,
and always will be, thank the God above us, power in the people supreme. Sometimes it sleeps, sometimes it seems the sleep of death;
but, sir, the sovereign power of the people never dies. It may be
suppressed for a time, it may be misled, be fooled, silenced. I think,
Mr. President, that it is being denied expression now. I think there
will come a day when it will have expression. The poor, sir, who are
the ones called upon to rot in the trenches, have no organized power, have no press to voice their will on this question of war and
peace; but, oh, Mr. President, at some time they will be
heard. . . . There will come an awakening; they will have their day
and they will be heard." On that day of awakening, hopefully, they
would remember not the glib, dishonest phrases of a hypocrite
President, but the dense honest utterance of the valiant senator
from Wisconsin.[36]

When La Follette finished his speech at 6:45 P.M., with tears of
grief and unspent anger streaming down his face, one reporter in
the press gallery turned to his friend and said: "That is the greatest
speech we will either of us ever hear. It will not be answered because it is unanswerable." A few hours later the Senate voted for
war 82 to 6—Norris, Stone, Gronna, Vardaman, and Henry Lane

of Oregon joining La Follette in a final courageous dissent. The next day the House voted with the Senate, 373 to 50. Woodrow Wilson at last had his war.[37]

Seek and ye shall find.

14

"The Old America That Was Free and Is Now Dead"

The triumph of Wilson and the war party struck the American Republic a blow from which it has never recovered. If the mainspring of a republican commonwealth—its "active principle" in Jefferson's words—is the perpetual struggle against oligarchy and privilege, against private monopoly and arbitrary power, then that mainspring was snapped and deliberately snapped by the victors in the civil war over war.

The sheer fact of war was shattering in itself. Deaf to the trumpets and the fanfare, the great mass of Americans entered the war apathetic, submissive, and bitter. Their honest sentiments had been trodden to the ground, their judgment derided, their interests ignored. Representative government had failed them at every turn. A President, newly reelected, had betrayed his promise to keep the peace. Congress, self-emasculated, had neither checked nor balanced nor even seriously questioned the pretexts and pretensions of the nation's chief executive. The free press had shown itself to be manifestly unfree—a tool of the powerful and a voice of the "interests." Every vaunted progressive reform had failed as well. Wall Street bankers, supposedly humbled by the Wilsonian reforms, had impudently clamored for preparedness and war. The Senate, ostensibly made more democratic through the direct election of senators, had proven as impervious as ever to public opinion. The party machines, supposedly weakened by the popular primary, still held elected officials in their thrall. Never did the powerful in America seem so willful, so wanton, or so remote from popular control as they did the day war with Germany began. On that day Americans learned a profoundly embittering lesson: They did not count. Their very lives hung in the balance and still they did not count. That bitter lesson was itself profoundly corrupting, for it transformed citizens into cynics, filled free men with self-loathing and drove millions into privacy, apathy, and despair.

Deep as it was, the wound of war might have healed in time had Wilson and the war party rested content with their war. With that war alone, however, they were by no means content. Well before the war, the war party had made its aims clear. It looked forward to a new political order distinguished by "complete internal peace" and by the people's "consecration to the State." It wanted an electorate that looked upon "loyalty" to the powerful as the highest political virtue and the exercise of liberty as proof of "disloyalty." The war party wanted a free people made servile and a free republic made safe for oligarchy and privilege, for the few who ruled and the few who grew rich; in a word, for itself. The goals had been announced in peacetime. They were to be achieved under cover of war. While American troops learned to survive in the trenches, Americans at home learned to live with repression and its odious creatures—with the government spy and the government burglar, with the neighborhood stool pigeon and the official vigilante, with the local tyranny of federal prosecutors and the lawlessness of bigoted judges, with the midnight police raid and the dragnet arrest.

In this domestic war to make America safe for oligarchy, Woodrow Wilson forged all the main weapons. Cherisher of the "unified will" in peacetime, Wilson proved himself implacable in war. Despising in peacetime all who disturbed the "unity of our national counsel," Wilson in wartime wreaked vengeance on them all. Exalted by his global mission, the ex-Princeton professor, whom one party machine had groomed for high office and whom another had been protecting for years, esteemed himself above all men and their puling cavils. He could no longer tolerate, he was determined to silence, every impertinent voice of criticism, however small and however harmless. Nothing was to be said or read in America that Wilson himself might find disagreeable. Nothing was to be said or read in America that cast doubt on the nobility of Wilson's goals, the sublimity of his motives, or the efficacy of his statecraft. Wilson's self-elating catch phrases were to be on every man's lips or those lips would be sealed by a prison term. "He seemed determined that there should be no questioning of his will," wrote Frederick Howe after personally pleading with Wilson to relent. "I felt that he was eager for the punishment of men who differed from him, that there was something vindictive in his eyes as he spoke."[1]

By the time Wilson reached Paris in December 1918, political liberty had been snuffed out in America. "One by one the right of freedom of speech, the right of assembly, the right to petition, the right to protection against unreasonable searches and seizures, the right against arbitrary arrest, the right to a fair trial . . . the principle that guilt is personal, the principle that punishment should bear some proportion to the offense, had been sacrificed and ignored." So an eminent Harvard professor of law, Zechariah Chafee, reported in 1920. The war served merely as pretext. Of that there can be little doubt. In a searing civil conflict that threatened the very survival of the Republic, Americans, under Lincoln, enjoyed every liberty that could possibly be spared. In a war safely fought three thousand miles from our shores, Americans, under Wilson, lost every liberty they could possibly be deprived of.[2]

Under the Espionage Act of June 1917, it became a felony punishable by twenty years' imprisonment to say anything that might "postpone for a single moment," as one federal judge put it, an American victory in the struggle for democracy. With biased federal judges openly soliciting convictions from the bench and federal juries brazenly packed to ensure those convictions, Americans rotted in prison for advocating heavier taxation rather than the issuance of war bonds, for stating that conscription was unconstitutional, for saying that sinking armed merchantmen had not been illegal, for criticizing the Red Cross and the YMCA. A woman who wrote to her newspaper that "I am for the people and the government is for the profiteers," was tried, convicted, and sentenced to ten years in prison. The son of the chief justice of the New Hampshire Supreme Court became a convicted felon for sending out a chain letter that said the Sussex Pledge had not been unconditional. Under the Espionage Act American history itself became outlawed. When a Hollywood filmmaker released his movie epic *The Spirit of '76,* federal agents seized it and arrested the producer: his portrayal of the American Revolution had cast British redcoats in an unfavorable light. The film, said the court, was criminally "calculated . . . to make us a little bit slack in our loyalty to Great Britain in this great catastrophe." A story that had nourished love of liberty and hatred of tyranny in the hearts of American schoolchildren had become a crime to retell in Wilson's America. The filmmaker was sentenced to ten years in prison for recalling the inconvenient past.[3]

Fear and repression worked its way into every nook and cranny of ordinary life. Free speech was at hazard everywhere. Americans were arrested for remarks made at a boarding house table, in a hotel lobby, on a train, in a private club, during private conversations overheard by the government's spies. Almost every branch of Wilson's government sprouted its own "intelligence bureau" to snoop and threaten and arrest. By 1920 the Federal Bureau of Investigation, a swaddling fattened on war, had files on two million people and organizations deemed dangerously disloyal. At the Post Office Department, Albert Burleson set up a secret index of "illegal ideas"—such as criticizing Gompers, the patriotic union leader—and banned from the mails any publication guilty of expressing one. Even if an independent paper avoided an "illegal idea," it could still be banned from the mails for betraying an "audible undertone of disloyalty," as one Post Office censor put it, in otherwise nonfelonious remarks. Under the tyranny of the Post Office, Socialist papers were suppressed outright and country editors sent to jail. Freedom of the press ceased to exist.[4]

Nor did the administration rely on its own bureaucratic resources alone. To cast the net of repression wider and draw the mesh finer, the Justice Department called on the "preparedness" clubs, shock troops of the war party, for help. Authorized by the Justice Department to question anyone and detain them for arrest, the prepareders fell eagerly to their task of teaching "consecration to the State" by hounding free men into jail. Where the "preparedness" clubs were thin on the ground, the Justice Department recruited its own vigilante groups—the Minute Men and the

American Protective League—to enforce with the police power
"the unity of our national counsel." By August 1917 Attorney
General Thomas Gregory boasted that he had "several hundred
thousand private citizens" working for him, "most of them as
members of patriotic bodies . . . keeping an eye on disloyal individuals and making reports of disloyal utterances, and seeing that the
people of the country are not deceived."[5]

Truth and falsity were defined by the courts. According to
judicial decisions, public statements were criminally false under the
Espionage Act when they contradicted the President's April 2 war
message, which became, at gunpoint, the national creed, the touchstone of loyalty, and the measure of "sedition," a crime that Wilson and the war party resuscitated 118 years after it had destroyed
forever the old Federalist oligarchy. This time it did not destroy oligarchy. It helped destroy "the old America that was free and is
now dead," as one civil libertarian was to put it in 1920. Under the
Espionage Act no one was safe except espionage agents, for under
the Act not a single enemy spy was ever convicted.[6]

The War Enemy Division of the Justice Department had more
important war enemies in mind. Every element in the country that
had ever disturbed the privileged or challenged the powerful Wilson and the war party were determined to crush. They were the enemy. "Both the old parties are in power," Lincoln Steffens wrote a
friend during wartime. "They are the real traitors these days. They
are using the emergency to get even with their enemies and fight
for their cause." Radicals were ruthlessly persecuted. The International Workers of the World was virtually destroyed in September
1917 when Justice Department agents arrested 166 I.W.W. leaders
for heading a strike the previous June. Eugene V. Debs, the Socialist Party's candidate for President, was sentenced to ten years' imprisonment for attributing the World War to economic interests in
a speech before a Socialist gathering. Under the cloak of "patriotic
bodies" and armed with the federal police power, reactionary local
businessmen and machine politicians crushed local radicals and
prewar insurgents. The wartime tyranny in Washington spawned
and encouraged a thousand municipal tyrannies.[7]

"It was quite apparent," Howe recalled in his memoirs, "that the
alleged offenses for which people were being prosecuted were not

the real offenses. The prosecution was directed against liberals, radicals, persons who had been identified with municipal ownership fights, with labor movements, with forums, with liberal papers that were under the ban." The entire prewar reform movement was destroyed in the war, said Howe, "and I could not reconcile myself to its destruction, to its voice being stilled, its integrity assailed, its patriotism questioned." The reformers "had stood for variety, for individuality, for freedom. They discovered a political state that seemed to hate these things; it wanted a servile society. . . . I hated the new state that had arisen, hated its brutalities, its ignorance, its unpatriotic patriotism."[8]

Most of all, Wilson and the war party were determined to corrupt the entire body of the American people, to root out the old habits of freedom and to teach it new habits of obedience. Day after day, arrest after arrest, bond rally after bond rally, they drove home with overwhelming force the new logic of "the new state that had arisen": Dissent is disloyalty, disloyalty a crime; loyalty is servility, and servility is true patriotism. The new logic was new only in America; it is the perennial logic of every tyranny that ever was. The new state affected men differently, but it corrupted them all one way or another. The official repression drove millions of independent-minded Americans deep into private life and political solitude. Isolated, they nursed in private their bitterness and contempt—the corrupting consolation of cynicism. Millions more could not withstand the force of the new state that had risen. It was easier, by far, to surrender to the powerful and embrace their new masters, to despise with the powerful the very opinions they themselves had once held and to hound with the powerful their fellow citizens who still held them—the corrupting consolation of submission. Millions more simply bowed to the ways of oppression, to official lies and false arrests, to "slacker raids" and censored newspapers, to saying nothing, feeling nothing, and caring nothing—the corrupting consolation of apathy.

"The war has set back the people for a generation," said Hiram Johnson. "They have become slaves to the government." Yet the tolling of the bells for armistice brought no release to a corrupted and tyrannized people. To rule a free republic through hatred and fear, through censorship and repression, proved a luxury that the victors in the civil war over war refused to relinquish with the outbreak of peace. On Thanksgiving Day 1918, two weeks after the armistice, the war party, as if on signal, began crying up a new danger to replace the Hun, a new internal menace to replace the German spy, a new object of fear and hatred, a new pretext for censorship and repression. "Bolshevism" menaced the country, declared William Howard Taft, although Communist Party members constituted a minuscule .001 percent of the American population. Bolshevik propaganda menaced America, declared a Senate committee in the middle of winding down its investigation of the nonexistent German propaganda menace. Purge the nation of "Reds," declared the National Security League, opening up its campaign against "Bolshevism" a month after completing its hunt for "pro-Germans" and three and a half years after launching its campaign for "preparedness." In Washington, the Wilson administration, too, joined in the new outcry against Bolshevism and continued to wage war unchecked against the liberties of the American people. The Post Office censorship machine continued to tyrannize the independent press. The Justice Department began deporting aliens suspected of belonging to "the anarchistic and similar classes," to cite the federal statute authorizing the mass deportations. For the first time in American history, guilt by association became a formal principle of law.[9]

Everything seemed possible to the powerful and the privileged, so cowed by fear, so broken to repression had the American people become. Wilson even took time out from his messianic labors in Paris to urge passage of a peacetime federal sedition law, "unprecedented legislation," as Harvard's Professor Chafee put it at the time, "whose enforcement will let loose a horde of spies and informers, official and unofficial, swarming into our private life, stirring up suspicion without end." The war was over but Wilson did not want the American people to regain their freedom of speech and disturb once more "the unity of our national counsel." Although Congress never voted on the bill, the state party machines followed the President's lead. After the armistice almost every state in the Union passed laws abridging free speech. The statutes were sweeping enough in some states to satisfy a dictator's requirements. In Connecticut it became a crime to say anything that in the words of the statute, "intended to injuriously affect the Government" of Connecticut or of the United States. Striking while the iron was hot, Wilson and the war party were determined, in the immediate aftermath of war, to set up the legal machinery of permanent repression and to reconquer for oligarchy the venerable terrain of liberty in America. Fourteen months after the armistice, the New York *World,* awakening from its Wilsonian raptures, cried out in alarm over the new "despotism of professional politicians." The newspaper wondered why the prewar reform spirit and the prewar insurgents had died away so completely. It wondered, too, why "no other country in the world is suffering so much from professional politics" as America. There was no cause whatever to wonder. The professional politicians had won the only war they cared about, the war against a free republic that Wilson had begun in 1915 in the name of America's "mission."[10]

Defeated in so many ways, Americans in 1919 enjoyed one grim victory of sorts. They witnessed and joined in the personal and political destruction of Woodrow Wilson, whose fall from the heights of glory was swifter and steeper than any other in our history. Ten months after an ecstatic Paris turned out to welcome the savior of the world, ten months after Europe paid him its fulsome homage, Woodrow Wilson was an utterly broken man, crippled in mind and spirit, thoroughly discredited and publicly reviled, his name a stench in his countrymen's nostrils, his deeds publicly denounced as crimes. Popular hatred, party interest, and the unbearable knowledge of what he had done to his country combined to encompass his ruin.

In December 1918, the President had sailed for Europe determined to secure "peace without victory" and to establish a League of Nations to safeguard the just, nonpunitive peace he intended to impose. He appeared to enjoy every prospect of a glorious success. It seemed impossible for Britain and France to withstand the American President's implacable will, to resist his incomparable prestige or the coercive force of their utter dependence on American money and food. So it appeared, but it was all an illusion. The most powerful man at the Paris peace conference was in fact the neediest. Wilson's own deeds had made him so. In the name of "permanent peace" and an "association of nations," he had deceived and betrayed his countrymen, had falsely maneuvered them into war, had robbed them of their peace, their hopes, and the lives of 116,708 of their sons. And because he had done all that, Wilson needed the League of Nations far more desperately than the world did, if indeed the world needed it at all. The League, magical catch phrase, was to justify his life; the League, glimmering panacea, was to set right his betrayals; the League, whose "Covenant" Wilson wrote in Paris, was to hallow Wilson's war. At the peace conference Wilson was neither fighting for the world nor for the good of America. The President whose ambitions transcended his country, whose "idealism" embraced the whole world, was merely fighting to save his own life. Without a League to justify him, Wilson faced truths too crushing to bear. Without a League he was a false messiah who had served himself and called it God's work, an anti-Moses who had led his people from the Promised Land into Egypt. If, as Clemenceau remarked, Wilson "thinks he is another Jesus Christ," it was because megalomania was the condition of Wilson's survival. If he was not mankind's savior then he was America's scourge. For Wilson there was no middle ground. It was either the League or moral annihilation. At the peace conference he was a weak and desperate man.[11]

The Allies held the one trump card that mattered: They had Wilson's life in their hands. They threatened his League, hinted at postponement, tormented him with doubts, while the demons of guilt crowded in upon their adversary, sapping his strength still further. Driven frantic by Allied demands for territory and pelf, Wilson in early April threatened to leave the conference and sail home. His bluff was pitifully transparent. He, of all men, could least afford to leave Paris with empty hands. A few days later Wilson caved in to the punitive demands of the Allies in order to save the League and himself. The surrender, however, proved fatal. A catch phrase no longer, Wilson's "association of nations" became in April 1919 a corrupted reality, hardly more than a concert of the victors to safeguard the spoils of victory. So much was obvious even to Wilson's well-wishers. "It was not for this," William Allen White wrote to a member of Wilson's Paris entourage, "that our Americans died."[12]

From that unbearable accusation Wilson fled to the solace of delusion. "The failure here is complete," Steffens reported from Paris, "but that does not matter. What matters is that the President does not see it so." In January Wilson had known quite well that a punitive peace meant an unjust League. What he knew then he denied now, but the demons of guilt could not be eluded so readily. In Paris, after his surrender, Wilson exhibited symptoms of incipient madness, the madness of a man in flight from reality and from himself. He accused his French clerks of spying on him. He accused his once-beloved Colonel House of betraying his secrets to the Allies. He became convinced that visitors were stealing his belongings. Betrayers and Judases lurked everywhere. Four months after coming to Europe as the savior of the world, Wilson began preparing his final sanctuary from the terrors of reality: Wilson the failed savior was to become Wilson the sublime martyr.[13]

Republican Party leaders were now prepared to assist his martyrdom. For years they had vouched for Wilson's deceits, endorsed his flimsy pretexts, and agreed that reality was whatever Wilson said it was. They agreed no longer. The Republican oligarchy was bent on returning to power. Postwar America, degraded and despoiled, was an America made safe for their rule. There would be no trouble with reformers: The prewar reform movement had been destroyed. There would be no perilous popular demands for governmental action: Americans had grown to hate their government so much they merely wanted it lifted off their backs. The Republican Party, however, was not in good odor. Popular hatred of Wilson and the war was its only real asset, and Republican leaders had no choice but to exploit it as best they could. That hatred, as yet unvoiced by a citizenry too cowed to appear "disloyal," was a palpable force in the country nonetheless. It surged powerfully through the Middle West. It burned with white heat among the downtrodden "hyphenates." It waxed strong, too, among America's demobilized soldiers. By June 1919 some 2.6 million of them had returned home from Europe, hating the war they had fought and the President who had conscripted them. If the Republicans could somehow identify themselves with that hatred, their triumph was assured and Wilson doomed. The President's power at home was almost as illusory as his power in Paris. For years it had rested on the bipartisan unity of the powerful and the cordon they had thrown up to protect him and his sophistries from the effective judgment of the American electorate. Without that protective cordon Wilson would stand, for the first time, within the electorate's reach, and millions of Americans were ready on signal to reach for his throat. It was not because Wilson had tried to keep America out of war that millions of Americans hated him, just as it was not because war had been forced upon him that he had failed so wretchedly in Paris.[14]

While Wilson was still at the peace conference, Republicans, led by Senator Lodge, launched their attack on the President through a concerted attack on his League. That a large majority of Republican senators favored a League of Nations in principle, that Wall Street supported Wilson almost unanimously, did not deter Republican leaders. For ventilating popular hatred, Wilson's League made the perfect outlet, and the party was not about to pass it up.

To attack Wilson's League was to attack Wilson's war, without incurring the dangers of doing so openly. Republicans assailed the League as a "breeder of war," denounced it as a "supergovernment" concocted by Wilson to snuff out American sovereignty. Unless altered by the Republican-controlled Senate, it would drag America, they said, into corrupt foreign conflicts under the pretense of international "obligation." The implication was clear. Wilson's League would inflict on Americans the kind of war they hated most—the one they had just fought. That Republican leaders had supported that war with the utmost enthusiasm, millions of Americans were past caring. Unrepresented for so long, they were meanly grateful for whatever crumbs men of power threw them.

To attack Wilson's League was to assault Wilson himself. Of the actual merits and defects of the League of Nations, millions of Americans cared little. They knew only that Wilson wanted it and that was reason enough to oppose it. As the Philadelphia *Public Ledger* complained: "The mere fact that President Wilson wants something is not an argument against it." Wilson was reaping what he sowed. The President had robbed Americans of what they had cherished most. Now, spitefully and vindictively, millions of Americans wanted him deprived of what he cherished most. "Nine out of ten letters I get in protest against this treaty," a pro-League senator complained, "breathe a spirit of intense hatred of Woodrow

Wilson. . . . That feeling forms a very large element in the opposition to this treaty." Licensed, as it were, by the Republican oligarchy, pent-up hatred of Wilson poured into the political arena. "No autocracy," shouted Republican foes of the League and audiences booed "the autocrat's" name to the rafters. "Impeach him! Impeach him!" a Chicago Coliseum audience screamed after Senator William Borah of Idaho finished assailing Wilson's League. It was no edifying spectacle, this picture of free men deliberating grave issues with little thought save personal vengeance. Yet here again Wilson reaped what he sowed. He had been the chief instrument of the Republic's degradation. Now hate-ridden millions howled for a degraded revenge.[15]

In July Wilson returned to America, mentally unhinged, morally bankrupt, and politically weak. Unless he acceded to some Republican demands for emendation and interpretive additions, the Treaty of Versailles (which included the League) faced defeat in the Senate, which had once again recovered its voice in foreign affairs. Wilson stood adamant. He would accept no alterations. He would yield not an iota to his Republican betrayers. The League, Wilson claimed, was "ninety-nine percent insurance against war," but compromise with his enemies for the sake of world peace was a price Wilson refused to pay. In the end as in the beginning, Wilson cared only for himself. Compromise would unleash the demons of guilt. It meant admitting that the treaty was flawed, his League corrupted, his war unhallowed. From that admission Wilson had been fleeing in terror since April. Having sacrificed America for the League's sake, Wilson was now prepared to sacrifice the League for his own. Defeat held irresistible attractions. The League, defeated in the Senate, would regain what it had lost at the peace conference: the pristine purity of a noble ideal. The League's defeat would shift from Wilson the burden of guilt that was crushing him. Who could accuse him of vainly inflicting war on his countrymen, after ignoble politicians made his noble war vain? Defeat of the League in the Senate would salvage the one ideal Wilson had ever served—his vainglorious idea of himself.[16]

The defeat, perforce, had to be a noble one, a defeat after heroic efforts to triumph. In the summer of 1919 Wilson drew up his plans for staging a heroic defeat. He decided to undertake a

10,000-mile speaking tour through the Middle West and West—the enemy camp—to arouse popular support for the treaty. Western Republicans who opposed the League root and branch would feel the wrath of constituents spurred to fury by the President's incomparable eloquence. So Wilson claimed. Others knew better. The President's cabinet advised against the tour. Politically it could only do harm. Attacking Republican senators in their home states would not soften Republican opposition to an unamended treaty. It would merely goad partisan Republicans into sterner resistance. The bipartisan days were over. If the President wanted the treaty ratified, his only course was to stay in Washington and quietly work out a compromise. One yielding message to Senate Democrats and ratification was certain. Wilson spurned his cabinet's advice. The message was never to come.[17]

Wilson's personal physician, too, pleaded with him not to go on the tour. A schedule calling for twenty-seven days' confinement in a railway car, ten daily rear platform speeches, and twenty-six major addresses would exhaust the stamina of a youthful Bryan. Wilson's own health was poor. His appearance was haggard, his hands trembled, his face twitched. At the Paris peace conference the sixty-three-year-old President had become an old man. The tour, Wilson's physician warned him, was sheer suicide. Wilson loftily spurned the warning. "The boys who went overseas," he told his doctor, "did not refuse to go because it was dangerous." Moreover, he added, "You must remember that I, as commander-in-chief, was responsible for sending our soldiers to Europe." Of course, Americans had not died in France because Wilson was titular head of the American armed forces. His real responsibility was too damning to put into words. Wilson preferred to speak instead of "destiny disclosed" and the "hand of God who had led us into this way," phrases that exalted himself—who was the hand of God?—while relieving him of blame.[18]

As a last resort, Wilson's physician urged the President to ease the tour by adding rest stops. The killing schedule was scarcely a necessity. To Wilson it was. He refused to add rest stops. When Joe Tumulty advised his "chief" that he would be sacrificing his life, Wilson replied grandly, "I will gladly make the sacrifice to save the Treaty." Even Wilson's display of valor was false. It was not dying he feared, but living. And it was not the treaty he was trying to save.[19]

In early September the President set off on his speaking tour—his road to Golgotha—in search of a martyr's death. Fate was to prove cruelly disobliging. The tour, a political disaster, brought Wilson not death but death-in-life.

Even before disaster struck him, Wilson on the stump showed clear signs of onrushing madness. The treaty he stood up to defend was not the Treaty of Versailles, it was the treaty of his dreams. "This incomparable consummation of the hopes of mankind," he called it. Grim reality he brushed aside. How did his vaunted "peace without victory" square with the Allies' annexation of territory and the reparations they were forcing Germany to pay? Wilson's answer was astonishing. The Treaty of Versailles, he assured his listeners, was the first treaty in history ever drawn up by the victors in war "that was not made in their own favor." Addressing the voters, Wilson was consoling himself. As the presidential train hurtled deeper into the West, Wilson fell deeper into fantasy, as if the train's solitary passage were hastening his own flight from reality. On September 17, Wilson described the treaty as an "enterprise of divine mercy," nothing less. The terrible meetings with Lloyd George and Clemenceau, meetings that had broken his will and destroyed his hopes, he now described as "a very simple council of friends . . . men who believed in the same things and sought the same objects." Speeding toward madness, Wilson on September 24 had virtually suppressed all knowledge of the actual treaty. The Allies, he assured a western audience, "did not claim a single piece of territory."[20]

The fantasy was now complete. The Treaty of Versailles had become for Wilson what he so desperately wished it had been—the peace without victory he had failed to achieve. In fantasy so deep and clung to so desperately no man can find safety or peace. The strain on Wilson was beyond enduring. Something had to snap and release him from torment. On September 25, after assuring a Colorado audience that American boys had died in France for the "liberation and salvation of the world," Wilson collapsed on the train, smitten with an excruciating headache. The rest of the tour was canceled. The presidential train rolled home, curtains drawn.

On October 2, at the White House, a blood clot on the brain struck down the President, paralyzing half his body. For three weeks Wilson lay near death, his condition kept secret by the White House entourage. Inevitably rumors sprouted. People promptly concluded that Wilson had gone mad, a testament to the impression his League speeches had made. There was an element of truth in the rumor, for Wilson's stroke had saved his sanity by the narrowest of margins. From October 2 until his death in 1924 Wilson was to be a mere shell of a man. Much of the time his mind wandered fruitlessly, or else it focused obsessively on his customary grievances—the treachery of his friends, the villainy of his opponents. Spasms of self-pity perpetually overwhelmed him; he often wept. His bitterness bordered on lunacy. When he recovered his strength somewhat he fired Secretary of State Lansing for trying to usurp the presidency; Lansing had called a cabinet meeting without him. He continued to console himself with delusions. Too sickly even to perform the routine duties of his office, he planned nonetheless to run for a third term. The people, he believed, would vindicate him. There was a deep irony in that desperate belief, for many years before, Wilson had written that the sovereignty of the American people was a mere legal fiction. Now, in extremis, it was the people's sovereign forgiveness—not God's—that he yearned for and needed. Such is the moral authority that a great Republic exerts even on its betrayers. Popular vindication, however, was just another fantasy of Wilson's. By the end of 1919 half the country would have cheered his impeachment. Hatred of Wilson had not abated while the President lay stricken; it had grown more intense. Pitiless toward others, Wilson aroused no pity in others. While the White House fell silent, anti-League orators publicly denounced "the crimes of Wilson."[21]

A madman and a criminal, that was what millions of Americans now thought of their President.

From his wheelchair in the White House Wilson had just power enough to perform one last major act. He could defeat the League of Nations—and he did. In mid-November, the Senate, following Lodge, added fourteen interpretive clauses or "reservations" to the Treaty of Versailles. For public consumption Republicans claimed that their reservations had drawn the poison from Wilson's League.

The reservations, in fact, were innocuous. Some were superfluous; others asserted the supremacy of the Constitution over the Covenant of the League; none altered anything substantially. For Republicans they served the dual purpose of exploiting hatred of Wilson without openly repudiating the official aims of the war. Republicans were maneuvering for power, not leading an insurrection.[22]

Innocuous though the reservations were, the ailing President rejected them outright. From the shrouded, secretive White House came instructions to Senate Democrats to unite against the treaty with Republican reservations. The Democrats were prepared to follow the President. They had gone too far with Wilson to turn back now; they had nothing to turn back to. On November 19, 1919, Democrats duly voted against the Republican-tinctured treaty. Republicans in turn voted down the unamended treaty. Since there was no third alternative before the Senate, America remained technically at war. For two months thereafter, Democrats and Republicans tried to reach some accord. With ratification threatening, Wilson struck again. On December 14, the White House issued a stern declaration: The President would accept "no compromise or concession of any kind." On January 8, Wilson repeated the instructions. Let the treaty be defeated now, he advised his party, and let the election of 1920 serve as a "great and solemn referendum" on his noble handiwork. Thanks to Wilson's instructions, no bipartisan accord was reached. On March 19, 1920, the two versions of the Treaty of Versailles once again came to a vote in the Senate. The results were the same as before. Democrats voted against the treaty with reservations; Republicans voted against the treaty without them. The second defeat was final. The United States was never to ratify the Treaty of Versailles nor to enter the League of Nations. This was Wilson's final achievement. After wreaking havoc on his country for the sake of the League of Nations, Wilson strangled the League at its birth. It was a noble catch phrase once more, untarnished, sublime, justifying everything.[23]

Contemporaries saw matters more clearly. The President was now discredited almost everywhere. His selfish, destructive course had disgraced him even in the eyes of admirers. With one year left of his term, he was utterly without power. In May Congress passed

a joint resolution terminating the war with Germany. Wilson ve-
toed it and Congress overrode his veto. A few weeks later, the ailing, half-mad President watched in disappointment as his party
nominated Governor James Cox, a party hack from Ohio, to run
for his office against Senator Warren G. Harding, a party hack
from the same state.

Cox never stood a chance of winning. Just as millions of Americans had cared nothing about the merits of the League of Nations,
so in 1920 they cared nothing about the merits of the candidates.
The chief issue of the 1920 election was Thomas Woodrow Wilson.
Wilson's enemies poured their support into Harding's campaign
headquarters and it flowed in a torrent. Hatred of the President
dominated the campaign. In the denunciations of Wilson the "dictator" and Wilson the "autocrat," Cox himself was virtually forgotten, buried, as the Springfield *Republican* put it, under a
"mountain of malice." With nothing to recommend him save the
fact that he was not a Democrat, Harding won the election with
16.2 million votes to Cox's 9.1 million. It was the most crushing
election victory ever won by a presdiential candidate of no distinction whatever. The 1920 election was indeed the "great and solemn
referendum" Wilson had called for, and it rendered its judgment
on Wilson; guilty as charged. So ended the political career of a
President whom Americans for years had been compelled to "stand
by," whose lies had been deemed in the courts to be truth itself,
whose honest critics had been denounced as "conspirators" and arrested as felons. On his last morning in office this terrible ruin of a
man was asked to pardon Eugene Debs, rotting his life away in a
federal penitentiary. Unforgiving, Wilson refused. He had pity only
for himself. Today American children are taught in our schools
that Wilson was one of our greatest Presidents. That is proof in itself that the American Republic has never recovered from the blow
he inflicted upon it.[2]

In 1920 Americans yearned for the "good old days" before Wilson and war, before everything had gone so wrong. They yearned in
vain. The war and the war party had altered America permanently
and since the war party had shaped America to serve its own interests, the change was a change for the worse. In postwar America

the "despotism of professional politicians" went unchallenged. Independent citizens ceased to pester the party machines. The "good citizens" whose rise to civic consciousness had spawned the progressive movement now spurned the public arena in disgust. Wilson's hymns to "service" had made public service seem despicable. Wilson's self-serving "idealism" made devotion to the public good seem a sham and a fool's game. "The private life became the all in all," a chronicler of the 1920s has written. "The most diverse Americans of the twenties agreed in detestation of public life." The Babbitt replaced the political insurgent and what was left of the free public arena was a Kiwanis club lunch. In 1924 three-quarters of the electorate thought it useless to vote.[25]

The nation's Republican rulers governed with impudence and impunity. A major administration scandal scarcely cost them a vote. They not only served the interests of the trusts, they boasted openly of doing so, for the "captains of industry" were now restored to their former glory as if the prewar reform movement had never existed. The Republican rulers even set about creating multicorporate cartels to enable the monopolists to govern themselves and the American people as well. This refurbished monopoly economy the rulers and their publicists praised fulsomely as the "American System," although it was a system prewar Americans had fought for thirty years and which the very laws prohibited. Herbert Hoover, the chief architect of the cartels, described the new economy as "rugged individualism," which was very like calling the sunset the dawn or describing Wilson's neutrality as "America First," for official lies and catch phrases dominated the country after Wilson's demise as much as they had in his heyday. The catch phrases were crass rather than lofty. That was the chief difference.

Magazines that once thrived on exposing the corrupt privileges of the trusts now retailed gushing stories of business "success," supplied recipes for attaining "executive" status, and wrote paeans in praise of big business, although it was even more corruptly privileged in the 1920s than it had been in the days of the muckraker. America basked in unexampled prosperity, the publicists wrote, although half the country was poor and the farmers desperate. In the 1920s the poor became prosperous by fiat. America had entered an endless economic golden age, proclaimed the magnates of Wall Street whose ignorant pronouncements were now treated with reverence and made front-page news. Peace had returned to America, but the braying of bankers, not the voice of the turtle, was heard in the land. There were other diversions, too, for the populace: Babe Ruth, Red Grange, Al Capone, and an endless stream of songs and movies extolling the charms of college life, although most Americans had never graduated from high school. In postwar America the entire country lived on fantasy and breathed propaganda.

Against the fictions and the lies, where were the voices of dissent? There were few to be heard. What had happened to America's deep enmity toward monopoly and private economic power? It had virtually ceased to exist. It was just strong enough to call forth a few euphemisms. Republicans labeled the cartels "trade associations" and that was that. When the indomitable La Follette ran for President in 1924 as a third-party candidate, it was hardly more than the swansong of a cause long lost. Outside a few of the old insurgent states (now known collectively as the "farm bloc," a mere special interest) the country fell silent. Apathy and cynicism were the universal state. The official propaganda of the 1920s meant little to most Americans, but by now they were inured to a public life that made no sense and to public men who never spoke to their condition. Like any defeated people, they expected their rulers to consider them irrelevant. Even when the Great Depression struck down the postwar economy (it was a house of cards) and toppled the tin gods of the 1920s, Americans remained as if dumbstruck. Foreign visitors to America in the early 1930s were astonished by the American people's docility, for we had never been docile before. In the 1893 depresssion America had looked like the Rome of the Gracchi; forty years later people whose life savings had been wiped out by the "American System" stood quietly on breadlines as if they had known breadlines all their lives.

Not all of this postwar degradation was destined to last. Some hope, in time, would return to the defeated and a semblance of civic courage to the servile. What did not return was the struggle for republican reform. That was the lasting achievement of Wilson and the war party. That was the irreparable damage they had done to the American Republic. They had destroyed once and for all the republican cause. Never again would the citizenry of this Republic enter the political arena determined to overthrow oligarchy (as Lincoln bid his countrymen do), to extirpate private power and eliminate special privilege.

Historians sometimes call this change "the end of American innocence," scarcely realizing (so dead is the republican spirit) what depths of cynicism that airy little phrase betrays. If the republican struggle for liberty and equality was "innocent," what then is "experience"? It means giving up the ancient faith that self-government is worth fighting for; it means growing indifferent to special privilege and private power while forgetting that privilege corrupts and private power enslaves. It means conceding that a few shall monopolize our politics while forgetting that oligarchies serve chiefly themselves. It means comporting ourselves with proper humility, demanding not an end to corrupt privilege, say, but merely a "piece of the pie" or a "piece of the action," a crumb of corruption for ourselves. Such was the new age of "experience" historians say we entered after the First World War and they are right. Senator Stone of Missouri had foreseen its arrival on that fateful April day when the Senate voted for war against Germany. He was opposed to war, he had told a colleague, not because of the costs or the deaths but "because if we go into it we will never again have this same old Republic."[26]

The new age revealed itself first in the degradation of the discontented. Of the generation that tasted the bitter betrayal of the war, most were too disheartened to speak out. In the early 1920s, there were still Americans angry enough to lash out against their lot, but they had grown too cowardly to fight their real enemies. So they bought white bedsheets from the local Ku Klux Klan and terrorized Negroes, Catholics, and Jews. A few prairie states were all that remained to uphold the old republican cause. The degradation of the discontented proved especially long-lasting. Seventeen years after the war's end, Americans who refused to suffer the shams of the professional politicians turned not to the old reform traditions of the country. They turned instead to the fascistic fulminations of Father Coughlin or to the greedy puerilities of Huey Long's "Share Our Wealth" movement. That, too, was part of our hard-won "experience." Millions of Americans followed a Louisiana dictator and cheered the language of dictatorship, something we had never done in our "innocence." That is how thoroughly the war party had triumphed. It spawned a generation of Americans who mirrored its own corruption, for it no longer cherished the American Republic and no longer fought for its principles.

What the war generation ceased to care about, its children were to forget almost entirely. Who was left to remind them? Over the long years since 1917 the "despotism of professional politicians" has suffered its own ups and downs, but it has never been menaced—as it was menaced for so long—by free men struggling to protect their own freedom and regain a voice in their own affairs. From the ruins of the war, the republican cause has never revived to rally free men. It has ceased to make a difference in our politics. What the Spanish-American War deflected and weakened, the World War obliterated. And who can measure the cost of that loss, both to ourselves and to humanity, in whose name both wars had been fought.

Notes

1: "The Eve of a Very Dark Night"

1. *Imperial Democracy: The Emergence of America as a Great Power* by Ernest May, 1961, quoted p. 251.
2. *Forty Years of It* by Brand Whitlock, 1914, p. 27.
3. Whitlock, p. 53. *Grand Old Party: Political Structure in the Gilded Age, 1880–1896* by Robert Marcus, 1971, p. 17.
4. *Twenty Years of the Republic* by Harry Peck, 1906, p. 529.
5. *William McKinley and His America* by H. Wayne Morgan, 1963, quoted p. 129. *Politics, Reform and Expansion, 1890–1900* by Harold Faulkner, 1959, pp. 96–110.
6. *Democracy and the Organization of Political Parties* by M. Ostrogorski, 1902, vol. 2, pp. 79, 103. *Party Organization and Machinery* by Jesse Macy, 1904, p. 48. For Republican Party leadership during the 1890s see *Boies Penrose* by Robert Bowden, 1937; *Boss Platt and His New York Machine* by Harold Gosnell, 1924; *Nelson W. Aldrich* by Nathaniel Stephenson, 1930; *John Coit Spooner, Defender of Presidents* by Dorothy Fowler, 1961; *William Boyd Allison* by Leland Sage, 1956; *Fram Hayes to McKinley: National Party Politics, 1872–1896* by H. Wayne Morgan, 1969; Marcus, *Grand Old Party*, 1971.
7. *Politics, Strategy and American Diplomacy* by John Grenville and George Young, 1966, p. 76.
8. Morgan, 1969, quoted p. 304.
9. *Expansionists of 1898* by Julius Pratt, 1936, quoted p. 151.
10. For the Democratic Party of the 1890s see *Origins of the New South, 1870–1913* by C. Vann Woodward, 1951; *The Whirligig of Politics: The Democracy of Cleveland and Bryan* by Joseph Hollingsworth, 1963; *Bourbon Democracy of the Middle West, 1865–1896* by Horace Merrill, 1953; *Bourbon Leader: Grover Cleveland and the Democratic Party* by Horace Merrill, 1957; *The Politics of Depression* by Samuel McSeveney, 1972.
11. *The Winning of the Midwest* by Richard Jensen, 1971, pp. 209, 219–222. McSeveney, p. 97.
12. Morgan, 1969, quoted p. 267.

13. Woodward, quoted p. 51; pp. 52–58. *The Populist Revolt* by John Hicks, 1931, pp. 51–52.
14. *Master of Manhattan: The Life of Richard Croker* by Lothrop Stoddard, 1931, quoted p. 84.
15. *Reform in Detroit* by Melvin Holli, 1969, pp. 10–14, 38–44, 138–143.
16. Merrill, 1953.
17. Morgan, 1969, quoted p. 194.
18. *The Letters of Grover Cleveland,* 1933, pp. 5–6, 70, 240.
19. *Hoke Smith and the Politics of the New South* by Dewey Grantham, 1958, quoted p. 57.
20. *Grover Cleveland* by Allan Nevins, 1932, p. 466. Woodward, pp. 238–241. Merrill, 1957, p. 158.
21. Woodward, quoted p. 243; p. 262.
22. Woodward, quoted pp. 259, 272; p. 266. Morgan, 1969, quoted p. 478.
23. *The Tolerant Populists* by Walter Nugent, 1963, quoted p. 98. *American Radicalism, 1865–1901* by Chester Destler, 1946, pp. 17–20.
24. Hicks, quoted p. 159. Woodward, quoted p. 247.
25. Hollingsworth, p. 10. Morgan, 1969, quoted pp. 448–449. *The Education of Henry Adams,* 1907 [1931 edition], p. 338.
26. Morgan, 1969, quoted p. 455. Peck, pp. 391–392.
27. *Missouri, the Center State* by Walter Stevens, 1915, vol. 2, quoted p. 431. "The Politics and Personalities of Silver Repeal in the United States Senate" by Jeanette Nichols, *American Historical Review,* vol. 61, 1935, pp. 22–28, 48. Woodward, quoted p. 273.
28. Morgan, 1963, quoted p. 481. *Pitchfork Ben Tillman* by Francis Simkins, 1944, quoted p. 315.
29. *The Politicos* by Matthew Josephson, 1938, p. 618. Hollingsworth, p. 27. Cleveland, *Letters,* pp. 351, 355. Woodward, quoted p. 279. Simkins, quoted p. 315.
30. Josephson, pp. 568ff.
31. Faulkner, 1959, p. 168. Morgan, 1969, quoted pp. 472, 476. *The Letters of Henry Adams,* vol. 2, p. 67.
32. Morgan, 1969, p. 478.

2: "The Malevolent Change in Our Public Life"

1. *The Relations of the United States with Spain, Diplomacy* by F. E. Chadwick, 1909, quoted p. 409.
2. *The Martial Spirit* by Walter Millis, 1931, pp. 17–23. Morgan, 1963, p. 327.
3. Nevins, 1932, quoted p. 624.
4. Millis, 1931, quoted pp. 30, 35. Pratt, 1936, p. 22. *Anti-Imperialism in the United States* by E. Berkeley Tompkins, 1970, quoted p. 75. *Henry Cabot Lodge* by John Garraty, 1953, quoted p. 152.

5. Pratt, 1936, quoted p. 229. Tompkins, p. 87. *The Letters of Theodore Roosevelt,* vol. 1, p. 746.

6. *The Presidential Election of 1896* by Stanley Jones, 1964, quoted p. 196. For the Democrats' "plan" see Woodward, p. 281; Jones, p. 49; *Bryan* by Louis Koenig, 1971, p. 142.

7. For "fusion" as a state party stratagem see, for example, Merrill, 1953, p. 92.

8. "The Populist Movement in Oregon" by Marion Harrington, *University of Oregon Masters' Theses,* 1935, quoted p. 35. Hollingsworth, pp. 8–9. Hicks, p. 317.

9. Jones, quoted p. 298. *Populism in the Old Dominion* by William Sheldon, 1935, pp. 96, 100, 121. Woodward, pp. 282ff. Hollingsworth, p. 8.

10. Koenig, p. 166. Jones, p. 207. *Eagle Forgotten: The Life of John Peter Altgeld* by Harry Barnard, 1938, quoted p. 353. For Tammany Hall's assistance to the "silver" Democrats see *My Quarter Century in American Politics* by Champ Clark, 1920, vol. 1, p. 389.

11. Sheldon, quoted p. 143. May, quoted p. 76; pp. 34–39. Josephson, quoted p. 624.

12. Cleveland, *Letters,* pp. 369, 383–386. Grenville, p. 158.

13. U.S. Department of State. *Papers Relating to the Foreign Relations of the United States, 1894, p. x.*

14. *U.S. For. Rel.,* 1894, pp. 803ff. For summaries of the Venezuela crisis see "Background of Cleveland's Venezuela Policy," by Nelson Blake, *American Historical Review,* vol. 47, 1942; "The Background of Cleveland's Venezuela Policy: A Reinterpretation" by Walter LaFeber, *American Historical Review,* vol. 66, 1961; Grenville, pp. 125–178; Peck, pp. 413ff; Nevins, 1932, pp. 630ff.

15. Blake, p. 259. Peck, p. 413. Grenville, pp. 140–146.

16. Stevens, vol. 2, quoted p. 440. Koenig, quoted p. 120. *A Diplomatic History of the American People* by Thomas Bailey, 1940, quoted pp. 478, 486.

17. Cleveland, *Letters,* p. 417.

18. Blake, pp. 259–261; quoted p. 262. Grenville, p. 48.

19. Garraty, 1953, pp. 155–156.

20. Grenville, pp. 148ff. Blake, quoted p. 266. *The Cuban Crisis as Reflected in the New York Press, 1895–1898* by Joseph Wisan, 1934, quoted p. 71.

21. Nevins, 1932, p. 670.

22. Peck, p. 389.

23. *Court and Constitution in the Twentieth Century* by William Swindler, 1969, pp. 3–17.

24. Nevins, 1932, quoted p. 634.

25. *U.S. For. Rel.,* 1895, pp. 545–562.

26. Blake, pp. 270ff. *Congressional Record,* 54th Congress, 1st session, pp. 108–109.

27. *U.S. For. Rel.,* 1895, pp. 563–576.

28. *U.S. For. Rel.,* 1895, pp. 542–545.

29. Peck, quoted p. 425. Garraty, 1953, quoted p. 161. Nevins, 1932, quoted pp. 641, 644, 658. *Life and Letters of John Hay* by William Thayer, 1916, vol. 2, pp. 141–142.

30. Adams, *Letters,* vol. 2, pp. 91–92. *Cong. Record,* 54th Cong., 1st sess., pp. 659–662, 912.

31. Adams, *Letters,* vol. 2, pp. 92–93. *Henry White* by Allan Nevins, 1930, quoted pp. 109–110. Grenville, p. 200.

32. Millis, 1931, quoted p. 39.

3:   *"The Broad Ground of a Common Humanity"*

1. *Cong. Record,* 55th Cong., 2d sess., p. 768; 54th Cong., 1st sess., p. 2588. *Notes of a Busy Life* by Joseph Foraker, 1916, vol. 2. p. 18.

2. *Cong Record,* 54th Cong., 1st sess., pp. 1972, 2119, 2249, 2058.

3. *Cong Record,* 54th Cong., 1st sess., pp. 1972, 1976. May, quoted p. 77.

4. *Cong. Record,* 54th Cong., 1st sess., pp. 2244.

5. *Cong. Record,* 54th Cong., 1st sess., pp. 2680, 3011, 2587–2594.

6. *Cong. Record,* 54th Cong., 1st sess., p. 3550.

7. *Cong. Record,* 54th Cong., 1st sess., pp. 2877, 3125.

8. *Cong. Record,* 54th Cong., 1st sess., p. 2719.

9. Grenville, pp. 192–193.

10. *Spanish-American Relations Preceding the War of 1898* by Horace Flack, 1906, pp. 22–30.

11. Wisan, pp. 95–153.

12. Ostrogorski, vol. 2, pp. 157–196. "Middle-Western Newspapers and the Spanish-American War" by George Auxier, *Mississippi Valley Historical Review,* vol. 26, 1940, pp. 524–529. Bowden, p. 167.

13. *Public Opinion and the Spanish-American War* by Marcus Wilkerson, 1932, pp. 55ff. Millis, 1931, quoted pp. 41–42; p. 77.

14. Wisan, p. 193.

15. Jones, pp. 192–197. Koenig, p. 174. Nevins, 1932, p. 691. Cleveland, *Letters,* p. 439.

16. Jones, pp. 207, 216. Koenig, pp. 174, 179ff.

17. Koenig, quoted p. 168; p. 182. *Henry Moore Teller* by Elmer Ellis, 1941, p. 271. Jones, quoted p. 213. Josephson, quoted p. 672.

18. Hicks, p. 345. Jones, quoted p. 71; pp. 82–84.

19. Hicks, quoted p. 344.

20. Koenig, quoted p. 217. Jones, quoted p. 298.

21. Morgan, 1963, quoted p. 184.

22. Marcus, pp. 208–211, 220. Morgan 1963, p. 188.

23. For the Democrats' failure to support Bryan's presidential bid see Marcus,

p. 242; Josephson, p. 689; Nevins, 1932, p. 711; Koenig, p. 238; McSeveney, pp. 171, 195, 207, 212. Woodward, quoted p. 289.

24. *Hanna* by Thomas Beer, 1929, pp. 172, 177, 196–197. Pratt, 1936, quoted p. 215.

25. Millis, 1931, pp. 62–65. *In the Days of McKinley* by Margaret Leech, 1959, p. 99. May, p. 81. Wilkerson, p. 70. Chadwick, quoted p. 485; p. 489. Garraty, 1953, quoted p. 182.

26. *Cong. Record,* 55th Cong., 1st sess., pp. 2–5. Peck, p. 518.

4: "An Uncommonly Dangerous Politician"

1. Thayer, vol. 2, p. 153. Adams, *Letters,* vol. 2, p. 191. Morgan, 1963, p. 478. Leech, p. 69. *Threshhold to American Imperialism: Essays on the Foreign Policy of William McKinley,* edited by Paolo Coletta, 1970, pp. 15–16.

2. Adams, *Letters,* vol. 2, p. 195.

3. Morgan, 1963, p. 64.

4. Jensen, p. 177. Leech, pp. 135, 368–369. Gosnell, pp. 250–256. Marcus, pp. 236–237, 240.

5. *Autobiography of Seventy Years* by George Hoar, 1903, vol. 2, pp. 47–51. *Fifty Years of Public Service* by Shelby Cullom, 1911, p. 275.

6. Faulkner, 1959, p. 263.

7. May, pp. 129–133. Leech, pp. 368–369. Millis, 1931, p. 58.

8. May, quoted p. 120. Garraty, 1953, quoted p. 177. May, p. 117.

9. Grenville, p. 279. May, p. 121.

10. Grenville, quoted p. 196. Cleveland, *Letters,* p. 488.

11. Roosevelt, *Letters,* vol. 1, p. 606. *Cong. Record,* 55th Cong., 1st sess., p. 949.

12. Millis, 1931, p. 89. Chadwick, pp. 495, 504. Flack, pp. 72–76.

13. *Cong. Record,* 55th Cong., 1st sess., pp. 881, 949ff.

14. *Cong. Record,* 55th Cong., 1st sess., p. 1081. *An Old-Fashioned Senator, Orville H. Platt* by Louis Coolidge, 1910, p. 268.

15. May, p. 121. Wisan, quoted pp. 295, 299.

16. *Cong. Record,* 55th Cong., 1st sess., pp. 1169, 1192; 2d sess., p. 780. Ellis, p. 298.

17. Millis, 1931, p. 77. Morgan, 1963, p. 340.

18. *U.S. For. Rel.,* 1898, pp. 507–508. Flack, pp. 72–76. Chadwick, p. 495.

19. *U.S. For. Rel.,* 1898, pp. 585ff.

20. *U.S. For. Rel.,* 1898, pp. 560–584. Morgan, 1963, p. 343.

21. Morgan, 1963, quoted p. 295. Hoar, vol. 2, pp. 307–308. Tompkins, p. 97. May, quoted p. 244.

22. Roosevelt, *Letters,* vol. 1, pp. 670, 679. Grenville, p. 277.

23. Morgan, 1963, pp. 346–347. Roosevelt, *Letters,* vol. 1, p. 746.

24. Grenville, quoted p. 255. Millis, 1931, p. 93.

25. *U.S. For. Rel.,* 1897, pp. vii–xxxiv; 1898, p. 645.

26. May, p. 116. Hollingsworth, pp. 112–115. Ellis, p. 326. *Midwestern Progressive Politics* by Russel Nye, 1959, pp. 218–219. Koenig, p. 257. Barnard, pp. 417–421. *Cong. Record,* 55th Cong., 1st sess., p. 871.

27. Millis, 1931, pp. 94–95. Wisan, quoted p. 387. Nevins, 1930, p. 153. Coletta, p. 46. Morgan, 1963, quoted p. 455. *America of Yesterday as Reflected in the Journals of John Davis Long,* 1923, p. 155.

28. Wisan, pp. 386–389. Nevins, 1930, quoted p. 130.

29. Chadwick, quoted p. 538.

30. Millis, 1931, p. 139.

31. Millis, 1931, p. 107.

32. *Cong. Record,* 55th Cong., 2d sess., pp. 2074–2088.

33. Millis, 1931, p. 141. *U.S. For. Rel.,* 1898, p. 684.

34. Millis, 1931, quoted p. 123. *Cong. Record,* 55th Cong., 2d sess., p. 2916. Coletta, p. 50. Morgan, 1963, p. 366. May, pp. 143, 152.

35. Millis, 1931, p. 127. Fowler, p. 227. May, p. 154. *U.S. For. Rel.,* 1898, pp. 711–713.

36. *U.S. For. Rel.,* 1898, pp. 727, 734, 735. Millis, 1931, p. 126.

37. *U.S. For. Rel.,* 1898, pp. 750–760.

38. Beer, quoted p. 202. *Cong. Record,* 55th Cong., 2d sess., pp. 3788, 3954–3959, 3787, 3702, 3962ff.

39. Adams, *Letters,* vol. 2, pp. 175–176.

5: *"The Almighty Hand of God"*

1. Coletta, quoted p. 184. Tompkins, quoted p. 166.

2. Morgan, 1963, quoted p. 411.

3. May, quoted p. 246.

4. Millis, 1931, p. 172. Morgan, 1963, p. 294. Hollingsworth, p. 140.

5. Millis, 1931, quoted p. 251.

6. May, p. 245. Millis, 1931, quoted p. 199. Pratt, 1936, quoted p. 326. "Papers of John Davis Long," *Massachusetts Historical Society Collections,* vol. 78, 1939.

7. Millis, 1931, p. 222. Morgan, 1963, quoted p. 467.

8. Millis, 1931, quoted pp. 225, 252.

9. Millis, 1931, quoted p. 252.

10. Millis, 1931, p. 253; quoted p. 336. *Cong. Record,* 55th Cong., 2d sess., p. 6018. Hollingsworth, quoted p. 140. Leech, quoted p. 349.

11. Millis, 1931, pp. 339–340. May, quoted p. 255.

12. Grenville, quoted p. 286. Millis, 1931, p. 198.

13. Millis, 1931, quoted p. 317. *Joseph Benson Foraker* by Everett Walters, 1948, quoted p. 152.

14. Pratt, 1936, quoted pp. 356, 332. Tompkins, quoted pp. 166–167, 197.
15. Morgan, 1963, quoted p. 451.
16. "Anti-Imperialism and the Democrats" by Harold Baron, *Science and Society,* vol. 21, 1957, p. 228. Hoar, vol. 2, p. 322. May, p. 256.
17. Koenig, p. 288.
18. Woodward, quoted p. 324. Hoar, vol. 2, quoted p. 305.
19. Coletta, pp. 132ff. *Diplomatic Memoirs* by John W. Foster, 1909, vol. 2, p. 257.
20. *U.S. For. Rel.,* 1898, p. 907.
21. Millis, 1931, quoted pp. 383, 385. Coletta, quoted p. 143.
22. Tompkins, pp. 185–188, 194. Hoar, vol. 2, p. 322.
23. *Thomas B. Reed* by Samuel McCall, 1914, quoted p. 253. *Twelve Against Empire* by Robert Beisner, 1971, quoted p. 152.
24. Foster, vol. 2, p. 207. Morgan, 1963, quoted p. 467.
25. Leech, quoted p. 464. May, pp. 5–6, 263–269.
26. *Selections from the Correspondence of Theodore Roosevelt and Henry Cabot Lodge,* 1925, vol. 1, p. 274.
27. Roosevelt, *Letters,* vol. 1, pp. 84–85, 479. *Harper's Weekly,* January 13, January 20, 1894. Nevins, 1932, p. 111. Koenig, p. 77. Holli, pp. 10–44. *A Study of Boss Politics: William Lorimer of Chicago* by Joel Tarr, 1971, pp. 25–26, 32.
28. Ostrogorski, vol. 2, p. 216. Beisner, quoted p. 124.
29. *Our Times* by Mark Sullivan, vol. 2, quoted p. 403 [1971 edition]. Koenig, pp. 370–373. Cleveland, *Letters,* pp. 549–550, 562–563.

6:   "The People Are Through with Party Government"

1. *The Corporate Ideal in the Liberal State, 1900–1918* by James Weinstein, 1968, quoted p. 9.
2. *The Era of Theodore Roosevelt* by George Mowry, 1958, quoted p. 42. *Robert M. La Follette* by Bela and Fola La Follette, 1953, vol. 1, p. 254. *Tyrant from Illinois: Uncle Joe Cannon's Experiment with Personal Power* by Blair Bolles, 1951, pp. 56–57.
3. Sullivan, vol. 2, quoted pp. 351–352.
4. *The Progressive Era in Minnesota, 1899–1918* by Carl Chrislock, 1971, p. 15. *The Quest for Social Justice, 1898–1914* by Harold Faulkner, 1931, p. 35.
5. Sullivan, vol. 3, quoted p. 84. *The Letters of Lincoln Steffens,* 1938, vol. 1, pp. 191–196.
6. *Businessmen and Reform* by Robert Weibe, 1962, quoted p. 44. *Privilege and Democracy in America* by Frederick Howe, 1910, pp. 59–62.
7. *Untimely Papers* by Randolph Bourne, 1919, pp. 211–212.
8. *Power and Responsibility: The Life and Times of Theodore Roosevelt* by

William Harbaugh, 1961, quoted pp. 166, 167, 229. Sullivan, vol. 3, quoted p. 23.

9. Sullivan, vol. 3, pp. 27–68.

10. *Charles Evans Hughes* by Merlo Pusey, 1951, vol. 1, pp. 185, 193. *The Politics of Provincialism* by David Burner, 1970, pp. 24–25. *The Progressive Movement* by Benjamin De Witt, 1915, p. 72.

11. *The Republican Roosevelt* by John Morton Blum, 1954, p. 58. Sullivan, vol. 2, quoted pp. 467–468.

12. Harbaugh, 1961, pp. 264–265. Mowry, 1958, quoted p. 210.

13. Nye, pp. 218–219. *The California Progressives* by George Mowry, 1951, quoted p. 120.

14. *Roosevelt-Lodge Correspondence,* vol. 2, pp. 259, 350–351.

15. Bolles, quoted p. 143; pp. 108–110. La Follette, vol. 1, quoted p. 261. Harbaugh, p. 353.

16. *Theodore Roosevelt and the Progressive Movement* by George Mowry, 1946, p. 33.

17. *Insurgency: Personalities and Politics of the Taft Era* by Kenneth Hechler, 1940, p. 93.

18. Roosevelt, *Letters,* vol. 7, p. 99.

19. Hechler, pp. 104, 108–109. Mowry, 1958, pp. 244–245.

20. *Roosevelt-Lodge Correspondence,* vol. 2, pp. 331–332, 337.

21. Mowry, 1946, pp. 87–127. "Conservatives in the Progressive Era" by Norman Wilensky, *University of Florida Monographs,* no. 25, 1965.

22. *Burrows of Michigan and the Republican Party* by William Orcutt, 1917, vol. 2, p. 322; quoted p. 289.

23. *Roosevelt-Lodge Correspondence,* vol. 2, pp. 367–374.

24. Howe, 1910, p. 68.

25. *Roosevelt-Lodge Correspondence,* vol. 2, pp. 367–374.

26. *History of the Progressive Party, 1912–1916* by Amos Pinchot, 1958, p. 23.

27. *TR and Will* by William Manners, 1969, pp. 209, 216. Weinstein, pp. 148–150. *Brandeis, A Free Man's Life* by Alpheus Mason, 1946, p. 373. Pinchot, pp. 94–95.

28. Pinchot, p. 92. *The Life and Times of William Howard Taft* by Henry Pringle, 1939, vol. 2, p. 655. Bolles, p. 175.

29. Wilensky, quoted pp. 13–14. Pinchot, quoted p. 160.

7: *"A Man of High Ideals but No Principles"*

1. *The Public Papers of Woodrow Wilson,* vol. 3, p. 5.

2. *The Origins of the Foreign Policy of Woodrow Wilson* by Harley Notter, 1937, quoted pp. 16, 37. *Wilson* by Arthur Link, vol. 1, quoted p. 35.

3. La Follette, vol. 2, p. 967.

4. Notter, quoted p. 107.

5. Link, vol. 1, quoted p. 27.
6. *John Sharp Williams* by George Osborn, 1943, pp. 137–188. *Joe Bailey, The Last Democrat* by Sam Acheson, 1932, quoted pp. 256–257.
7. Osborn, 1943, pp. 110–111, 197.
8. Roosevelt, *Letters,* vol. 7, p. 420. *Cobb of the "World"* by John Heaton, 1924, pp. 40, 42, 45, 56, 70, 93, 163.
9. "Democratic Factions and Insurgent Republicans" by Herbert Croly, *North American Review,* vol. 191, 1910. For useful information about the prewar Democratic Party see *The La Guardia Years* by Charles Garrett, 1961, p. 11; *Labor and the Progressive Movement in New York State, 1897–1916* by Irwin Yellowitz, 1965, pp. 167, 192–193, 213–214, 232; "Joseph Folk of Missouri" by Louis Geiger, *University of Missouri Studies,* vol. 25, 1953, pp. 140–141, 153; *Law-Making in America* by Lynn Haines, 1912, pp. 45–46; *A. Mitchell Palmer, Politician* by Stanley Coben, 1963, p. 39; *Populism to Progressivism in Alabama* by Sheldon Hackney, 1969, pp. 314–316; La Follette, vol. 1, p. 449; Roosevelt, *Letters,* vol. 7, pp. 149–152; Woodward, pp. 391, 447ff.
10. Link, vol. 1, pp. 99–104.
11. Roosevelt, *Letters,* vol. 7, p. 592. Link, vol. 1, pp. 98–130. *Fighting Years: Memoirs of a Liberal Editor* by Oswald Villard, 1939, p. 219. *Liberalism in the New South* by Hugh Bailey, 1969, quoted pp. 202, 204.
12. Link, vol. 1, quoted p. 358.
13. *Woodrow Wilson, Life and Letters* by Ray Stannard Baker, vol. 2, quoted p. 223. Link, vol. 1, quoted p. 121.
14. Link, vol. 1, quoted p. 152. Acheson, quoted p. 285.
15. Link, vol. 1, pp. 184–185, 187, 189.
16. Link, vol. 1, quoted pp. 373, 381, 382.
17. Link, vol. 2, quoted p. 277.
18. Wilson, *Public Papers,* vol. 3, p. 200.
19. Link, vol. 2, p. 443.
20. La Follette, vol. 1, pp. 487–488. *American Democracy and the World War* by Frederic Paxson, 1936, vol. 1, quoted p. 100.
21. *The Intimate Papers of Colonel House,* edited by Charles Seymour, vol. 1, pp. 120, 297.
22. Link, vol. 2, quoted p. 350.
23. Wilson, *Public Papers,* vol. 3, pp. 45ff.
24. Link, vol. 2, p. 361.
25. Link, vol. 2, quoted pp. 379–380.
26. Link, vol. 2, quoted p. 367.
27. Link, vol. 2, p. 372; quoted p. 380. Wilson, *Public Papers,* vol. 3, pp. 64–69.
28. *Elihu Root* by Philip Jessup, 1938, vol. 2, quoted p. 256. Link, vol. 2, pp. 373–377.
29. Bailey, 1940, p. 605. Link, vol. 2, quoted p. 391.
30. *Revolution: Mexico 1910–1920* by Ronald Atkin, 1970, p. 189.
31. Atkin, quoted pp. 189–190. Wilson, *Public Papers,* vol. 3, p. 117. Link, vol. 2, quoted p. 396.

32. Wilson, *Public Papers,* vol. 3, pp. 98ff. Atkin, quoted p. 193.
33. *Wilson As I Knew Him* by Joseph Tumulty, 1921, quoted pp. 152–153.
34. Link, vol. 2, pp. 402–407. *Cong. Record,* 64th Cong., 1st sess., pp. 1318ff.
35. Wilson, *Public Papers,* vol. 3, pp. 104, 124–134.
36. La Follette, vol. 1, p. 500. Link, vol. 4, quoted p. 128.

8: *"The Noblest Part That Has Ever Come to a Son of Man"*

1. Link, vol. 3, quoted pp. 18–19. For the state of American public opinion at various stages of the European war see Link, vol. 3, pp. 6–30; vol. 5. p. 303; Roosevelt, *Letters,* vol. 8, pp. 969–970; La Follette, vol. 1, p. 638; Weinstein, p. 234; *America Enters the War* by Charles Tansill, 1938, p. 659.
2. Paxson, vol. 1, p. 165.
3. Link, vol. 3, pp. 9, 12, 25; vol. 4, p. 42.
4. *U.S. For. Rel. Supplement,* 1914, pp. 100–101.
5. House, *Intimate Papers,* vol. 1, pp. 93, 114.
6. *U.S. For. Rel. Supplement,* 1914, pp. 551–552. Tumulty, quoted pp. 228, 231. House, *Intimate Papers,* vol. 1, p. 276. Link, vol. 3, pp. 43, 203.
7. Link, vol. 3, quoted pp. 6, 48.
8. Link, vol. 3, quoted p. 56; vol. 2, p. 325. Roosevelt, *Letters,* vol. 7, p. 75 footnote 1. Wilson, *Public Papers,* vol. 3, pp. 164–167. House, *Intimate Papers,* vol. 1, p. 297.
9. *Road to War: America 1914–1917* by Walter Millis, 1935, quoted p. 102. House, *Intimate Papers,* vol. 2, p. 92.
10. *Propaganda for War* by Horace Peterson, 1939, quoted p. 83. Millis, 1935, quoted p. 84. For critical studies of American neutral rights and the British blockade see *Neutrality for the United States* by Edward Borchard and William Lage, 1937; *The American Defense of Neutral Rights, 1914–1917* by Alice Morrissey, 1939; *The Allied Blockade of Germany, 1914–1916* by Marion Siney, 1957; Tansill, *America Enters the War,* 1938.
11. *U.S. For. Rel. Supplement,* 1914, pp. 219–220. Link, vol. 3, pp. 116–117.
12. *U.S. For. Rel. Supplement,* 1914, pp. 225–232.
13. House, *Intimate Papers,* vol. 1, pp. 307–308. Link, vol. 3, pp. 108–112.
14. *U.S. For. Rel. Supplement,* 1914, pp. 232–233. Borchard, p. 64. Morrissey, p. 29.
15. *U.S. For. Rel. Supplement,* 1914, pp. 237, 244–246, 248–250. Tansill, p. 148. U.S. Department of State, *Papers Relating to the Foreign Relations of the United States. The Lansing Papers,* vol. 1, pp. 252, 257.
16. *U.S. For. Rel. Supplement,* 1914, pp. 464, 465–466. Millis, 1935, quoted pp. 117–118.
17. Wilson, *Public Papers,* vol. 3, p. 200. Link, vol. 2, quoted p. 471.
18. House, *Intimate Papers,* vol. 1, p. 374. Link, vol. 3, quoted p. 219. Millis, 1935, pp. 138–140. Tansill, pp. 443–453.

19. *U.S. For. Rel. Supplement,* 1915, pp. 93–94, 96–97.
20. *Neutrality, Its History, Economics and Law* by Edgar Turlington, 1935–36, vol. 3, p. 39. Millis, 1935, pp. 134–135.
21. Borchard, pp. 136–139.
22. Morrissey, quoted p. 53.
23. *Lansing Papers,* vol. 1, pp. 196–198.
24. *U.S. For. Rel. Supplement,* 1915, pp. 98–100. Tansill, quoted p. 236 footnote.
25. Peterson, p. 112.

9: *"I Cannot Understand His Attitude"*

1. House, *Intimate Papers,* vol. 2, p. 84.
2. House, *Intimate Papers,* vol. 2, pp. 54–55. Link, vol. 5, quoted p. 414.
3. *U.S. For. Rel. Supplement,* 1915, pp. 22–23.
4. Bourne, 1919, p. 53.
5. House, *Intimate Papers,* vol. 2, p. 64. Millis, 1935, quoted pp. 179–180. Tumulty, pp. 257–258.
6. *U.S. For. Rel. Supplement,* 1915, pp. 127–128. Link, vol. 3, quoted p. 342.
7. *Lansing Papers,* vol. 1, pp. 295, 353–354. *U.S. For. Rel. Supplement,* 1915, pp. 107–112, 152–156. Link, vol. 3, pp. 116–117. Morrissey, p. 86.
8. Tansill, quoted pp. 251–252.
9. Link, vol. 3, quoted p. 349.
10. *Lansing Papers,* vol. 1, pp. 365–368. Borchard, p. 38.
11. *Lansing Papers,* vol. 1, pp. 368, 370–372. Tansill, quoted p. 138.
12. Lansing Papers, vol. 1, p. 369.
13. *Lansing Papers,* vol. 1, p. 372.
14. *Lansing Papers,* vol. 1, pp. 374–376.
15. Borchard, pp. 94–95. *U.S. For. Rel. Supplement,* 1915, pp. 104–105, 122, 137.
16. *Lansing Papers,* vol. 1, pp. 332–333.
17. *Lansing Papers,* vol. 1, p. 376. Link, vol. 3, p. 363.
18. *U.S. For. Rel. Supplement,* 1915, pp. 159, 365–366, 368.
19. Tansill, quoted p. 259. *Lansing Papers,* vol. 1, pp. 377–378.
20. *The Memoirs of William Jennings Bryan* by W. J. and Mary B. Bryan, 1925, p. 397.
21. Millis, 1935, quoted pp. 156–157.
22. Millis, 1935, quoted pp. 172, 175. Bailey, 1940, quoted p. 628.
23. Tansill, quoted pp. 276–277. *Lansing Papers,* vol. 1, p. 386.
24. Tumulty, pp. 232–233. Link, vol. 3, quoted p. 412.
25. House, *Intimate Papers,* vol. 1, pp. 442, 434; vol. 2, pp. 5–6. Villard, p. 258.
26. Wilson, *Public Papers,* vol. 3, pp. 318–322.
27. *Lansing Papers,* vol. 1, pp. 392–394. *U.S. For. Rel. Supplement,* 1915, pp. 393–396.

28. *U.S. For. Rel. Supplement,* 1915, p. 397.
29. Link, vol. 3, quoted p. 397.
30. *Lansing Papers,* vol. 1, pp. 392–394, 408–410, 411.
31. *Lansing Papers,* vol. 1, pp. 408–410, 422–426.
32. Link, vol. 3, quoted pp. 436–437 footnote 87. *U.S. For. Rel. Supplement,* pp. 402, 461–462.
33. *Lansing Papers,* vol. 1, pp. 452–454. *U.S. For. Rel. Supplement,* 1915, p. 462.
34. *U.S. For. Rel. Supplement,* 1915, pp. 419–421, 436–438.
35. *Lansing Papers,* vol. 1, pp. 436–437. Link, vol. 3, pp. 438–440.
36. Link, vol. 3, p. 425. Millis, 1935, quoted p. 190.
37. Villard, pp. 275–276. Link, vol. 3, quoted p. 426. *Bryan and World Peace* by Merlo Curti, 1931, p. 220. Koenig, p. 554.
38. *U.S. For. Rel. Supplement,* 1915, pp. 463–466, 469.
39. Link, vol. 3, quoted pp. 439–440. *Beveridge and the Progressive Era* by Claude Bowers, 1932, quoted p. 484. *Lansing Papers,* vol. 1, pp. 460–463.
40. *Lansing Papers,* vol. 1, pp. 457–459.
41. *U.S. For. Rel. Supplement,* 1915, pp. 480–482.
42. Millis, 1935, quoted p. 195. House, *Intimate Papers,* vol. 2, pp. 60–61.
43. House, *Intimate Papers,* vol. 2, p. 49.

10:   *"Never Before Were More Lies Told"*

1. New York *World,* August 29, 1915.
2. *Preparedness, 1914–1917* by Samuel Hubbard, 1923, quoted p. 101. Mowry, 1951, p. 275. Pringle, vol. 2, p. 873. "Origin and Activities of the National Security League, 1914–1919" by Robert Ward, *Mississippi Valley Historical Review,* vol. 47, 1960, pp. 55–56.
3. Bourne, 1919, pp. 36, 211–214. *World,* December 28, 1915. Pinchot, p. 216.
4. Roosevelt, *Letters,* vol. 8, p. 960.
5. *Cong. Record,* 64th Cong., 1st sess., pp. 143–144, 3715, 3717, 676.
6. *World,* October 2, December 3, 1915.
7. *Cong. Record,* 64th Cong., 2d sess., p. 4777.
8. Roosevelt, *Letters,* vol. 8, pp. 920–921. Peterson, quoted p. 21.
9. Mowry, 1951, quoted p. 248. Preparedness pamphlets comprise a sizable literature but their tone, their arguments, and their general political outlook are well expressed in book-length works such as *Americanism* by David Jayne Hill, 1916; *Straight America, A Call to National Service* by Frances Kellor, 1916; *Americanization* by Royal Dixon, 1916; *Selected Articles on National Defense* by Corinne Bacon, 1915.
10. Link, vol. 3, p. 590.
11. Link, vol. 3, p. 590. *Inviting America to War* by Allan Benson, 1916, p. 96.
12. *World,* September 10, 1915. *Cong. Record,* 64th Cong., 1st sess., p. 239.
13. *World,* July 19, December 31, 1915.

14. *World,* August 11–18, 1915. *Leonard Wood* by Hermann Hagedorn, 1931, vol. 2, pp. 157–160.
15. *World,* September 26, October 10, 1915.
16. *Cong. Record,* 64th Cong., 1st sess., p. 463. *World,* September 10, 1915.
17. Roosevelt, *Letters,* vol. 8, p. 965 footnote 2.
18. Link, vol. 4, pp. 24–25.
19. Link, vol. 3, p. 590. *World,* July 18, 1915. Tumulty, pp. 260–261. House, *Intimate Papers,* vol. 2, pp. 19–20.
20. *World,* July 24, August 5–6, 1915. Governors' Conference, *Proceedings,* no. 8, 1915, pp. 126, 250–251.
21. Link, vol. 3, quoted p. 555.
22. *World,* August 15–17, 1915.
23. *World,* September 12, 1915.
24. Grantham, p. 286. *World,* November 7, 1915.
25. *World,* November 10, 15, 1915. Benson, p. 85.
26. Wilson, *Public Papers,* vol. 3, pp. 373–374.
27. Wilson, *Public Papers,* vol. 3, pp. 375–381.
28. Wilson, *Public Papers,* vol. 3, pp. 384–392.
29. Link, vol. 4, pp. 23–24. Tansill, quoted p. 606 footnote 67.
30. Paxson, vol. 1, quoted p. 297. Wilson, *Public Papers,* vol. 3, pp. 406–428 (italics mine).
31. Link, vol. 3, quoted pp. 586, 577 footnote 80. *Lansing Papers,* vol. 1, p. 474.
32. House, *Intimate Papers,* vol. 2, pp. 70–71, 75. *U.S. For. Rel. Supplement,* 1915, pp. 578–589. Borchard, quoted p. 39.
33. House, *Intimate Papers,* vol. 2, pp. 87–89.
34. House, *Intimate Papers,* vol. 2, p. 84.
35. House, *Intimate Papers,* vol. 2, pp. 170–171. Link, vol. 4, p. 114.
36. House, *Intimate Papers,* vol. 2, pp. 85–86.
37. Link, vol. 4, quoted p. 108. House, *Intimate Papers,* vol. 2, p. 91.
38. Tansill, p. 454. House, *Intimate Papers,* vol. 2, pp. 99, 176–177, 183, 260–262. "The British Response to the House-Grey Memorandum" by John Cooper, *Journal of American History,* vol. 59, 1973. Link, vol. 4, pp. 118–130.
39. Millis, 1935, quoted p. 249. House, *Intimate Papers,* vol. 2, pp. 100–101.
40. *Lansing Papers,* vol. 1, pp. 488–489.
41. House, *Intimate Papers,* vol. 2, pp. 145–146.
42. *U.S. For. Rel. Supplement,* 1916, p. 649. *Lansing Papers,* vol. 1, p. 502.
43. Tansill, quoted pp. 391–392.
44. *Lansing Papers,* vol. 1, pp. 221–222.

11: *"We Do Not Covet Peace at the Cost of Honor"*

1. Curti, p. 235. *World,* December 15, 1915. Grantham, quoted p. 301. *Cong. Record,* 64th Cong., 1st sess., p. 2468.

2. Osborn, 1943, pp. 247, 254–258. *World,* August 21, 1915. *Cong. Record,* 64th Cong., 1st sess., pp. 1356–1357, 2481, 3597, 3636.

3. *Cong. Record,* 64th Cong., 1st sess., p. 505.

4. *Cong. Record,* 64th Cong., 1st sess., pp. 876, 1635–1636.

5. *Cong. Record,* 64th Cong., 1st sess., pp. 272ff, 463, 697, 745, 876, 922, 1573.

6. *U.S. For. Rel. Supplement,* 1914, pp. 576–577, 611–612. Tansill, quoted p. 413; p. 428. Borchard, pp. 86–89, 100. Morrissey, p. 14.

7. *Lansing Papers,* vol. 1, pp. 330–331.

8. House, *Intimate Papers,* vol. 2, pp. 73–74.

9. *Lansing Papers,* vol. 1, pp. 331–333. *U.S. For. Rel. Supplement,* 1915, pp. 652–654.

10. *Lansing Papers,* vol. 1, pp. 334–335.

11. *U.S. For. Rel. Supplement,* 1916, pp. 146–148.

12. Link, vol. 4, pp. 144–150.

13. *U.S. For. Rel. Supplement,* 1916, p. 151. Link, vol. 4, p. 152.

14. *World,* February 11, 13, 15, 1916.

15. *U.S. For. Rel. Supplement,* 1916, p. 170. Borchard, quoted p. 108.

16. Wilson, *Public Papers,* vol. 4, pp. 1–121. *World,* January 31, February 2, 1916. *Cong. Record,* 64th Cong., 1st sess., p. 2123. Tansill, p. 464. *Claude Kitchin and the Wilson War Policies* by Alex Arnett, 1937, p. 87.

17. *Cong. Record,* 64th Cong., 1st sess., pp. 3518, 3486.

18. *Cong. Record,* 64th Cong., 1st sess., pp. 3702, 3706; Appendix, pp. 364–365.

19. Tansill, quoted p. 466. Link, vol. 4, pp. 167–168. *Cong. Record,* 64th Cong., 1st sess., pp. 3318–3319; Appendix, p. 832. *World,* February 23, 1916.

20. Tansill, quoted p. 467. *New York Times,* February 24, 1916. *World,* February 24, 1916.

21. *La Follette's Magazine,* March 1916. Arnett, quoted p. 161. Link, vol. 4, p. 169. *Cong. Record,* 64th Cong., 1st sess., p. 3408.

22. *Cong. Record,* 64th Cong., 1st sess., p. 3410.

23. *Cong. Record,* 64th Cong., 1st sess., p. 2762; Appendix, p. 832. *World,* February 24, 1916. Tansill, p. 471.

24. *U.S. For. Rel. Supplement,* 1916, pp. 177–178.

25. *Cong. Record,* 64th Cong., 1st sess., p. 3408. *New York Times,* February 25, 1916.

26. *World,* February 25, March 1, 1916. *New York Times,* February 25, 1916. *Cong. Record,* 64th Cong., 1st sess., pp. 3407, 3479, 3637.

27. *Cong. Record,* 64th Cong., 1st sess., p. 3483.

28. *Cong. Record,* 64th Cong., 1st sess. p. 3405; Appendix, p. 681.

29. *Cong. Record,* 64th Cong., 1st sess., p. 3886.

30. *Cong. Record,* 64th Cong., 1st sess., pp. 3463ff.

31. *New York Times,* March 6, 1916.

32. *Cong. Record,* 64th Cong., 1st sess., pp. 3634–3638, 3688.

33. *Cong. Record,* 64th Cong., 1st sess., pp. 3712ff.

34. Benson, p. 117. "Progressive Republican Senators and the Submarine Crisis" by Walter Sutton, *Mid-America,* vol. 47, 1965, quoted p. 86.

12: "A Hopelessly False Position"

1. Link, vol. 4, quoted pp. 134–135.
2. House, *Intimate Papers*, vol. 2, pp. 164, 170, 292.
3. Link, vol. 4, p. 137.
4. *U.S. For. Rel. Supplement*, 1916, pp. 149–200, 210. *World*, February 28, 1916. House, *Intimate Papers*, vol. 2, pp. 254–255. Siney, p. 256. Link, vol. 4, pp. 227–228.
5. Wilson, *Public Papers*, vol. 4, pp. 169–177.
6. *Lansing Papers*, vol. 1, pp. 537–538. House, *Intimate Papers*, vol. 2, pp. 226–227, 230. Link, vol. 4, pp. 236–238.
7. Link, vol. 4, pp. 244–245.
8. Link, vol. 4, p. 245; quoted p. 249.
9. *U.S. For. Rel. Supplement*, 1916, pp. 232–234.
10. Wilson, *Public Papers*, vol. 4, pp. 153–159.
11. Link, vol. 4, pp. 254–255. Morrissey, quoted p. 124. *Searchlight on Congress*, 1916, vol. 1, no. 4.
12. Link, vol. 4, p. 265. *U.S. For. Rel. Supplement*, 1916, pp. 244–248, 252. Borchard, pp. 123–124. Tansill, p. 510.
13. Link, vol. 4, quoted p. 257.
14. *U.S. For. Rel. Supplement*, 1916, pp. 257–260.
15. Tansill, quoted p. 514.
16. *U.S. For. Rel. Supplement*, 1916, p. 263.
17. Tumulty, p. 159.
18. Link, vol. 5, pp. 13–14; vol. 4, p. 322. *Joe Tumulty and the Wilson Era* by John Morton Blum, 1951, pp. 107–108.
19. Link, vol. 4, pp. 319–322; vol. 5, p. 3. *Cong. Record*, 64th Cong., 1st sess., pp. 2822–2827. Roosevelt, *Letters*, vol. 8, p. 1005. Mowry, 1946, p. 320. Pusey, vol. 2, pp. 327–328.
20. Paxson, vol. 1, pp. 340–341. Villard, quoted p. 317.
21. Pusey, vol. 2, p. 342. Link, vol. 5, p. 100. House, *Intimate Papers*, vol. 2, p. 369. *The Democratic Party, A History* by Frank Kent, 1928, p. 421.
22. Pusey, vol. 2, quoted p. 332. Morrissey, pp. 141–148. Link, vol. 5, pp. 65–66. House, *Intimate Papers*, pp. 371–372. Paxson, vol. 1, p. 361. Burner, p. 31.
23. Paxson, vol. 1, p. 348. Morrissey, pp. 141–153. Link, vol. 5, pp. 73–77.
24. Link, vol. 4, pp. 322–345; vol. 5, pp. 60–65. Wilson, *Public Papers*, vol. 4, pp. 275–291.
25. Wilson, *Public Papers*, vol. 4, p. 330.
26. Link, vol. 5, p. 106.
27. House, *Intimate Papers*, vol. 2, pp. 371–372. Link, vol. 5, quoted pp. 111, 102.
28. Link, vol. 5, quoted p. 111.

13: "The National Conscience Is Clear"

1. *The Making of a Reporter* by Will Irwin, 1942, p. 324. *Thomas Woodrow Wilson, A Psychological Study* by Sigmund Freud and William Bullitt, 1967, p. 179.
2. House, *Intimate Papers,* vol. 2, pp. 256–257, 270–275, 282–292, 304, 316.
3. Link, vol. 5, p. 73 footnote 106.
4. Link, vol. 5, p. 187. House, *Intimate Papers,* vol. 2, pp. 390–392.
5. House, *Intimate Papers,* vol. 2, pp. 335–336. Link, vol. 5, pp. 165–167, 177, 189. *U.S. For. Rel. Supplement,* 1916, pp. 28–29, 46–47, 55, 267. Tansill, pp. 609–613. Morrissey, p. 160.
6. Tansill, quoted p. 606. *U.S. For. Rel. Supplement,* 1916, p. 71.
7. House, *Intimate Papers,* vol. 2, pp. 394–395. Link, vol. 5, pp. 199–200.
8. Link, vol. 5, pp. 206, 209.
9. *U.S. For. Rel. Supplement,* 1916, pp. 85–86, 94–95. Link, vol. 5, p. 210.
10. Link, vol. 5, quoted p. 217.
11. *U.S. For. Rel. Supplement,* pp. 97–99. Link, vol. 5, pp. 221, 232, 239. Millis, 1935, pp. 370–373. Morrissey, p. 172.
12. *U.S. For Rel. Supplement,* p. 118.
13. House, *Intimate Papers,* vol. 2, pp. 412–413. Link, vol. 5, pp. 250–251, 256–257, 278–279.
14. *U.S. For. Rel. Supplement,* 1917, pp. 24–29.
15. Millis, 1935, pp. 386, 389–391. Tansill, quoted p. 645.
16. Millis, 1935, quoted p. 392.
17. Millis, 1935, quoted p. 395. Link, vol. 5, p. 310.
18. *The Zimmermann Telegram* by Barbara Tuchman, 1958, p. 162.
19. Link, vol. 5, pp. 312–313.
20. *Cong. Record,* 64th Cong., 2d sess., quoted p. 4998. Morrissey, p. 187.
21. Millis, 1935, quoted p. 402.
22. Millis, 1935, p. 402.
23. Tuchman, quoted p. 146.
24. Acheson, quoted pp. 345–346. Tuchman, quoted p. 177.
25. Tuchman, quoted pp. 168, 173. Millis, 1935, quoted p. 408.
26. Wilson, *Public Papers,* vol. 4, pp. 428–432.
27. *Cong. Record,* 64th Cong., 2d sess., p. 4745.
28. Tuchman, pp. 173–175. Millis, 1935, pp. 407–408.
29. Wilson, *Public Papers,* vol. 4, p. 435; vol. 5, p. 365. La Follette, vol. 1, pp. 628–629.
30. Millis, 1935, quoted p. 413.
31. Link, vol. 5, p. 414. Millis, 1935, quoted p. 422.
32. Millis, 1935, quoted p. 419.

33. Millis, 1935, p. 436.
34. *Cong. Record,* 65th Cong., 1st sess., pp. 102–104.
35. Millis, 1935, p. 440.
36. *Cong. Record,* 65th Cong., 1st sess., pp. 223–234.
37. Pinchot, pp. 128–129.

14: *"The Old America That Was Free and Is Now Dead"*

1. *Confessions of a Reformer* by Frederick Howe, 1925, p. 284.
2. *Freedom of Speech* by Zechariah Chafee, 1920, pp. 335–336.
3. Chafee, pp. 10, 38, 57–84.
4. *Drifting Sands of Party Politics* by Oscar Underwood, 1928, p. 355. "The Nation-wide Spy System," *American Civil Liberties Union,* 1924. *Aliens and Dissenters* by William Preston, 1963, quoted p. 147. Villard, p. 327.
5. *The Challenge to American Freedoms* by Donald Johnson, 1963, quoted p. 65. Preston, p. 156.
6. "The Old America and the New," *American Civil Liberties Union,* 1920.
7. Steffens, *Letters,* vol. 1, pp. 428–429. Preston, p. 123.
8. Howe, 1925, pp. 278–279.
9. *Into the Twenties* by Burl Noggle, 1974, pp. 91–92; quoted p. 95.
10. Chafee, p. 227; also chapter 4. *A Liberal in Wartime* by Walter Nelles, 1940, quoted p. 182. Heaton, pp. 346–348.
11. Freud, quoted p. 243.
12. Noggle, quoted p. 137. *A Time for Angels* by Elmer Bendiner, 1975, p. 140.
13. Steffens, *Letters,* vol. 1, p. 472. *When the Cheering Stopped* by Gene Smith, 1964, p. 49. Freud, pp. 263–264.
14. Noggle, p. 26. *The United States and the League of Nations* by Denna Fleming, 1932, p. 334.
15. *Woodrow Wilson and the Great Betrayal* by Thomas Bailey, 1945, quoted pp. 72, 128. *Wilson and the League of Nations,* edited by Ralph Stone, 1967, quoted p. 35.
16. Freud, pp. 279–280.
17. Fleming, p. 334. Bailey, 1945, pp. 93–95.
18. Bailey, 1945, quoted p. 100. Smith, quoted p. 49.
19. Bailey, 1945, quoted p. 100. Smith, pp. 61, 82.
20. Freud, pp. 285–290.
21. Fleming, quoted p. 381.
22. Bailey, 1945, pp. 157–169. Stone, p. 22.
23. Fleming, quoted pp. 403–404. Stone, p. 33. Bailey, 1945, p. 277.
24. Fleming, pp. 467–469.
25. Nye, p. 287. Blum, 1951, pp. 153, 167, 187, 245. Burner, pp. 34–64. *Babbitts and Bohemians* by Elizabeth Stevenson, 1967, pp. 71–72.
26. La Follette, vol. 1, quoted p. 654.

Bibliography

Abrams, Richard. "Woodrow Wilson and the Southern Congressmen, 1913–1916," *Journal of Southern History,* vol. 22, 1956.

Acheson, Sam. *Joe Bailey, The Last Democrat,* 1932.

Adams, Frank. *Texas Democracy,* 4 vols., 1937.

Adams, Henry. *The Education of Henry Adams,* 1907 [1931 edition].

———. *Letters,* 2 vols., 1930–1938.

Alexander, De Alva. *History and Proceedings of the House of Representatives,* 1916.

Allen, Frederick Lewis. *The Big Change,* 1952.

American Academy of Political and Social Science. *Annals,* vol. 56, 1916.

American Civil Liberties Union. "The Old America and the New," 1920.

———. "The Nation-wide Spy System," 1924.

Arnett, Alex. *Claude Kitchin and the Wilson War Policies,* 1937.

Atkin, Ronald. *Revolution: Mexico 1910–1920,* 1970.

Auxier, George. "Middle-Western Newspapers and the Spanish-American War," *Mississippi Valley Historical Review,* vol. 26, 1940.

Bacon, Corinne. *Selected Articles on National Defense,* 1915.

Bailey, Hugh. *Liberalism in the New South,* 1969.

Bailey, Thomas. *A Diplomatic History of the American People,* 1940.

———. *Woodrow Wilson and the Great Betrayal,* 1945.

Baker, Ray Stannard. *Woodrow Wilson, Life and Letters,* 8 vols., 1927–1929.

Barnard, Harry. *Eagle Forgotten: The Life of John Peter Altgeld,* 1938.

Baron, Harold. "Anti-Imperialism and the Democrats," *Science and Society,* vol. 21, 1957.

Barrett, James. *Joseph Pulitzer and His World,* 1941.

Bass, Herbert. *"I Am a Democrat": The Political Career of David Bennett Hill,* 1961.

Bates, Josephine, "Make America Safe," 1916.

Beaver, Daniel. *Newton Baker and the American War Effort,* 1966.

Beck, James. "Where There Is No Vision," 1916.

Beer, Thomas. *Hanna,* 1929.

Beisner, Robert. *Twelve Against Empire,* 1971.

Belmont, Perry. *An American Democrat,* 1940.

Bemis, Samuel. *The United States as a World Power,* 1950.

Bendiner, Elmer. *A Time for Angels*, 1975.

Benson, Allan. *Inviting America to War*, 1916.

Billington, Monroe. "The Gore Resolution of 1916," *Mid-America*, vol. 47, 1965.

Blake, Nelson. "Background of Cleveland's Venezuela Policy," *American Historical Review*, vol. 47, 1942.

Blakeslee, George. *The Problems and Lessons of the War*, 1916.

Blum, John Morton. *Joe Tumulty and the Wilson Era*, 1951.

———. *The Republican Roosevelt*, 1954.

Bolles, Blair. *Tyrant from Illinois: Uncle Joe Cannon's Experiment with Personal Power*, 1951.

Borchard, Edward, and William Lage. *Neutrality for the United States*, 1937.

Bourne, Randolph. *Untimely Papers*, 1919.

Bowden, Robert. *Boies Penrose*, 1937.

Bowers, Claude. *Beveridge and the Progressive Era*, 1932.

Bryan, William Jennings, and Mary B. *The Memoirs of William Jennings Bryan*, 1925.

Burner, David. *The Politics of Provincialism*, 1970.

Carnegie, Andrew. *Autobiography*, 1920.

Carr, Raymond. *Spain, 1808–1936*, 1966.

Chadwick, F. E. *The Relations of the United States with Spain, Diplomacy*, 1909.

Chafee, Zechariah. *Freedom of Speech*, 1920.

Chamber of Commerce of the State of New York, "Report on the Common Defense," 1916.

Child, Clifton. *The German-Americans in Politics, 1914–1917*, 1939.

Chrislock, Carl. *The Progressive Era in Minnesota, 1899–1918*, 1971.

Church, Charles. *History of the Republican Party of Illinois*, 1913.

Clark, Champ. *My Quarter Century of American Politics*, 2 vols., 1920.

Cleveland, Grover. *Letters*, 1933.

Coben, Stanley. *A. Mitchell Palmer, Politician*, 1963.

Coletta, Paolo (ed.). *Threshhold to American Internationalism: Essays on the Foreign Policy of William McKinley*, 1970.

The Commoner.

Congressional Record.

Coolidge, Louis. *An Old-Fashioned Senator, Orville H. Platt*, 1910.

Cooper, John. "The British Response to the House-Grey Memorandum," *Journal of American History*, vol. 59, 1973.

Cortissoz, Royal. *The Life of Whitelaw Reid*, 2 vols., 1921.

Cotner, Robert. *James Stephen Hogg*, 1959.

Cox, James M. *Journey Through My Years*, 1946.

Cramer, C. H. *Newton D. Baker*, 1961.

Croly, Herbert. "Democratic Factions and Insurgent Republicans," *North American Review*, vol. 191, 1910.

———. *The Promise of American Life*, 1909.

Cullom, Shelby. *Fifty Years of Public Service*, 1911.

Curti, Merlo. *Bryan and World Peace*, 1931.

Daniels, Josephus. *Editor in Politics*, 1941.

———. *Cabinet Diaries, 1913–1921*, 1963.

Davis, Elmer. *History of the New York Times*, 1921.

Dawes, Charles. *A Journal of the McKinley Years*, 1950.

Dawson, Thomas. *Life and Character of Edward Oliver Wolcott*, 2 vols., 1911.

De Conde, Alexander. "The South and Isolationism," *Journal of Southern History*, vol. 22, 1956.

Depew, Chauncey. *My Memories of Eighty Years*, 1922.

Destler, Chester. *American Radicalism, 1865–1901*, 1946 [1966 edition].

De Witt, Benjamin. *The Progressive Movement*, 1915 [1968 edition].

Dixon, Royal. *Americanization*, 1916.

Ellis, Elmer. *Henry Moore Teller*, 1941.

Ewing, Cortez. *Congressional Elections, 1896–1944*, 1947.

Faulkner, Harold. *The Quest for Social Justice, 1898–1914*, 1931 [1971 edition].

———. *Politics, Reform and Expansion, 1890–1900*, 1959.

Flack, Horace. *Spanish-American Relations Preceding the War of 1898*, 1906.

Fleming, Denna. *The United States and the League of Nations*, 1932.

Flint, Winston. *The Progressive Movement in Vermont*, 1941.

Folwell, William. *A History of Minnesota*, 4 vols., 1926.

Foraker, Joseph. *Notes of a Busy Life*, 2 vols., 1916.

Foster, John W. *Diplomatic Memoirs*, 2 vols., 1909.

Fowler, Dorothy. *John Coit Spooner, Defender of Presidents*, 1961.

Freud, Sigmund, and William Bullitt. *Thomas Woodrow Wilson, A Psychological Study*, 1967.

Fuess, Claude. *Carl Schurz, Reformer*, 1932.

Garraty, John. *Henry Cabot Lodge*, 1953.

———. *The New Commonwealth, 1877–1890*, 1968.

Garrett, Charles. *The La Guardia Years*, 1961.

Geiger, Louis. "Joseph Folk of Missouri," *University of Missouri Studies*, Vol. 25, 1953.

George, Alice. "The Teaching of Patriotism in Home and School," 1916.

Gosnell, Harold. *Boss Platt and His New York Machine*, 1924.

Governors' Conference. *Proceedings*, no. 8, 1915.

Grantham, Dewey. *Hoke Smith and the Politics of the New South*, 1958 [1967 edition].

Grenville, John, and George Young. *Politics, Strategy and American Diplomacy*, 1966.

Griffin, Solomon. *People and Politics Observed by a Massachusetts Editor*, 1923.

Grinder, Robert. "Progressives, Conservatives and Imperialists: Another Look at Senate Republicans, 1913–1917," *North Dakota Quarterly*, vol. 41, 1973.

Guthrie, Mildred. "Anti-War Minority Group in Congress, 1916–1917," *The Historian*, vol. 2, 1940.

Hackney, Sheldon. *Populism to Progressivism in Alabama*, 1969.

Hagedorn, Hermann. *Leonard Wood*, 2 vols., 1931.

————. *The Bugle That Woke America,* 1940.

Haines, Lynn. *Law-Making in America,* 1912.

Harbaugh, William. *Power and Responsibility: The Life and Times of Theodore Roosevelt,* 1961.

Harper's Weekly.

Harrington, Marion. "The Populist Movement in Oregon," *University of Oregon Masters' Theses,* 1935.

Haworth, Paul. *America in Ferment,* 1915.

Heaton, John. *Cobb of the "World,"* 1924.

Hechler, Kenneth. *Insurgency: Personalities and Politics of the Taft Era,* 1940.

Hendrick, Burton. *The Life and Letters of Walter Hines Page,* 3 vols., 1923.

Hicks, John. *The Populist Revolt,* 1931.

Hill, David Jayne. *Americanism,* 1916.

Hirshson, Stanley. *Farewell to the Bloody Shirt,* 1962.

Hoar, George. *Autobiography of Seventy Years,* 2 vols., 1903.

Holbo, Paul. "Presidential Leadership in Foreign Affairs: William McKinley and the Turpie-Foraker Amendment," *American Historical Review,* vol. 72, 1967.

Holbrook, Franklin, and Livia Appel. *Minnesota in the War with Germany,* 2 vols., 1928–1932.

Holcombe, Arthur. *The Political Parties of Today,* 1924.

Holli, Melvin. *Reform in Detroit,* 1969.

Hollingsworth, Joseph. *The Whirligig of Politics: The Democracy of Cleveland and Bryan,* 1963.

House, E. M. *The Intimate Papers of Colonel House,* edited by Charles Seymour, 4 vols., 1926–1928.

Houston, David. *Eight Years with Wilson's Cabinet,* 2 vols., 1926.

Howe, Frederick. *Privilege and Democracy in America,* 1910.

————. *Confessions of a Reformer,* 1925.

Hubbard, Samuel. *Preparedness, 1914–1917,* 1923.

Irwin, Will. *The Making of a Reporter, 1942.*

Isaac, Paul. *Prohibition and Politics in Tennessee, 1885–1920,* 1965.

Jaffe, Julian. *Crusade Against Radicalism: New York During the Red Scare, 1914–1924,* 1972.

Jensen, Richard. *The Winning of the Midwest,* 1971.

Jessup, Philip. *Elihu Root,* 2 vols., 1938.

Johnson, Donald. *The Challenge to American Freedoms,* 1963.

Jones, Stanley. *The Presidential Election of 1896,* 1964.

Josephson, Matthew. *The Politicos,* 1938 [1963 edition].

Kellor, Frances. *Straight America, A Call to National Service,* 1916.

Kent, Frank. *The Democratic Party, A History,* 1928.

Koenig, Louis. *Bryan,* 1971.

Kohlsaat, H. H. *From McKinley to Harding,* 1923.

Kolko, Gabriel. *The Triumph of Conservatism,* 1963.

La Feber, Walter. "The Background of Cleveland's Venezuela Policy: A Reinterpretation," *American Historical Review*, vol. 66, 1961.

La Follette, Bela and Fola La Follette. *Robert M. La Follette*, 2 vols., 1953.

La Follette's Magazine.

Lambert, John. *Arthur Pue Gorman*, 1953.

Leech, Margaret. *In the Days of McKinley*, 1959.

Link, Arthur. "The Wilson Movement in Texas, 1910–1912," *Southwestern Historical Quarterly*, vol. 48, 1944.

———. "The Underwood Presidential Movement of 1912," *Journal of Southern History*, vol. 11, 1945.

———. "The Progressive Movement in the South, 1870–1914," *North Carolina Historical Review*, vol. 23, 1946.

———. *Wilson*, 5 vols., 1947–1965.

Lodge, Henry Cabot. *War Addresses*, 1917.

Long, John D. *America of Yesterday as Reflected in the Journals of John Davis Long*, 1923.

———. "Papers of John Davis Long," *Massachusetts Historical Society Collections*, vol. 78, 1939.

McAdoo, William. *Crowded Years*, 1931.

McCall, Samuel. *Thomas B. Reed*, 1914.

McKay, Seth. *Texas Politics, 1906–1944*, 1952.

McSeveney Samuel. *The Politics of Depression*, 1972.

Macy, Jesse. *Party Organization and Machinery*, 1904.

Mann, Arthur. *Yankee Reformers in the Urban Age*, 1954.

Manners, William. *TR and Will*, 1969.

Marburg, Theodore. *Development of the League of Nations Idea*, 2 vols., 1932.

Marcus, Robert. *Grand Old Party: Political Structure in the Gilded Age, 1880–1896*, 1971.

Martin, Roscoe. "The People's Party of Texas," *The University of Texas Bulletin*, no. 3308, 1933.

Mason, Alpheus. *Brandeis, A Free Man's Life*, 1946.

May, Ernest. *Imperial Democracy: The Emergence of America as a Great Power*, 1961.

Merk, Frederick. *Manifest Destiny and Mission in America History*, 1963.

Merrill, Horace. *Bourbon Democracy of the Middle West, 1865–1896*, 1953 [1967 edition.]

———. *Bourbon Leader: Grover Cleveland and the Democratic Party*, 1957.

Miller, William D. *Mr. Crump of Memphis*, 1924.

Millis, Walter. *The Martial Spirit*, 1931.

———. *Road to War: America 1914–1917*, 1935.

Moore, J. Hampton. *Roosevelt and the Old Guard*, 1925.

Morgan, H. Wayne. *William McKinley and His America*, 1963.

———. *From Hayes to McKinley: National Party Politics, 1872–1896*, 1969.

Morrissey, Alice. *The American Defense of Neutral Rights, 1914–1917*, 1939.

Mowry, George. *Theodore Roosevelt and the Progressive Movement*, 1946.

———. *The California Progressives*, 1951.

———. *The Era of Theodore Roosevelt*, 1958.

Myers, Gustavus. *The History of Tammany Hall*, 1917.

National Security League. *Annual Report*, 1916.

Nelles, Walter. *A Liberal in Wartime*, 1940.

Nevins, Allan. *Henry White*, 1930.

———. *Grover Cleveland*, 1932.

———. *Study in Power*, 1953.

New York Times.

New York *World.*

Nichols, Jeanette. "The Politics and Personalities of Silver Repeal in the United States Senate," *American Historical Review*, vol. 61, 1935.

Nixon, Herman. *The Populist Movement in Iowa*, 1926.

Noggle, Burl. *Into the Twenties*, 1974.

Norris, George. *Fighting Liberal*, 1944.

Notter, Harley. *The Origins of the Foreign Policy of Woodrow Wilson*, 1937.

Nugent, Walter. *The Tolerant Populists*, 1963.

Nye, Russel. *Midwestern Progressive Politics*, 1959.

Ogg, Frederic. *National Progress, 1907–1917*, 1918.

Orcutt, William. *Burrows of Michigan and the Republican Party*, 2 vols., 1917.

Osborn, George. *John Sharp Williams*, 1943.

———. *Woodrow Wilson, The Early Years*, 1968.

Ostrogorski, M. *Democracy and the Organization of Political Parties*, 2 vols., 1902 [1964 edition.]

Parker, George. *Recollections of Grover Cleveland*, 1911.

Paxson, Frederic. *American Democracy and the World War*, 3 vols., 1936–1948.

Peck, Harry. *Twenty Years of the Republic*, 1906.

Peterson, Horace. *Propaganda for War*, 1939.

Pinchot, Amos. *History of the Progressive Party, 1912–1916*, 1958.

Pratt, Julius. *Expansionists of 1898*, 1936 [1964 edition].

———. *America's Colonial Experiment*, 1950.

Preston, William, *Aliens and Dissenters*, 1963.

Pringle, Henry. *The Life and Times of William Howard Taft*, 2 vols., 1939.

Pusey, Merlo. *Charles Evans Hughes*, 2 vols., 1951.

Republican Club of the City of New York. "Report of the Committee on National Affairs," 1915.

Reynolds, George. *Machine Politics in New Orleans, 1897–1926*, 1936.

Richardson, Leon. *William E. Chandler, Republican*, 1940.

Roosevelt, Theodore. *America and the World War*, 1915.

———. *Selections from the Correspondence of Theodore Roosevelt and Henry Cabot Lodge*, 2 vols., 1925.

———. *Letters*, 8 vols., 1951–1954.

Russell, Francis. *The Shadow of Blooming Grove*, 1968.

Sage, Leland. *William Boyd Allison*, 1956.

Searchlight on Congress.

Seitz, Don. *Joseph Pulitzer, His Life and Letters*, 1924.

Sheldon, William. *Populism in the Old Dominion*, 1935.

Simkins, Francis. *Pitchfork Ben Tillman*, 1944.

Siney, Marion. *The Allied Blockade of Germany, 1914–1916*, 1957.

Smith, Gene. *When the Cheering Stopped*, 1964.

Stealey, O. O. *Twenty Years in the Press Gallery*, 1906.

Steffens, Lincoln. *The Struggle for Self-Government*, 1906.

———. *Letters*, 2 vols., 1938.

Stephenson, George. *John Lind of Minnesota*, 1935.

Stephenson, Nathaniel. *Nelson W. Aldrich*, 1930.

Stevens, Walter. *Missouri, the Center State*, 4 vols., 1915.

Stevenson, Elizabeth. *Babbitts and Bohemians*, 1967.

Stimson, Henry. "The Individual's Duty Toward Preparedness," 1916.

Stoddard, Lothrop. *Master of Manhattan: The Life of Richard Croker*, 1931.

Stone, Ralph (ed.). *Wilson and the League of Nations*, 1967.

Sullivan, Mark. *Our Times*, 6 vols., 1926–1935 [1971 edition].

Sundquist, James. *Dynamics of the Party System*, 1973.

Sutton, Walter. "Progressive Republican Senators and the Submarine Crisis," *Mid-America*, vol. 47, 1965.

Swanberg, W. A. *Citizen Hearst*, 1961.

Swindler, William. *Court and Constitution in the Twentieth Century*, 1969.

Tansill, Charles. *America Enters the War*, 1938.

Tarbell, Ida. *The Nationalizing of Business*, 1936.

Tarr, Joel. *A Study of Boss Politics: William Lorimer of Chicago*, 1971.

Taylor, A. J. P. *The Origins of the Second World War*, 1961.

Thayer, William. *Life and Letters of John Hay*, 2 vols. 1916.

Thompson, Charles. *Party Leaders of the Time*, 1906.

Tompkins, E. Berkeley. *Anti-Imperialism in the United States*, 1970.

Trattner, Walter. "Progressivism and World War I: A Reappraisal," *Mid-America*, vol. 44, 1962.

Traver, Harry. "Are We Americans Cowards or Fools?" 1915.

Tuchman, Barbara. *The Zimmerman Telegram*, 1958 [1966 edition].

Tumulty, Joseph. *Wilson as I Knew Him*, 1921.

Turlington, Edgar. *Neutrality, Its History, Economics and Law*, 4 vols., 1935–1936.

Underwood, Oscar. *Drifting Sands of Party Politics*, 1928.

Union League Club of New York. "Report of the Committee on National Defense," 1915.

U.S. Department of State. *Papers Relating to the Foreign Relations of the United States*, 1894–1900.

———. *Papers Relating to the Foreign Relations of the United States, Supplement*, 1914–1917.

———. *Papers Relating to the Foreign Relations of the United States. The Lansing Papers, 1914–1920,* 2 vols., 1939–1940.

Vare, William. *My Forty Years in Politics,* 1928.

Villard, Oswald. *Fighting Years: Memoirs of a Liberal Editor,* 1939.

Violette, Eugene. *A History of Missouri,* 1918.

Wall, Joseph. *Henry Watterson,* 1956.

Walters, Everett. *Joseph Benson Foraker,* 1948.

Ward, Robert. "Origin and Activities of the National Security League, 1914–1919," *Mississippi Valley Historical Review,* vol. 47, 1960.

Weinstein, James. *The Corporate Ideal in the Liberal State, 1900–1918,* 1968 [1969 edition].

Whitlock, Brand. *Forty Years of It,* 1914.

———. *Letters and Journals,* 1936.

Wiebe, Robert. *Businessmen and Reform,* 1962 [1968 edition].

Wilkerson, Marcus. *Public Opinion and the Spanish-American War,* 1932.

Wilensky, Norman. "Conservatives in the Progressive Era," *University of Florida Monographs,* no. 25, 1965.

Willis, E. F. "The Foreign Policy of Sir Edward Grey," *The Historian,* vol. 1, 1939.

Wilson, William. *Cabinet Diaries,* 1957.

Wilson, Woodrow. *Public Papers,* 6 vols., 1925–1927.

Wisan, Joseph. *The Cuban Crisis as Reflected in the New York Press, 1895–1898,* 1934.

Woodward, C. Vann. *Origins of the New South, 1877–1913,* 1951 [1966 edition].

Yellowitz, Irwin. *Labor and the Progressive Movement in New York State, 1897–1916,* 1965.

Index